Political Aesthetics in the Era of Shakespeare

RETHINKING THE EARLY MODERN

Political Aesthetics in the Era of Shakespeare

Edited by
Christopher Pye

Northwestern University Press
Evanston, Illinois

Northwestern University Press
www.nupress.northwestern.edu

Printed in the United States of America

10 9 8 7 6 5 4 3 2 1

Library of Congress Cataloging-in-Publication Data

Names: Pye, Christopher, 1953– editor.
Title: Political aesthetics in the era of Shakespeare / Christopher Pye [editor].
Other titles: Rethinking the Early Modern.
Description: Evanston, Illinois : Northwestern University Press, 2020. | Series: Rethinking the Early Modern.
Identifiers: LCCN 2020001351 | ISBN 9780810142176 (paperback) | ISBN 9780810142183 (cloth) | ISBN 9780810142190 (ebook)
Subjects: LCSH: Shakespeare, William, 1564–1616—Political and social views. | Shakespeare, William, 1564–1616—Aesthetics. | English literature—Early modern, 1500-1700—History and criticism. | Aesthetics—Political aspects. | Politics and literature—Great Britain—History.
Classification: LCC PR3017 .P57 2020 | DDC 822.3/3—dc23
LC record available at https://lccn.loc.gov/2020001351

CONTENTS

Part Three: Island Voices

Introduction

Early Modern Political Aesthetics

Christopher Pye

The interest in political aesthetics reflected in this volume bears witness to a significant shift in literary studies generally and early modern studies in particular. From about the 1980s until relatively recently, the turn to political concerns in literature was dictated by forms of cultural materialism that staked their claims at least in some measure against consideration of the aesthetic dimensions of the work. This was true particularly for early modern scholarship, which tended during this time to treat the work as something akin to an anthropological artifact, bolstering such an approach with the conviction that the aesthetic was the construction of a latter era. "The autonomous self and text are mere holograms, effects that intersecting institutions produce."[1] The claim for "an autonomous aesthetic order" is an anachronism, and whatever the fluidity of the relation between text and context, the literary work must in the end be construed as "an historically and socially determined event, performed *in* the world and *upon* the world."[2]

Recent scholarship has challenged those assumptions on historical grounds. Critics have shown that a developed and self-conscious awareness of the literary as literary extends well back into the Renaissance, whether that is a matter of heightened attention to the field of representation as a self-referential discursive system,[3] on sensate judgment as a form of evaluation,[4] on the techne of artistic practice,[5] or on localized instances of the reflexive metadramatic and metapoetic turn by which "aesthetic discourse [comes to] emerge as a separate way of talking or writing, separate from rhetoric, philosophy, or theology."[6] Understood in sociological terms, that appearance of an autonomous literary domain can be seen to respond to the historic separation of art from sacred iconicity, as well as the gradual shift from personal patronage to the anonymous market. The ambiguous character of that emergent literariness is particularly evident in the poetic "defense," an "anxious" genre, as Robert Matz has shown, motivated by threats from without—the perception of literature's relative social marginality—and from within: the sense of the instability attending autonomous literature's severance from empirical grounding that is hard to separate from literature's distinctive mystery and power.[7] Erotic verses harbor a "je ne sais quoy," Montaigne writes, "more amorous than love itself."[8]

The political stakes of such a protoaesthetic have also been explored in recent scholarship. Victoria Kahn recovers a seventeenth-century political aesthetic interval before the eighteenth-century separation between political science proper and an aesthetic ideology of the "man of feeling" whose powers will be defined explicitly against political judgment. During that interim, a heightened cognizance of the status of fiction and fictionality is associated with a new awareness of the constitutive function of language implied by contract, and thus too with a developing conception of an autonomous political subject.[9] Recovering Hans Blumenberg's surprising promise for political theology, Graham Hammill traces the significance of the tradition of the Mosaic constitution for sixteenth-century conceptions of human governance in the form of a growing consciousness of the "persuasive capacities of metaphor and narrative to shape life through belief," capacities Hammill associates with the function of image and fantasy within the extralegal act by which political community founds itself.[10]

But the promise of political aesthetics in its recent incarnations extends beyond the revised understanding of the instrumental aims of fiction implied by Kahn's analysis, or even a conception of the political stakes of the aesthetic based on art's capacity to reflect the world. To see that, we need to consider how recent versions of aesthetic philosophy have taken on the perennial riddle posed by political readings of art: how is it possible to pursue such forms of political contextualizing without sacrificing the singularity of the work, its ways of functioning according to its own distinctive logic? Conventional solutions have resolved the matter by forms of compromise—for instance, by opting for partial or impure versions of aesthetic autonomy.[11] Aesthetic philosophers such as Theodor Adorno and Jacques Rancière have pursued a more surprising course, though a course aesthetic philosophy implied from its outset. These thinkers suggest in their different ways that it is precisely by taking seriously art's claim to a radical autonomy that one arrives at its most profound political claims. I want to turn to Rancière in particular in what follows in order to recover the original grounds and promise of aesthetic thought and to engage issues that run throughout the essays, concerns about the aesthetic's relation to social formation, the limits of representability, and the politics of sensible experience.

For Adorno and Rancière alike political aesthetics has meant a return to what had been aesthetic philosophy's original vocation, a means for reconceiving possibilities of social rapport as well as the most fundamental phenomenological organization of the world. Rather than being a tool for political ends, the aesthetic becomes, for Rancière, the sphere within which subjectivities and communities take shape according to historically and politically distinct orderings of the sensible domain itself, what he terms the "distribution of the sensible." The problem of the aesthetic bears directly on "the sensory fabric of 'being together' " that defines the human as an irreducibly political category.[12] According to aesthetics thus conceived, a textured engagement with the artwork as artwork—that is, in its referentially untethered condition—draws us closer to rather than further from our condition as political beings, even while it expands the reach of political theory to the most irreducible dimensions of affective life, the "here and now of the distribution of space and time" with all the forms of equality and exclusion, visibility and invisibility, necessarily entailed in such an allocation.[13]

In many ways, Rancière's exploration of the communal dimensions of phenomenal experience recovers and reorients what had always been the stakes of Kantian aesthetics, or attempts to coordinate those transcendental claims with a political-historical framework—I'll return to the difficulty of that conjunction later. For Kant, the aesthetic was not concerned with describing the empirical determinates of artistic judgments. Rather, aesthetic judgment is bound up with the conditions of phenomenal experience as such. Situated beyond the spheres of cognitive understanding on the one hand and the purely formal, nonempirical imperatives of reason that underpin ethical action on the other, and intended to bridge those apparently incommensurable domains, aesthetic judgment for Kant sought to explain the means through which the sheer particulars of sensible apprehension become available to a form of comprehension that is communicable to others yet not mediated by established cognitive norms.

Such a form of understanding, as Kant conceives it, is not a matter of assimilating the particular to a universal—it doesn't sublate or dissolve the particular into concepts. Rather, the "subjective universality" involved in aesthetic judgment sustains the contingently particular and the universal in a kind of "relationless relation" realized, not in any cognizable content—not conceptually—but rather in the purely formal movement through which the mind comes to itself via the reflective act of aesthetic judgment itself, a movement that entails imaginative transport as much as it does ideational consolidation. That "reflective judgment" is, for Kant, irreducible: it amounts to the precondition for all phenomenal perception. At the same time, precisely because it is a purely formal and relational enactment aesthetic judgment implies a heteronomy and sociality at subjectivity's core, a constitutive sociality unmediated by normative categories that Kant terms the sensus communis. Aesthetic judgment involves, then, a form of communicability in advance of communicated content, and an other-directedness inherent in the most intimate forms of phenomenal apprehension.

A law without law, the aesthetic opens a register of experience that falls outside the web of subsumptive cognition determining the objectively knowable world. In that sense, the Kantian aesthetic entails a version of imaginative free play whose utopian promise aesthetic philosophy from Schiller to Fredric Jameson has sought to conceive in realizable form. The problem is that it opens that free space only to the extent that the aesthetic remains a separate, autonomous domain. Nor is that paradox a mere contingency: it bears on a heterogeneity that marks aesthetic experience at its defining core.

To see that, we need to return to the question of what, precisely, we mean by "aesthetic autonomy." Aesthetic autonomy isn't autonomy constituted as against a world beyond, a definition that would contradictorily make autonomy a relationally defined category. More ambitiously, aesthetic autonomy swallows up its own beyond, incorporating difference as its internal measure and condition. Artworks "bear what is opposed to them in themselves," Adorno writes.[14] Understood in these compassing terms, aesthetic autonomy troubles the very distinction between autonomy and heteronomy. "The autonomy of aesthetic experience, which founds the idea of art qua autonomous reality, is . . . accompanied by the elimination of all pragmatic criteria for extricating the domain of art from that of non-art, the solitude of the work from the forms of collective life."[15]

Taken in that capacious sense, autonomy becomes the very condition of the work's implication in the world. Because for Adorno the rationalized domain of instrumental reason and the purposely purposeless space of the aesthetic are mutually constitutive—because those categories are dialectically bound—the aesthetic is from the outset entangled with the extra-aesthetic, all the more bound for the insistence with which the work seeks to maintain the autonomy that defines it.[16] That dialectical character is what vexes those forms of cultural materialist analysis that explicitly stake themselves against "mere aestheticization";[17] in doing so, such accounts reproduce the divisive procedure through which the aesthetic constitutes itself in the first place. As the mechanism that gathers in and sets in play such divisions as its founding ambition, aestheticization is the process that at once establishes and endlessly undoes the distinctions through which we would categorize it, distinctions between concept and sense, idea and materiality, the work and its theorization.

That at once divided and all-enveloping vocation—what Bernstein terms "the antinomy of autonomy"—underlies what has been the permanent irony of aesthetics's long history as a category.[18] Consider the last critically significant effort to formulate a political aesthetics in relation to early modern literary studies: New Historicism, or, according to Stephen Greenblatt's preferred term at the time, "cultural poetics." That method amounted to an aesthetics insofar as it sought to extend interpretive modes of attention beyond the literary work to the larger symbolic field of a culture. And yet while it represented itself as a poetics, it nevertheless defined itself explicitly against aesthetics proper, staking itself on the detail resistant to what it took to be the universalizing theoretical conceptualizations of aesthetics proper; New Historicism legitimized itself in some large measure through the evocation of such fascinating remainders—the "touch of the real" as the "oddly marginal or eccentric"—a practice that of course entailed its own aesthetic frisson.[19]

The paradox is that in such a procedure New Historicism placed itself squarely within the aesthetic tradition. "Aesthetics proper" has always been an impure aesthetics. Aesthetics is not just a matter of judging the art object's sensuous particulars. Rather, it registers or enacts its encounter with the radically particular, with what remains incognizably singular, as the inassimilable limit of its own conceptualizing procedure. Aesthetic consciousness is consciousness that precipitates from the repeated cognition—or attempted cognition—of its own limits; that is the self-inclusive, self-negating ground of the aesthetic's claim to autonomy. In that sense, aesthetics is a philosophical procedure founded over and against itself, one that repeatedly undoes the ideology it enables: thus the historical resilience of an operation founded on its capacity to derogate itself.[20] Those materialist critiques that have sought a more direct integration of life and art by repudiating aesthetics repeat the self-negating logic of aesthetic ideology itself both in the disavowal that energizes them and in the fiction of mimetic transparency such a division and disavowal paradoxically underwrites.

For thinkers such as Adorno and Rancière, the larger social claims of the aesthetic inhere in that divided and self-exceeding—the "dissensual"—character of its operation. For Adorno, whose focus is the modern work in the context of capitalist forces of production, that irreconcilable dimension of the aesthetic is played out in the work's relation to the world it at once repudiates and absorbs. In its claims to autonomy, the modern work replicates and if anything exacerbates the most inhuman dimensions of the technical, autonomic workings of capitalist exchange relations—the work is an "absolute commodity." And yet in the very absoluteness of that embrace, art inevitably conjures the repressed traces of another, foreclosed world, a world long gone or perhaps still to come.[21] In that sense, the politics of the aesthetic is for Adorno attached to a sociological orientation—Marx and Weber are the points of reference—and bound up with a teleological trajectory extending from a forgotten past to an as yet unrealizable future, thus the intractable pathos of Adorno's account.[22]

Rather than being governed by a prior sociological framework, the aesthetic for Rancière bears on the constitution of the social as such.[23] Coincident with the severing of the work from an instrumental function, the phenomenal dimension that emerges with what Rancière terms the modern "aesthetic regime" suspends the normative hierarchical oppositions organizing sensory life in any given political dispensation and in doing so teases out from the "multiplicity of folds and gaps in the fabric of common experience" the promise of unrealized forms of life and community.[24] The aesthetic dissolves the distinction between *poiesis* and *aesthesis*, making and reception. But it accomplishes that utopian equivalence only by virtue of enacting the division that defines it, the dehiscence by which phenomena become reflectively cognizable: "*Poesis* and *aesthesis* stand henceforth in immediate relation to each other. But they relate to one another through the very gap of their ground. They can only be brought together by a human nature that is lost or that is yet to come."[25] That division and deferral doesn't befall the sensible; it is the condition of its coming to being as a knowable phenomenon, what simultaneously enables and erodes the fiction of transparently available experience. The familiar reproach against aesthetic theory—that it severs us from the immediate experience of the artistic work—fails to recognize that experience itself is from the outset already divided from itself.

In that divisive process, the aesthetic structures the relation between art and life according to its own self-contradictions. Expanding beyond itself precisely insofar as it divides and withdraws itself, the aesthetic work becomes in all its opaque singularity the never fully legitimate manifestation of the intelligible conditions for community as such, understanding community at the level of "the very tissue of ordinary sensory experience."[26] At the same time, whatever community aesthetics thus opens will always be a community in excess of itself—a self-divided, contestatory, and thus a definitionally political formation.

In its concern with minimal levels of sensory apprehension, political aesthetics would seem to be consistent with the recent preoccupation in literary studies generally and Renaissance studies in particular with embodiment, affect, and bodily sensation. At the same, by situating the politics of phenomenal experience in relation to the inescapable problem of grounds, political aesthetics also brings to view the unacknowledged ideological stakes of such work insofar as that work is committed to a claim for "the mind's embeddedness in the body," or a fluid "reciprocity between books, bodies and selves," with all such formulations imply of a transparent rapport or direct translatability between material sensation and cognition.[27] Materialist critics in the field who have sought a vantage "outside metaphysics, in the materials of the physical book itself," risk reproducing in such a valorization of the material thing "itself" one of metaphysic's founding binarisms.[28]

Indeed, political aesthetics suggests how thoroughly such analyses, often articulated in the name of being historically true to a pre-Cartesian dispensation, remain within the terms of the grandest of grand nineteenth-century Burckhardtian narratives of the era. For Burckhardt's *Kulturgeschichte* with its commitment to a developmental procedure through which the multiplicity of particulars is at once retained and sublated into a figure of universal acculturation—the emergence of the Renaissance individual—simply realizes in full-blown Hegelian mode the aesthetic operation informing even the most ostensibly "materialist" claim to find in the sensory particular a direct and transparent expression of human life, the possibility of something like the embodied mind or "passionate cognition."[29] To cite sixteenth-century humoreal writings in the service of such arguments leaves unexamined the aesthetic ideology underpinning those writing's organicist tropes, as well as the aesthetic ideology implied by the mimetic claim that such tropes show us how people "actually" responded to literature.[30]

To provide a more concrete sense of what's involved in the aesthetic transformation Rancière is describing—a shift from thematic preoccupations governed by norms of mimetic verisimilitude to the interpretive reorientation implied by a fully aesthetic logic—I turn to a passage from Shakespeare in which the literary defense genre is explicitly engaged: Rosalind's "apology" at the close of *As You Like It*, the moment where she does and doesn't step aside from play and role to "conjure" us directly:

> It is not the fashion to see the lady the epilogue; but it is no more unhandsome than to see the lord the prologue. If it be true that good wine needs no bush, 'tis true that a good play needs no epilogue. Yet

> to good wine they do use good bushes, and good plays prove the better by the help of good epilogues. What a case am I in then, that am neither a good epilogue nor cannot insinuate with you in the behalf of a good play! I am not furnished like a beggar, therefore to beg will not become me. My way is to conjure you; and I'll begin with the women. I charge you, O women, for the love you bear to men, to like as much of this play as please you. And I charge you, O men, for the love you bear to women—as I perceive by your simpering, none of you hates them—that between you and the women the play may please. If I were a woman I would kiss as many of you as had beards that pleased me, complexions that liked me, and breaths that I defied not. And I am sure, as many as have good beards, or good faces, or sweet breaths will for my kind offer, when I make curtsy, bid me farewell.[31]

Rosalind's words recall one of the more cunningly defensive moments in Sidney's well-known defense: "But the poet, as I said before, never affirmeth; the poet never makes any circles about your imagination, to conjure you to believe for true what he writes; he citeth no authorities of other histories, but even for his entry calleth the sweet Muses to inspire into him a good invention—in troth, not laboring to tell you what is or is not, but what should or should not be."[32] The epilogue brings to view the irony perhaps already at work in his predecessor's trope, where the delimiting and defensive operation of Sidney's literary apology may in fact be slyly reenacting the seductions of the conjurer's circle.

For what promises in the epilogue to be a simple gathering in of all parties, men and women alike, turns out to be a considerably more ambiguous form of enlistment. Why do we clap at the end? For the manly men—the good-bearded sorts—the impulse might well be aggressive, a matter of bidding farewell indeed to the approaches of the curtsying figure. After all, she had already let the mask drop: "If I were a woman." In that sense, clapping would be of the spell-breaking sort, a matter of drawing the line on what has been a thoroughly ambiguous fiction.[33] But of course she never said she was a man, only "if I were a woman," and thus never stepped aside from the play's infinitely iffy, infinitely conjectural world, where the opposite of "if I were a woman" is only ever "if I were a man." "'If' is the only peace maker," said Touchstone, resolutely (5.4.91–92). That irreducible conditionality is consistent with literature's functioning absent mimetic grounding, which is to say as a purely aesthetic formation. And with that ungrounding comes a resituating of the locus of meaning from the work "in itself" to the interpretive act dictated by the illimitable domain the now unbounded work opens. For if we feel trapped by Rosalind's approach at the close, it's by virtue of our having snared ourselves; it is, in other words, precisely the audience's desire to draw a line on the fiction, to know it as separable and autonomous, that renews its power to inscribe itself beyond such limits. We are guilty in defense, as King Henry V says of the encircled citizens of Harfleur.

What seemed a primitive ploy—to clap to banish the fiction winds up signifying one's approval—turns out to obey a more intractable logic. In relation to the prospect of infinite conjecture—a sphere where, as Touchstone puts it, "the truest poesy is the most feigning"—one can only draw the line: that is what lets us call this an effect of fiction at all and thus claim a space of judgment beyond—that's the condition of our own claim to autonomous subjecthood.[34] And that is what reinscribes us, thus determining fiction as limitless. Just as the purely supplementary and quintessentially literary figure who "comes between" men and women constitutively divides even as it joins them, so what turns us from what we want shows us the way to our desire, shows us, that is, how such veering is precisely "as we like it"; indeed, the epilogue shows the groundless grounds of desire as such. And in that, the play articulates the limitlessly conditional condition, at once self-divided and self-sufficient, of an emerging aesthetic consciousness: not a matter of knowing as against not knowing, but of knowledge as the knowledge that we do not know, the Montaignean recognition that knowing our blindness doesn't protect us from enacting it.

A slight, dismissably literary effect, the epilogue instances at the same time and by virtue of that very insubstantiality a shift in the logic and politics of figuration. Rather than being given in advance and mimetically reflected in the artwork, self and world become what is actively constituted in the unstable movement of the work's autonomous/heteronomic formation.[35] In that sense, the "literary" takes on the character of an event, understanding event, including the historical event, not as a matter of what is thematically representable but as what opens even as it remains inassimilable to the field of cognizable representations—as what *inscribes* itself. And with that performative turn, the political consequences of the aesthetic shift from an instrumental framework, a Horatian paradigm of persuasion to right action enunciated from an implicitly transcendental posture of choice, to a politics of complicity in which every act is already inscribed within an open structure of forces.[36] Autonomy—the work's severance from any ground beyond itself—translates into a politics of radical implication.

While the promise of post-Kantian aesthetic thought for a politically oriented criticism is evident in a generalized way both in the extension of the work beyond its borders and in the penetration of political critique into the most intimate reaches of affective and communal experience, the Shakespearean example confronts us with an obvious historical problem. For at least according to Rancière's reckoning, the "aesthetic regime" is a post–eighteenth century phenomenon, a correlative to modern democratization. According to Rancière's tripartite historical scheme of representational orders, the Renaissance belongs to the "representative regime," the historical interval during which, no longer ruled by Platonic equation between representation and truth claims, art as art can be said to have come to view, but in a form governed by extrinsic norms of verisimilitude, generic appropriateness, and adequation between representational modes and subject matter—in other words, an era in which art remains regulated by all the norms appropriate to a fully hierarchical vision of community.[37] In one regard, Rancière's categorization reflects a peculiarly French conception of cultural history, oriented around neoclassical concerns with verisimilitude, concerns that have little bearing on a designation such as "early modernism." But in a purely epistemological sense, the representative regime accurately describes all those modes of Renaissance self-conscious *poiesis* falling within the ambit of Sidney's well-known dictum that literature never lies because it never affirms. The metapoetic or metadramatic turn of literary self-consciousness implied by such a conception of an art that knows itself as art wouldn't in itself imply a posture outside such a normative regime. Indeed, insofar as they confirm literature as a self-reflective space, such moments of literary self-consciousness could be seen to underwrite the mimetic logic that sustains the representative regime's ordered relation between making and reception.

And yet it is difficult to maintain that early modern reflexive literariness remains within the stabilizing terms of mimesis. Think for instance of the conclusion of *The Winter's Tale*, where the scene of Hermione's return as a living statue—one of the more developed of the frequent Renaissance instances of art reflecting back on its own conditions—enacts all those suspensions of the hierarchical relations between active and passive, possession and nonpossession, viewer and viewed, living and dead that Kant for one associates with the indeterminate space of aesthetic judgment: "Would I were dead, but that methinks already— . . . / Would you not deem it breathed? . . . / No settled senses of the world can match / The pleasure of that madness."[38] Or consider the dumb-show scene in *Hamlet*, where in the pantomime of the ear-poisoning crime the work can be seen to expose its own grounds as the abyssal reflex of the auditor's own audition. These are thematized or mimetically objectified reflections on art as art. But, like Rosalind's epilogue, they also figure literature performatively, as an art that finds at its generative source nothing other than the elusive trace of the audience's fatally absorbed response.

How do we make sense of this prematurity of the aesthetic, the fact of its apparent arrival before its articulation either as a philosophical category or as an explicit ideological program? In fact, Rancière's sequencing isn't absolute: he allows for the coexistence of regimes of representation in a work, and we can certainly read such Shakespearean moments as historically anticipatory.[39] But it may be important to hold on to the anachronistic awkwardness implied by the nonce category, "early modern aesthetics," for it suggests how directly for us that era may be bound up with the contradictory relation between aesthetics and the process of historicization as such.

Realized in advance of its appearance as a fully articulated ideology and at the limits of historicism as an explanatory procedure, the "early modern aesthetic" needs to be read at least in part in ways that move beyond familiar empirical-sociological accounts of its causes. One factor within an array of social factors, the aesthetic is also bound up with the more fundamental process through which early modern society first constitutes itself as a phenomenal form. In an extended reading of Carl Schmitt, the Italian political theorist Carlo Galli argues that the early modern "moment" consists in the reversal through which a dispensation in which space, understood as a given, ontotheological form, determines politics becomes one in which the political determines space, which is to say the space of sociality as such. Galli's point is not simply that modern society is divided, conflictual, and thus open to a multiplicity of interpretations. The argument is rather that society is deontologized—that it doesn't exist except as a function of the force that would totalize it and thus grant it the fiction of an immanent form.[40] Without secure transcendent reference, the social becomes the unstable drama of its auto-foundation, the divisive, self-exclusive movement through which it constitutes itself in a form that doesn't escape, in Claude Lefort's phrase, the "enigma" of its "external/internal articulation." "The social," Lefort writes, "can't be dissociated from the problem of its institution."[41] Irreducibly relational, which is to say without being or essence, the *ordini nuovi* of modern political society is constitutively overdetermined; it remains incapable of totalization and structured in relation to the limit or void that opens it. The sociological division of classes, as well as the division between civil society and state, must in that sense be understood as a function of a prior, only ever retroactively apprehensible division that opens the space or interval of the social as such and marks it as irreducibly political.[42]

That auto-foundational process—the means through which society seeks to realize itself in phenomenal form—is a fundamentally aesthetic one. The artwork may well remain bound to a hierarchized society during the era, but that society was itself constituted via an intrinsically unstable aesthetic mechanism. Rather than serving an emerging state as Burckhardt claims, aestheticization is coterminous with the social field as such, realizing society's political character in the divisions and asynchrony of its own persistent failure to ground itself. To read modern society's institution by way of the aporia of aesthetic grounding is pointedly to suspend the question as to whether such an "event" is a matter of developmental origination or of retroactive allegorization. And that irresolvability is precisely the measure of the historicity of the problem of institution, for it acknowledges the fact of our own inscription within the mechanism of historicization rather than allowing us the transcendental and thus ahistorical posture implied by the reduction of history to any narrative schematization, including Rancière's.

Such a claim for the aesthetic's relation to modern political society returns us to Burckhardt, but Burckhardt with a difference. Rather than being realized through the hand of the prince, rather than serving an instrumental function, the political aesthetic inscribes social agents within an opening they do not themselves create, one that by definition exceeds them.[43] That creationist dimension of the early modern aesthetic is of a piece with its conception as *poiesis*, but a *poiesis* that persistently slips beyond its securing analogy with divine fiat[44]—if Renaissance instances of aestheticization can seem surprisingly "modern," suggesting a supervening mechanism that exceeds any authorial hand, that may be because they occupy an ambiguous interval between transcendent authority and a strongly developed ideology of human authorship.

The distinction between early modern aesthetic formations and aestheticization's later variants has to do with this formative, ontological dimension. During a later era in which it is fully articulated as an ideology of human social-political fulfillment—a form of life—the aesthetic's destabilizing potential will be managed in part by its translation into a purely sociological phenomenon, one among an array of discursive formations—exactly the kinds of explanatory narratives against which Rancière's analysis militates. Thus for instance Carl Schmitt's equivalence between aesthetic indetermination and the depoliticization of society in the liberal era, or the familiar equation between aesthetic autonomy and mere commodification on the one hand and the atomized, self-determining bourgeois subject on the other.[45]

Aestheticization does of course have boundaries. But within the time of its "prehistory" those defining limits are best understood not within the terms of an already constituted sociological framework but in relation to the foundational narratives political theology claims for itself. Traditional accounts of such a relation, associating aesthetics with a valorization of human agency, read theology and aesthetics in oppositional terms, understanding the aesthetic as a strong marker of secularization.[46] But Julia Lupton and Graham Hammill imply a more intricate complicity between political theology and political aesthetics: "What is at stake for political theology is not the truth of religion but the status of theology as operative fiction whether conceived as an instrument of civil religion, a thesaurus of absolute metaphors, or the part played by myth, fantasy, and affect in the founding and sustaining of collectives."[47] In associating political theology with creativity, they affiliate theology not with the legitimizing norms of already established religious institutions but with the prior constitutive and potentially resistant act that opens the system of norms and equivalencies in the first place. Rather than entailing "legitimation by analogy," political theology issues "in moments in which imagination reclaims the forces of making against sovereignties both statist and divine by staging the very effects of sovereign power in and as what literature does."[48]

What remains to unpack in such an account is the precise relation between theology and aesthetics in this "operative fiction." It's certainly the case that political theology and political aesthetics share a common vocation in their mutual capacity to open prospects beyond an empirically given world—that is where their political potential lies. But in both cases it may be a mistake to read those "forces of making" in entirely instrumental terms. The familiar analogy between aesthetic creation and divine fiat holds because aestheticization implies an insistent movement beyond the hand of those who would instantiate it, though in the case of the aesthetic, that's an exorbitant movement that nevertheless remains radically immanent—thus the proximity between political aesthetics and Merleau-Ponty's project of imagining subjectivity neither as a function of an embodied community nor via transcendental reference but as constituted within the at once internal and external "flesh of the social."[49]

But to the extent that theology becomes *political* theology by suspending a fixed transcendental reference, by becoming, in Walter Benjamin's terms, a messianism without messiah, to the extent that that suspension is what opens a space between institutional religion and theology, it can be hard to know the difference between political theology and political aesthetics as projects. Perhaps we can grasp that distinction only by putting pressure on the very impulse to rely on "legitimation by analogy," the impulse to read the relation between theology and fiction by way of *analogy* at all. For to conceive that relationship in terms of equivalence or identity is to lose track of the stakes of an instituting act whose force is precisely to realize the conditions for such structures of equivalency, the structures on which identity and norms are based.[50] Instead, political aesthetics and political theology should be read in terms of the knotted coimplication by which each exposes the limit of the other and thus returns each to its enabling condition.

On the one hand, a theological remainder can be seen to haunt modern aesthetics insofar as aesthetics inevitably betrays itself in its dream of absolute autonomy. Against the aesthetic's claim to the power to fully harbor its own limit, to know that it does not know and thus translate that limit into a matter of aesthetic *consciousness*, political theology recalls the aesthetic to a prior and radically heterogeneous mandate definitionally incapable of internalization: a voice beyond. On the other, aesthetics vexes political theology, exposing the element of forced and arbitrary phenomenalization at work in any attempt to convert the recursive and limitlessly conditional "as if" of theology into a founding event and thus to translate illimitability into a vectored narrative oriented around beginnings and ends, even if those messianic ends remain permanently deferred. There's nothing merely abstract about the need to retain the promise of those enabling aesthetic tensions and aporiai, particularly in an era of resurgent fundamentalism and the return of a politics committed to eroding truth claims in order to enlist them all the more fiercely in the service of a radically homogenizing fantasy of the nation as one people.

Whether it's a matter of tracing the emergence of an explicit aesthetic turn at the boundary between cognitive and noncognitive reception in *Two Noble Kinsmen*, describing the appearance of an aesthetic of the political "part that has no part" in *Julius Caesar*, or locating the aesthetic at the boundaries of social and economic exchange in *Timon of Athens*, the essays that follow pursue the promise of political aesthetics through an intensified attunement to the stakes of form and the generative limits of the representable. The collection is divided into three parts, each bearing out in one way or another claims for the historical and political cogency of a distinctive early modern political aesthetic.[51]

Part 1, "An Early Modern Aesthetic," engages the emergence of the aesthetic as a historical issue, each of the essays extending the purview of aesthetics from the Enlightenment to the longer arc of early modern political and ethical formation. Andrew Sisson's "'No Toy But Was Her Pattern': Renaissance Friendship and the Rise of Aesthetics in *The Two Noble Kinsmen*" traces the emergence of the aesthetic in the shift from forms of sensuous judgment sustained by already established social bonds to aesthetic judgment as that which exceeds and ultimately proves itself to be the condition for any such normative ideational formations. With that, aesthetics asserts itself as the at once singular and universal ground of any judgment, the cognitive and the noncognitive becoming each other's irresolvably antithetical conditions. Attending particularly to the apparently inassimilable status of the Jailer's Daughter's mad fixation in the play, Sisson's essay ultimately traces the mechanism through which fleeting impulses become translated into the fabric of sociality itself.

My "'No cause, no cause': *King Lear* and the Space of the World" finds similar evidence for the preexistence of something like the Kantian aesthetic transformation, though for me that turn enacts a distinctive early modern aesthetic insofar as it also troubles the logic through which we would make such a turn historically narratable. Out of the contradictions of its fablelike opening, the play stages the separating out of the features of the modern political and subjective field: on the one hand, biopolitical governmentality, on the other the autonomous and infinite transcendental subject—something on the order of Kantian aesthetic subjectivity. At the same time, in the contingency of that staged opposition between atemporal allegory and historicization, the play unsettles the story of political-aesthetic origination it sets forth. That disturbance of narratability is related to a more untoward aesthetic—the dark lining of Kantian aesthetic consciousness—that unbinds subjectivity even as it intimates possibilities of being-in-common at the limits of tragedy in either its classical or Christian iterations.

Shifting focus to the eighteenth century, Russ Leo's "Thomas Rymer, Poetic Justice, and the Limits of Representation: Dispatches from the Representative Regime of Art" finds in Rymer's tragic theory the theological stakes informing neoclassical aesthetic thought, what Rancière terms the representative regime. Tragic mimesis is not a matter of faithful empirical representation but of the more profound correspondence between Aristotelian laws of universality, probability, and necessity and God's providential designs, designs not evident through nature or history alone. Judged according to such a conception of "poetic justice," the formal shortcomings of Shakespeare and his contemporaries—faults of plot and causal logic rather than decorum—become not just aesthetic but theologico-political problems. But here too mimesis necessarily encounters its representational limits. Steering between poetic fanatics on the one hand and deists on the other, Rymer invokes that limit because of the need to represent God's designs as natural, but not to make the equation so absolute that nature is exposed as mechanically dictated. Ultimately, poetic justice can't be disassociated from a certain indeterminate "surplus mystery," a fact that aligns Rymer's critical theory with the larger modern aesthetic project of aligning *poiesis* with an organizing *aesthesis* serving to bridge the gap between theological treatments of religious experience and more critical approaches to sensory experience.

Shifting from the historical register to structural accounts of the politics of representation, part 2, "Aesthetics and the Politics of the Representable," explores the way the aesthetic becomes manifest at the constitutive margins of the social domain, whether that limit is figured in the person of the poor, the pleb, or the misanthrope. Bringing Rancièrean political aesthetics directly to bear on *Julius Caesar*, Tracey Sedinger's "Shakespeare and the Plebs" suggests the way in which the humanist rhetorical tradition informing Brutus's metaphoric and Antony's metonymic reasoning is ultimately derailed in the play by the emergence of an aesthetic of the socially marginalized embodied in the plebs, "the part that has no part" within the representational space of the socius. The play figures the emergence of an aesthetic register specifically as a function of the social "distribution of the sensible," evoking political violence as a function of the obstructed agency of those who remain unrepresentable. The consequent dissolution of social order means a reduction of spirit and character to "bloody marks" even as it opens a potentially liberatory political recognition on the part of the audience. That recognition amounts for Sedinger to a lesson in the divergence between sensibility and intelligibility—in that sense, it's a harbinger of political-aesthetic possibilities to come.

Joan Pong Linton's "Timon's Hunger in the Forest: Toward a Political Aesthetics of Being beside Oneself" similarly looks to a figure inhabiting the limits of the social imaginary to tease out theater's deepest political aesthetic promise, now in the context of a play that asserts its claim as fiction to imagine what consequences a changing economy has for the epistemological status of self and society. Focusing on the scene in which the famished misanthrope uncovers gold while digging for roots, Linton finds in that evocation of earth's own "most operant poison" the play's deepest biopolitical and aesthetic stakes; even as it realizes the physiological basis for the misanthrope's egocentric *poiesis* or self-making, Timon's being "beside himself" with hunger evokes the promise of a fully relational sociality embodied ultimately in the audience's vicarious—at once identificatory and critically distanced—theatrical engagement. Insofar as a play is able to structure audience engagement in terms of an aesthetic *commoning* of hunger, theater will have realized its potential as political event.

In "From Political Theology to Political Aesthetics in *A Midsummer Night's Dream*," Jennifer R. Rust opens the question of the relation between those two critical approaches even while, picking up a thread from Sisson, she extends the collection's reflections on the rapport between aesthetics and affect theory. The essay uncovers a quasi-autonomous aesthetic in Bottom's synesthetic vision-speech, an aesthetic that resists the ruler's attempts to instrumentalize it, thus suggesting the possibility of social "compacts" extending beyond sovereign control. Consistent with the radical dimensions of Pauline thought, Bottom aestheticizes the First Letter to the Corinthians, not by dissolving the incarnational body in the name of community but by suggesting that it can be assembled—"rewired"—otherwise. Such a figural and material aesthetic resists secularization even as it symptomizes it, and it does so insofar as it eschatologically exceeds its own phenomenal moment through a temporal transport Rust associates with the kind of redistribution of the sensible against which the sovereign's rationalizing discourse stakes itself. In the "rude mechanics'" play at drama's close, the resurgence of an apocalyptic dimension, as well as the dissolution of spatial and temporal boundaries such a perspective implies, exposes the arbitrariness of all political dispensations.

Adopting an Adornian sociological perspective to a Rancièrean attention to the limits of symbolization as such, Joel M. Dodson's "'Need makes good schollers': Spenser and the Poverty of Aesthetics" conceives early modern aesthetics not simply as the anticipation of Kantian autonomy but as a category in its own right, an aesthetic underwritten by poverty and exigency in advance of and conditioning the possibility of the modern politics of abundance and class distinction. Tracing the trope of "need" through the humanist curriculum and focusing on Spenser's *The Faerie Queene*, the essay explores the way the privative "cut" of the aphorism opens the passage into aesthetic purposelessness even as it necessarily conjures the forgotten—and unforgettable—remainder that enables it, a remainder termed "the scholar's need." To engage such a relation between scholarly privation and aesthetic emergence is to bring to view "that which clings forever to the back of the mimetic regime and its 'golden world' legacy."

More than that of any other Shakespeare play, *The Tempest*'s critical reception has seemed to presume an unnegotiable divide between political and aesthetic readings, a tradition of reading the play as about art apparently superseded by postcolonial lines of enquiry. For that reason, part 3, "Island Voices," takes that play as a testing ground for the promise of an alternative political-aesthetic paradigm. Considering the play's engagement with the epic tradition, Lydia C. Heinrichs's "'I . . . Will Cry It O'er Again': Virgil, *The Tempest*, and the Aesthetics of Imitation" explores the complex relation between aesthetics and *imitatio*, arguing that the Renaissance emphasis on the imitation of artistic convention and the estranging historicity of Rancière's purportedly modern aesthetic regime are in fact by no means mutually exclusive. Focusing on the figure of Dido, the essay argues that the internally divided and reiterative temporality of supposedly anti-Virgilian works such as Ovid's in fact suggest not so much an alternative to the Virgilian epic narrative as its very structural principle; it's a principle that achieves success, she argues, only by repeatedly reevoking a past that eludes burial. Those anxieties about the uncanny recurrences of history inform *The Tempest*'s own fantasy of realizing a fully self-originating, self-legitimating, and autonomous sociohistorical order. The equally necessary demands of internal consonance and heterogeneity sustaining such a vision ultimately crystallize in the form of an encompassing aesthetic formation that riddles the very distinction between outside and inside, mimesis and *aesthesis*, thus eroding the play's imperial aesthetic program from within.

While Heinrichs harks back historically to uncover the play's formal logic, Hugh Grady's "The Political, the Aesthetic, and the Utopian in *The Tempest*: A Shakespearean Dialectic Unfolded" adopts a critical framework aligned more with Adorno, Benjamin, and Ernst Bloch than with Rancière to explore the way Shakespeare's late play dialectically counters a Machiavellian political universe through a utopian meta-aesthetic explicitly associated with a coming secular Enlightenment. Without foreclosing the darker realities of the Machiavellian world, utopian aesthetic consciousness and the distancing it implies afford characters in the drama possibilities of a defamiliarized perception of the political, even as it provides the audience with a space of critical reflection necessary to imagine possibilities beyond the ravages of instrumentalized politics.

Colby Gordon's "A Diversity of Sounds, All Horrible': The Political Aesthetics of Soundscapes in *The Tempest*" echoes Rust's exploration of the politics of the sensorium, shifting the terrain of political-aesthetic analysis of the play from the formal preoccupations of the previous two essays to the drama's phenomenological textures, and finding in those textures both the grounds and the limits of monarchic power. In instances such as his strategic use of Ariel's intoxicating songs to subdue Ferdinand, Prospero fashions his sovereignty out of a specifically acoustic mode of enchantment. Pairing the play with Thomas Adès's operatic adaptation, the essay explores the aesthetic dimensions of princely charisma, locating Prospero's acoustic experiments in relation to the history of liturgical acclamations of kingship traced by Ernst Kantorowicz. At the same time, the island conjures its own resistant variants of aesthetic power, moments when the inhuman sonic spirits of the isle assume an agential role in scripting the actions, teasing out the fantasies and impeding the projects of the shipwrecked arrivals. Ultimately, sound traverses bodies, binding together human, animal, plant, and meteorological actors in a sonorous ecology, a consonant—and dissonant—commons.

Like Grady, in "Shakespeare's *Sturm*, Caliban's *Drang*: Walter Benjamin and *The Tempest*," Julia Reinhard Lupton adopts a Benjaminian orientation to uncover the glimmer of utopian possibilities in the island drama. But while for Grady the play's aesthetic anticipates a secularized Enlightenment, Lupton, tracing out "Prince Caliban's" affiliation with biblical prototypes from Adam to David, aligns the play with the "messianic archeology" of Benjamin's baroque *Trauerspiel*. And, while other essays in the collection associate the aesthetic break with forms of judgment shorn of secure referential grounding—a *fundamentum in re*—Lupton aligns the contingency of baroque aesthetic allegorization precisely with the inescapable insistence of the creaturely domain, a domain in which the light of grace lingers but only as filtered through "the swamp of Adamic guilt." Caliban is marked by that luminously fallen condition, a condition of messianic immanence. But in his capacity to mount a counternarrative to Prospero's exclusionary regime, the monster intimates a resistant project founded on an aesthetic associated not with sovereign autonomy but with an autopoetic convergence of the island's own sounds and voices, a specifically political aesthetic insofar as it is aligned with the relational and communal nature of being as such.

Notes

We are grateful to the volume's readers, Christopher Warley and Ryan Netzley, as well as our editors at Northwestern: Trevor Perri, Maia Rigas, Feisal Mohamed, and Michael Ashby.

1. H. Aram Veeser, ed., *The New Historicism* (New York: Routledge, 1989), xi.

2. Louis Montrose, "Professing the Renaissance: The Poetics and Politics of Culture," in Veeser, *The New Historicism*, 23; emphasis in original.

3. Robert Williams, "Italian Renaissance Art and the Systematicity of Representation," *Rinascimento* 43 (2004): 327.

4. David Summers, *The Judgment of Sense: Renaissance Naturalism and the Rise of Aesthetics* (Cambridge: Cambridge University Press, 1987), 9.

5. Victor Stoichita, *The Self-Aware Image: An Insight into Early Modern Meta-Painting* (Cambridge: Cambridge University Press, 1996), 16.

6. Clark Hulse, "Tudor Aesthetics," in *The Cambridge Companion to English Literature, 1500–1600*, ed. Arthur F. Kinney (Cambridge: Cambridge University Press, 2000), 32–33. Recent examples of a renewed interest in form in the early modern context include Stephen Cohen, ed., *Shakespeare and Historical Formalism* (London: Ashgate Publishing, 2007); Mark Rasmussen, ed., *Renaissance Literature and Its Formal Engagements* (New York: Palgrave, 2002); Heather Dubrow, *Deixis in the Early Modern English Lyric* (New York: Palgrave, 2015); and Rachel Eisendrath, *Poetry in a World of Things: Aesthetics and Empiricism in Renaissance Ekphrasis* (Chicago: University of Chicago Press, 2018).

7. Robert Matz, *Defending Literature in Early Modern England* (Cambridge: Cambridge University Press, 2000), 22, 52–53, 58–85.

8. Michel de Montaigne, *The Complete Essays of Montaigne*, trans. Donald Frame (Stanford, Calif.: Stanford University Press, 1948), 645. See also Richard Scholar, *The Je-Ne-Sais-Quoi in Early Modern Europe: Encounters with a Certain Something* (Oxford: Oxford University Press, 1985), 261.

9. Victoria Kahn, *Wayward Contracts: The Crisis of Political Obligation in England, 1640–1674* (Princeton, N.J.: Princeton University Press, 2004), 57–58.

10. Graham Hammill, *The Mosaic Constitution: Political Theology and Imagination from Marlowe to Milton* (Chicago: University of Chicago Press, 2012), 11, 19.

11. For an especially cogent argument for such an approach, see Hugh Grady, *Shakespeare and Impure Aesthetics* (Cambridge: Cambridge University Press, 2009).

12. Jacques Rancière, *The Emancipated Spectator*, trans. Gregory Elliott (London: Verso, 2011), 56.

13. Rancière, *The Emancipated Spectator*, 19.

14. Theodor Adorno, *Aesthetic Theory*, ed. and trans. Robert Hullot-Kentor (Minneapolis: University of Minnesota Press, 1997), 344. "The relation between what autonomously belongs to art and what is heteronomous is an internal relation" (J. M. Bernstein, *The Fate of Art: Aesthetic Alienation from Kant to Derrida and Adorno* [University Park: Pennsylvania State University Press, 1992], 11).

15. Jacques Rancière. *The Politics of Aesthetics*, trans. Gabriel Rockhill (London: Continuum, 2004), 42.

16. In its claims for the universal aestheticization of *all* experience in late capitalism, and thus its "dedifferentiation" from extra-aesthetic discourses, Sianne Ngai's account of contemporary aesthetic categories would seem to relinquish this founding antimony in Kant's as well as in Adorno's analysis of aesthetic autonomy, a fact that makes it fair to ask whether she is describing aesthetic phenomena or rather affective categories bearing a mimetic or symptomatic relation to the commodified world they evoke—such categories allow "a more direct reflection" of society. Nevertheless, the splitting at the defining core of aestheticization recurs in her account in the unresolvable indeterminacy of the evaluative and descriptive dimensions of aesthetic judgment, an indeterminacy related to what she ultimately refers to as the "articulation of aesthetic and extra-aesthetic judgments underpinning all specifically aesthetic discourse" (*Our Aesthetic Categories: Zany, Cute, Interesting* [Cambridge, Mass.: Harvard University Press, 2015], 19–22, 40, 47).

17. See, for example, Douglas Bruster, *Shakespeare and the Question of Culture: Early Modern Literature and the Cultural Turn* (New York: Palgrave Macmillan, 2003), 41, 53.

18. Bernstein, *The Fate of Art*, 205.

19. Catherine Gallagher and Stephen Greenblatt, *Practicing New Historicism* (Chicago: University of Chicago Press, 2000), 6, 36.

20. "Our contemporaries strive in vain to denounce the term *aesthesis*, since those who honored it were the first to do so" (Jacques Rancière, *Aesthetics and Its Discontents* [Cambridge: Polity Press, 2009], 11). See also Marc Redfield, "Island Mysteries," in *Art History Versus Aesthetics*, ed. James Elkins (New York: Routledge, 2006), 273–74, 283.

21. According to Christopher Warley's Adorno-influenced reading, that conjuring limit is form and what it calls up is the inevitable specter of class (*Reading Class through Shakespeare, Donne and Milton* [Cambridge: Cambridge University Press, 2014]). Rachel Eisendrath also forwards a particularly suggestive Adornian account of early modern aesthetics as a response to the "emptying out of experience entailed in the emerging empiricist worldview" (*Poetry*, 21).

22. On Adorno's pathos and its relation to the totalizing perspective that subtends even his valorization of the fragment, see Thierry de Duve, "Resisting Adorno, Revamping Kant," in *Art and Aesthetics after Adorno*, ed. Jay M. Bernstein et al., 249–99 (Berkeley: University of California Press, 2010).

23. Indeed, for Rancière sociology as a discipline emerges as a reaction to the aesthetic regime, its distinctions a response to the aesthetic's socially dissolvative effects (*The Politics of Aesthetics*, 13).

24. Jacques Rancière, *Dissensus: On Politics and Aesthetics* (London: Bloomsbury, 2015), 21.

25. Rancière, *Aesthetics and Its Discontents*, 8.

26. Rancière, *Aesthetics and Its Discontents*, 31.

27. Catherine Craik and Tonya Pollard, *Shakespearean Sensations: Experiencing Literature in Early Modern England* (Cambridge: Cambridge University Press, 2013), 4, 9.

28. Margreta de Grazia and Peter Stallybrass, "The Materiality of the Shakespearean Text," *Shakespeare Quarterly* 44, no. 3 (Autumn 1993): 280.

29. Craik and Pollard, *Shakespearean Sensations*, 20. It is worth noting the way in which even those antihumanist accounts that recognize the mediated character of the thing can revert in their formulation of a materialist derivation to versions of aestheticized pathos, evocations, for instance, of the subject as a being that comes to itself "in suffering, in feeling its own corporeal and sensual receptivity as it intently plies its object" thus recognizing its own object status in relation to others (Margreta de Grazia, Maureen Quilligan, and Peter Stallybrass, eds., *Subject and Object in Renaissance Culture* [Cambridge: Cambridge University Press, 1996], 4).

30. For a counterexample, John Parker, in "What a Piece of Work Is Man: Shakespearean Drama as Marxian Fetish, the Fetish as Sacramental Sublime," *Journal of Medieval and Early Modern Studies* 34, no. 3 (Fall 2004): 643–72, forwards an especially subtle Adornian account of the Renaissance stage that does recognize the fully dialectical character of the thing itself; in this instance, the play. Against those accounts that have taken commodification as a sacrifice of the rich particularity of the sensuous world, Parker rightly argues that the commodity assumes its magically fetishistic hold precisely because it gathers that particularity into itself by way of a mechanism of sublation through which the concrete becomes all the more sensuously potent for its entering into the severed and universalizing domain of exchange. That (for Parker) "aesthetic" effect is an illusion, but no more of one than sense certainty itself. My only hesitation concerns the series of equivalencies governing Parker's analysis: sense certainty as the equivalent of the commodity form, the commodity fetish as the equivalent of the aestheticization, the aesthetic as equatable with the hold of religious belief, and so on. Is the aesthetic (to limit the focus to that category) assimilable to a logic of sublimation, or even to relations of exchange; indeed, can it be made *equivalent*?

Even at the point where it fetishistically exceeds human volition, the commodity is inscribed within the structures of exchange that define it. The aesthetic suspends object desire as such, as we know from Kant, and thus functions always at once within and beyond the promised returns of exchange—thus the association between the aesthetic and the death drive, a point Lacan develops in his analysis of *Antigone*. I return to the distinctions, as well as the commonalities, between aesthetics and religious faith at the close. A different though equally suggestive analysis vis-à-vis political aesthetics derives from early modern theatricality studies. I'd argue that when Henry S. Turner advocates for a new conception of form beyond literariness that would be at once "intuitive and informed," that would involve at once generalization and particularization, and by virtue of which we would experience the object as what we are "unprepared for but for which we have, at the same time, somehow been made ready," he is in fact describing in a very precise way the logic of aesthetic consciousness ("Generalization," in *Early Modern Theatricality*, ed. Henry S. Turner [Oxford: Oxford University Press, 2013], 14–15).

31. *As You Like It*, in *The Norton Shakespeare*, ed. Stephen Greenblatt, Walter Cohen, Jean E. Howard, and Katharine Eisaman Maus, 2nd ed. (New York: Norton, 2008). Subsequent parenthetical citations of Shakespeare's works in the introduction are to this edition.

32. Gavin Alexander, ed., *Sidney's "The Defence of Poesy" and Selected Renaissance Literary Criticism* (London: Penguin Books, 2004), 34.

33. The association of the circle of the stage with the conjurer's circle and of applause with the clap through which the magus brought the demonic event to a close was, since Marlowe, conventional.

34. Or, as Lisa Freinkel describes the Shakespearean turn, the possibility of "a lie that lies like truth" (*Reading Shakespeare's Will: The Theology of Figure from Augustine to the Sonnets* [New York: Columbia University Press, 2002], 203).

35. Such an account obviously militates against the trend in recent early modern criticism to construe reading itself as "an embodied practice," as if the body were an already given category capable of subsuming the interpretive act (Craik and Pollard, *Shakespearean Sensations*, 17). On the relation between art's ineffectuality and its strength, see Adorno, *Aesthetic Theory*, 29, 39.

36. What's at stake is something distinct from the forms of interpretive participation implied by Lorna Hutson's account of sixteenth-century literature's newfound inferential spaces; the issue isn't imaginative investment, it's subjective constitution. Similarly, the focus on inscription should be distinguished from Rachel Eisendrath's emphasis on Renaissance aesthetics as a recuperation of the subjective dimension of experience. At the same time, aesthetic logic is distinct from the sheer referential openness William West describes in his account of "intertheatricality." Where there is interpretation there is subjecification, and where there is subjectification there is closure, no end of closure. See Lorna Hutson, *Circumstantial Shakespeare* (Oxford: Oxford University Press, 2015), 1–22; Eisendrath, *Poetry*; and William N. West, "Intertheatricality," in Turner, *Early Modern Theatricality*.

37. Rancière, *The Politics of Aesthetics*, 22.

38. *The Winter's Tale*, ed. Stephen Orgel (Oxford: Oxford University Press, 1996), 5.3.63–73. See also Christopher Pye, *The Storm at Sea: Political Aesthetics in the Age of Shakespeare* (New York: Fordham University Press, 2015), 136–38.

39. Rancière, *The Politics of Aesthetics*, 50.

40. Carlo Galli, *Political Spaces and Global War*, ed. Adam Sitze, trans. Elizabeth Fay (Minneapolis: University of Minnesota Press, 2010), 17–19.

41. Claude Lefort, "The Permanence of the Theological-Political," in *Democracy and Political Theory*, trans. David Macey (Minneapolis: University of Minnesota Press, 1988), 225, 232. On political "disincorporation" more broadly, see Claude Lefort, *The Political Forms of Modern Society: Bureaucracy, Democracy, Totalitarianism*, trans. David Thompson (Cambridge, Mass.: MIT Press, 1986), 303–6.

42. Claude Lefort, *Machiavelli in the Making*, trans. Michael Smith (Evanston, Ill.: Northwestern University Press, 2012), 140, 297–98. For an especially subtle reading of class in just such terms, see Warley, *Reading Class*. On power becoming "an immanent dimension of history" for early modern political thought, see Hammill, *The Mosaic Constitution*, 123–24.

43. The divisive self-institution of political society articulates human personhood as that which "opens onto itself by being held in an opening it does not create" (Lefort, "Permanence," 223).

44. Colleen Ruth Rosenfeld, in *Indecorous Thinking: Figures of Speech in Early Modern Poetics* (New York: Fordham University Press, 2018), 4, 9, describes early modern *poesie*'s tendency to disarticulate its own instrumental foundation, with figures of speech coming to "drive thinking and act as the constitutive engines of . . . imaginative worlds." *Poesie* converges with *aesthesis* at the point where the distinction between the term's noun and verb forms become undecidable.

45. Terry Eagleton, *The Ideology of the Aesthetic* (Oxford: Wiley-Blackwell, 1991).

46. For a polemical instance of such a reading, see J. M. Bernstein, "Remembering Isaac: On the Impossibility and Immorality of Faith," in *The Insistence of Art: Aesthetic Philosophy After Early Modernity*, ed. Paul A. Kottman, 257–88 (New York: Fordham University Press, 2017).

47. Julia Reinhard Lupton and Graham Hammill, eds., *Political Theology and Early Modernity* (Chicago: University of Chicago Press, 2012), 5.

48. Lupton and Hammill, *Political Theology*, 5.

49. Maurice Merleau-Ponty, *The Visible and the Invisible* (Evanston, Ill.: Northwestern University Press, 1997), 139.

50. The kind of identificatory logic implied by the provocative equivalencies informing Parker's account of the relations among theater, monetary returns, and religious faith ("What a Piece of Work Is Man").

51. Particular thanks to Andrew Sisson for help thinking through the collection's conception and sequencing.

Part One

An Early Modern Aesthetic

"No Toy But Was Her Pattern"

Renaissance Friendship and the Rise of Aesthetics in *The Two Noble Kinsmen*

Andrew Sisson

In *The Two Noble Kinsmen*, Shakespeare and Fletcher adapt *The Knight's Tale*, following the plot with a fidelity unusual in period dramatizations of Chaucerian material but introducing two major changes of emphasis and one wholly novel element.[1] First, they cast the kinsmen, Palamon and Arcite, in the mold of the humanist discourse of ideal friendship, based in absolute equality and dedication to a shared concept of virtue. The cousins are made to voice and enact the commonplaces of this tradition, drawn from Cicero and other classical sources and exemplified for the English Renaissance by Thomas Elyot's rendition of the tale of Titus and Gisippus.[2] Their friendship, which Chaucer takes more or less for granted, is juxtaposed with others (Theseus and Pirithous, Emilia and Flavina) staged or recalled in the play; and their falling out over a common object of desire is presented as at once the loss and the paradoxical continuation of this cherished solidarity. Second, whereas in Chaucer's tale the pervasive atmosphere of ritualized ceremony is bound to the theme of the providential control of human affairs, in the play the latter concern is minimized if not trivialized, even as the ceremonial character of the action is insisted on all the more explicitly. The effect is to bring into the play something of the formal and aesthetic approach characteristic of the masque, its preoccupation with abstract compositions and specular relationships—as, in fact, the play is structured around a central Morris-dance scene that reprises part of a masque presented earlier in the year.[3]

In making these two moves together—or such will be my argument—Shakespeare and Fletcher develop Renaissance friendship's inherent potential to become a protoaesthetics. The peculiar structure of friendship discourse is such as to give it an opening onto the conceptual field that will develop as "the aesthetic" in the subsequent century and a half, though to pass through that opening may require an impulse to read friendship discourse against its own priorities. I propose that in *The Two Noble Kinsmen* that impulse is embodied in Shakespeare and Fletcher's third major departure from their source: the character of the Jailer's Daughter, whom they invent to replace the obscure "freend" who helps Palamon break from prison. Renaissance friendship represents what will come to be called aesthetic judgment as an expression of the (ideal, hypothetical) social forms in which it is situated. The Daughter's madness, by contrast, is the aspect judgment takes on when it loses its embeddedness and acquires its own autonomy, forcing a reconceiving of the terms of social consensus in order to accommodate it; the search for those terms is the enterprise we know as aesthetics.

The rise of the aesthetic in the later seventeenth and eighteenth centuries, culminating in Alexander Baumgarten's codification of the term in his 1750 *Aesthetica*, is a story that has been told often and variously. Here I offer only the briefest of sketches by way of indicating the background against which the subsequent analysis will unfold.[4] A first precondition for aesthetic modernity is the weakening of beauty's status as an index of metaphysical fullness, only ambiguously distinguished from goodness or truth, and its redefinition as a quality of *sensation*, capable of being elicited equally by natural objects or works of art. To locate beauty in sensation in turn means locating it in some way beyond the jurisdiction of reason, a division ratified by Descartes's conception of the subject as the agency that sifts the clear and distinct from the obscure and confused. Sensation is a field of impressions in which I am passively immersed before I am actively scrutinizing, which means also that it is a field in which "I" am not yet altogether present. And yet I experience this immersion not simply as an anarchic flux of more and less pleasing qualities but rather as organized by attractions that exercise a compelling power over me in ways I find difficult to articulate: what this period agreed to call the je ne sais quoi.[5] Why do certain empirically trivial differences between one object and another—Pascal's famous example is the length of Cleopatra's nose—so often lead to such overwhelmingly distinct subjective effects?[6]

Leibniz is the pivotal figure who proposes both that this question might admit of a systematic answer and that the practices of the arts might play a central role in supplying it. For Leibniz the je ne sais quoi marks out a cognitive domain not anticipated by Descartes's divisions: that of ideas simultaneously "clear" and "confused," possessing not conceptual distinctness but rather the kind of representational value a painter points to when he prefers one composition to another without being able to give a further analysis of the judgment.[7] From such evaluations we can derive principles accounting for sensation's internal organization, analogous to the way in which logic accounts for the intellect's method of arranging its products in a satisfying order. This is precisely the rationale for Baumgarten's coinage: aesthetic contains the bylaws of *aisthesis* as logic contains the laws of *logos*. The premise of aesthetics, then, is that objects in the domain of sensation have an implicit and inherent normativity. They can be judged normatively, as beautiful, sublime, ugly, and so forth, just insofar as the norms in question are not specified as abstract principles to which we assent in advance of our encounters with the objects to which they apply, but rather are realized through those encounters in their rich particularity. The name usually given to the system or totality of those norms, as well as to the condition of the subject well trained to realize them through her particular judgments, is *taste*.

On the one hand, then, the aesthetic appears to promise a socially predictable and reproducible, quasi-lawful system of taste. On the other hand, what authorizes us to think of this domain as possessing a kind of self-organizing power to begin with is the intersubjective closure of the je ne sais quoi, the certain something that can be articulated only as inarticulacy. It is this curious fact that links the constitution of the aesthetic to that of humanist friendship, which likewise offers the reproducibility of judgment as an image of social consensus while severely limiting the possibility of its communication.

What is most notable about friendship in the Renaissance tradition is its being a relationship defined invariably in terms of the sharing of judgment.[8] According to Cicero, "the whole essence"—or force, *vis*—"of friendship" consists in "the most complete agreement in policy, in pursuits, and in opinions."[9] In Elyot's tale of Titus and Gisippus the protagonists' "willes and appetites daily more and more so confederated them selfes, that it semed none other, whan their names were declared, but that they hadde onely chaunged their places, issuinge (as I mought saye) out of the one body, and entringe in to the other."[10] But what sort of judgment is it, exactly, that friends are supposed to share? At first glance, this appears to mean agreement on literally everything: "There should be between them complete harmony of opinions and inclinations in everything without exception."[11] But this formulation by Cicero's Laelius comes with a qualification: there can be complete harmony only when "the characters of friends are blameless." This is an equally consistent assertion in the literature of friendship. Not only must friends agree subjectively concerning everything to be desired but also that which they find desirable and wish to pursue must objectively be the good; friendship between those who agree in badness would be not simply counterproductive but actually inconceivable, *nisi in bonis amicitiam esse non posse*.[12]

However, we would not likely wish to stake friendship merely to, say, agreement in condemning a murderer or approving of the punishment of a thief. The common reason that tracks natural or positive law seems too widely and too weakly shared to account for that special intensity of agreement that leads friends continually to discover new objects for their assessments to converge upon. Friendship depends on judgment, but this judgment finds itself suspended in midair, between a merely accidental similarity of morally neutral inclinations, on the one hand, and a merely abstract consistency with a universally shared moral law, on the other.[13] What friends share, in a word, is *taste*—not because the literature of friendship places any special emphasis on friends' opinions about art but because the attempt to define friendship implies a peculiar pressure on those acts of judgment that can be seen to participate in the general good even as they mark the bounds of a particular sensibility.

The judgment of taste is certainly a besetting preoccupation of *The Two Noble Kinsmen*, an astonishing amount of which is given over to characters' gathering to discuss the relative appeal of other characters' performances—in dancing, singing, wrestling, or simply bearing oneself pleasingly. In other of the romances beauty can be taken for an index of transcendence; *The Two Noble Kinsmen* stays planted in the realm of sense's relative perfection, the polishing or refinement of experience as opposed to its transfiguration. This is expressed in two overlapping groups of metaphors tracing throughout the play: one of swimming, sailing, buoyant motion in a fluid medium; the other of the management of horses and other conveyances, the producing of an impression of facility while directing the movements of a restive apparatus. Gerald, the comic pedant and Morris-dance director who fancies himself extracting edifying order from the "coarse frieze capacities" and "jean judgments" of his charges, tells them to "swim with your bodies, / And carry it sweetly and deliverly" (3.5.8, 128–29).[14] He thus picks up on the preferred idiom of the play's protagonists, as in this speech in which Palamon in prison laments losing the pleasure of being seen in displays of physical grace:

> Never more
> Must we behold those comforts, never see
> The hardy youths strive for the games of honor,
> Hung with the painted favors of their ladies,
> Like tall ships under sail; then start amongst 'em

And, as an east wind, leave 'em all behind us,
Like lazy clouds, whilst Palamon and Arcite,
Even in the wagging of a wanton leg,
Outstripped the people's praises, won the garlands
Ere they have time to wish 'em ours. Oh, never
Shall we two exercise, like twins of honor,
Our arms again, and feel our fiery horses
Like proud seas under us. (2.2.8–20)

This instance is particularly telling in its way of tacking between universality and exclusivity, suggesting both that the kinsmen's excellence lies in what is obvious to sense and that it is their capacity to discern their own distinction that singles them out from the crowd.

The play in general shows a remarkable capacity to convert all manner of affective and dramatic facts into the language of aesthetic discrimination. For instance, when Emilia registers that Pirithous is missing his friend Theseus, she does so by noticing his "careless execution" in "sports" demanding "seriousness and skill" (1.3.27–29). Or, more strikingly, when Theseus gives an account of the kinsmen's offstage *agon*, the play's climactic moment, he does so not by narrating events but by offering an aesthetic metaphor for the doubtfulness of judgment:

I have heard
Two emulous Philomels beat the ear o'th' night
With their contentious throats, now one the higher,
Anon the other, then again the first,
And by and by out-breasted, that the sense
Could not be judge between 'em. (5.3.123–28)

Passages such as this one have often been used to motivate a quasi-biographical reading in which the emulous rivalry between the protagonists is taken as an allegory for the play's own origins as a product of collaborative authorship.[15] Alternatively, Shakespeare and Fletcher's emphasis on artful performance and judgment might be seen in sociohistorical terms as a sign of the play's address to an increasingly differentiated courtly audience able to recognize itself through the possession of a shared language of style.[16] But both approaches risk underrating the degree to which the sociality of aesthetic judgment is itself a matter under investigation in *The Two Noble Kinsmen*, as well as the variety of distinct, even antithetical models the play assembles for understanding it.[17] In what remains of this essay, I offer an inventory of these models, beginning with how the sharing of taste is treated in the humanist literature of friendship and the ways in which this paradigm continues to inform the play. I then turn to the opposing model—or antimodel—implied in Shakespeare and Fletcher's conception of the Jailer's Daughter. Finally, I seek to show how *The Two Noble Kinsmen* most nearly anticipates the episteme of the aesthetic when it imagines drawing these opposites together in an unstable relation.

Consider first the widely imitated tale of Titus and Gisippus, included in Elyot's *The Boke Named the Governour* to "ministre to the redars singuler pleasure and also incredible comforte to practice amitie" (133).[18] Titus is a young Roman patrician sent to Athens to learn philosophy, where he is housed with a local notable's son named Gisippus. Already alike in age, "stature, proporcion of body, fauour, and colour of visage, countenaunce and speche," as their friendship deepens Titus and Gisippus become so similar as to appear virtually indistinguishable (134). One day Gisippus introduces Titus to his fiancée, Sophronia. Titus is instantly inflamed but conceals this and pines away until, near death, he confesses his plight to Gisippus. Why, he laments, did Gisippus reveal to him the woman he loved, knowing "that what ye liked was euer to me in lyke degree pleasaunt?" (139). Gisippus finds this reasoning not only persuasive but obvious in hindsight—"I remembered nat the commune astate of our nature, ne the agreeablenesse, or (as I mought saye) the unitie of our two appetites"—and without hesitation arranges through a kind of bed trick to wed Sophronia to Titus instead (140). After several further twists of fortune, Titus reciprocates Gisippus's generosity by confessing to a crime for which Gisippus stands accused; the willingness of each friend to die in the other's place is so moving that the real criminal comes forth to confess.

However much friendship as a social form may be *conceptually* dependent upon the sharing of judgments, then, the *narrative* conventions of friendship literature work in the opposite way. Elyot's narrative, having first presented erotic desire as essentially a matter of aesthetic judgment, goes on to define that judgment as a reflex of the friends' preexisting social solidarity. *Of course* Titus and Gisippus would be attracted to the same woman; after all, Titus and Gisippus are friends! The lesson, we might say, is that the social structure of friendship proves sufficient to absorb without remainder the acts of judgment that nominally determine it. Precisely because Titus's love for Gisippus's fiancée can be interpreted as merely emblematic of an underlying relationship between the two men, that relationship can also supply the script for resolving whatever tensions their identity of object choice may have created.

In *The Two Noble Kinsmen*, any such resolution is of course ruled out by the nature of Chaucer's plot. Yet in some respects Shakespeare and Fletcher are still inside Elyot's paradigm, in which the judgment of the senses is conceived as a determined effect of the relationships that underlie and justify it. Most obviously, Arcite makes exactly Titus's argument after becoming infatuated with the woman Palamon has pointed out to him through the window of their prison cell: "Am I not liable to those affections, / Those joys, griefs, angers, fears, my friend shall suffer?" (2.2.193–94). Less explicit but more telling is the scene in which Emilia, hoping to prevent the kinsmen's death match by choosing one, studies their portraits at length but ultimately finds that she can articulate no basis on which to judge one against the other:

> What a mere child is Fancy,
> That, having two fair gauds of equal sweetness,
> Cannot distinguish, but must cry for both! (4.2.52–54)

As Eugene Waith points out, this stalling of judgment seems clearly meant to enforce upon us what he calls "the absolute equality which is the basis for the perfect friendship of Palamon and Arcite."[19] Emilia, in Waith's reading, cannot decide because at a deeper level she *gets it*—by contrast with the Jailer's Daughter, who vulgarly supposes that she likes one boy better than the other and so demonstrates her ignorance of humanist pedagogy—and what Emilia gets is that the kinsmen must really be equals because they really are friends. Again, a scene of aesthetic judgment functions to emblematize the terms of a social relationship that precedes it and enables its interpretation.

The Jailer's Daughter is indeed well chosen as Emilia's opposite, but in a much more than merely casual sense. Whereas Emilia can find between the kinsmen no distinction significant enough to motivate a differential judgment, the Daughter gives absolute significance to a distinction overwhelmingly available to no one but herself. In the Daughter's first scene she, her father, and her would-be suitor, the Wooer, watch as the kinsmen appear at the cell window above. The Jailer misidentifies Palamon as Arcite; the Daughter corrects him, then adds, "It is a holiday to look on them. Lord, the diff'rence of men!" (2.1.58–59). This consciousness of "the diff'rence of men" will grow into a terrifying fixation upon Palamon and his imagined sexual potency, yet the difference the Daughter sees never does become quite apparent to anyone else. Her absolute preference for Palamon is set off against the more publicly prominent discourse of Emilia's indecision or Theseus's "emulous Philomels," insistently invested in the kinsmen's essential sameness. Moreover, whatever it is that the Daughter fixates upon is so far from being intelligible to others *as* a difference that she ultimately happily accepts as "Palamon" a person—the lower-class Wooer—who in every way apparent could not be less like him. The Daughter's attunement to the infinitesimal difference that makes Palamon appealing beyond all other men coincides with her blindness to the empirical chasm between him and the man she takes for his substitute.

If Arcite's and Emilia's citations of the narrative conventions of Renaissance friendship show judgment resolved without remainder into a social form, here we see judgment given such a radical autonomy that it seems to refer to nothing but the self as its own groundless ground. The Daughter is a case par excellence of what we might, following Christopher Pye, call vanishing-point subjectivity.[20] Literally, she enters the play pointing to Palamon framed by the window, the place from which in the next scene Palamon will point out Emilia to Arcite. Alex Davis has illuminatingly discussed this as an "elegantly chiasmic structure" through which "the audience's attention passes into the prison house and is there turned inside out."[21] In that sense, the visible-invisible minimal difference that marks out "Palamon" might be analogized to the point of indistinction that in perspective space closes the visual field and offers it up as infinite. It would be as precipitous to heap on the Jailer's Daughter all the weight psychoanalytic criticism will subsequently give to this particular metaphor as it would be obtuse to fail to notice how, as she becomes more isolated in her fantasies, these take the form of figurative elaborations of the first specular scene. Most striking in this context is what amounts to a pastiche of the "Dover Cliff" episode in *King Lear*:

> Yonder's the sea, and there's a ship. How't tumbles!
> And there's a rock lies watching under water.
> Now, now, it beats upon it; now, now, now,
> There's a leak sprung, a sound one. How they cry!
> Open her before the wind, you'll lose all else.
> Up with a course or two, and tack about, boys. (3.4.5–10)

The most compelling element here is the rock "watching under water," invisible and yet somehow summative of the scene's availability to vision. The Daughter's desire, it seems, is at once to possess a visual field identical with the whole of reality and to include in that field an element marking it as hers, as irreducibly structured by her own presence to it.

In the Jailer's Daughter it is as if the judgment friends are said to share had gained autonomy at the cost of producing an organization of experience seemingly impossible to reproduce or communicate. If this calls to mind the je ne sais quoi, it is perhaps not insignificant that that figure's intellectual history has a peculiar relation to dramatic material of much this kind. The most influential seventeenth-century text on the subject, Dominique Bouhours's *Les entretiens d'Ariste et d'Eugène* (to which Leibniz's philosophical treatment is a response), concurs with Pascal in identifying Corneille as the je ne sais quoi's iconic spokesman.[22] Bouhours's dialogue begins with a discussion of friendship, which the protagonists understand to consist in an incalculable power by which their conversation continually invents new objects pleasing to both. Ariste argues that all attempts to supply a causal principle for this "indefinable something" are merely empty circumlocutions covering its essential quality of resistance to specification. One poet, he says, has grasped this point better than the philosophers, and he proceeds to quote Corneille's *Rodogune*:

> There are strong bonds of hidden, tender liking,
> Through whose sweet pow'r each lover finds his own;
> Each to each is join'd at glances' striking
> By something hidden, never to be known.
> [*Par ces je ne sais quoi, qu'on ne peut expliquer*.][23]

The situation in Corneille's play is that two brothers who are also classical friends, equal in their devotion to virtue and each other, have both fallen in love with the princess Rodogune. What Ariste quotes is Rodogune's confession to her maid that, in spite of the brothers' perfectly balanced merits, she in fact finds herself drawn exclusively and overwhelmingly to one of them. She thus in a way occupies the Jailer's Daughter's structural position in an externally similar type of plot, although in both social decorum and narrative development the two scenarios drastically diverge.

Rodogune keeps her feeling a secret, one she reveals only when the progress of the intrigue has so differentiated the brothers as to give her preference a retrospectively objective basis. *The Two Noble Kinsmen*, by contrast, makes the Daughter's unreciprocated desire for Palamon into a point of subjective closure that cannot be hidden because it expresses itself in each new fantasy image spun out of its absent presence. And yet it's precisely here that the play proposes that the Daughter's mind can be comprehended as a formal system like that of an aesthetic object, restored to its composure by supplying the missing element around which it is structured. Just as the Daughter returns the Morris to order by filling the spot left vacant by one dancer's absence, so too is the Daughter returned to something like sanity when the Wooer steps into the right formal space, the empty plenitude that is "Palamon." And the content he fills it with is, precisely, the aesthetic. The Doctor instructs the Wooer as follows:

> Sing to her such green songs of love as she says Palamon hath sung in prison; come to her stuck in as sweet flowers as the season is mistress of, and thereto make an addition of some other compounded odors which are grateful to the sense. All this shall become Palamon, for Palamon can sing, and Palamon is sweet and ev'ry good thing. (4.3.82–88)

"All this shall become Palamon" wonderfully encapsulates the point: to become Palamon is just to be becoming, for Palamon here has turned into a kind of placeholder for whatever pleases the aesthetic sense.

What is at one level a pure marker of recalcitrant subjectivity can at another be treated as a kind of generic frame for a heterogeneous but orderly set of contents, the common heading under which to range comely flowers and sweet love songs. There is a curious anticipation of this maneuver in the turn taken by the Daughter's reveries when she is overheard by the Wooer just before her return home. She multiplies her own Palamon obsession into the image of "a hundred black-eyed maids that love as I do," drawn by their shared feeling into a stylized version of the Morris, going off to "dance an antic 'fore the Duke" with "chaplets on their heads of daffadillies . . . cherry lips and cheeks of damask roses" (4.1.72–75). The Doctor's technique in a sense simply follows the line of this imaginative movement—developed yet more strangely in the Daughter's vision of Palamon fathering a clan of two hundred castrati to "sing the wars of Theseus" (133)—offering the aesthetic object as a kind of generic interpretation of the subjectivity secreted in the je ne sais quoi. That, at any rate, is the gambit of the Daughter's cure: a successful translation of the fathomless "diff'rence of men" into just that difference that can be comprehended by the judgment of beautiful forms.

Groundless desire and reproducible form are thus drawn, in the Jailer's Daughter's story, into an embrace not unlike that described by Jacques Rancière in his influential interpretation of the aesthetic's emergence as a discursive regime. For Rancière this regime's distinguishing feature is that art comes to be conceived primarily in terms of a paradoxical identity between cognition and noncognition, as the place of "thought that is present outside itself" or "thought of that which does not think."[24] At one level this account is continuous with the Leibnizian tradition, insofar as it suggests that aesthetic objects' cognitive value resides not in decorum or proportion ordering experience from outside but rather in some hidden formative power inhering in sensation's own confused contents. In Rancière's version, however, what develops from this is not a discrete sphere of "sensuous cognition" with its own set of representational norms parallel but not reducible to those of discursive reason. Rather, the aesthetic is a permanently unstable coincidence of opposites, an interpretive space defined by the symmetrical moves by which thought and nonthought may each be revealed as the other's hidden truth. The trivial and seemingly random detail may disclose a legible pattern, through which cognition's work is carried on beyond its own domain; the most refined work of form may resolve to an unaccountable drive, which finds itself only in losing all relation to its ends.[25]

Rancière's way of putting the point helps us to recognize the most striking anticipations of the project of modern aesthetics in those moments when the play conceives of judgment neither on the purely social model of friendship discourse nor as the absolute subjectivity of the Daughter's specular scenes, but rather as a kind of rapid shuttling between antitheses.[26] If that project's novelty lies in its concern to explain how intersubjectively stable values can arise from the most contingent features of subjective experience, we may perhaps approach its prehistory by looking to moments in which the two terms are set in consciously paradoxical or oxymoronic relation.[27] We have observed one of these in the translation of inarticulate will into aesthetic system implied by the process of the Daughter's cure. Such a translation is presented more overtly, and rejoined to the amicable ideal's explicit sociality, in being made the basis of the friendship that the play imagines at length but cannot quite stage. Before the main action has begun, Emilia, in a speech that has attracted much attention, recalls her eleven-year-old self's love for a playfellow:

What she liked
Was then of me approved, what not, condemned—
No more arraignment. The flower that I would pluck
And put between my breasts—Oh, then but beginning
To swell about the blossom—she would long
Till she had such another, and commit it
To the like innocent cradle, where, phoenix-like,
They died in perfume. On my head no toy
But was her pattern; her affections—pretty,
Though happily her careless wear—I followed
For my most serious decking. (1.3.64–74)

In this speech the friends' conventional agreement in all things is modified by emphasizing its asymmetry: what for the one friend is a barely registered inclination becomes a matter of conscious study for the other. The absence of debate over competing tastes does not preclude the reflective activity of elaborating ad hoc expressions of taste into principles or even something like a system. What is a "toy" for you may become a "pattern" for me, if I can grasp enough of its inner character to find what makes it a choice for *this* and not *that*, and so reproduce it for myself. What is "careless wear" for me may become "serious decking" for you, but in the process it has to lose its spontaneous character and assume something of the solidity of a rule.

In this scenario aesthetic judgment, though fundamentally social, is not reducible to the sociologism whereby the shared taste of objectively similar people precedes the acts of judgment that express it. But neither is aesthetic judgment, though fundamentally individual, reducible to the psychologism whereby each judgment of particulars only confirms its subject in her incommunicable particularity. Rather, Emilia and Flavina's friendship suggests a sociability that is not the ground of aesthetic activity so much as its product: society as the collective elaboration of the normative logic deeply implicit in what we observe of the unreflective inclinations of others. With the aspiration to such a sociability we are on the threshold of what the philosophy of the Enlightenment would seek to achieve through the discourse of the aesthetic.

To describe Emilia's recollection in this way is, however, to raise the question of its status in the play's larger economy of meaning. Certainly there is not much obvious internal warrant for reading it as historical prolepsis; on the contrary, the friendship involved is presented as in several senses without a future. Generically it belongs to the type of youthful homoeroticism that in Shakespearean comedy frequently appears as destined to fall before the imperatives of conjugal maturity. Yet even by the standards of the pairings it otherwise most resembles, Emilia and Flavina's friendship is distinguished by the degree to which it takes ephemerality as the principle of its own self-conception. Helena in *A Midsummer Night's Dream* remembers herself and Hermia as "artificial gods" conspiring to make one flower in one sampler, concurrence conferring solidity on their joint intentions.[28] Emilia describes a mimesis fixated on the specifically transient detail, seeking to approach the friend's ungraspable particularity by reproducing it in ever more fragmentary and evanescent signatures of style, the flower plucked and placed so as to die in just the manner of its mate.

Such a mode of relation implies a yet more pointed contrast with that of the male protagonists introduced in the scene before. In Arcite and

Palamon's first appearance they plan their escape from Creon's Thebes, the moral miasma of which is summed up in a fashion system that Palamon describes as pure heteronomy, the compulsion of an entirely arbitrary series of unjustified preferences. Tell me, he demands,

> Why mine own barber is unblessed, with him
> My poor chin too, for 'tis not scissored just
> To such a favorite's glass? What canon is there
> That does command my rapier from my hip
> To dangle't in my hand, or to go tip-toe
> Before the street be foul? (1.2.53–58)

Palamon traces the performance of a stereotyped sprezzatura to its origin in a "canon" of taste reductively imagined as the pure willfulness of those who control access to social prestige. The specious casualness of a gesture like dangling one's rapier is vitiated by its inhabitation by a certain external violence, the sword being "commanded" to leave its natural position. At the same time, the command's lawlike status is undermined by arising from that ultimate sphere of fleeting and underdetermined affective choice, the world of court favoritism that serves as a parody of genuine friendship.

Palamon, then, defines his and Arcite's friendship by opposing it to the sort of potentiation of the ephemeral that constitutes the whole consistency of Emilia and Flavina's. What this early scene presents is not Arcite and Palamon's sharing of taste—that will come later—so much as their agreement in the more generalized morality meant to ground and justify the convergence of their faculties. That morality is, indeed, so very accessible as to center on the propositions that society does not do enough for disabled veterans and that courtiers are odious. In the humanist model, as we have seen, the intensity of friends' participation in a more broadly intelligible moral accord is precisely what the sharing of sensible judgment serves to emblematize. Given that model, however, any system of taste that acquires collective power without being grounded in such a prior cognitive structure might well appear as a kind of tyranny. In the reified guise of court fashion, taste comes to look like an inversion of the proper relations between fickle liking and durable rule. A properly aesthetic sociability, in which judgments of sense constitute an autonomous formative element, can in this context justify itself only by accepting the condition of transience to the point of being propelled out of the play's present altogether.

The role *The Two Noble Kinsmen* assigns to the aesthetic as a social form is thus complexly rendered but ultimately equivocal. Reluctantly accepting the obligation to serve Creon's perverted regime, Arcite and Palamon equate this with surrender to the power of chance, "that never-erring arbitrator," foreshadowing the mishap that will ultimately strike Arcite down in his moment of triumph at the play's climax (1.2.114). Yet this invocation of the formula of *virtus* and *fortuna* is complicated by the way in which the catastrophe turns out to be set within the same framework of inscrutable impulse and emergent system that appears more positively in Emilia and Flavina's aesthetic relations. The conjuncture of "toy" and "pattern" recurs once more in Pirithous's remarkable speech recounting the accident, which has left Arcite near death and so opened the way for Palamon to take his place with Emilia.

The way the event happens in *The Knight's Tale* is that Saturn, god of mischances, sends a demon to startle Arcite's horse, and Arcite, momentarily distracted, is thrown from his saddle. The narration in *The Two Noble Kinsmen* is far more intricate than Chaucer's and begins with an extended evocation of Arcite's virtuosity as a horseman, "trotting the stones of Athens, which the calkins / Did rather tell than trample" (5.4.55–56). The figure of horse and rider is at one level clearly meant to summon up the symbolism of reason and sense, higher faculties exerted over lower, that conventionally attaches to it. Yet the passage's emphasis falls instead on sense's reflexive capacity, its responsiveness to its own immanent regularity. "Counting / The flinty pavement, dancing as 'twere to th' music / His own hoofs made," the horse does not seem to be governed by the rider's higher-order rationality so much as driven by some indwelling potential to produce a spontaneous approximation of it (58–60). But then his foot strikes—apparently—send up a spark, and at this eruption from within the rapture of his own performance the horse "took toy," reverting "to what disorder / His power could give his will" (66–67). I say "apparently" because in Pirithous's narration the spark is really a hypothesis, the barest physical equivalent for the minimal difference that divides the ordered pattern of the horse's dance from the capricious "toy" of its dissolution. It is, in other words, the purest form of je ne sais quoi—which is, indeed, how Pirithous presents it. "I comment not," he says, "what envious flint, / Cold as old Saturn," might have "darted a spark," nor "what fierce sulphur else" might have produced the same disastrous effect (59–65).

Significantly, Arcite does not fall from his horse. Rather, the creature's very inability to unseat his rider leads him to rise up and come over backward, until finally Arcite is crushed beneath his weight. It is as if to say that what the catastrophe announces is not a *parting* of sense from reason but rather their entrance into a new and paradoxical configuration, of which "toy" and "pattern" are the infinitely reversible yet inseparably bound elements. Confining Chaucer's divinities to an ambivalent simile, Shakespeare closes off the opening to causal exteriority that drives *The Knight's Tale*'s meditations on fortune and providence. What is at stake is, rather, the emergent autonomy of a sphere formerly seen to receive its order from without. The play solves the problem of choosing one kinsman over the other, unresolvable when referred to the moral scheme guaranteeing their equality, by relocating its arbitrariness within the very constitution of beauty as a socially communicable value. Reversing the direction of Emilia's recollection, Pirithous's speech suggests that if the forms inferred from fugitive impulse can be the fabric of sociability, then sociability itself may as easily collapse back into the subjective will from which it began. For all this vision's deep pessimism, could there be a better image for the advent of the aesthetic? The rider, no longer struggling to keep hold of a restive animal that threatens to throw him off, instead finds himself bound to a sensuous double that rises to its feet and leaves him suspended in midair, so that "Arcite's legs, being higher than his head, / Seemed with strange art to hang" (78–79).

Notes

1. Helen Cooper, "Jacobean Chaucer: *The Two Noble Kinsmen* and Other Chaucerian Plays," in *Refiguring Chaucer in the Renaissance*, ed. Theresa M. Krier, 189–209 (Gainesville: University Press of Florida, 1998).

2. See Eugene M. Waith, "Shakespeare and Fletcher on Love and Friendship," *Shakespeare Studies* 18 (1986): 235–50. Other important treatments of the friendship theme include Barry Weller, "*The Two Noble Kinsmen*, the Friendship Tradition, and the Flight from Eros," in *Shakespeare, Fletcher, and "The Two Noble Kinsmen,"* ed. Charles H. Frey, 93–108 (Columbia: University of Missouri Press, 1989), and Laurie Shannon, *Sovereign Amity: Figures of Friendship in Shakespearean Contexts* (Chicago: University of Chicago Press, 2002), 90–122.

3. Specifically, the second antimasque from Francis Beaumont's *Masque of the Inner Temple and Gray's Inn*, performed for the wedding of Princess Elizabeth and the Elector Frederick. For text and commentary, see Lois Potter, ed., *The Two Noble Kinsmen* (London: Bloomsbury, 2015), 382–99. On ritualism and masque influence in the play, see Northrop Frye, "Romance as Masque," in *Shakespeare's Romances Reconsidered*, ed. Carol McGinnis Kay and Henry Jacobs, 11–39 (Lincoln: University of Nebraska Press, 1978); Julie Sanders, "Mixed Messages: The Aesthetics of *The Two Noble Kinsmen*," in *A Companion to Shakespeare's Works*, vol. 4, ed. Richard Dutton and Jean Howard, 445–61 (Oxford: Blackwell Publishing, 2005).

4. The argument of this paragraph is much indebted to that of Christoph Menke, *Force: A Fundamental Concept of Aesthetic Anthropology*, trans. Gerrit Jackson (New York: Fordham University Press, 2013).

5. See Richard Scholar, *The Je-Ne-Sais-Quoi in Early Modern Europe: Encounters with a Certain Something* (Oxford: Oxford University Press, 2005).

6. Blaise Pascal, *Pensées*, no. 162, quoted in Menke, *Force*, 7.

7. For context, see Jeffrey Barnouw, "The Beginnings of 'Aesthetics' and the Leibnizian Conception of Sensation," in *Eighteenth-Century Aesthetics and the Reconstruction of Art*, ed. Paul Mattick Jr., 52–95 (Cambridge: Cambridge University Press, 1993).

8. Contrasting critical assessments of this tradition include Shannon, *Sovereign Amity*, and Lorna Hutson, *The Usurer's Daughter: Male Friendship and Fictions of Women in Sixteenth-Century England* (London: Routledge, 1994).

9. Cicero, *De Amicitia*, trans. William Armistead Falconer (London: Heinemann, 1923), iv.15 (p. 125).

10. Thomas Elyot, *The Boke Named the Governour*, ed. Henry Croft (1829; repr., New York: Franklin, 1967), 2.134; hereafter cited parenthetically.

11. Cicero, *De Amicitia*, xvii.61 (p. 171).

12. Cicero, *De Amicitia*, v.18 (p. 127).

13. An interpretation of the history of aesthetics as the search for a public philosophy that would resolve this antinomy is the main theme of Terry Eagleton's *The Ideology of the Aesthetic* (Oxford: Blackwell Publishing, 1990).

14. All references to the play cite *The Complete Works of Shakespeare*, ed. David Bevington, 5th ed. (New York: Pearson Longman, 2004).

15. See especially Donald K. Hedrick, "'Be Rough With Me': The Collaborative Arenas of *The Two Noble Kinsmen*," in Frey, *Shakespeare, Fletcher*, 45–77, and Jeffrey Masten, *Textual Intercourse: Collaboration, Authorship, and Sexualities in Renaissance Drama* (Cambridge: Cambridge University Press, 1997), 49–60.

16. A provocative argument situating *The Two Noble Kinsmen* at a key transitional moment in the Jacobean theater's social address is offered by Douglas Bruster, "The Jailer's Daughter and the Politics of Madwomen's Language," *Shakespeare Quarterly* 46, no. 3 (1995): 277–300.

17. For period conceptions of what would come to be called aesthetic judgment, see David Summers, *The Judgment of Sense: Renaissance Naturalism and the Rise of Aesthetics* (Cambridge: Cambridge University Press, 1987).

18. Elyot's source is a Latin translation of the eighth story of the tenth day of Boccaccio's *Decameron*. On the narrative's literary history and influence, see Louis Sorieri, *Boccaccio's Story of "Tito e Gisippo" in European Literature* (New York: Institute of French Studies, 1937).

19. Waith, "Shakespeare and Fletcher," 244.

20. Christopher Pye, *The Vanishing: Shakespeare, the Subject, and Early Modern Culture* (Durham, N.C.: Duke University Press, 2000).

21. Alex Davis, "Living in the Past: Thebes, Periodization, and *The Two Noble Kinsmen*," *Journal of Medieval and Early Modern Studies* 40, no. 1 (2010): 179.

22. On Corneille's paradigmatic status for seventeenth-century theorists, see Scholar, *Je-Ne-Sais-Quoi*, 155. Leibniz's use of Bouhours is discussed in Barnouw, "Beginnings," 87–91.

23. Dominique Bouhours, "The Je Ne Sais Quoi from 'The Conversations of Aristo and Eugene' (1671)," in *The Continental Model: Selected French Critical Essays of the Seventeenth Century, in English Translation*, ed. and trans. Scott Elledge and Donald Schier (Ithaca, N.Y.: Cornell University Press, 1970), 183. For the quotation, see Pierre Corneille, *Rodogune*, trans. William G. Clubb (Lincoln: University of Nebraska Press, 1974), 1.5.359–62.

24. Jacques Rancière, *The Aesthetic Unconscious*, trans. Debra Keates and James Swenson (Cambridge: Polity Press, 2009), 6. Cf. Jacques Rancière, *The Politics of Aesthetics: The Distribution of the Sensible*, trans. Gabriel Rockhill (London: Continuum, 2004), 20–30.

25. Rancière, *The Aesthetic Unconscious*, 31–42.

26. This is not to say that Rancière would necessarily take the same view of the historical material presented here. His remarks on the je ne sais quoi treat it essentially as a "supplement" to what he terms the representative regime, or what might more familiarly be called the discourse of classicism, one brought in to guarantee the fit between the arts' repertoire of cultivated techniques and their affective medium of reception. The passage to a conception of aesthetic experience as constitutively split, at once a kind of cognitive activity and its negation, Rancière places later and associates in a perhaps somewhat tendentious fashion with the fall of the ancien régime in politics. See Jacques Rancière, *Aisthesis: Scenes from the Aesthetic Regime of Art*, trans. Zakir Paul (London: Verso, 2013), 10–11.

27. For a similar formulation of the problematic of aesthetic modernity, see Luc Ferry, *Homo Aestheticus: The Invention of Taste in the Democratic Age*, trans. Robert de Loaiza (Chicago: University of Chicago Press, 1993), 7–25.

28. *A Midsummer Night's Dream*, in Bevington, *Complete Works of Shakespeare*, 3.2.203.

“No Cause, No Cause”

King Lear and the Space of the World

Christopher Pye

Against familiar conceptions of the historical boundaries and depoliticizing vocation of aesthetic thought, I want to suggest here that it is precisely through the category of the aesthetic that the political stakes of early modernity are most directly engaged, whether we understand those stakes in terms of historical causes or the politics of our own attempts to give narrative form to such causes. Bound up with the emergence of representation’s claims to autonomous, even autogenerative, powers, the aesthetic also coincided historically with a distinctly early modern transformation in the social field: on the one hand, a shift in conceptions of the grounds of sovereignty from questions of genealogical legitimacy to the formal indivisibility of its authority;[1] on the other, although of a piece with that turn, a reconception of the social domain itself as a self-creative and self-founding space, a space articulated through a process whose very groundlessness aligned it with the logic of aestheticization.[2]

At the same time, that very association between aesthetics and autogeneration suggests why the political dimension of political aesthetics only fully appears at the point where the problem of the aesthetic passes beyond such narratives of historical causation. Precisely in its claim to a world-creating autonomy, aesthetics, like sovereignty, is structured on a claim to compass and enact its own grounds of emergence, and in doing so inevitably poses the question of its own causes. Ultimately, “early modern aesthetics,” like sovereignty, must be situated at once in and beyond the historicizing narratives through which we would locate it. On the one hand, I argue that in *King Lear*, my focus here, something like historical aesthetics—that is, aesthetics in the Kantian sense of aesthetic *consciousness*—comes to view as the subjective or transcendental pendant to the division and externalization of the social domain associated with the appearance of modern historical society, society conceived in relation to the contingency of its own foundation. On the other, the play stages that genealogical narrative explicitly against the more unstable and temporally unplaceable allegory of sovereign origination that opens the drama. That elliptical opening unsettles the play's narrative trajectories even as it draws us close to the unseen grounds of theater's affective hold. Aesthetics functions to mediate that relation between historical causation and a more opaque causeless cause; whether *King Lear* conveys the historical emergence of the aesthetic or whether that aesthetic break must always have already occurred for any such narrative of origination to become possible is the very question aesthetics opens and pointedly suspends.

The novelty and fragility of such a mechanism of aesthetic self-grounding is evident in the way consciousness is haunted in the play by a dimension of aesthetic transformation that remains resistant to interiorization—Kantian subjectivity's dark remainder, as it were. Necessarily demonized in relation to the play's thematic and developmental preoccupations, that untoward aesthetic recurs at the close as the very condition for the drama's conceiving possibilities of community and rapport beyond the traditional economies of tragedy, classical or Christian. Ultimately, the political stakes of the drama can't be separated from that constitutive, historical/ahistorical dimension of aestheticization; those stakes are to be sought neither in the play's diegetic narrative nor in its mimetic reference to an already presumed world beyond but in the inhuman force that opens such worlds in the first place.

Of course, to make claims for the origins of sovereignty in *King Lear* will seem counterintuitive. Isn't the play about the *undoing* of the sovereign's claim to all-encompassing power, Cordelia's "nothing" the grit in the mechanism of kingship that sets the tragedy in motion? With her act of defiance, Cordelia breaks open the king's narcissistic absorption in a ritualized enactment terrifying in the extent of its phenomenological reach. "I love you . . . Dearer than eyesight," Goneril declares.[3]

And yet, as I have argued in another context, the calamity that marks the opening of the drama may be hard to distinguish from sovereignty's initiating condition.[4] If the drama of the era insistently gravitates toward the act by which sovereignty undoes itself, that is because that act intimates something about the grounds of sovereign power as a formal conception.[5] Rather than being the delusion of a figure too long absorbed in his role and thus blind to its limits, Lear's fantasy of overseeing his own end is the recourse through which relationally defined sovereignty would exceed and compass its own bounds thereby constituting itself as radically self-inclusive and therefore autonomous. In that sense, the play's ritual opening allegorizes something like the transition from suzerainty—a matter of feudal bonds—to "modern" sovereignty conceived vis-à-vis autonomy and self-relation, sovereignty as, in Jean-Luc Nancy's formulation, "an infinite institution that nevertheless includes within it the imperious necessity of the finite moment of its institution."[6]

By the logic of such constitutive finitude, institution and end become indistinguishable. "I would unstate myself to be in due resolution," Gloucester says (1.2.99–100); sovereign self-certainty demands just such a passage beyond the limit, a self-seeing by virtue a self-undoing. In that regard, Lear's is the act that sets in train all those self-consuming, self-generating mechanisms the drama plays out, acts in which resolution and dissolution, cure and punishment, become indistinguishable. Echoing his obscurely self-knowing reference at the drama's opening to the "barbarous Scythian" who "makes his generation messes / To gorge his appetite," Lear declaims of his thankless daughters, "Is it not as this mouth should tear this hand / For lifting food to't?" (1.1.117–19, 3.4.15–16). "I will punish home," Lear says, preparing to revenge himself against his own flesh and blood, healing and renewing the divisions that haunt him (3.4.16). In that sense, Lear's "darker purpose" at play's opening is only the first of the play's manifold "monsters of the deep" "that prey on [themselves]" (4.2.313).[7]

Such implied equivalency between cure and disease suggests the immunological—or autoimmunological—paradigm that has been associated in recent political theory less with sovereignty than with the shift away from a transcendentally conceived sovereign affiliated with law and prohibition to the immanent and self-perpetuating workings of biopower, where force is endlessly reconstituted through its own resistance.[8] And yet Lear's "punish[ing] home"—a conclusive punishment, but also a reverting punishment—suggests the ways in which that immunological mechanism inevitably exceeds the biopolitical framework within which it is often described, revealing biopower as an epiphenomenal derivative of sovereignty, not its historical replacement, and early modern sovereignty itself as an irreducibly political-aesthetic phenomenon.[9]

The aesthetic, rather than biopolitical, dimensions of sovereign formation at this historical juncture can be brought to view by considering the most far-reaching recent efforts to articulate the assumed transition from sovereign power to biopower: Giorgio Agamben's project attempting to integrate a Foucauldian genealogy of biopower with the post-Hegelian tradition through which the concept of sovereignty has been traditionally articulated. For Agamben, sovereignty involves an immunological mechanism, but one that ultimately binds it to a supervening biopolitical dimension. That mechanism is associated with the aporetic gesture by which sovereignty founds itself, the gesture by which sovereignty institutes itself precisely through what it at the same time excludes; that is, by constituting its own defining limits from within. Because that mechanism of "inclusive exclusion"—what Agamben terms the "sovereign ban"—is constitutive, it is itself without "positive content," without referent because it constitutes "the structure of reference in general."[10] And yet in the course of Agamben's various narratives, that founding mechanism does nevertheless assume an object: "bare life" as the correlate, indeed "the first and immediate reference," of the sovereign ban.[11]

Bare life is without essence: it is a definitionally indeterminate category, existing always in the "zone of indistinction" between *zoe* and *bios*, natural and politically determined life, thus falling neither within nor beyond the juridical domain. And yet by granting phenomenally substantialized form to that indeterminate condition, by translating it into sovereignty's object at all, Agamben is able to convert a repetitive and necessarily open mechanism—the process by which sovereignty at once constitutes and endlessly consumes itself—into a drama of "capture" in which life is caught within law, and through which the sovereign becomes at once the effect of the operation of the ban and its arbiter.[12] Recuperating a purely formal operation in these agonistic terms, Agamben is able to recast the entire Enlightenment project and its preoccupation with thinking the incognizable limits of cognition—what is "in force without significance"—as one more turn in the dire advance of biopower's expansive inscription of life, Kant becoming a way station in the inevitable biopolitical trajectory toward the Nazi death camps.[13] Moreover, once sovereignty's nonground becomes "capturable" as a phenomenally legible form, a reiterative operation becomes capable of historical narrativization. What had bypassed the claims of reference in its unbounded operation now becomes fully determinate spatially and temporally, traceable in an epochal arc culminating in the delimiting confines of the death camp and the immanent being of the *Muselmann*.

What would it mean to conceive the inclusive exclusion through which early modern sovereignty founds itself absent such hypostatic tethering? It would mean conceiving sovereignty not biopolitically but politico-aesthetically. Associated specifically with signification severed from its referential and instrumental functions, the aesthetic concerns the way in which a discursive field institutes itself "from within," as it were, instituting its limits in precisely the movement by which it exceeds them. Understanding sovereignty in political-aesthetic terms implies a framework at once narrower than Agamben's, relating as it does to the specifically early modern formalization of the problem of the sovereign, and larger, insofar as it bears not on a given phenomenal point of reference such as "bare life" but on the mechanism of phenomenalization as such, the means through which a signifying field becomes immanently realizable in the first instance—thus the aesthetic's relation to the era's preoccupation with the problem of social-symbolic foundations generally.[14]

Conceiving Lear's creative and destructive act in political-aesthetic terms means reimagining that moment vis-à-vis the drama as a whole. The gesture of casting Cordelia out remains motivationally illegible: Lear can be read as the most knowing character in the drama, ensuring the marriage based on love precisely by casting his daughter beyond his cannibalistically incestuous and absorptive ken—recall his reference to the "barbarous Scythian"—or, of course, as the most self-ignorant. The contradiction arises not for characterological reasons but because Lear's opaque gesture enacts the institution of the drama as a space in which the characters as knowing subjects will be constituted: it is that constitutive expulsion that opens up the vectored space of recognition and return in relation to which characterization becomes possible. In that sense, the act allegorizes the auto-generative opening within which sovereignty itself becomes knowable, sovereign ritual coinciding with the phantasy of autotelic fiction, a fiction that constitutes itself from within.

That groundless and purely self-generative dimension crystallizes in the moment of banishment. To make claims for sovereignty's creative force prompts the obvious retort: it's not Lear's act but Cordelia's—her "nothing"—that sets the drama in motion. And yet Cordelia's response needs to be understood in terms of her equivocal status in relation to the drama up to this point. Critics generally read the king's theatricality in those opening moments as an index of his narcissism and blindness, an absorption terrifying because of its illimitable scope. "I do love you . . . / Dearer than eyesight, space and liberty" (1.1.55–56). We know to be fearful because we see all this for the consuming fiction that it is. The problem is the king sees it as that as well, as do his daughters—everyone knows; Lear makes clear the kingdom has already been divided, the ritual proof of love no more than a ritual. Or it's fiction and it's not, a display and a real test. Which is to say the characters are in precisely the position we are in relation to theater: knowing and absorbed. That's the epistemological condition of illimitable fiction.

The coincidence between Lear's fabulation and the play's is evident in Cordelia's formal status to this point in the drama, the fact that all her words are spoken as asides. She is "subjectivized"—indeed, one can feel she is the only independent, fully subjectivized character to this point—precisely insofar as she speaks from beyond the swallowing space of the king's ritual enactment. And yet to say that is to say she is entirely dependent on that space, defined in relation to it; she is, like us, the play's included exception.

The critical moment in relation to sovereignty and to the play is the moment that exception is indeed included, the impossible moment at which sovereignty's founding status as inclusive exemption is dramatically enacted. Cordelia's "Nothing" joins—she enters the play—but as a refusal to join, and what emerges from the moment is a function not of any signifiable content—it's virtually contentless—but purely of the empty redounding of the exchange. The dialogue amounts to an entire miniaturized creation ex nihilo, the scene of drama's convergent and divergent auto-generation. "What can you say to draw / A third more opulent than your sisters'?"

> LEAR: Speak.
> CORDELIA: Nothing, my Lord.
> LEAR: Nothing?
> CORDELIA: Nothing.
> LEAR: Nothing will come of nothing. Speak again. (1.1.86–90)

Nothing happens in this reechoing parlay; nothing comes of nothing. Lear enjoins Cordelia to speak again as if no exchange had transpired. And yet nothing does indeed come of nothing, one might say. The chiasmus of the exchange—the doubling-back movement from speaking to speaking again—suggests how much the scene bears on the condition of the speech act as such. Precisely insofar as the king declares the resistant response to be no response he reduces his own speech in its purest, most singular and uncontested form to a mere speaking again. At once relationally defined and originary, sovereignty is that constitutive and redundant "speak." As the originative force of address as such, the king's speech is the performative that in commanding a response from the other constitutes the other as other. And yet even in doing so, because it is itself purely a function of that possibility of exchange, sovereign speech initiates itself as what will have been from the outset a speaking again. Which is to say that at its foundation and in its most absolute, world-creative form sovereignty proves itself an irreducibly fictitious condition.

Vexing the distinction between command and response, assertion and question, the exchange crystallizes the problem of the sovereign decision. The sovereign is he who decides on the exception, Carl Schmitt asserts.[15]

Because the sovereign is the one who above all excepts himself, becomes what he is insofar as he has already exceeded himself, the sovereign is he whose decision is inevitably his own and not his own, whose act is secretly known in advance—now, Lear begins the scene, "we shall express our darker purpose"—and for all involved seems to arise purely out of the blue. "Reserve thy state / And in thy best consideration check / This hideous rashness," Kent exclaims referring specifically to the division of the kingdom, even though he knew and spoke calmly of that event in advance. Instituted for the first time as what will have already been in place, the finitely infinite theater of the sovereign act inscribes all in just such a knowing and blind, clear-eyed and absorbed, condition.

Sovereignty and fiction alike orient themselves in relation to the task of getting the measure of that groundless origination. The indeterminacy of the act becomes apparent in the disturbances of agency that follow from it. "Hence and avoid my sight / So be my grave my peace, as here I give / Her father's heart from her" (1.1.125–27). Is Lear giving or taking back here? Extrusion or inclusion? Is he speaking from the space of the other or from his own? After speaking of his giving/taking of his heart, Lear's thoughts turn immediately to the suitors, as if the double aims of the opening scene—banishment and the love match—had always been one, his taking of his heart his gift:

> . . . here I give
> Her father's heart from her. Call France. Who stirs?
> Call Burgundy. [*Attendants rush off.*]
> Cornwall and Albany,
> With my two daughters' dowers, digest this third. (1.1.126–29)

The phrase "*this* third," whose uncertain reference the Arden edition notes, echoes the conclusion of the king's words of banishment: "Here I disclaim all my paternal care, / . . . / And as a stranger to my heart and me / Hold thee from *this* forever" (1.1.114–17; emphasis added). The Arden edition note at this point reads, "*This*: this moment; but . . . possibly indicating a gesture. Does Lear point to his heart, the map or the coronet?" The possibility of self-reference is complicated by Lear's having implicitly distinguished "this" from "my heart and me." If "this" is Lear, where is he?

Sovereign power is bound to such unstable claims of reference. The king's indicating lines chime with the deixis that had been the very measure of his potency in the scene: "Of all these bounds, even *from this line to this*, / With shadowy forests and with champaigns riched, . . . / We make thee lady" (63–66; emphasis added). That gesture has elicited topical claims for the drama, critics seeing there an allusion to contemporary concerns over the division of the kingdom.[16] And yet understanding the king's initiating act in relation to the play's own self-grounding means seeing in that divisive indication—"from this line to this"—a reference not just to the world but also to the inscriptive *poiesis* out of which worlds are created from sheer lines. The indicating gesture is thus equivalent to *nomos*, law conceived as the primordial division from which sovereign authority derives. The instabilities of reference in the opening moments of the play is a consequence of that designation's very inclusiveness, the fact that the sovereign himself must be seen as a function of that inscriptive demarcation.[17] Lear's inaugurating division amounts to the epideictic mark that inscribes all, including its own indicating—all *this*: the scene, the play, the speaker. Sovereignty condenses to an act whose creative force and radical, cannibalistic incorporativeness is a function of the divisive ungrounding that brings it forth: a giving/taking of itself and of the world.

It is the burden of the political-aesthetic to make that impossible ground phenomenally available, to make sheer difference cognizable at all. The coincidence between the world-creating pronouncement and the play's larger aesthetic status is apparent if we include in the deictic marker's scope the audience's own relation to the drama. The ambiguity of reference extends to the temporal condition of the indicator, "this" as "this moment," this instant of utterance. "This" is the moment of the character's speaking as well as the "now" of our theatrical reception; the one by virtue of the other. That one could be surprised by an event that was also a foregone conclusion is the measure of an act that places all at once ahead and behind itself, within and beyond its frame. In its instituting end, sovereignty moves at once forward and backward, toward death by moving toward infancy: "'tis our fast intent," Lear says, to confer our power on younger strengths "while we unburdened crawl toward death" (1.1.39–40).

That ahead and behind time opens the space in which the play unfolds. Because sovereignty constitutes itself in passing beyond its own limit—because that is the condition for the possibility of totality as such—the drama of sovereignty is definitionally apocalyptic. But because that limit is constitutive and thus already passed from the outset, the absolute limit is also no limit; the end of time and at the same time what all earthly time remains within an apocalyptic framework: a meantime: "Meantime we shall express our darker purpose," Lear declares, introducing the stagily world-dissolving opening scene as a mere interlude (1.1.35). End-time, like the time of the play itself, is absolute and it is empty: Kent: "Is this the promised end?" Edgar: "Or image of that horror?" (5.3.261–62)

The temporal ellipsis that undoes sequential narrative is also the creative engine of drama as aesthetic formation. Consider the conclusion of the Fool's pronouncement about the coming redemption and dissolution of the world. "This prophecy Merlin shall make, for I live before his time" (3.2.95). Again, nothing happens here. The Fool's prophecy turns out to be only the prophecy of a prophecy, and one that remains emptily self-referential at that: Merlin's prophecy derives from the textual source—Geoffrey of Monmouth—from which the Fool himself derives. But again, nothing *happens*, happens as an event. To situate himself where he is he must have moved ahead of Merlin—he arrives where he is by being in advance of his time. And his time is our time—we get our bearings for once in this moment of direct address. Which is to say, we too arrive ahead of ourselves. This is lowbrow apocalypticism: time redeemed as time undone. But it is also the condition of voice at all in the play, the secret grounds of momentousness and sovereign singularity.

Reading the opening scene of the play as the allegory of its own founding alters one's account of the stakes of what follows in the drama. The casting out of Cordelia constitutes the space of deferral that enables the drama to translate the temporally unstable recursiveness of the opening—the minimal condition of aesthetic formation—into a developmental narrative form, and thus to assume the character of a vectored and thematically coherent drama. The complexity of the "recognition" scenes marking the end of the drama—scenes of recognition as repeated misrecognition—derives from the fact that that promised return involves not just a homecoming between the parted but a reenactment of the inclusive exclusion from which character and drama emerge and on which they depend. The drama that does unfold within that space is able to manage the contradictions of the opening, to translate groundless allegory into narratable form, only by separating out and distributing the dimensions of the aporetic act from which the drama devolves. Something like the landscape of political modernity is legible in that attempted distribution of sovereignty.

On the one hand, constitutive abdication is translated into a power based on its disseminative movement beyond itself. "Inform her of my particular fear, / And thereto add such reasons of your own / As may compact it more," Goneril says to her subordinate, Oswald, one of many instances in the play of investing the mediator with full authority (1.4.333–35). "Put on what weary negligence you please, / You and your fellows; I'd have it come to question" (1.3.13–14). Set against the king's legal absolutism—"Acquaint my daughter no further with anything . . . than comes from . . . out of the letter"—such force derives from a calculatedly dispersive self-banishment: tell him I am sick, tell him I am not home, the malevolent daughter says, turning the unhoused king back on himself (1.5.2–4). Such homelessness is an epistemological as well as a thematic concern, consistent with the passage of events in the play into the register of untethered rumors, accounts of external and internal divisions that we may or may not have already witnessed. That unmooring opens the possibility that we are receiving what we already knew as "strange news," that, as for the king, the play's opacities have become our own (2.1.87).

That disseminative conception of force, a correlate of the heteronomous or self-emptying dimension of the sovereign act as evoked at the opening, intimates what in the Foucauldian idiom is described as the modern emergence of governmentality or biopower, the "making immanent and pluralization" of power associated with the undoing of transcendentally localized sovereign authority.[18] In other words, the play shows us biopolitics as a contingent strategy for the management of sovereignty's contradictions. For Foucault, as for the play, that transition entails a shift from a sovereign potency orientated around the question of origination to a version of mediated force within which one is always already inscribed, in which power, indistinguishable from its mediating forms, becomes inseparable from the circulation of rumor and groundless report.[19]

Although historically connected to the technical and bureaucratic machinery of institutions of state, such a capillary extension of power beyond formal law into the texture of life is of a piece with the play's and the era's engagement with natural law, whether understood as beneficent or as nature's ravenous laws of destruction. Ultimately, such a naturalization of law merely reinscribes the contradictions played out at the opening in a different register. Consider the aporia of natural law as Björn Quiring has described it: conceived at once as the law of the particularized instance in cases where positive law has no purchase and as the transcendent ground of that universal law, natural law becomes during the era the law of its own exception.[20] Thus nature's tendency in the play to devolve into various versions of cannibalizing monstrosity: the "monsters of the deep" "that prey on [themselves]."

Counterposing that model of dispersive power, the play articulates particularly through Edgar's acts of self-abjection a power that centripetally consolidates itself in relation to its own negation. Edgar sustains his disguise even after overhearing his father say he would choose to live if only he could see his son again, not merely out of sadistic aggression or emotional self-protectiveness but in order to maintain the mechanism that enables his narcissistic recuperation of power from its repeated evacuation. When Edgar looks back up the cliff from which his father imagines he has fallen, the demon he sees is the exorcised figure of his father's suicidal impulses. But it is also a self-description of the "fiend" who has led his father there; the scene is for Edgar one of auto-exorcism. The self-recognition here is absolute yet leads to no change—the disguise remains in place, Gloucester uncured. And nothing changes because the act's sole aim is self-cognition, an exorcising exteriorization of self and world in order to claim to see them fully.

In that sense, Edgar realizes *avant la lettre* the fiction of Kant's infinite, and infinitely negational, subjectivity—the subject as correlate of Edgar's vertiginous view down the cliff face. Ultimately, that subjective construction depends on the claim to be able to enact death by seeing it face-to-face, to make it one's own. "Edgar I nothing am" (2.2.192). Such a negative, infinite subject coincides with the translation of the atemporal and referenceless allegorization of the play's opening into something historically novel: aesthetic *consciousness*—that is, the aesthetic understood in its historically specifiable sense as the attempt to recuperate that very groundlessness as the condition of a newly imagined subjectivity.

Whereas Foucault speaks of a transition from transcendence to biopolitical immanence, historically speaking those two structures—governmentality and transcendence—were the opposed and mutually reinforcing faces of a single political universe that emerged, Marx argues, with the distribution of productive forces constitutive of modern capitalism: on the one hand, the autonomic workings of the mechanism of state, on the other, the self-creating claims of the purportedly autonomous subject. With the individual defined in relation to particularized interests, with its being, precisely, "individuated," the field of so-called common interests is cast as a separate sphere—the social domain itself is exteriorized. At the same time, that cleavage within the social inhabits the individuated subject as well; because engagement in the conditions of life take on for the first time an accidental and contingent character, the subject's own deeds "become an alien power opposed to him."[21]

Indeed, as Claude Lefort argues, the subject constituted within such a definitionally divided society—modern, historical society—is itself sustained through that reenacted cleavage, the movement by which self-consciousness becomes defined as self-differential and contingent; with that, the subject becomes a definitionally *historical* being.[22] It wouldn't be wrong to see in protean Edgar's ascent at the close of the play something like the transition to a new dispensation. Aesthetic consciousness is critical to that historical transformation. Defining the space of subjective inwardness as against a newly exteriorized world, it is the aesthetic that translates, or seeks to translate, that founding and necessarily inapprehensible division into phenomenal form. In that sense, the aesthetic coincides with the process of historicization as such.

But the distribution of the play's initiating contradictions across now narratable forms hardly resolves the impasse of sovereignty. Precisely because the separating out of immanence and transcendence lets those categories become distinct, world-creating functions, each its own infinitude, such a distinction inevitably poses the question of what horizon those worlds share.

That problem of horizons—a shift from the question of the being of the sovereign to that of the phenomenal consistency of the world as such—is precisely what aesthetic consciousness seeks to negotiate.[23] Viewed one way—literally, *down*—the "Dover Cliffs" scene can be seen as the play's attempt to comprehend its own limit and vanishing point in terms that anticipate Kant quite precisely:

> The murmuring surge
> That on th'unnumbered idle pebble chafes,
> Cannot be heard so high. I'll look no more,
> Lest my brain turn and the deficient sight
> Topple down headlong. (4.6.20–24)

The mind turns back on itself at the point where phenomenal perception sublimely exceeds itself and undoes its own ground in its unsupported extension: "The murmuring surge . . . Cannot be heard so high." With that passage beyond what it deceptively took to be its own perceptual grounding, the subject according to Kant discovers the supersensible dimension that must have been its transcendent condition all along. Such a recognition is by definition a missed recognition; lured by the particulars of the view down, and thus caught within the self-referential metonymic chain that constitutes its absorptive power—the "samphire gatherer" diminished to the size of his own "head," the "anchoring barque" to its "cock" or dinghy, the cock to its buoy—we realize too late that we never knew on what ground we stood, that we have been caught in the "murmuring" of "what cannot be heard so high." And with that systematic self-exceeding movement, a groundless drama seeks to constitute itself from within by incorporating its own boundary; in the infinitude of the cliff scene, the tragedy folds within itself the fatal horizon that marks its close. In other words, the play explicitly enters the limitlessly self-comprehending, self-exceeding space of the aesthetic, now dramatized as the condition of subjective consciousness.[24]

That space is illimitable—at once closed and infinitely open—because its captivations aren't easily passed beyond, for the inscribing effect is initiated precisely by the claim to know it for what it is. If mad Lear suffers from literalism—"nothing will come of nothing"—blind Gloucester presumes the world figuratively masks a truth to be revealed by the penetrative gaze: "Come, if it be nothing, I shall not need spectacles," he says, falling for the letter ploy that precipitates his tragedy (1.2.35–36). Gloucester may be gullible, but it's the gullibility of the hermeneut, the one who imagines truth is staked on its concealing limits, as distinct from kings who imagine all is exposed before their all-knowing gaze. When Edgar looks back up the cliff face to describe the fiend who has led the old man to the brink, that monster's eyes like "two full moons" might describe the consuming and consumed gaze of the one given over to the particulars of the view down, seizing detail upon detail and thus caught in the passage's vertiginous chain. Then again, that precipitous viewing is impelled here, as in Kant, by the desire to compass the totality, by the limitless promise of the limit. In that sense, the monstrous eye could also describe the all-mastering gaze of Edgar, the one who led his father to the cliff and who as their controlling director presumes to know such theatrical effects for what they are. "Why I do trifle with his despair / Is done to cure it" (4.6.33–34). In the end, the empirically particularizing and the totalizing gaze are the same, both premised on a claim to know the limit, to know representation as mere representation.

And, in its multiplicitousness—"he had a thousand noses"—that monster might equally be the reflexive image of the audience itself, the fiend's consuming eye a reflection either of our own blind absorption or our claim to all-knowing theatrical distance. "Great thing of us forgot! / Speak, Edmund, where's the King? And where's Cordelia?" Albany declares, after the headlong concatenation of events toward the end.[25] If even at the very close we lose track of the chief object of our investment and thus of the tragedy itself, that may be because of our absorption. "An interlude!" Goneril declared as the adulterous intrigues were about to come to light, and one might have good reason to distract oneself with the dire end approaching. But one could equally say the audience loses the end precisely in its fixed attention to it, for in the context of the play's manifold indeterminacies of time and space it is the blazoned promise of closure—of a face-to-face with death—that gives absorptive power to the final duel and Edgar's killingly punctual tale of his father's end, the events that led our attention astray.[26] Insofar as those forms of attention—averting death, confronting death, immanent absorption and transcendent cognizance—turn out to be indistinguishable, the play's ensnarements would seem to become irreducible: in attempting to make it the object of our fixed gaze, death eludes us, but in our eluding it—keeping it at bay—death returns to us in the inwardly marking form of guilt. Thus the hold of a newly manifest aesthetic logic.

But that Kant is so explicitly anticipated in Edgar's view down makes it all the more significant that we pass from this seemingly illimitable view with its implacable logic to a revision of it, now as something phenomenally other. Edgar, in a new disguise, looks back up the cliff face to describe the fiend that has led us to this fatal place:

> As I stood here below methought his eyes
> Were two full moons. He had a thousand noses,
> Horns whelked and waved like the enridged sea.
> It was some fiend. (4.6.69–72)

The fantastical description has been taken to represent Edgar's play on his father's credulousness, a "trifl[ing] with his despair." And yet we've been warned about claiming to know what is and isn't fiction, and the description itself raises the question of the boundaries of fantasy. It's a view up and still a view down toward the "enridged sea"; it's a view out and a reflexive view back, its monstrous eyes figuring the theatergoers own ravenous gaze now as spectacle. In that sense, it is another of the play's many scenes of optical extrusion, of "sight / Toppl[ing] down headlong"—think of Gloucester's blinding. But here that desubjectifying effect assumes a very different form.

Though infinite, the view down operated according to a calculable logic, the self-referential chain functioning according to a system of indefinitely extended substitutions: this for that, this for that.[27] "Dreadful trade," Edgar says of the samphire gatherers, perhaps picking up on the logic of exchange underlying the scene; the economic trope will come to the fore later in the language of coining associated with the "handy-dandy" reversibility of justice.[28] The systematic infinitude of perspectivalism, a geometric and rhetorical rather than a strictly optical operation, is structured by that internally referential substitutive ordering—what Derrida terms in relation to Kant's analytic "economimesis." And such a mimetic "this-for-that" economy is also what underwrites the sacrificial logic that lets Kant translate a potentially limitless mechanism into an affirmative passage from one distinct realm into another, the giving up of the sensory to achieve in its place the supersensory, just as it underwrites Edgar's ability to cast such moments as instances of self-purifying exorcism. With that, the aesthetic becomes at once boundless and internalized.[29]

Shakespeare's fiend dissolves that mimetic presumption. The exorcized demon is more than Edgar's negative image; he's is the undoing of the logic of negation—the claim to a face-to-face with his own limit—to which Edgar's infinitely self-exceeding selfhood aspires. Rather than involving a reversal of positions, a seeing oneself as object of the gaze, the consuming eyes-like-full-moons elide seeing and showing, as if with that collapsing of sight and spectacle the perspective cone itself were inverted.[30] We move from the systematic passage beyond limits in order to be reinscribed within them to a phantasmic space the boundaries of which are everywhere and nowhere. Rather than a part of the whole, the part—the horn—now becomes more than the whole—the sea itself—because it's an all-consuming spectacle: the subject is from the outset already dispersed within it. And that scene is itself nothing but the multiple instances of the whelklike turning from nature to artifice, animate to inanimate—flesh to horn, sea to enridged stone—that figures the viewer's own reflexive turning around in and on the scene. The view conjures in that sense the autonomic spiraling through which image becomes image, phantasy, phantasy.[31] Shakespeare draws upon the passage in Golding's translation of *Metamorphoses* where the image's superhuman hold is associated with its ongoing, recursive gyre: "Joves ymage which the Lybian folke by name of Hammon serve, / Is made with crooked welked hornes that in ward still do terve."[32] The dispersive scene suggests the horizonless opening from and against which transcendental consciousness—Edgar's consciousness—must seek to constitute itself.

The view from beyond the perspectival world conjures the demonic remainder of the process by which sovereignty seeks to translate itself into the newly minted citizen-subject of pure exchange, an inward and infinite being who, like Edgar the endless self-fashioner, stakes itself on the claim to master exchangeability as such. That vexed transition coincides with a significant early modern transformation in political space, what Carlo Galli describes as the shift from politics as a function of already given social spaces to space as a function of the political; that is, to the political becoming the always open question of its own terrain.[33] Constitutive and yet without fixed transcendental reference, a function of its own creative divisions, the self-exceeding space of modern sociality is the space of an emergent aesthetic consciousness, for it is aestheticization that makes those formative negations—the inaugurating "nothing" of social relationality—available to phenomenal consciousness, even as it inevitably conjures the untoward limits of such a process of world creation.

I'm tempted to take the inward-"terving" demon as a figure for that temporally impossible category "early modern aesthetics." In its attempt to recursively construct the story of its own grounds through an orchestrated distinction between allegory and narrative temporalization, the play conjures an inscribing remainder that it can't internalize even as a horizon structure. Associated with demonic threat and the limits of the play as a character-centered form, that inhuman aesthetic paradoxically returns at the close as the condition for the play's most radical reimagining of possibilities of social rapport.

As I have suggested in a different context, against the presumption to absolute mimetic correspondence implicit in Edgar's punctual narration of his father's death, where father and son, self and other, event and its telling, life and death all coincide in a fatal clinch, the play articulates toward its close versions of recognition-as-misrecognition that retain the ellipses of time and self from which the drama had emerged, scenes such as Lear's first, tentative reencounter with Cordelia, where he seems to coincide with his daughter only insofar as he fails to coincide with himself—"I will not swear these are my hands" (4.7.55).[34]

The logic of the encounter-as-missed-encounter culminates with Lear's death. If the play begins before it begins, as it were, it also ends beyond its ending.[35] And in that boundary crossing—the formal enactment of the self-exceeding, inclusive/exclusive logic of sovereignty and aesthetics equally—the tragedy moves beyond classical models of recognition and Christian sacrifice alike.

> O thou'lt come no more,
> Never, never, never, never, never!
> Pray you, undo this button. Thank you, sir.
> O,o,o,o.
> Do you see this? Look on her, look, her lips,
> Look there, look there! [*Dies.*]
> EDGAR: He faints! My lord, my lord! (5.3.306–10)

What the king sees on Cordelia's mute lips is a corrective to his initial presumption: "Nothing will come of nothing: speak again." Nor are we in a position to say he sees nothing; we have been forewarned about the dangers of presuming where to draw the line on fiction. The resources of cognizable meaning in the opposition between reading literally—nothing is nothing—and reading figuratively—Gloucester's nothing as mask or substitute for something—are vacated here at the end in a performative crisscrossing of death's limit that dissolves the boundary between fictive and real, self and other, subject and object. The long-awaited "recognition" occurs not in the play but where the play exceeds the audience's ability to compass its limits, and thus to constitute itself in relation to its boundary. In that incognizable recognition, death reveals itself as what is at once absolute—the unpassable limit of consciousness and being—and as what, precisely because it is the condition of cognition as such, has already been crossed. End-time as mean-time, mean-time as end-time.

The violence of deictic indication is still here: "look there"; it is that effort to mark death—to compass it face-to-face—that for king and audience renews the transgressing of representational limits, as it does at the play's opening. And yet that marking occurs in relation to an outright uncertainty of reference associated now with theater's promise. Where are we looking? Mirror? Feather? Lips? "Undo this button," Lear says: Cordelia's or Lear's? Is that unbuttoning the act that allows breath, or the one that revives the "suffocation of the mother"—"down, your place is below"—and thus kills? Are we moving toward death or away? "Look there, look there": look ultimately only at looking, perhaps, as one would look in an empty mirror, in a reflex that at once reiterates theater's evacuating effect and opens its world-creating space.[36]

The uncanniness of the effect is a consequence of the radical nature of the boundary crossing it entails. "Lend me a looking glass; / If that her breath will mist or stain the stone, / Why then she lives" (5.3.259–61). "Oh, you are men of stones!" (255). In the Quarto, that translation between animate and inanimate affects the most intimate resources of breath, materially inscribing the pure vocative of speech even as it opens speaking to its generative iterations beyond all characterological limits. "O, o, o, o," Lear declaims. "O, let him pass," says Kent. "O he is gone," says Edgar (5.3.309, 312, 314)—we recall the Fool's reference to women making "mouths in a glass" (3.2.35). In the arresting emptiness of the mirroring stone the audience's own response or nonresponse is also already inscribed. Neither subjective nor objective, belonging neither to one subject nor the other, the inapprehensible breath in the mirror is what initiates any such oppositional ordering and thus amounts to subjectivity's causeless cause.

The ethics of the scene is bound up with that causelessness—Cordelia's "no cause"—for it is the unbinding of causation that moves the drama beyond the recoils of self-protective force and thus at least in some measure beyond sacrifice's fiery wheel. And it frees to the extent that it assumes the form of a "still . . . terv[ing]" aesthetic mechanism that works of its own accord, the effect of a techne that elides the human-nature divide: a stone, a mirror, a feather, a play. Bypassing phenomenal apprehension insofar as it constitutes its condition, that inhuman mechanism passes beyond an ethic based on mimetic or speculative equivalence.[37] As in the earlier reunion, Lear meets Cordelia where he passes beyond himself, but now in the form of an encounter at the limit of narratability. "Are you with me?" Lear had said earlier. He is with Cordelia, and we are with him—never more proximate to him—insofar as he addresses us from across an infinite divide.[38] He doesn't return to us nor does Cordelia return to him in the form of reverting conscience. Rather, Cordelia is with Lear as what was from the outset in his condition as sovereign subject at once inward and alien to him, which is to say as definitionally phantasmic. A theater oriented around such a rapport doesn't take place according to a securely situating logic of correspondence. Indeed, it doesn't "take place" at all; that is, it doesn't occupy an already given subjective or objective space. Rather it opens space—creates and decreates world—in the interval that constitutes each.

By virtue of such creationism, *King Lear* suggests the prospect of a version of community whose promise is indissociable from its instability, where whatever appears of equivalence is at once opened and undone by a force that is already displacing it toward another scene and time. The possibility of such rapport is a function of the play's engagement with an aesthetic that animates and disarticulates the play from start to finish. Because *King Lear* institutes itself as sovereignly self-inclusive fiction, no Shakespeare play more explicitly exceeds its own boundaries, submitting itself to the spiraling contingency from which it emerges; the most autonomous of fictions, it is also the most heteronomous. All Shakespeare plays have varied textual manifestations. Only with *Lear* has that meant a division of the kingdom; that is, a critical division over whether *King Lear* was, in fact, a single play. The formative divisions at the play's end are themselves divided across the play's manifestations, the "O, o, o's" appearing in the Quarto alone, the pointing to Cordelia's lips in the Folio. The decisive reference of the play, the reference that opens it as a drama, is to an appearance that has us looking there and there.[39] Ultimately the historical claim of the play lies neither in what the play constructs diegetically nor in the play's referential correspondence to an already presumed world securely beyond it but in the inapprehensible force that inscribes itself in the movement of noncoincidence that opens and suspends the distinction between play and world. It is as causeless that the play manifests its historicity.

That formal condition is a political matter. As critics have noted, the most significant distinction between the two versions of the play concerns whether the threat to the kingdom arises from without—an imminent French invasion in the earlier Quarto—or from within, a matter of internal divisions in the Folio. The significance of that distinction extends beyond questions related to censorship or whether the drama was played before the king. It is indissociable from the founding of the play itself, its inclusive/exclusive, breached and breachless character as an explicitly *aesthetic* fiction—everything that makes it as sovereign fiction by definition "strange news" to itself. The possibility of a stable political conceptualization, as well as the possibility of narrative historicization, depends on maintaining a cognizable distinction between those variants, between an inside and an outside, a self-same and a contingent. And yet the force necessary to maintain such a distinction will inevitably amount to a "punishing home," a renewal of the fragmentation it fends against. Early modern aesthetics doesn't arise as an instrument in that political drama. It is located instead in relation to the opaque violence that constitutes and undoes those conceptual distinctions and thus at the point where historicity converts to historicization and where the space of the political opens in the first instance.

Notes

1. A shift manifest among other places in Jean Bodin. See Russ Leo, "'Natures freedome,' the Art of Sovereignty, and Mustapha's Tragic Insolubility: Fulke Greville and Jean Bodin among the Ottomans," in *Fulke Greville and the Culture of the English Renaissance*, ed. Russ Leo, Katrin Röder, and Freya Sierhuis (Oxford: Oxford University Press, forthcoming).

2. Christopher Pye, *The Storm at Sea: Political Aesthetics in the Time of Shakespeare* (New York: Fordham University Press, 2015), 29–31.

3. *King Lear*, ed. R. A. Foakes (London: Arden Shakespeare, 1997), 1.1.55–6. Subsequent parenthetical citations are to this edition.

4. Christopher Pye, "*Green World / No World*: *King Lear*, Ecocriticism, and the Politics of Finitude," *Shakespeare Jahrbuch* 11 (2017): 3–6.

5. On the persistence of that staging of the monarch's self-destruction, see Franco Moretti, *Signs Taken for Wonders* (London: Verso, 1988), 42–60.

6. Jean-Luc Nancy, *The Creation of the World, or Globalization*, trans. François Raffoul and David Pettigrew (Albany: State University of New York Press, 2007), 100. Marx comments on the shift with absolutism to a purely structural and relational conception of sovereignty: "One man is king only because other men stand in relation of subjects to him. They, on the other hand, imagine they are subjects because he is king" (*Capital: A Critique of Political Economy*, vol. 1, trans. Ben Fowkes [Harmondsworth, U.K.: Penguin Books, 1976], 149n22). See also Kojin Karatani, *Transcritique: On Kant and Marx*, trans. Sabu Kohso (Cambridge, Mass.: MIT Press, 2005), 271.

7. The identity between vivification and numbing in the play's recurrent instances of self-wounding that Giulio Pertile subtly explores suggests the intimate reach of such a political-symbolic autoimmune logic ("*King Lear* and the Uses of Mortification," *Shakespeare Quarterly* 67, no. 3 [Fall 2016]: 319–43).

8. On biopower as immanence, see Roberto Esposito, *Terms of the Political: Community, Immunity, Biopolitics*, trans. Rhiannon Noel Welch (New York: Fordham University Press, 2013), 67–78. For biopower and the immunological paradigm in the early modern context, see Roberto Esposito, "Biopolitics," in *Biopolitics: A Reader*, ed. Timothy Campbell and Adam Sitze (Durham, N.C.: Duke University Press, 2013), 328–30.

9. Kathleen Biddick also critiques familiar periodizations of sovereignty, seeing in the formation untimely residues of a foreclosed medieval and non-Christian ground (*Make and Let Die: Untimely Sovereignties* [New York: Punctum Books, 2016], 110–11, 127). See also Kathleen Davis, *Periodization and Sovereignty: How Ideas of Feudalism and Secularization Govern the Politics of Time* (Philadelphia: University of Pennsylvania Press, 2008).

10. Giorgio Agamben, *Homo Sacer: Sovereign Power and Bare Life*, trans. Daniel Heller-Roazen (Stanford, Calif.: Stanford University Press, 1998), 29.

11. Agamben, *Homo Sacer*, 107.

12. Agamben, *Homo Sacer*, 26, though the instrumentalizing language of capture recurs at such moments throughout Agamben's oeuvre—see *The Kingdom and the Glory*, trans. Lorenzo Chiesa, with Matteo Mandarini (Stanford, Calif.: Stanford University Press, 2011), 251; and *The Use of Bodies*, trans. Adam Kotsko (Stanford, Calif.: Stanford University Press, 2016), 237, 265.

13. Agamben, *Homo Sacer*, 51.

14. On aesthetics and phenomenalization, see Paul de Man, *Aesthetic Ideology*, ed. Andrzej Warminski (Minneapolis: University of Minnesota Press, 1996), 61–69. On its connection with early modern social formation, see Christopher Pye, *The Storm at Sea: Political Aesthetics in the Age of Shakespeare* (New York: Fordham University Press, 2015), 29–31.

15. Carl Schmitt, *Political Theology: Four Chapters on the Concept of Sovereignty*, trans. George Schwab (Chicago: University of Chicago Press, 2006), 1, 12–14.

16. Seeing in the moment, for instance, an allusion to James I's comments addressed to his son on the risks of dividing kingdoms such that you "leave the seed of division and discord among your posteritie" (*Basilikon Doron*, in *The Political Works of James I*, ed. Charles Howard McIlwain [Cambridge, Mass.: Harvard University Press, 1918], 37). For topical readings of the moment, see Leah S. Marcus, *Puzzling Shakespeare: Local Reading and Its Discontents* (Berkeley: University of California Press, 1988), 149, and James Shapiro, *The Year of Lear* (New York: Simon and Schuster, 2015), 33–45.

17. Carl Schmitt, *The Nomos of the Earth in the International Law of Jus Publicum Europaeum*, trans. G. L. Ulmen (New York: Telos Press, 2006), 67–79. The nomic "this" corresponds in this context to the incognizably singular deixis that in Kant and Marx alike precedes and conditions the possibility of any exchange or symbolization whatsoever. See Karatani, *Transcritique*, 107–8.

18. Roberto Esposito, *Bios: Biopolitics and Philosophy*, trans. Timothy Campbell (Minneapolis: University of Minnesota Press, 2008), 36.

19. Michel Foucault, *Security, Territory, Population: Lectures at the Collège de France, 1977–1978*, ed. Michel Senellart (New York: Picador, 2007), 259, 268.

20. Björn Quiring, *Shakespeare's Curse: The Aporias of Ritual Exclusion in Early Modern Royal Drama* (London: Routledge, 2014), 170–72. On natural law and contingency/particularization, see R. S. White, *Natural Law in English Renaissance Literature* (Cambridge: Cambridge University Press, 1996), 51–54.

21. Karl Marx, *The German Ideology* (Amherst, N.Y.: Prometheus Books, 1998), 53, 87.

22. Claude Lefort, "The Permanence of the Theological-Political," in *Democracy and Political Theory*, trans. David Macey (Minneapolis: University of Minnesota Press, 1988), 225.

23. On world as horizon of phenomenalization, see Martin Heidegger, *Being and Time*, trans Joan Stambaugh (Albany: State University of New York Press, 2010), 347–49.

24. Jacques Rancière, *Aesthetics and Its Discontents* (Cambridge: Polity Press, 2009), 6–12.

25. Stephen Booth, *King Lear, Macbeth, Indefinition, and Tragedy* (New Haven, Conn.: Yale University Press, 1983), 11–12, sees in the moment a trial of the audience.

26. On the dangerous lure of the "familiar and neatly 'literary' ending" in the play, see Katharine Eisaman Maus, *Being and Having in Shakespeare* (Oxford: Oxford University Press, 2013), 129.

27. On the "algebra" of the construction, see Jonathan Goldberg, "Perspectives: Dover Cliff and the Conditions of Representation," in *Shakespeare and Deconstruction*, ed. G. Douglas Atkins and David M. Bergeron (New York: Lang, 1988), 250.

28. On the relation between economy and justice in the scene, see Pye, "*Green World / No World*."

29. Emmanuel Kant, *Critique of Judgment*, trans. Werner S. Pluhar (Indianapolis: Hackett, 1987), 129; Jacques Derrida, "Economimesis," *Diacritics* 11, no. 2 (Summer 1981): 2–25.

30. On the uncanny crossing of seeing and spectacle in the "pulsatile, spread-out function of the gaze," see Jacques Lacan, *Four Fundamental Concepts of Psychoanalysis*, trans. Alan Sheridan (New York: Norton, 1977), 89. Philip Armstrong, *Shakespeare's Visual Regime: Tragedy, Psychoanalysis and the Gaze* (Houndmills, Basingstoke, Hampshire, U.K.: Palgrave, 2000), 52–53, associates the view up with the presence beyond the perspectival construct of the disquieting gaze of the Other.

31. For a marvelous meditation on the spiral in Shakespeare, see François-Xavier Gleyzon, *Shakespeare's Spiral: Tracing the Snail in "King Lear" and Renaissance Painting* (Lanham, Md.: University Press of America, 2010).

32. *Ovid's Metamorphoses: The Arthur Golding Translation, 1567*, ed. John Frederick Nims (Philadelphia: Paul Dry Books, 2000), 124, bk. 5, ll. 416–17. The figure's status as the play's own cryptic counterimage is evident in the reference to the North African god Ba'al Hammon, the Lord of Two Horns, for whom according to Greco-Roman accounts the citizens of Carthage burned their children as sacrificial offerings. The image would thus figure Lear's self-consuming involution as the very grounds of sovereignty's potency.

33. Carlo Galli, *Political Spaces and Global War*, ed. Adam Sitze, trans. Elizabeth Fay (Minneapolis: University of Minnesota Press, 2010), 17–19.

34. Pye, "*Green World / No World*," 23, 26–28.

35. On the failed promise of finality in the play, see Booth, *King Lear*, 13.

36. On the exchange opening "a life beyond sight and empirical presence," see Simon Palfrey, *Poor Tom: Living "King Lear"* (Chicago: University of Chicago Press, 2014), 237.

37. On a noninstrumentalized techne as that which "gives man entry into something which, of himself, he can neither invent nor in any way make," see Martin Heidegger, "The Question Concerning Technology," in *Basic Writings*, ed. David Farrell Krell (New York: Harper and Row, 1977), 313.

38. On nearness—actual proximity—as that which preserves the far as its condition, see Martin Heidegger, "The Thing," in *Poetry, Language, Thought*, trans. Albert Hofstadter (New York: Harper and Row, 1971), 177–78.

39. In one regard, we engage history when we simply "look there" in the mirror. Richard Wilson, *Free Will: Art and Power on Shakespeare's Stage* (Manchester, U.K.: Manchester University Press, 2013), 262–63, associates that prop with the play's circumstance as the first by Shakespeare's newly elevated company to be played directly before King James. The device looks forward to *Macbeth*, where the mirror's confirming, expropriative function in relation to sovereignty is more gaudily evoked.

Thomas Rymer, Poetic Justice, and the Limits of Representation

Dispatches from the Representative Regime of Art

Russ Leo

In the preface to his signal 1725 edition of *The Works of Shakespear*, Alexander Pope castigates recent critics who measure Shakespeare's works against the standards of Aristotle's *Poetics*. After all, Pope argues, "our Authors had no thoughts of writing on the model of the Ancients" before Ben Jonson; until Jonson "brought critical learning into vogue," English "Tragedies were only Histories in Dialogue; and their Comedies follow'd the thread of any Novel as they found it, no less implicitly than if it had been true History."[1] The *Poetics*, in other words, was virtually inaccessible to most Tudor playwrights, to say nothing of antique comedies or tragedies. Under these circumstances, Pope alleges, Shakespeare could not have imitated antique forms.[2] "To judge therefore of *Shakespear* by *Aristotle's* rules," Pope claims, "is like trying a man by the Laws of one Country, who acted under those of another," particularly since Shakespeare "writ to the *People* . . . without that knowledge of the best models, the Ancients, to inspire him with an emulation of them."[3] Invoking "the *People*," Pope emphasizes "that Stage-Poetry of all other is more particularly levell'd to please the *Populace*, and its success more immediately depending upon the *Common Suffrage*."[4] In this sense Pope implies that the *Poetics*, even if it had been accessible, would nevertheless have been irrelevant to Shakespeare's trade. As a "*Player*," Shakespeare based his poetry "upon other principles than those of *Aristotle*."[5]

Among the host of then-modern critics to whom Pope responds in his 1725 preface—René Rapin, the Abbé d'Aubignac François Hédelin, John Dryden, John Dennis, Charles Gildon, and Nicholas Rowe, among others—it is Thomas Rymer who most thoroughly excoriates Shakespeare on Aristotelian grounds.[6] In *A Short View of Tragedy* (1693), for instance, Rymer delivers an exacting critique of *Othello*, a tragedy in which he admittedly finds "some burlesk, some humour, and ramble of Comical Wit, some shew, and some Mimickry to divert the spectators" but which in its "tragical part" is "plainly none other, than a Bloody Farce, without salt or savour."[7] Rymer's is evidently not a popular opinion. "From all the Tragedies acted on our English Stage," he concedes, "*Othello* is said to bear the Bell away"—that is, it is regarded as exemplary among his contemporaries.[8] But Rymer nevertheless proceeds to illustrate how *Othello* is "fraught . . . with improbabilities," neglecting the Aristotelian mandates concerning probability, necessity, and irrationality in plot, the very "soul of tragedy"; the "*Characters* or Manners," moreover—Aristotelian *ethos*, or ἦθος—"are not less unnatural and improper, than the Fable was improbable and absurd."[9] *Othello*, and "this sort of Poetry" in general, Rymer insists, offer nothing of substance to the audience, nothing useful or edifying; "instead of settling the mind, and purging our passions," he argues, the tragedy works "to delude our senses, disorder our thoughts, addle our brain, pervert our affections, hair our imaginations, corrupt our appetite, and fill our head with vanity, [and] confusion."[10] But Rymer is most critical when he accuses Shakespeare of being careless with the details of plot and thus impugning nothing less than divine justice. Rymer coins an important critical term to illustrate how Aristotelian considerations of plot and causality are inextricable from notions of providence and theodicy: "poetic justice."

To the letter Rymer calls this "Poetical Justice."[11] Charles Gildon introduces the more familiar "poetic justice" in his 1691 *History of the Athenian Society* when he paraphrases Aristotle's claim in the *Poetics* that "Sophocles said he created characters as they ought to be, Euripides as they really are" (1460b.35): "'tis said of Sophocles, and Euripides," Gildon writes, "that one represented the Accidents of Human Life, without regard to that Poetic Justice, as they too often happen; the other, as they ought to have been."[12] But Gildon undoubtedly recalls Rymer's theses on "poetical justice" in *The Tragedies of the Last Age Consider'd and Examin'd by the Practice of the Ancients, and by the Common Sense of All Ages* (1678), a concept that is rarely, if ever, recognized for what it is: a meditation on deism and natural religion as well as an investigation of enthusiasm and the reasonableness of Christianity. This notion of poetic justice also subtends Rymer's 1693 attack on *Othello* and makes the stakes of the critique much more clear.

"Poetic justice" rings of confidence as Rymer, as if by mandate, defends nothing less than God's providence against Shakespearean distortions of plot and nature. But Rymer writes at an impasse, his turn to "poetic justice" as much an attempt to buttress imperiled Aristotelian assumptions about mimesis and the philosophical province of tragedy as it is a treatment of providence and the reasonableness of Christianity. Rymer endorses principles on art and criticism that Jacques Rancière identifies with the representative regime of art, a regime that finds its "first theoretical legitimation . . . in Aristotle's elaboration of the notion of *mimesis*."[13] And as Pope's indictment makes clear, Rymer defends this representative regime of art against emergent alternatives. Incisively, Rancière recognizes that, for Aristotle, "to pretend is not to put forth illusions but to elaborate intelligible structures," structures that the tragedian presents by way of a series of actions and affects that are carefully arranged according to probability or necessity.[14] This sense of *mimesis*, or imitation, is essential to the representative regime of art. Critics who, like Rymer, remain faithful to Aristotle's *Poetics* identify and adjudicate among works of art based on their presentations of the world. But as Rancière makes clear, the work of art does not merely reproduce the world: it organizes perception, securing a correspondence between a particular fictional presentation of nature and a particular way of perceiving or comprehending nature, an αἴσθησις, or *aisthesis*. The work of art is never simply an imitation of nature but a presentation (under the pretense of "representation") of nature that renders certain aspects visible, others invisible, certain aspects intelligible, others unintelligible. Insofar as the work of art is representative of nature, the poet effectively establishes and fortifies a relationship "between a *poiesis* and an *aesthesis*," "between an autonomous arrangement of actions and the bringing into operation of affects specific to the representative situation and it alone."[15] Rymer's "poetic justice" belongs to the representative regime of art. Rancière helps us see what is at stake in Rymer's poetics, particularly as Rymer turns to providence and justice to address what appear to him and his cohort as the very limits of representation.

The connection between Rymer and Rancière is hardly remote. Rancière undoubtedly reads the *Poetics* as a foundational presentation of the representative regime of art, identifying Aristotle's work—particularly his interpretation of *Oedipus*—as a marked departure from both Sophoclean and Platonic approaches to art and *aesthesis*. But Rancière consistently turns to neoclassicism to explain both the representative regime of art and its discontents, operating under the assumption that Aristotelian *mimesis* finds "its emblem in classical French tragedy, and its systematization in the great treatises of the French eighteenth century, from [Charles] Batteux to [Jean-François de] La Harpe by way of Voltaire's *Commentaires sur Corneille*."[16] Thus Rymer's contemporaries rank among the most important advocates of the representative regime of art, arguably more so than Aristotle himself. Rancière's representative regime of art is, albeit tacitly, an early modern phenomenon, identified in large part with neoclassicism. Indeed, his most substantive claims about the representative regime of art emerge from his reading of Pierre Corneille's 1659 *Oedipe*.[17] And because Corneille effectively collated Aristotelian statements concerning plot and character, giving new force and consistency to the *Poetics*, Rancière reckons his *Oedipe* to be *more* representative of the representative regime of art than the *Poetics* itself.[18] Corneille is able to realize Aristotelian notions of causality in plot and character (again, Aristotelian *ethos*, or ἦθος), wherein what is at stake is not simply a representation of nature but rather "an ordered deployment of meanings, an adjusted relationship between what is understood or anticipated and what comes as a surprise," the very "logic of gradual, thwarted revelation [that] excludes the abrupt emergence of speech that says too much, speaks too soon, and makes too much known."[19] Corneille's depiction of probability and necessity in nature as well as consistency in character is in fact a lens through which elements of nature are rendered more or less visible or intelligible, "a system of relations that defines, more fundamentally, the representative order itself."[20] Put simply, representative art does not merely imitate nature; it lays the groundwork by which nature is appropriately intelligible and palpable as such. And Corneille's *Oedipe* is "a masterpiece of representative logic," a seamless work, the "perfection of a certain art and the presupposition that grounds it."[21] It is emblematic of the representative regime of art at large.

Rymer's criticism is also emblematic of the representative regime of art. If Corneille enables Rancière to mark the culmination of this regime, however, Rymer's engagements with tragedy and theodicy help us understand the limits of representation as well as how and why it gives way to a properly *aesthetic* regime of art. This study proceeds with an account of Rymer's 1678 work *The Tragedies of the Last Age*, demonstrating how Rymer interprets Aristotle as well as how his critical treatment of Shakespeare and his contemporaries involves a turn to enthusiasm and fanaticism. Rymer collates criticism with faith, defending the reasonableness of tragedy and Christianity, guarding against fanatics in both religion and poetry. As he moves from this endorsement of reason against enthusiasm, Rymer not only illustrates the degree to which reason confirms the truth of Scripture but also equates Aristotle's statements about universality, probability, and necessity in tragedy with God's providence. It is here that he lays bare his assumptions about reason, directed against emergent deist claims about justice as well as unsuitable tragic plots. As Rymer proceeds, moreover, he faces the limits of representation—not representation per se but rather the capacity of a representative regime of art to present the deity. The tragic plot should be an expression of poetic justice—that is to say, of God's justice, of theodicy—and it is on this ground that he excoriates Shakespearean tragedy. But to this end he duly charges the tragedian with an onerous task: demonstrating God's providence, rendering God as comprehensible in tragedy as in nature, but without reducing God to nature. In order to make this claim, Rymer retrieves Aristotle's ancient formal distinction between history and tragedy, identifying the latter alone as suitable to the representation of God's providence. This marks an impasse in the history of the representative regime of art. As if paradoxically, the emergence of the term "poetic justice" corresponds with the moment when the terms and limits of representation, to which Rancière devotes due attention, are most apparent to its most ardent advocates. The study ends with an account of the consequences of Rymer's work as well as its import to aesthetic philosophers in the eighteenth century. Tragedy, for Rymer, must serve theodicy. It is on this ground that he excoriates Shakespearean tragedy, to a purpose: to establish poetry and poetics as philosophical projects, even at the expense of theology. If modern aesthetic philosophy bridges a gap between theological treatments of religious experience and more critical approaches to sensation and experience, Rymer's theses on poetic justice warrant attention for the crucial part they play in this story.

The Reasonableness of Tragedy

The Tragedies of the Last Age is a careful commentary on the *Poetics* and its import in modernity as well as a critical study of "the choicest and most applauded *English Tragedies* of this last age."[22] While Rymer mentions Shakespeare's *Othello* and *Julius Caesar* as well as Jonson's *Catiline His Conspiracy* at the outset of the treatise, he devotes most of the work to three tragedies by Francis Beaumont and John Fletcher: *The Tragedy of Rollo, Duke of Normandy*; *A King and No King*; and *The Maid's Tragedy*. Despite the popularity of these plays, Rymer finds them wanting. He does not, however, render judgment on either the "phrase and expression" or the "*mechanical part*" of a work, on the "*Machines, Actors, Dances* and circumstances which are meerly *accidental* to the *Tragedy*."[23] He restricts his critique largely to plot, censuring those poets and tragedians who pay insufficient attention to "the *Fable* or *Plot*, which all conclude to be the *Soul* of a *Tragedy*; which, with the *Ancients*, is always found to be a *reasonable Soul*; but *with us*, for the most part, a *brutish*, and often worse than *brutish*."[24] This is in one sense a critical paraphrase of the *Poetics*. But to the letter Rymer emphasizes that the plot should conform to reason, not to the *Poetics*. Aristotle's work is salient to playwrights and critics insofar as it enables them to see what is reasonable about tragedy, insofar as it underlines tragedy's philosophical province. Thus Rymer does not merely uphold the standards and exempla of antique tragedy or criticism against degraded modern varieties. In fact, he begins with the assumptions that "our *Philosophers* agreed well enough with theirs, in the main," and that one need not "be some *Aristotle*, and *Doctor* of *Subtilties*, to form a right judgment in this particular"; instead, "common sense suffices" to understand and adjudicate among aspects of plot in tragedy.[25] Rymer recapitulates Aristotle's foundational claim, that "it is not the poet's function to relate actual events, but the kinds of things that might occur and are possible in terms of probability or necessity . . . Consequently, poetry is more philosophical and more elevated than history, since poetry relates more of the universal, while history relates particulars."[26] But Rymer also emphasizes that tragedy should treat the universal, probable, and necessary in nature, just as philosophers ancient and modern alike train our attention to such things. Aristotle and his acolytes are not uniquely able to access things universal, probable, or necessary. Nor do modern philosophers or tragedians lack resources to understand tragedy. The problem is that, whereas ancient tragedians depicted such matters with clarity and sophistication, "our Poets have forc'd another way to the *wood*; a *by-road*, that runs directly cross to that of *Nature*, *Manners* and *Philosophy* which gain'd the *Ancients* so great veneration."[27] Ancient poets, in other words, recognized the philosophical province of tragedy; modern poets neglect philosophy at large, both ancient *and* modern, and are attentive only to the whims and demands of diverse audiences, to "what will *please*."[28]

Thus Pope risks imprecision when he claims that to judge "*Shakespear* by *Aristotle's* rules is like trying a man by the Laws of one Country, who acted under those of another." He intends to challenge the scope of Aristotelian poetics, but, for Rymer, "*Aristotle's* rules" are in no sense particular to the *Poetics*. They are, rather, observations on universality, necessity, and probability, precisely those elements of tragedy (to follow Pope's analogy) that remain true in every country, which pertain not to human laws but to God and nature. Rymer does not judge Shakespeare "by *Aristotle's* rules," nor does he take recourse to any empirical logic of audience satisfaction to evaluate tragedy. He turns, rather, to reason and "common sense." He makes this clear in his preface to his 1674 translation of René Rapin's *Reflections on Aristotle's Treatise of Poesie*, noting that

> what *Aristotle* writes on this Subject, are not the dictates of his own magisterial will, or dry deductions of his Metaphysicks: But the Poets were his Masters, and what was their practice, he reduced to principles. Nor would the *modern* Poets blindly resign to this practice of the *Ancients*, were not the Reasons convincing and clear as any demonstration in *Mathematicks*. 'Tis only needful that we understand them, for our consent to the truth of them.[29]

Poetics and criticism alike, Rymer implies, are not empirical but rather mathematical exercises. What is best in both ancient and modern tragedy is philosophical and precise, honed to produce the same effects in Athens as in London, on men and women who have "the same *affections* and *passions* in both places, and the same *springs* than give them *motion*."[30] Tragic theses on the passions are "founded on a Philosophy never contraverted, but alike current at *Malmsbury* as at *Athens*"; both Hobbes and Aristotle, in other words, enable the tragedian to understand the movement of the passions and their place in the philosophy of nature.[31] Antique tragedy is not inherently better, but Sophocles and Euripides were indeed more attentive to philosophy than their modern counterparts Shakespeare, Jonson, Beaumont and Fletcher. They were thus more able to write effective, edifying tragedy. It is in this sense that Rymer takes it as incontrovertible "that *Athens* was more *civiliz'd* by their *Philosophers*, than we with both our *Philosophers* and *twelve Apostles*."[32]

Rymer's reference to Christianity is crucial as he develops the notion that poetry—and tragedy in particular—is an important intellectual resource, demonstrating probability and necessity in nature. Underscoring poetry as a matter of reason, skill, and method, he denies that poetic acumen is a species of inspiration, a divine frenzy or madness akin to prophecy. Rymer does not merely dispense here with antique Platonic assumptions concerning poetry, periodically in vogue across the Renaissance; he recalls Henry More's important study of the nature and the causes of the "distemper of *Fantastrie* and *Enthusiasme*," *Enthusiasmus Triumphatus* (1656), wherein More defines enthusiasm as "nothing else but a misconceit of being *inspired*," "*A full, but false perswasion in a man that he is inspired*."[33] Enthusiasm, according to More, is an expression of melancholy, a complexion that poets and enthusiasts share.[34] Indeed, More even suggests that while "a *Poet* is an *Enthusiast in jest*," assuming that the poetic claim to divine inspiration is a familiar (and relatively harmless) conceit, "an *Enthusiast* is a *Poet in good earnest*; Melancholy prevailing so much with him, that he takes his no better than Poeticall fits, and figments for divine inspiration and reall truth."[35] The poet exercises skill and boasts only in jest about the source of inspiration. When poets praise the muses, they do so conventionally, not in earnest; the "jest" takes the place of, without negating, a deliberate reflection on their craft. The enthusiast, however, produces a powerful fiction that they seriously attribute to the Spirit. Proceeding confidently, such enthusiasts have "the greatest power to delude the people," acting as if they were truly inspired by God.[36] The "*Mock-prophets* and false *Messiasses*" that distort and abuse Christian doctrine are such enthusiasts, from "the vain and idle *Enthusiasmes* of David George [Joris]" and "the tumultuous *Anabaptists* in *Germany*" to his own countrymen who base their authority on "*Extasies and Raptures with triumphant joy and singing*," on "*Mystical interpretations of Scripture, Quakings*, and *Visions*, all which are easily resolved into effects of Melancholy."[37] More offers, in turn, guidance on how to distinguish between genuine inspiration and enthusiasm. He insists that revelation should confirm, not contradict, the "*Spirit of illumination*, which resides in the soules of the faithful [as] a Principle of the purest Reason that is communicable to the humane Nature"; he claims, moreover, that "if any man shall pretend to the discovery of a Truth by inspiration that is of no good use or consequence to the Church of God, it is to me little less then [*sic*] a Demonstration, that he is *Fanatical*."[38] Reason and the Church provide criteria with which to recognize and reject enthusiasm, a play of "Fancy, which testifies nothing of the *Truth* or *Excellence* of any thing, and therefore ought not, nor cannot be assented to by any but mad men or fools."[39]

Rymer never defines poetry as a species of enthusiasm, as either "the *Child* of *Fancy*," "*blind* inspiration," "pure *enthusiasm*," or "*rapture* and *rage* all over." Poetry is, rather, an exercise of knowledge, a skill that may be "school'd and *disciplin'd* by *Reason*."[40] Following More, Rymer makes explicit the connection between poetry and religion, guarding against excessive fancy in either enterprise.

> *Fancy* . . . in Poetry, is like *Faith* in Religion; it makes far discoveries, and soars above reason, but never clashes, or runs against it. Fancy leaps, and frisks, and away she's gone; whilst *reason* rattles the chains, and follows after. *Reason* must consent and ratify whatever by *fancy* is attempted in its absence; or else 'tis all null and void in law. However, in the contrivance and *oeconomy* of a Play, reason is always principally to be consulted. Those who object against reason, are the *Fanaticks* in Poetry, and are never to be sav'd by their good works.[41]

In Rymer's remarkable analogy Christian faith is actually akin to fancy. He does not degrade faith. "Faith" may indeed name a steadfast belief in God's benevolence grounded in Scripture and reason. But Rymer also invites us to consider the supposed "faith" of the enthusiast, the fanatic or would-be prophet who believes he receives direct revelation from God, even if these revelations contradict Scripture and reason. When Rymer's contemporary Edward Stillingfleet imagined a world without Scripture, for instance, a world in which "*God* had left the *matters* of *Divine revelation* unrecorded at all, but left them to be discovered in every age by a *spirit of prophecy*," he admitted that "we cannot but conceive that an innumerable company of *croaking Enthusiasts* would be continually pretending *commissions* from heaven, by which the minds of men would be left in continual *distraction*, because they would have no certain *infallible rules* given them, whereby to difference the *good and evil spirit* from each other."[42] Rymer also maligns a faith that "leaps, and frisks" in the absence of reason, lacking the force of law, a poetic indictment of religious enthusiasm and fanatics' pretensions to ecclesiastical authority and political power. Just as the religious enthusiast or fanatic, in other words, impugns the reasonableness of Christianity (a preoccupation for Restoration divines like Stillingfleet and John Tillotson as well as philosophers like John Locke, Lodewijk Meyer, and John Toland), so too does the fanciful poet or critic deny the reasonableness of poetry. As Rymer's analogy turns on his arraignment of religious enthusiasm he insists that reason is fundamental to poetic practice as well, particularly in the "the contrivance and *oeconomy* of a Play." Reason is absolutely necessary to tragic plot. This fact is lost on those fanatic tragedians who follow only their fancy and thus produce defective plots. Their work undermines the project of tragedy. But here Rymer also suggests that the failures of English tragedians are not merely poetic. Jonson, Shakespeare, and Beaumont and Fletcher are "*Fanaticks* in Poetry," certainly, but insofar as their deficient plots also challenge divine providence, their poetic shortcomings are also theologico-political problems.

Providence, between History and Tragedy

To give substance to his comparison between faith and fancy, Rymer proceeds to describe the relationship between tragedy and philosophy in antiquity. Like most of his contemporary critics, Rymer accepts that "Tragedy was originally, with the Ancients, a piece of *Religious* worship, a part of their *Liturgy*."[43] Tragedy developed across antiquity in tandem with the cult of Dionysus before it assumed a more extensive dramatic function, instructing audiences about virtue. At this point Sophocles and Euripides, Rymer claims, taught "by *examples*, in a graver way, yet extremely *pleasant* and *delightful*."[44] And this is specifically the pleasure of effective mimesis. Referring to the *Poetics*, Rymer notes that "many things naturally unpleasant in the World in *themselves*" nevertheless give "*delight* when well *imitated*," his examples being "the *last Judgment*, of *Mich. Angelo*" as well as "the *Massacre* of the Innocents, the *Baptist's* head, &c."[45] But pleasure is not produced merely by depicting historical figures that audiences recognize. The Baptist's head, in a biblical tragedy, is only a sign, "an *Index*," that points to the historical episode recorded in Matthew 14 and Mark 6. Unless audiences are familiar with this particular episode, "the *head* of the *Baptist* can say no more to us, than the *head* of *Goliath*."[46] Ancient poets thus worked to depict or imitate the more enduring and universal aspects of nature. Recognizing the limits of history and its relevance to diverse audiences, they "refin'd upon the History" and "thence contriv'd something more *philosophical*, and more *accurate* than *History*"—namely, poetry, and tragedy in particular, which Rymer (roughly quoting *Poetics* 1451b.6) calls "Σπουδαιότερον καὶ φιλοσόφικότερον [*sic*]."[47] This involves a search for "design" in history, an effort to depict "the *universal* and *eternal truths*" that subtend history.[48]

On these grounds, Rymer argues, Aristotle and the antique tragedians *reformed* tragedy. They seized poetry and philosophy alike from "the *men* of *sense*," who were preoccupied with discussions "of *Atoms* and *empty Space*," advocates of a "*Mechanical* Philosophy" who were content to see "the same *end* happen to the *righteous* and to the *unjust*, *vertue* often opprest, and *wickedness* on the Throne."[49] Sophocles and Euripides, in other words, wrested tragedy from antique materialists for whom there was no design in nature, no governing deity or notion of providence giving direction to the world. Tragedians and critics responded to these materialists in their attention to plot. In particular, they recoiled from the "*unequal* distribution of rewards and punishments" in tragedies, aspects of plot that "did perplex the *wisest*, and by the *Atheist* [were] made a scandal to the *Divine Providence*"; "They concluded," in turn,

> that a *Poet* must of necessity see *justice* exactly administred, if he intended to please. For, said they, if the World can scarce be satisfi'd with God Almighty, whose holy will and purposes are not to be *comprehended*; a *Poet* (in these matters) shall never be pardon'd, who (they are sure) is not *incomprehensible*; whose *ways* and *walks* may, without *impiety*, be penetrated and examin'd.[50]

Ancient tragedians, Rymer claims, made it their ethical task to justify the ways of God to men, participating in the work of theodicy so crucial to philosophers at the end of the seventeenth century.[51] They did so, however, at the level of plot, *in fiction*, precisely because audiences would not tolerate an inexplicable deity. It is thus in tragedy that poets depict providential design and justice. Tragedy depicts things universal, necessary, and probable in order to underscore the work of the deity in nature. The tragedian renders God, or at least providence, comprehensible. Yet Rymer also suggests that while audiences will "scarce be satisfi'd" with an unintelligible deity, neither are they satisfied with poets who are "not *incomprehensible*." Almost paradoxically, the poet assumes both the office and obscurity of the deity. The poet must demonstrate God's design in nature, but not so thoroughly that nature is laid bare as a machine, without some surplus mystery to attribute to providence. The poet should thus construct plots that enable audiences to recognize providence while also imitating the unexpected and astonishing (but not improbable) means by which God works in nature. With this in mind, the able critic must exercise belief and piety in their examination of the tragedy.

The tragic plot, in other words, should demonstrate God's providence, rendering God as comprehensible in tragedy as in nature, but without reducing God to nature. Christianity is reasonable, but Rymer, like More and Stillingfleet, understands "reason" as a faculty that ultimately confirms the truth of Scripture as well as of Christian Doctrine. Thus, as Rymer traces the development of Greek tragedy and its importance among his contemporaries, he imports the same terms and concepts that his contemporaries used to combat deism. As Isabel Rivers and Robert E. Sullivan make clear, "deism" is in fact an elusive and ambiguous term used to describe a religion grounded in reason to the extent that believers might come to know the one true God by means of reason alone, without Christian revelation.[52] Since the deist God was evident in nature, deism was often referred to as natural religion. And whereas many philosophers and theologians argued that Christianity is itself fundamentally rational, often to the exclusion of Scripture, miracles, and enthusiasm, their opponents—even latitudinarians like Stillingfleet and Tillotson—saw this as an attack on the tenets of Christianity. In his *Religio Laici* (1682), for instance, Dryden claims that "deism, or the principles of natural worship, are only the faint remnants or dying flames of revealed religion in the posterity of Noah, and that our modern philosophers, nay, and some of our philosophizing divines, have too much exalted the faculties of our souls, when they have maintained that by their force mankind has been able to find out that there is one supreme agent or intellectual being which we call God . . . without the benefit of divine illumination."[53] Deism is thus primitive, appropriate only in the absence of revelation (among the heathen, for instance, or those figures and cultures that lacked knowledge of the God of Scripture). But an inappropriate deism nevertheless persists among modern Christians who, instead of following Scripture and other forms of revelation, place far too much faith in their own faculties as well as in a degraded determination of reason. Dryden develops this argument in poetry, in his *Religio Laici*:

> The deist thinks he stands on firmer ground;
> Cries 'εὕρηκα, the mighty secret's found:
> God is that spring of good, supreme and best,
> We made to serve, and in that service blessed;
> If so, some rules of worship must be given,
> Distributed alike to all by Heaven,
> Else God were partial, and to some denied
> The means his justice should for all provide.
> This general worship is to praise and pray,
> One part to borrow blessings, one to pay;
> And when frail nature slides into offence,
> The sacrifice for crimes is penitence.
> Yet since th' effects of Providence we find
> Are variously dispensed to human kind,
> That vice triumphs, and virtue suffers here
> (A brand that sovereign justice cannot bear)
> Our reason prompts us to a future state,
> The last appeal from Fortune, and from fate,
> Where God's all-righteous ways will be declared,
> The bad meet punishment, the good reward.' (42–61)[54]

In Dryden's poem, the deist comprehends the existence of God by reason alone, reducing God to the source "good, supreme and best"—that is, to an abstract principle. As a principle, they reckon that a perfectly good and just being must distribute itself equally among its creations, "Else God were partial." Dryden's deist proceeds to deliver a proof for the existence of an afterlife. God is perfect and just, not partial; a perfect and just God distributes good evenly; but God does indeed "variously dispense" the "effects of Providence" among human beings in history; in order for God to remain good and just, this apparent partiality in history requires the exercise of justice in an afterlife. Hence, while it might seem that "vice triumphs, and virtue suffers here / (A brand that sovereign justice cannot bear)," this is simply because God's goodness and justice are actually evident in the afterlife, where (appropriately) "The bad meet punishment, the good reward." The deist God exercises sovereign justice. But the deist does not look to Scripture to confirm the existence of heaven or hell. Rather, "Our reason prompts us to a future state." Reason alone lays bare God's just design as the deist undermines more primitive appeals to fortune or fate, including orthodox positions. We find a similar argument in Louis-Armand de Lom d'Arce, the baron de Lahontan's magnificent *Nouveaux voyages dans l'Amérique septentrionale* (1702), for instance, where the (deist) Huron affirm the immortality of the soul without access to Scripture or the resources of Revelation. Assuming that God is an "infinitely perfect being" (*Etre infiniment parfait*), "neither unusual nor capricious," they deduce that he would not preordain some to happiness and others to misery and slavery without the promise of another life.[55] Lahontan's Huron thus articulate a deist argument proving the immortality of the soul and the life of the world to come, an argument grounded in reason, not revelation, and presuming the existence of a just, constant, and rational deity.

Rymer's tragedian attends to remarkably similar criteria in the composition of a plot. The Greek tragedians, seeing that the "*unequal* distribution of rewards and punishments did perplex the wisest, and by the *Atheist* was made a scandal to the *Divine Providence*," sought to underscore Divine Providence by seeing "*justice* exactly administred" in their plots. Rymer calls this "*Poetical Justice*," as the careful design of the plot underscores God's abiding design in nature, inspiring wonder though men are neither subject to chance nor contingency.[56] The tragedian, like the deist, produces proof of God's justice without taking recourse to revelation, without direct reference to Scripture or Christian doctrine. Yet whereas the deist turns to nature, the tragic poet constructs plots that demonstrate God's providence, with accuracy and philosophical depth. This is where the apparent similarity between the tragedian who administers poetic justice and the deist ends. The deist, Rymer implies, looks for God's providence in "History," where they observe "the same *end* happen to the *righteous* and to the *unjust, vertue* often opprest, and *wickedness* on the Throne."[57] Deists ground their proof of the existence of the afterlife on this vision of the world, on these notions of history and nature: injustice and inequity in "History" *must* be rectified in an afterlife, "Else God were partial." Rymer sees this as unacceptable. The deist god is not a benevolent providential deity whose justice is evident in nature; it is an abstraction that is at times reducible to nature, at times entirely alien to "History." Drawing directly from Aristotle's *Poetics*, Rymer sees their notion of "History" as perilously limited and limiting, as a record only of "particular *yesterday-truths*," "imperfect and improper to illustrate the *universal* and *internal truths*" of nature.[58] Such truths—manifest signs of God's providence—are not evident in "History" as such. They are, rather, the stuff of tragedy, and the tragedian, who is charged with the mimesis not of discrete events but of design and the unity of action, is poised to depict God's providence in a more precise, philosophical, and *satisfying* way. As Rymer develops this notion he argues that "in former times *Poetry* was another thing than *History*, or than the *Law* of the Land."[59] Whereas history and law alike deal with particular applications of justice or to contingent episodes and events, "*Poetry* discover'd crimes, the *Law* could never find out; and punish'd those the *Law* had acquitted. The *Areopagus* clear'd *Orestes*, but with what *Furies* did the *Poets* haunt and torment him? and what a wretch made they of *Oedipus*, when the *Casuist* excus'd his *invincible* ignorance?"[60] Poetry, in other words, was invested in natural right, in the gods' justice (now God's justice), which is not necessarily expressed in any one instance of historical judgment but which is nevertheless universal. Poetic justice renders God's design visible in tragedy, a form that is never simply a depiction of a series of contingent events. The deist relegates "justice" to an afterlife, abstracting God entirely from the realm of the sensible. Rymer's tragedian renders providence visible, palpable, and demonstrable in poetry.

The poet is nevertheless limited insofar as they can distribute perfect poetic justice only over the course of a tragic plot. The very form of tragedy places restrictions on a poet as well as on an audience's ability to comprehend justice or feel satisfaction. The poet must "have a strict eye on their Malefactor, that he transgrest not too far," in order that an exact justice can be served in the work.[61] The tragedian should thus take care not to make the sinner or criminal too reprobate, or too despicable, for under those circumstances it is not enough that the "Malefactor" be tried and condemned according to the law of a particular country. "For though *historical Iustice* might rest there," Rymer reasons, "yet *poetical Iustice* could not be so content."[62] Poetical justice is a more thorough, universal judgment. While a particular nation might demand the life of a criminal in recompense for a crime, this might actually be too lenient in light of his offense. Poetical justice would thus "require that the satisfaction be compleat and full" within the span of a plot; such justice is achieved only when "the *Malefactor* goes off the *Stage*, and nothing left to God Almighty, and another World."[63] Thus the tragedian cannot take recourse to an "afterlife" to resolve the plot, cannot reserve punishment for another place and time. This is how the deist accounts for God's justice, relegating it to "another World." Poetic justice must be rendered in the plot itself, which places limits on the sorts of crime and punishment that a tragedian can adequately depict in a complete plot, particularly since it is difficult for "Spectators [to] trust the *Poet* for a *Hell* behind the *Scenes*; the fire must roar in the conscience of the *Criminal*, the *fiends* and *furies* be *conjur'd* up to their faces, with a world of *machine* and horrid spectacles."[64] The antique tragedians Euripides and Sophocles knew this well, depicting only the sort of criminals and crimes that could accept due punishment onstage, satisfying justice historical and poetical, particular and universal, in the span of a single plot. This is not to say that the ancients "were squeamish, or unacquainted with any of these great *lumping* crimes in that age"—consider, Rymer reminds his readers, "their *Oedipus*, *Orestes*, or *Medea*," all of whom committed crimes against nature—but that they took great care to see their offenses appropriately punished within the span of a single plot.[65] It is only in this sense that tragedy observes "that constant order, that harmony and beauty of Providence, that necessary relation and chain, whereby the causes and the effects, the vertues and rewards, the vices and their punishments are proportion'd and link'd together; how deep and dark soever are laid the Springs, and however intricate and involv'd are their operations."[66]

Rymer does not deliver his promised critique of *Othello* in *The Tragedies of the Last Age*. He offers a thorough reading of Shakespeare's tragedy only in 1693, in *A Short View of Tragedy*, a far less-focused work save for Rymer's careful reading of *Othello*. Before he turns to Shakespeare's work Rymer rehearses many of the claims about tragedy that appeared in his 1678 tract while offering a much more extensive history of tragedy and criticism. Much of this history, particularly his studies of Continental tragedy after the Reformation, subtends Rymer's critique of Shakespeare. While the critic does not produce an interlinear commentary, he comes close. Indeed, Rymer walks through *Othello*, act by act, detailing Shakespeare's sins against nature and philosophy, with reference not only to the *Poetics* but also to other relevant poetics of tragedy. He accuses Shakespeare of "un-hallowing the Theatre, profaning the name of Tragedy; And instead of representing Men and Manners, turning all Morality, good sence, and humanity into mockery and derision."[67] His gravest error, however, lies in the catastrophe of the tragedy, as Shakespeare violates the principle of poetic justice that Rymer outlines in his 1678 treatise.

The decisive problem lies with Desdemona's death, as Rymer wonders "what unnatural crime *Desdemona*, or her Parents had committed, to bring this Judgment down upon her"—that is, "to Wed a Black-amoor, and innocent to be thus cruelly murder'd by him."[68] This leads him, in turn, to ask, "What instruction can we make out of this Catastrophe? Or whither must our reflection lead us? Is not this to envenome and sour our spirits, to make us repine and grumble at Providence; and the government of the World? If this be our end, what boots it to be Vertuous?"[69] Rymer duly offers a revised ending à la Nahum Tate's 1681 *King Lear* wherein Desdemona merely faints, appearing dead to Othello, who promptly kills himself; "touch'd with remorse," Rymer would have Othello "honestly cut his own Throat, by the good leave, and with the applause of all the Spectators. Who might thereupon have gone home with a quiet mind, admiring the beauty of Providence; fairly and truly represented on the Theatre."[70] But providence is not depicted in the resolution of the play, in the particular details of either Othello's or Desdemona's fate. Providence does not pertain to particular details at all but rather to reason and nature. The depiction of providence rests on the tragedian's treatment of necessity, in the plot and in nature at large. Desdemona has not behaved unnaturally so her death is *unnecessary*. Moreover, Rymer alleges that

> from this Scene to the end of the Play we meet with nothing but blood and butchery, described much-what to the style of *the last Speeches and Confessions of the persons executed at Tyburn*: with this difference, that there we have the *fact*, and the due course of Justice, whereas our Poet against all Justice and Reason, against all Law, Humanity and Nature, in a barbarous arbitrary way, executes and makes havock of his subjects, *Hab-nab*, as they come to hand.[71]

Rymer tacitly recognizes that a certain justice is served in *Othello* and, in comparing the remainder of act 5 to the scaffold confessions at Tyburn, recalls his earlier distinction between historical justice and poetic justice. But Shakespeare does not satisfy either form. In fact, he proceeds "against all Justice and Reason, against all Law, Humanity and Nature" to depict a series of actions that is episodic and random, which violates any sense of probability or necessity in tragedy or providence. It is not only the content of *Othello* that Rymer finds objectionable. It is primarily Shakespeare's inability to realize any probability or consistency in his plot. Rymer abhors what he sees as excessive violence in *Othello* not because it is bombastic or spectacular (he suggests, remember, that Shakespeare might have avoided this critique had his Othello "honestly cut his own Throat" onstage—a gory proposition, indeed) but because the terms of the plot do not call for it. It is not a matter of decorum but rather causality and economy.

What Does It Take to Represent Providence?

Rymer delivers a totalizing critique of *Othello*, citing Shakespeare with crimes not only against art but also against nature and providence. His poetics affords him these resources, enabling him to collate probability and necessity in tragedy with nature itself. Laying claim to Aristotle's *Poetics*, Rymer's is at once a critical and a theologico-political indictment of Shakespeare and his cohort, of popular tragedy, and of an alternative regime of art and identification that privileges craft, performance, and the resources of the company.[72] On its own terms, Rymer's critique is devastating. It might seem strange, then, that I have described his as an impasse: in what must have appeared to him as a moment of triumph, how is it that Rymer points to the limits of the representative regime of art? In the first case, like Rancière's Corneille, Rymer delivers a poetics that lays bare the logic of the representative regime of art. Nowhere is this clearer than at the moment when he insists that, in order to see poetic justice administered in the plot, the tragedian must at once render providence comprehensible and imitate God's incomprehensibility. As I said before, as if paradoxically the poet assumes both the office and obscurity of the deity. As Rancière makes clear, the work of art, considered with respect to the representative regime of art, is never simply a representation of nature. It is a double articulation, a presentation not only of the work but also of a particular way of perceiving or comprehending nature, a *poiesis* and an *aesthesis*, organizing the field of vision, sensation, and intelligibility. If Rymer's "poetic justice" is a strong statement on behalf of the representative regime of art, his insistence that the tragedian imitate God's incomprehensibility is a stronger endorsement yet—the point at which the tragedian is responsible not only for the poetic presentation of nature but also for the terms of probability and necessity themselves, the economy of appropriate actions and affects, the causal relationships between them, and the terms of visibility, sensation, and comprehension. The poet can render providence intelligible and sensible—that is to say, beautiful or terrifying—within the scope of a single plot only because they establish the terms of intelligibility and sensibility, to say nothing of probability and necessity. What is both "incomprehensible" *and* imitated by the poet is the articulation of the universal, of the logic of the universal. Drawing together discourses on providence and poetic acumen Rymer reveals the dual operation of mimesis in the representative regime of art.

So too does Rymer render providence subject to poetic criteria. As Rymer collates faith and fancy, the reasonableness of Christianity and the philosophy of tragedy, it may seem at first that poetic statements rely on established notions of reason and revelation, as if Rymer merely extends the claims of theology to address relevant aspects of tragedy. But this is not how either *The Tragedies of the Last Age* or *A Short View of Tragedy* takes shape. Rymer refers obliquely to philosophical notions of reason, but (with the exception of the ancient materialists from whom Euripides and Sophocles saved tragedy) he readily admits that little has changed in metaphysics or philosophical anthropology in the interim between Aristotle and his contemporary Hobbes (Hobbes would have been surprised to learn he was ostensibly an Aristotelian). A cynical reader might take this as evidence that Rymer lacked familiarity with the history of philosophy, that he understood little about the relationship between the *Poetics* and the larger Aristotelian corpus, to say nothing of materialisms ancient or modern. Maybe this is true. But what is more relevant to the present discussion is the degree to which this matters: not much. Rymer accords poetics, and specifically the poetics of tragedy, a certain autonomy, accepting that representation ultimately expresses an *aisthesis*, organizing intelligibility and sensation, in a manner that is not necessarily dependent on an established philosophy or theology. While it would be too much to say that Rymer affirms the autonomy of either art or criticism it is nevertheless the case that his poetics is not in the service of any theology. His idiosyncratic comparison between faith and fancy, as well as his flirtation with deism, makes this patently clear.

And it is here that we might see why, if not how, a regime of representation gives way to alternatives in the eighteenth century, particularly with respect to their competing accounts of providence and religious experience. Historians of art and philosophy generally identify Alexander Gottlieb Baumgarten and Christian Wolff as the earliest purveyors of aesthetic philosophy, developing theses on sensation and experience not only in conversation with slightly earlier philosophers like the Earl of Shaftesbury but also with Pietists, Methodists, and other sects that articulated religious experience in decidedly aesthetic and affective terms. Preoccupied with sublimity, enthusiasm, and genius, these later figures reject the norms of mimesis that ground Rymer's poetics, which hold his particular approaches to *poiesis* and *aisthesis* together and which subtend his theses on providence, plot, and poetic justice. Take, for example, *A Letter Concerning Enthusiasm* (as well as the first and second miscellanies expounding the brief *Letter*), in which Shaftesbury, like Rymer, collates discussions of poetry, fanaticism, and enthusiasm. Like Rymer, Shaftesbury affirms that "inspiration is a real feeling of the Divine Presence and enthusiasm a false one," but rather than adjudicate between the true and the false he claims that "the passion they raise is much alike."[73] Enthusiasm, Shaftesbury maintains, is "a very natural honest passion, and has properly nothing for its object but what is good and honest."[74] What is at stake here is not a simple difference of opinion but rather a signal matter of focus and method. Rymer's poetic justice relies on a notion of representation that renders affects and actions more or less appropriate in relation to the imitation of nature—a mimesis that is in fact a statement about nature that organizes visibility and comprehension. The representation, the tragedy, dictates whether affects or passions are "natural" or appropriate under given circumstances. Shaftesbury, in contrast, begins with the natural affect and traces its career in history, without immediate recourse to a governing representation of the universal. From this vantage point, tragedy, to say nothing of Scripture and revelation, is best seen not as complete action depicting justice but rather as a play of historical affects and actions—precisely the opposite of Rymer's Aristotelian thesis on plot and form. Rymer's preoccupation with tragedy gives way to an acute account of affects in history, a science that Rymer (after Aristotle and his early modern interpreters) degrades but that affords Shaftesbury and his contemporaries more adequate resources to understand religious experience in increasingly *aesthetic* terms. Rymer's representation of providence, as an expression of the representative regime of art, ultimately reveals itself as a particular, historical articulation of cause and effect, of passion and action, and divine justice. The representative regime of art, in turn, discloses its limits: art does not merely relate god or nature, it effectively takes their place while simultaneously establishing conditions under which "God" and "nature" become intelligible.

Notes

1. Alexander Pope, "The Preface of the Editor," *The Works of Shakespear in Six Volumes, Collated and Corrected by the Former Editions, by Mr. Pope*, volume 1 (London: Jacob Tonson, 1725), vi.

2. Pope's claim here is patently false. See, for instance, Tanya Pollard, *Greek Tragic Women on Shakespearean Stages* (Oxford: Oxford University Press, 2017); Micha Lazarus, "Sidney's Greek Poetics," *Studies in Philology* 112, no. 3 (2015): 504–36; and my own *Tragedy as Philosophy in the Reformation World* (Oxford: Oxford University Press, 2019).

3. Pope, "The Preface of the Editor," vi–vii.

4. Pope, "The Preface of the Editor," v.

5. Pope even flirts with the notion that Shakespeare eschewed imitation altogether, introducing him as "an Original," "not so much an Imitator, as an Instrument, of Nature"—undermining the Aristotelian dictum, that "Poesie in general, is a picture or imitation of an action." Shakespeare, Pope suggests, does not merely "imitate" or "copy" nature. Instead Shakespeare's characters "are so

much Nature her self, that 'tis a sort of injury to call them by so distant a name as Copies of her"; his poetry, an intuitive expression of "life and variety," as if Shakespeare participates directly in nature and creation. Pope, "The Preface of the Editor," vii, ii-iv; and René Rapin, *Reflections on Aristotle's Treatise of Poesie*, trans. Thomas Rymer (London: T. N. for H. Herringman, 1674), 76.

6. See J. C. Eade, *Aristotle Anatomised: The "Poetics" in England, 1674–1781* (Frankfurt am Main: Lang, 1988), 7–28; John Dale Ebbs, *The Principle of Poetic Justice Illustrated in Restoration Tragedy* (Salzburg: Institut für Englische Sprache und Literatur, 1973), 60–71; and Thomas Rymer, *The Critical Works of Thomas Rymer*, ed. Curt A. Zimansky (New Haven, Conn.: Yale University Press, 1956), vii–li.

7. Thomas Rymer, *A Short View of Tragedy: It's Original, Excellency, and Corruption; With Some Reflections on Shakespear, and Other Practitioners for the Stage* (London: Baldwin, 1693), 146.

8. Rymer, *Short View of Tragedy*, 86.

9. Rymer, *Short View of Tragedy*, 87, 92; Aristotle, *Poetics*, trans. Stephen Halliwell, in *Aristotle: Poetics; Longinus: On the Sublime; Demetrius: On Style* (Cambridge, Mass.: Harvard University Press, 1995), 52–53, 58–63, 124–25.

10. Rymer, *Short View of Tragedy*, 146.

11. Thomas Rymer, *The Tragedies of the Last Age* (London: Tonson, 1678), 23–27, 37.

12. Aristotle, *Poetics*, 128–29; Charles Gildon, *The History of the Athenian Society* (London: Dowley, 1691), 9.

13. Jacques Rancière, *The Aesthetic Unconscious*, trans. Debra Keates and James Swenson (Cambridge: Polity Press, 2009), 51.

14. Jacques Rancière, *The Politics of Aesthetics: The Distribution of the Sensible*, trans. Gabriel Rockhill (London: Continuum, 2004), 36.

15. Jacques Rancière, *The Future of the Image*, trans. Gregory Elliott (London: Verso, 2007), 115; Jacques Rancière, *Aesthetics and Its Discontents*, trans. Steven Corcoran (Cambridge: Polity Press, 2009), 6–7; Jacques Rancière, *Disagreement: Politics and Philosophy*, trans. Julie Rose (Minneapolis: University of Minnesota Press, 1999), 17, 57–58.

16. Rancière, *The Aesthetic Unconscious*, 51.

17. Rancière, *The Aesthetic Unconscious*, 51.

18. Rymer also accords Corneille's 1659 work a special status. After testifying in the dedication to *A Short View of Tragedy* that "my zeal goes no higher than the Doctrine of *Horace*, and *Aristotle*; and the Primitive Fathers of *Dramatick Poetry*," Rymer takes the side of the ancients—and in this case Sophocles's *Oedipus*, "reckon'd in the degree of perfection"—against his contemporaries, in particular against "that [*Oedipus*], by *Corneille*, and by others of a Modern Cut, *quantum Mutatus*!" How much has changed, in other words, since antiquity; the august and acute tragedy of old has given way to flawed and degraded modern examples. Suffice it to say that Corneille's *Oedipe* is no less representative for Rymer than it is for Rancière. Rymer, *A Short View of Tragedy*, A4^{r}, A4^{v}.

19. Rancière, *Future of the Image*, 114.

20. Rancière, *Future of the Image*, 117.

21. Rancière, *Future of the Image*, 117.

22. Rymer, *Tragedies*, 1.

23. Rymer, *Tragedies*, 2, 6.
24. Rymer, *Tragedies*, 4.
25. Rymer, *Tragedies*, 4.
26. Aristotle, *Poetics*, 58–61.
27. Rymer, *Tragedies*, 3.
28. Rymer, *Tragedies*, 5.
29. René Rapin, *Reflections on Aristotle's Treatise of Poesie*, trans. Thomas Rymer (London: Herringman, 1674), A4^{v}.
30. Rymer, *Tragedies*, 6. On the tension between poetry and philosophy among Rymer's French contemporaries, see Joseph M. Levine, *Between the Ancients and the Moderns: Baroque Culture in Restoration England* (New Haven, Conn.: Yale University Press, 1999), 153–83.
31. Rymer writes specifically about the passions here when he conflates antique Athens and modern Malmesbury. But his is nevertheless a remarkable claim considering the obvious differences between Aristotle's and Hobbes's philosophies. Rymer evidently knew Hobbes and was familiar enough with his philosophy to compose the Latin preface for his *Historia ecclesiastica* (published posthumously in 1688). See Rymer, *Tragedies*, 99, and Rymer, *Critical Works*, xv, 284–86.
32. Rymer, *Tragedies*, 7.
33. Henry More, *Enthusiasmus Triumphatus; or, A Discourse of the Nature, Causes, Kinds, and Cure, of Enthusiasme* (London: Flesher, 1656), 1, 2.
34. The Third Earl of Shaftesbury, Anthony Ashley Cooper, fundamentally agrees, claiming that "there is a melancholy which accompanies all enthusiasm" (*Characteristics of Men, Manners, Opinions, Times*, ed. Lawrence E. Klein [Cambridge: Cambridge University Press, 1999], 9).
35. More, *Enthusiasmus Triumphatus*, 20.
36. More, *Enthusiasmus Triumphatus*, 20.
37. More, *Enthusiasmus Triumphatus*, 22, 23, 24.
38. More, *Enthusiasmus Triumphatus*, 54, 55.
39. More, *Enthusiasmus Triumphatus*, 54.
40. Rymer, *Tragedies*, 8.
41. Rymer, *Tragedies*, 8.
42. Edward Stillingfleet, *Origines Sacrae, or a Rational Account of the Grounds of Christian Faith, as to the Truth and Divine Authority of the Scriptures* (London: Mortlock, 1662), 109.
43. Rymer, *Tragedies*, 11.
44. Rymer, *Tragedies*, 13–14.
45. Rymer, *Tragedies*, 14–15.
46. Rymer, *Tragedies*, 15.
47. Rymer, *Tragedies*, 15–16.
48. Rymer, *Tragedies*, 14, 16.
49. Rymer, *Tragedies*, 13, 14.
50. Rymer, *Tragedies*, 14.
51. Gottfried Wilhelm Leibniz, with whom Rymer corresponded as he composed his *Foedera*, coined the term "theodicy" in his foundational work *Essais de theodicée sur la bonté de Dieu, la liberté de l'homme et l'origine du mal* (1710).
52. Robert E. Sullivan, *John Toland and the Deist Controversy: A Study in Adaptations* (Cambridge, Mass.: Harvard University Press, 1982), 205–34; Isabel

Rivers, *Reason, Grace, and Sentiment: A Study of the Language of Religion and Ethics in England, 1660–1780, Volume 1: Whichcote to Wesley* (Cambridge: Cambridge University Press, 1991), 44–45.

53. John Dryden, *Religio Laici*, in *Dryden: Selected Poems*, ed. Paul Hammond and David Hopkins (London: Routledge, 2007), 260–61.

54. Dryden, *Religio Laici*, 281–82.

55. Baron de Lahontan, *Voyages du baron de Lahonton dans L'Amerique Septentrionale*, 2nd ed., 2 vols. (The Hague: L'Honoré, 1705), II.116.

56. Rymer, *Tragedies*, 23.

57. Rymer, *Tragedies*, 23.

58. Rymer, *Tragedies*, 14.

59. Rymer, *Tragedies*, 25.

60. Rymer, *Tragedies*, 25.

61. Rymer, *Tragedies*, 26.

62. Rymer, *Tragedies*, 26.

63. Rymer, *Tragedies*, 26.

64. Rymer, *Tragedies*, 26.

65. Rymer, *Tragedies*, 25–27.

66. Rymer, *Tragedies*, 140–41.

67. Rymer, *Short View of Tragedy*, 111–12.

68. Rymer, *Short View of Tragedy*, 137 (given in the text as 141).

69. Rymer, *Short View of Tragedy*, 137 [141]–38.

70. Rymer, *Short View of Tragedy*, 138.

71. Rymer, *Short View of Tragedy*, 143 [139]–44.

72. Although it is far beyond the scope of this essay, I would argue that Shakespeare, Beaumont, Fletcher, and their contemporaries belong to a historical regime of art and artistic production that Rancière does not identify in his oeuvre, a regime that was shaped by the exigencies of performance in London at the turn of the seventeenth century. Pope had something very right in his comment on Shakespeare and Aristotle: namely, that Shakespearean drama challenges critical judgments proper to the representative regime of art. Yet while there are certainly *aesthetic* productions and interpretations of Shakespeare's work—that is, Shakespeare is no stranger to the aesthetic regime of art—we should also be mindful of the meaningful distinctions between early modern and modern milieux, never presuming that Shakespeare or his audiences share later aesthetic assumptions about art or politics.

73. Shaftesbury, *Characteristics*, 27

74. Shaftesbury, *Characteristics*, 355.

Part Two

*Aesthetics and the
Politics of the Representable*

Shakespeare and the Plebs

Tracey Sedinger

In the "Life of Brutus" (from *The Lives of the Noble Grecians and Romans Compared*), Plutarch records the growing dissension between Brutus and Cassius in the eastern Mediterranean (after Julius Caesar's assassination), the product of temperamental differences as well as of the stress of campaigning so far from Rome. During one particularly vitriolic argument, Marcus Phaonius, a "counterfeate . . . Philosopher" and "a friend and follower of *Cato* while he liued," tries to play the role of Homer's Nestor, and intrudes into Brutus's chamber in order to upbraid the two generals.[1] In spite of himself, his efforts at diplomacy actually succeed, insofar as general laughter at him ends the argument.

When Shakespeare wrote *Julius Caesar* (1598), he retained this episode, but, in keeping with his general practice of abridging his source materials, he transferred it to the eve of the Battle of Philippi (42 B.C.E.). More mysteriously, he changed Marcus's elective vocation from *philosopher* to *poet*. Whereas Marcus Phoanius had some claim on Brutus's attention (Cato had been his father-in-law), the intrusion of Shakespeare's unnamed poet lacks any such justification and appears merely to provide opportunities for both Brutus and Cassius to insult his alleged failures of both rhyme and meter. Though David Daniell (editor of the Arden Third Series *Julius Caesar*) argues that this episode provides some necessary levity in a scene dominated by interpersonal conflict, Cassius and Brutus's excoriation of a man who rightfully criticizes their failure to cooperate hardly seems funny. Perhaps the poet's translation of Homer is not of the best ("Love and be friends, as two such men should be, / For I have seen more years, I'm sure, than ye"), but the moral is nevertheless appropriate to the occasion.[2] So why did Shakespeare not only include the scene but make its victim a poet?

Famously, *Julius Caesar* is not kind to poets, as made clear in an earlier—and remarkably horrific—scene, when another poet, Cinna, is ripped apart by a plebeian mob (3.3). Equally famously, the play is preoccupied with rhetoric, as when Brutus and Mark Antony deliver what are usually referred to as "funeral orations" during 3.2.[3] Though Elizabethan poetics owed much to classical and humanist rhetorical theory, by the time Shakespeare was writing in the 1590s, it was clear that a poetic practice with the stage as its primary locus raised problems with the relationship between passion, morality, and politics that humanist rhetorical norms were incapable of articulating, let alone resolving. In response, Shakespeare elaborated an alternative theatricality characterized by an antihumanist refusal to discipline his audiences' feelings, beautiful or ugly, noble or ignoble—a rejection of rhetorical discipline in favor of aesthetic emancipation with unpredictable political effects. And as one of the first plays that Shakespeare wrote for the Globe, during a decade when even monarchical republicanism was losing its legitimacy, *Julius Caesar*'s subject matter was especially well suited to his exploration of these issues.[4]

Toward a Political Aesthetics

In a series of lectures given at the New School for Social Research in 1970, Hannah Arendt argued that if Kant could be said to have a political philosophy, it could be found in his *Critique of Judgment*, which was first published in 1790, one year after the storming of the Bastille.[5] Central to her argument was Kant's promotion of a sensus communis that propelled his critical philosophy beyond its methodological individualism, including his emphasis on the reality of freedom and autonomy.[6] In the third *Critique*, Kant developed a mode of judgment (reflective) neither conceptual nor objectively valid, based on the feeling of pleasure occasioned, not by the beauty of the work of art, but by the free play of the faculties of the imagination and understanding as produced by the object associated with that judgment.[7] Though reflective judgment lacks logical validity, it still feels proleptically, universally valid because it rests on what Kant called sensus communis:

> The idea of a **communal** sense, i.e., a faculty for judging that in its reflection takes account (*a priori*) of everyone else's way of representing in thought, in order **as it were** to hold its judgment up to human reason as a whole and therefore avoid the illusion which, from subjective private conditions that could easily be held to be objective, would have a detrimental influence on the judgment. Now this happens by one holding his judgment up not so

> much to the actual as to the merely possible judgments of others, and putting himself into the position of everyone else, merely by abstracting from the limitations that contingently attach to our own judging; which is in turn accomplished by leaving out as far as it is possible everything in one's representational state that is matter, i.e., sensation, and attending solely to the formal peculiarities of his representation or his representational state.[8]

As a regulative idea, sensus communis lacks a concrete materialization in the world, even though, as Arendt points out, publicity (and presumably those other features of a public sphere) is absolutely necessary for it to operate. As a consequence, later readings, such as Jean-François Lyotard's or J. M. Bernstein's, adduce a very different, elegiac relationship between judgment and politics, one marked less by the normative communicability of such judgments than by the obstruction that Kant's subjectivism (beauty's derivation from the free play of the faculties) poses to publicity. For these writers, common sense is not community—and no amount of communicability can make up for the corrosive impact of political modernism's social divisions on the human capacity for being together.

Despite substantial differences, Arendt, Bernstein, and Lyotard comprehend a political modernism defined by a fundamental contradiction between individual autonomy and a lost or coming community on whose behalf sensus communis operates. Aesthetic judgment marks an absent plenitude, whether prepolitical or premodern, destroyed by Weberian processes of rationalization and administration: hence Bernstein's delineation of the melancholic loss that defines Kantian aesthetics; Arendt's return to ancient Greece for a politics uncontaminated by social questions; and Lyotard's focus on sublimity as a kind of absolute negation.[9] But as Shakespeare scholars must recognize, cultural divisions—and their concomitant social divisions—precede political modernism, which suggests that a more complex account of the historical emergence of aesthetic discourse and the phenomena it comprehends might be in order. History is never simply a forward march; as Benjamin's angel of history makes clear, we always look back even as we are being blasted into a ruinous future that we cannot see.

When considered as an ideology, aesthetics has often been taken as a spurious universality that obscures fundamentally unjust distinctions between people. But as Kant argued, sensus communis requires the exclusion of "everything in one's representational state that is matter, i.e., sensation."[10] Moreover, the discourse of taste disciplines (or "refines") individual, intrasubjective sensibility, in order to exclude what Sianne

Ngai has called ugly feelings, the affects or passions that corrode the highly normative moral and political values of community and commonality. But one does not necessarily need an anti-aesthetic in order to contest the normativity of beauty, sublimity, and form. Though aesthetics is usually defined as a philosophical discourse on art and the concomitant experiences of beauty and sublimity, in point of fact the term was first used to describe a much broader class of phenomena. Alexander Baumgarten (usually credited with the first use of the term) defined "aesthetic" as "the science of things perceived," a systematic comprehension of the knowledge to be gained through the senses, in opposition to a rationalist tradition that defined truth as pure conceptuality—the clear and distinct idea.[11] Kant's first use of the term appears in the *Critique of Pure Reason*, in a section devoted to the "Transcendental Aesthetic," or the necessary role that sensibility plays in the understanding's production of knowledge. And his *Critique of Judgment* is not a philosophy of artworks, despite its focus on beauty and sublimity.

This wider significance is deployed with especial rigor and sophistication in the work of Jacques Rancière, who restores to aesthetics its initial occupation with sense and sensibility and their connections to particular political dispositions and institutions. For Rancière, sensibility is always already implicated within modes of sociality, of being-in-common, a problematic evident within his sustained interrogation of the conditions of possibility of thought, feeling, and perception as informed by historical modes of sociality—or *le partage du sensible*: "the system of self-evident facts of sense perception that simultaneously discloses the existence of something in common and the delimitation that defines the respective parts and positions within it."[12] As David Panagia has noted, *partage* can be translated as "distribution" (as it is in *Politics of Aesthetics*), an economic process by which goods (commodities, certainly, but also anything deemed desirable and marketable) are distributed to the members of a community; but also as "partition," a more agonistic, even antagonistic, process that endangers the commonality so often seen as necessary for social being.[13] Distribution implies possession and a fundamental lack of equity in the access that members of a social formation have to even those "things"—such as time or space—that are supposedly held in common.

But community for Rancière is, and always has been, contested, antagonistic, "dissensual," insofar as it remains divided between those who have a recognized, institutionalized part in the common and those who don't. Whether his work is historical (his investigations into the lives of nineteenth-century workers) or philosophical (his interrogations of Althusser, Bourdieu, Lyotard), at its center is always a recognition of

(1) an asymmetrical (non)relation between those who speak and those who are spoken for, and a concomitant intellectual division between thought or understanding, versus (in)sensibility and feeling; and (2) the peculiar position of those who are both included (i.e., they contribute to the well-being of the community) and excluded (but they have no explicit, symbolized role in the administration of that community).[14] Following Marx and Engels's analysis in *The German Ideology*, Rancière prioritizes the divisions between manual and intellectual labor, sensibility and intelligibility, that have shaped both premodern and modern forms of sociality and (de)formed a philosophical discourse that may be said to be, still, a series of footnotes to Plato. His work complicates a narrative of political modernism in which aesthetics is a supplemental fantasy or response to the social ruptures of capital, bureaucracy, and instrumental reason. Rancière therefore provides a historically nuanced set of concepts for analyzing a Shakespearean political aesthetic defined less as a discourse about the value of ornament, design, beauty, sublimity, etc., than as a reflection on the intersection of sensibility with sociality—on subjects' feelings, ugly or beautiful, with and about others.

It may seem anachronistic to discuss Shakespeare's own theatrical practice in the context of *aesthetics*; after all, early modern poetry (including drama) owed much to the *rhetoric* that dominated the Tudor grammar school's curriculum.[15] But as I argue via a reading of *Julius Caesar*, long before the Romantics rejected rhetoric in favor of aesthetics, Shakespeare interrogated the deleterious social and political effects that early modern rhetorical practice and theory had for a theatrical experience available to both queen and clown. In contrast to a patrician rhetorical social imaginary in the process of dissolution (both within and without the play), Shakespeare foregrounded the ugly feelings associated with the plebeians—"the unacknowledged republic" (Goldie), or the part that has no part (Rancière)—in order to explore the problem of affective normativity that early modern rhetoric *and* poetics were incapable of resolving.[16]

The Tragedy of Republican Rhetoric

For many scholars *Julius Caesar* is the prototype for Shakespeare's later, greater tragedies, marking a watershed in his development as a writer and revealing for the first time what Cynthia Marshall has called "the deeply characterological drama," centered on Brutus, that still defines his legacy.[17] And Shakespeare's increasingly sophisticated deployment of persuasive discourse is crucial here: for though the play focuses on the *political* functions of rhetoric during a world-shattering historical crisis, rhetoric is also the primary medium through which social relations, especially between Roman patrician men, are conducted. Rhetoric—as both persuasion and tropology—underwrites the complex interplay of recognition and misrecognition that makes Brutus in particular exemplary of tragic character as an aesthetic and moral totality. But Marshall, Garry Wills, and many other critics neglect that key index of Brutus's purported political failure and his eventual tragic end: the role that the plebeians play in the initial legitimation and subsequent delegitimation of his actions. The plebs, I argue, are the fulcrum on which *Julius Caesar*'s narrative trajectory rests; examining the part they play—in Rome, in Shakespeare's play—is crucial to understanding Shakespeare's cogent analysis of an unusually toxic mixture of elite rhetorical sophistication, populism, and the degeneration of agonistic political disagreement into endgame violence. For the plebs' responses to patrician rhetorical display illustrate how one of the most prized of rhetorical qualities—energeia, or what Sir Philip Sidney called forcibleness—can degenerate into a force so destructive that neither rhetorical norms nor poetic interpretive practices can cope with the conflagration.

For much of the sixteenth century, Ciceronian ideals were central not only to Tudor pedagogical programs but also to the monarchical republicanism that dominated the political imaginary.[18] For Cicero, rhetoric, in both its forensic and deliberative forms, was the Roman Republic's lifeblood, a practice (as opposed to an instrument) on which the virtue of justice (the primary end of all political associations) was founded.[19] As he repeatedly insisted long after his tenure as consul was over, Cicero had triumphed over Rome's enemies (Catiline's conspiracy) with speech alone (and a few well-timed, possibly extralegal executions). In *Brutus* (a dialogue with Marcus Junius Brutus, the Brutus of *Julius Caesar*), Cicero suggests that his interlocutor's distant ancestor, Lucius Junius Brutus (the Brutus of *The Rape of Lucrece*), could have founded the remarkable institution of the Roman Republic and its law courts only with eloquence as opposed to violence; and he concludes with an elegy for a lost republic that has deprived his (and our) Brutus of the opportunity to display his persuasive powers in Rome's public institutions.[20] But Cicero is a remarkably minor figure in *Julius Caesar*. For Andrew Hadfield, his marginalization suggests that the conspirators' actions are unrepresentative of republican ideals, especially public discussion of common issues.[21] Shakespeare and his literate audience members, however, would surely have known of the historical Cicero's support for Caesar's assassination, expressed, for example, in book 3 of *De Officiis*, one of the most popular of classical texts in early modern England.[22] In a play full of miscommunication, Cicero's secondhand and incomprehensible Greek (the result of the kind of philhellene education to which Cicero and his party, the optimates, or *viri boni*, were inclined) further marginalizes the rhetorical master.[23]

Instead, Antony—a soldier and a libertine—is the play's most accomplished orator. Ros King has insightfully argued that his speeches "dramatize the dangers and failure of oratory"—a judgment with which I concur.[24] But despite their historical enmity, Antony's oratory is quite Ciceronian. In *De Oratore*, his most substantial exploration of rhetoric's technical, ethical, and political aspects, Cicero repeatedly images the relationship between orator and auditor as one of *poiesis*, or making, in which the audience is not a participant but the raw material: "because it is in calming or kindling the feelings of the audience that the full power and science of oratory are to be brought into play."[25] Though the people—or "the vulgar" (*vulgus*)—may lack the critical judgment to discern the true orator from the false, M. Antonius, one of the dialogue's two primary speakers (and Mark Antony's grandfather), nevertheless argues that appealing to emotion is far more effective than appealing to reason, since "men decide far more problems by hate, or love, or lust, or rage, or sorrow, or joy, or hope, or fear, or illusion, or some other inward emotion, than by reality, or authority, or any legal standard, or judicial precedent, or statute."[26] Cicero was, of course, aware of Plato's critique of rhetorical manipulation, but *De Oratore* attempts to refute this view by insisting on the orator's probity, his exceedingly wide knowledge of all sorts of subject matter, and the extensive and rigorous discipline (of his body, his voice, his memory) that he must undergo to excel as a public speaker.[27] Cicero depicts a republic that, though owing something to Polybius's ideal of a mixed government, places ultimate authority in the hands of the *viri boni*, the good men whose merit has made them worthy of piloting the ship of state.[28] For Cicero rhetoric is nothing less than philosophy.

In keeping with Ciceronian prescription (and in contrast to later, post-Kantian aesthetics), Tudor rhetoric continued to emphasize the importance of passion to persuasion, via the quality of energeia, the power of words to move the reader or auditor. Energeia was central to an educational program devoted to what Sidney called "the end of well-doing and not of well-knowing only."[29] Readers—and later auditors or spectators—have to be moved to pursue virtue and eschew vice, as in Sidney's example of Lucretia, whose dead body inspired Lucius Junius Brutus to cast out the Tarquins and establish the Roman Republic.[30] But in contrast to George Puttenham (who translated energeia as "efficacy" or "a strong and virtuous operation"), Sidney recognized that language could arouse ugly as well as beautiful feelings, could move toward violence, sweet or bitter.[31] Philip Stubbes had complained in *The Anatomie of Abuses* that "the arguments of tragedies, is anger, wrath, immunitie, crueltie, iniurie, incest, murther & such like."[32] Similarly, Sidney noted that the passions, virtues, and vices that poetry depicts and arouses are numerous, ranging from homesickness (Ulysses) to anger (Ajax) to pride (Agamemnon) to cruelty (Atreus). Ideally, however, "high and excellent Tragedy" should "openeth the greatest wounds, and showeth forth the ulcers that covered with tissue; that maketh kings fear to be tyrants, and tyrants manifest their tyrannical humours."[33] For example, during a performance of Euripides's *The Trojan Women*, Sidney writes, Alexander, tyrant of Pherae, "was not ashamed to make matters for tragedy yet could not resist the sweet violence of a tragedy."[34] But Alexander—or his "hardened heart"—did resist the translation of tears into mercy, since he left the theater so that the other spectators should not see him weeping while he was busy slaughtering so many citizens.[35]

Despite Alexander's failure to realize the moral lesson to which he was moved, this episode does reveal the affective and moral complex (or Rancière's distribution of the sensible) that bolstered Sidney's ideal of a Protestant monarchical republic, as encapsulated within the sweet violence of a tragic form that represents virtue and vice in decorous and class-appropriate ways. Confronted with the diversity of represented passions and possible imitative responses, Sidney relies on form—style, genre, and their respective contents—to prompt the correct response. For example, comedy unites a particular generic form with a scurrilous style, therefore prompting one to laugh at (and presumably reject) the represented vice. Hence his excoriation of tragicomedy's hybridity, its "mingling of kings and clowns"—an indecorous admixture on disturbing display in the *New Arcadia* when a group of discontented "clowns and other rebels," stirred into revolt by a sleazy former actor (of tragedies, no less), storm into their king's pastoral retreat only to be massacred by the book's two princely protagonists.[36] Anticipating a trope evident in *Julius Caesar*'s 1.1, Sidney identifies the "clowns" not by name but by occupation and describes with glee the injuries that often reflect and ridicule their labor. Sidney's rhetorical choices exemplify his poetic strictures, insofar as, through a kind of alienation, they aim to provoke cruel laughter, as opposed to pity.[37] For Sidney, external criteria—such as generic distinctions that respect the "natural" social distinctions of patrician and plebeian—ultimately (should) limit the destructive social and political impact that too much energeia can have. And if that fails, a few heads—or hands—can roll.

In contrast, Thomas Heywood's 1612 *An Apology for Actors* attempts to harness energeia's potentially antisocial impact for a militaristic nationalism. For Heywood, the theater transcends both painting and poetry as the most vivid and forceful medium for the presentation of exemplary figures and the virtues they embody. *Enargeia* (a vivid presentation) abets energeia (Sidney's "forcibleness), "as if the Personater were the man Personated, so bewitching a thing is liuely and well spirited action, that it hath power to new mold the harts of the spectators and fashion them to the shape of any noble and notable attempt."[38] In contrast to Sidney (and in keeping with a very different medium), Heywood does not attempt to limit the audience for such rhetorical power through generic strictures; tragedy has both patrician and plebeian spectators. But he never defines what might constitute a "noble and notable attempt," with the result that he is incapable of making moral distinctions even among his bloody heroes like "*Hector* all besmered in blood, trampling vpon the bulkes of Kinges."[39] And because imitation plays such an important role in the transmission of heroic values from one generation to the next, energeia is repeatedly translated into physical violence. For it was through personating former heroes that Hercules, Theseus, Alexander, and Julius Caesar became future heroes. When Julius Caesar was cast as Hercules Furens, he was so overcome by the passion he was personating that he killed one of his fellow actors (his servant) onstage.[40] Heywood's image of a will so forceful that it overruled the distinction between the imitator and the imitated reminds us of how fundamentally ambiguous Caesar's reputation actually was—which is in keeping with the other emperors, including Caligula, Nero, Vitellus, Domitian, and Commodus, who took to the stage. Energeia without limit becomes a recipe for tyranny.[41]

Heywood's lack of discrimination—his inability to provide normative criteria for the passions that theater arouses—highlights the importance of a critical discourse on what Sianne Ngai has called ugly feelings, specifically centered on the physical and metaphorical violence that prevailed in both content and form on the early modern stage. That such feelings were central to Shakespeare's theater is obvious; after all, the plot of *Hamlet* rests upon the Dane's belief that a secret murderer will respond so powerfully to represented violence that his guilt will out. Though Ngai's "ugly feelings" are specific to the more purportedly democratic aesthetics of late modernity, her conception is, I think, still quite pertinent to Shakespeare's plays. As opposed to grand classical passions (Ngai's distinction), modern subjects experience ugly feelings as lesser (envy, as opposed to jealousy, or resentment instead of anger, for example), and therefore shameful. What makes a feeling ugly is not simply a normative taxonomy of positive and negative, greater and lesser, emotions but an internal moral judgment about the unseemliness of such a feeling. And what generates that judgment is the subject's social marginalization, that he or she somehow lacks the right to such feelings. Ugly feelings are therefore inherently political, insofar as they constitute "interpretations of predicaments," responses not only to real or perceived injustice but also to the very problem of articulating a wrong in an inhospitable discourse. And absent that possibility, what ugly feelings reveal is an "obstructed agency . . . *whether the agency obstructed in individual or collective*."[42]

Many of Shakespeare's plays are full of "ugly feelings" that have, over the centuries, driven readers, spectators, actors, and critics to regard their socially marginalized subjects as somehow lesser: servants (Margaret in *Much Ado About Nothing*), commoners (Iago and his "motiveless malignity"), bastards (Don John in *Much Ado*, Edmund in *King Lear*), the plebeians of *Julius Caesar*. With few exceptions, the view that the plebs are little more than a mob manipulated by the more central (and appealing) patrician characters predominates in Shakespeare criticism.[43] Even those critics who focus more exclusively on the plebs usually conclude that their transformation into a mob explicitly and intentionally condemns populism or democracy.[44] But such analyses isolate the plebeians from the total political situation. The plebs are a contradictory if not incoherent group—but no more so than a tragic character who ends up stabbing his father figure in the groin (Brutus) or a patrician general who imagines that the destruction of all Italy is a worthy response to his beloved friend's murder (Antony). Why feelings should so regularly be held up as exemplary of ugliness is not completely explicable—except, perhaps, in the way that their obstructed agency cannot be registered from within the characterological drama that still defines Shakespeare's legacy.

The Shoemaker's Holiday

Socrates famously banned the tragedians from his ideal republic, in part because their subject matter (the sometimes contemptible actions of heroes like the angry, weepy Achilles) endangered a moral character shaped through imitation; in part because playing undermined the fixity of occupation and place that defined the social order.[45] In the republic, no one can undertake more than one job. Foremost among Socrates's examples of this desirable specialization is the shoemaker, who paradoxically manufactures the means by which others—with income and leisure—frequent the public streets on the political business from which he is barred.[46]

Coincidentally, *Julius Caesar*'s opening scene also uses a shoemaker to assert a highly contested plebeian right to frequent Rome's public spaces. Shakespeare's play is profoundly preoccupied with space, how it is organized, experienced, and shared, which was also evident in Shakespeare's earlier *The Rape of Lucrece*, when Tarquin's "enforced" penetration into Lucrece's private chamber anticipates the violation of her body.[47] Tyranny feeds on the "deep policy" (1815) that had led Brutus (Lucius Junius) to act the fool; and its end—and the foundation of the republic—is indexed by the public display of Lucrece's body and the "publish[ing of] Tarquin's foul offence" (1852). But this sense of an established shared space—a public thing—is already endangered in *Julius Caesar*; that the republican-minded conspirators whisper together (inaudible even to the audience) and meet secretly at night, in private and secluded spaces, ironically anticipates their eventual failure. In fact, the plebeians, led by a shoemaker, are most invested in the public nature of shared space and time—in contrast to those patrician elements that would deny them their holiday.

Who the plebeians are is one of the central conflicts of 1.1. The First Folio's stage directions label them (in 1.1) as "commoners," which, at least for Flavius and Murellus, the people's tribunes, identifies them as "mechanical," "idle creatures" whose being is limited to manufacture:

> Hence! Home, you idle creatures, get you home!
> Is this a holiday? What, know you not
> (Being mechanical) you ought not walk
> Upon a labouring day, without the sign
> Of your profession? (1.1.1–5)

But the shoemaker, who emerges as the spokesperson for his fellow mechanicals, contests this reduction: "I am but as *you would say* a cobbler . . . Truly, sir, all that I live by, is with the awl" (1.1.10–11, 22; emphasis added). His pun on "awl/all" refuses the tribunes' reduction of his being to the tools of his profession and highlights the importance of his work: in urban environments shoes provide a crucial material support for the republic, making it possible for citizens, whether plebeian or patrician, to move about the streets on public business. And on that basis he claims the same authority over the tribunes that the tribunes attempt to exercise over him: "A trade, sir, that I hope I may use with a safe conscience, which is indeed, sir, a mender of bad soles . . . Yet if you be out, sir, I can mend you" (1.1.13–14, 16–17). Shoemaking provides not grounds for subordination but for equality, as manifested in the witticisms aimed at the magistrates who attempt to police his behavior.

In Rancière's terms, the shoemaker exemplifies the process of subjectivization fundamental to a politics defined as a struggle over who can speak, who can be seen; the people refuse the partitioning of space and time, and the accompanying distribution of goods, by insisting on the equality of all speaking beings. For Rancière equality, the basic presupposition that appears whenever one speaks with another, is the only universal that politics knows. One must speak *with* (as opposed to *to*)—but one must also speak *for*, as is evident in Rancière's own historical examples, including his account of the events leading up the establishment of the tribunate.[48] As a process of subjectivization (as opposed to subjection or interpellation), speech emancipates the plebs from a natural order of all-consuming work defined as subordination.[49] Politics happens when the plebs—the part (of the people) that has no part (in the republic), the part without representation—insist that they too share in the community.[50] Politics is contingent and often ephemeral, appearing when and where one would least expect, and often "failing" to modify its immediate context, the sedimented administrative practices and institutions, the management of social groups and interests, called the police. "Police" owes much to policy—but it also carries with it Foucauldian connotations of discipline and surveillance. And though Rancière often treated the two as an opposition, increasingly he has detailed a relationship of mutual implication that enables the occasionally desirable conversion of politics into policy, of speech into constitution.

Rancière has been criticized for ignoring the historical specificity of the institutions and cultures that shape the political lives of both individuals and collectives.[51] But his emphasis on the dissensual impact of speech—the fact that it can bring together as well as separate individuals who share the same physical space but experience it very differently—is, I think, an exceedingly useful insight, especially in light of Shakespeare's revisions to his source material. For, in contrast to Plutarch's far more equivocal account, Shakespeare explicitly rendered the relationship between tribune and plebeian in act 1 as purely oppositional: as optimates, partisans of the dead Pompey's elite republican faction, Flavius and Murellus side with a republicanism that is both antipopulist and antiplebeian.[52] Shakespeare thus highlights a multitude of past and present antagonisms—Pompey versus Caesar, Pompey's adherents versus Caesar's adherents, tribunes versus plebeians, patricians versus plebeians—that contest the most basic conditions of republican possibility: public space and time.

Wit is a kind of merry warfare, reflecting and mediating the inevitable disagreements occasioned by living together. In other words, it embodies Rancière's conception of an aesthetic community as a form of "being apart together"—an experience of social being that evades the police-oriented oppression of more organic communitarianisms.[53] But in *Julius Caesar* the agonism of dissensual experiences in a shared space soon gives way to outright antagonism and violence, beyond a political field structured by the politics-policy opposition. Shakespeare's staging of one of the most important scenes in Julius Caesar's accession to near-monarchical power—Mark Antony's proffering of a crown in the marketplace—enacts an emerging division between the "secret" republicanism (an oxymoron, if ever there was one) of resentful patricians and a plebeian crowd whose own intentions remain disturbingly opaque. In Plutarch's "Life of Caesar," the plebeians remain highly invested in republican institutions, cheering only when Caesar refuses the crown.[54] But Brutus and Cassius conclude that the offstage plebeian noise approves Caesar's desire to be king. Caska's later account contradicts their assumptions but still betrays a peculiar ambivalence toward the plebeians, who are both part and no part of Rome's republican institutions:

> And then he [Mark Antony] offered it a third time; he [Julius Caesar] put it the third time by; and still as he refused it the rabblement hooted, and clapped their chopped hands, and threw up their sweaty nightcaps, and uttered such a deal of stinking breath because Caesar refused the crown that it had almost choked Caesar; for he swooned and fell down at it. And for mine own part, I durst not laugh, for fear of opening my lips and receiving the bad air. (1.2.241–49)[55]

Caska's depiction of the plebeian body and its emissions betrays his resentment at being forced to share a public space with those who are responsible for its "bad air"—what Oliver Arnold has called "the politics of halitosis."[56] "And for mine own part": though the most obvious meaning of the phrase would be the standard, "As far as I was concerned," it is also probable that Caska puns not only on "part" as in portion—his portion of the public air—but also on part as in role: "If the tag-rag people did not clap him and hiss him according as he pleased and displeased them, as they use to do the players in the theatre, I am no true man" (1.2.257–60). Imagining the bond between Caesar and the plebeians as a theatrical one suggests less the willful Caesar of Lucan's *Pharsalia* than the aging actor past his prime, dependent upon the lowliest groundling for his continued support. And despite the apparently clear preference that these bad-breathed plebeians show for Rome's republican institutions, Caska can see only a populist spectatorship, a kind of poisonous codependency in which sensibility is divorced from reason.

Patrician ambivalence toward the plebeians—contempt cast in sensuous terms, combined with the recognition that they nevertheless remain a crucial component of the republic—betrays a fault line running throughout Shakespeare's play. As a tragedy, *Julius Caesar* remains bound to a narrative structure dominated by elite protagonists; it therefore "translates," if you will, a social and political crisis into the subjective intentions and actions of patrician individuals, whose own psychological struggles—the problem, we might say, of Brutus's misrecognition—become the primary narrative focus (e.g., Cynthia Marshall's "deeply characterological drama"). But when one compares *Julius Caesar* with Plutarch's *Lives*, one can see how Shakespeare's various revisions and conflations allot a more substantial role to the plebs, in act 3 as well as in act 1—and provide a position from which patrician actions become subject to both diegetic and extradiegetic judgment. Brutus's and Antony's speeches in 3.2 therefore assume a singular importance that they lacked historically, making the plebs the sole arbiters of the conspirators' actions.[57] Furthermore, Shakespeare highlights the tension, indeed the conflict, between Brutus, ostensibly the man of reason, and the plebs, ostensibly the men and women of passion—a broken relationship not in evidence in Plutarch's "Life of Brutus."[58] Plutarch's Brutus understood well the value of appealing to the people's sensibility. Shakespeare's Brutus does not—an example of the tragic misrecognition that sets him on the long road to Philippi.

For Brutus operates within the long shadow cast by his ancestor, Lucius Junius Brutus. Cassius, for one, recognizes how susceptible Brutus remains to this anxiety of influence: "There was a Brutus once that would have brooked / Th'eternal devil to keep his state in Rome / As easily as a king" (1.2.158–60). But the earlier Brutus's total dedication to the republic constituted a more ambiguous historical exemplar than Cassius acknowledges. After the republic's foundation, a group of patrician youths, including Brutus's own sons, attempted to restore the monarchy; Brutus condemned all the conspirators to death and watched his sons die in the marketplace. Despite the episode's patriotic exemplarity (for Livy), Plutarch criticizes this action as too impossibly hard-hearted.[59] And the assumption that reason should dominate the unruly and inferior passions was hardly culturally dominant in the early modern period; the Renaissance discovered anti-Stoicism as well as Stoicism.[60]

In this context, Brutus's ethical status becomes more problematic, insofar as his constancy is admirable *and* appalling, effective *and* self-defeating.[61] Nowhere is this more evident than in the sacrifices he makes in order to preserve his constancy and fulfill the imaginary mandate of his illustrious ancestor. Though Brutus has a gift for friendship evident in almost all his interactions, from Cassius to Caesar to Portia to Lucius, he propounds a sacrificial logic that demands not only the ritual slaughter of his friend Julius Caesar but also the gradual alienation of his own, most intimate feelings:

> Let's be sacrificers but not butchers, Caius,
> We all stand up against the spirit of Caesar,
> And in the spirit of men there is no blood.
> O that we then could come by Caesar's spirit
> And not dismember Caesar! But, alas,
> Caesar must bleed for it. And, gentle friends,
> Let's kill him boldly, but not wrathfully:
> Let's carve him as a dish fit for the gods,
> Not hew him as a carcass fit for hounds.
> And let our hearts, as subtle masters do,
> Stir up their servants to an act of rage
> And after seem to chide 'em. (2.1.165–76)[62]

Brutus intends his sacrifice to restore a lost freedom. But in point of fact, his sacrificial rhetoric is anything but emancipatory, dependent as it is on what Rancière calls the representational regime, a neo-Aristotelian distribution of the sensible that aligns intelligibility (concepts or meanings) with the sensible images (including sound images) that they inform. For Brutus insists on interpretive norms that discipline affective response and restrict reception to decipherment. Like Sidney's imaginary Lucretia, he attempts to offer what "is fittest for the eye to see"—not a sensible image but an idea, the self-evident truth of which will be secured by the conspirators' noble intentions.[63] Brutus thus revises the projected action—the brutal, bloody murder of an older man—into a morally innocuous ideal: the eradication of a tyrannical spirit that had opposed the generally accepted republican values of "Peace, Freedom, and Liberty" (3.1.110). Despite its apparent cruelty, sacrifice is highly idealistic.

For Brutus, this subjective ordering of one's faculties duplicates the late republic's social hierarchy, a Rome in which everyone has a part ("Romans, countrymen, and lovers"), and therefore makes his own sacrificial logic meaningful—an exercise in morality as opposed to perversion. And given his centrality to the play's action, as well as his tragic stature, some critics have argued that this logic is not Brutus's but the play's.[64] But *Julius Caesar* interrogates and rejects that model. Brutus imagines that he sacrifices a variety of parts (his friend, his father, his family, and his feelings) on behalf of a whole—but it is clear from the very beginning that, in the absence of shared public spaces and discourses, there is no whole. And as a consequence, Mark Antony will soon demystify Brutus's idealization of a peaceful community that paradoxically requires the bloody murder of an old and feeble man.[65]

The Passionate Plebeian

Brutus's and Antony's speeches are commonly called funeral orations, but they are in fact more forensic than epideictic, insofar as each speech lays out an argument for Caesar's guilt or innocence. And Naomi Conn Liebler, following Nicholas Visser, suggests that the plebs reasonably choose the "right" side—Antony's side.[66] But though both Liebler and Visser provide an important corrective to decades (perhaps centuries) of criticism denigrating the plebs, the conclusion that the plebs are rational when they choose Antony over Brutus is, nevertheless, problematic—not because the plebs are irrational beings of pure sensibility but because neither speech makes (or can make) its case. As Shakespeare undoubtedly knew, the historical record was remarkably unclear about Caesar's motives—which left Plutarch himself undecided about his alleged tyranny.

Brutus and Antony depend on rhetorical strategies both persuasive and tropological to make a case unsupported by the evidence. But each speech also displays a different self-reflexive understanding of how rhetorical representation works (or should work)—especially in the relations between the sensible materiality of speech and the intelligibility of its import. Both Brutus and Antony rely on implication and absence, but their respective "nothings" take quite different forms. In keeping with a sacrificial logic, Brutus's speech foregrounds a metaphorical axis that asks its auditors to disregard the tenor of the sensible world in favor of the vehicle, the intelligible reality of his (and Caesar's) intentions, as based on his own honor, an essence that is not seen. Hence his (or Shakespeare's) surprising choice of prose: though it may reflect a correlation of linguistic form with social status, as well as Plutarch's description of Brutus's preference for a Spartan (or laconic) style, it is also an effort to render prosaic what is, after all, a shocking, violent event.[67] George Puttenham had argued that verse is more appealing because it resembles music; prose, less so because we hear it all the time.[68] Prose makes Brutus's reasons self-evident.

In contrast, Antony embraces a metonymical indirection that makes a fetish of the sensible, redirecting the plebs' attention away from what they cannot see to what they can: Caesar's body, a constant reminder of the cost of Brutus's devotion to Rome. Speaking Puttenham's more sensuously pleasing verse and addressing the plebs as "Friends, Romans, countrymen" (3.2.74), he builds a rapport based on an apparent social equality, underwritten by what Joy Connolly has called "the consensual fantasy of membership in an ideal civic body."[69] Unlike Brutus, Antony focuses less on the abstraction of "Rome" and more on the singularity of one human being, Caesar, and his actions, as well as his own intense love and grief for his dead friend: "My heart is in the coffin there with Caesar, / And I must pause till it come back to me" (3.2.107–8). He thus invites the plebs to identify with him, to feel that most basic of emotions—pity—even before he invokes their gratitude for Caesar's bequests of cash and a public park.[70] And as Antony displays Caesar's bloody robe, he tells a story that emphasizes not Roman liberty but the violence that a group of younger men unleashed on an elder, linking each rent to the sword that made it and concluding with "the most unkindest cut of all" (3.2.181). His loving description of Caesar's mantle, a kind of ekphrasis, makes "visible" for the plebs a bloody and violent event that neither he nor they have witnessed, and calls forth their tears—the mimetic twin of the blood with which Brutus had bathed his hands.[71] His theater makes Caesar's fall their (and our?) fall, a populist logic that reinforces the substantial horizontal identifications of his opening line, all united in their oppression by "bloody treason," a prosopopeia that transforms the conspirators' supposed bid for freedom into a betrayal of the highest order.

Under Antony's influence, the plebs reject Brutus's sacrificial logic and become invested in—fixated upon—the bloody corpse before them: "O piteous spectacle"; "O most bloody sight!" (3.2.198). In an earlier apostrophe, Antony had imaged Caesar's wounds as dumb mouths in need of his tongue to speak the curse that will take later, spectral form as Caesar's ghost:

> O pardon me, thou bleeding piece of earth,
> That I am meek and gentle with these butchers . . .
> Over thy wounds now I do prophesy
> (Which like dumb mouths do ope their ruby lips
> To beg the voice and utterance of my tongue)
> A curse shall light upon the limbs of men . . . (3.1.254–55, 259–62)

Now, before the plebs, the wounds speak (silently) through showing: "I tell you that which you yourselves do know, / Show you sweet Caesar's wounds, poor poor dumb mouths, / And bid them speak for me" (3.2.215–17). Anticipating Heywood, Antony fosters a theatrical union of sight and sound in order to move the plebs while appearing not to move them. But corpses do not speak for themselves, and what they show is not self-evident—which is one of the reasons why they require such ekphrastic symbolizations as the funeral oration and the monument.[72] As a *poetic* figure, ekphrasis makes vivid what is actually absent; in speaking to the mind's eye, it ultimately subordinates the concrete, visual image of this too-much-loved earth to speech—which is why Sidney claimed priority for the right poet's creation of a golden world. Antony's goal, of course, is less the creation of a golden world than hell on earth, the "bleeding piece of earth" (3.1.254) of Caesar's remains generalized to all of Italy ("That this foul deed shall smell above the earth / With carrion men, groaning for burial" [3.1.274–75]). His oration confronts not the mind's eye but the actual eye with the blunt reality of death, disguises the corpse's lack of significance by attributing to it all too much significance—a self-evident meaning that need only be shown, not told.

Antony thus persuades the plebs that he is not persuasive. And then the peculiar counterfactual:

> But were I Brutus,
> And Brutus Antony, there were an Antony
> Would ruffle up your spirits and put a tongue
> In every wound of Caesar that should move
> The stones of Rome to mutiny. (3.2.219–23)

Antony concludes with the paradoxical suggestion that were he Brutus, and Brutus he, he (Antony or Brutus?) would be able to persuade the plebs to mutiny against himself (whether he were Brutus or Antony). And in the next line, the first plebeian exclaims, "We'll burn the house of Brutus" (3.2.224). In casting Caesar's murder as a form of treason, Antony unleashes the very patriotism to which Brutus had appealed, underwritten by an identification of the plebs with the stones of Rome (3.2.223) that he (Antony) had earlier denied (3.2.143). And the appeal to prosopopeia—"Mischief, thou art afoot: / Take thou what course thou wilt" (3.2.252–53)—indexes their real reduction to the instruments of Antony's will, as opposed to their imaginary belief that they remain free agents. In other words, the plebs depart from the subjectivation that public speech embodies and succumb to an Althusserian interpellation characterized by the misrecognition of their own historical role.

Once the plebs become "Rome" in its entirety, their earlier demand for equality (based on the demos) is transformed into an exclusionary violence (based on the ethnos), their pity for Caesar so all-consuming that it leaves no room for pity for others, such as Cinna the poet. And because the plebs are the part with no part, because their tribunes have been put to silence, they are left with no legitimate political outlet for their discontent. Pity gives way to the inhuman vengeance demanded by a talking corpse, as represented in Shakespeare's play by a singular event that significantly comments on what rhetoric means for the arts.[73] As Norman Holland has argued, the scene with Cinna and the plebs replays—and therefore responds to—the conspirators' murder of Caesar in the Capitol.[74] Like Caesar, Cinna is isolated in the face of the crowd, with neither friends nor fans—only critics who aim to "pluck but his name out of his heart and turn him going" (3.3.33–34). Similar to the persistent, ironic distinction between Caesar's increasingly frail body and his name, the Fourth Plebeian condemns Cinna simply for being named Cinna—a name, indelibly inscribed on his heart, that both is and is not essential to his being. Releasing him from the tyranny of his name conflates freedom with death and thus anticipates Brutus's inability to free Rome from a tyranny that is not, in fact, limited to one man. If the plebeians murder "the wrong man," perhaps the patricians did too: Caesar may be dead, but his name and his ambitions live on in a kind of political hauntology, in which the signifier floats free in search of a body. And as the wrong man, Cinna can be guilty of nothing political—only poetical.

That vengeance is exercised upon the body of an undeserving poet is, I think, a decisive comment on why rhetoric can provide a model neither for poetry nor theater. When Cinna insists that he is not a conspirator but a poet, Fourth Plebeian responds with, "Tear him for his bad verses, tear him for his bad verses" (3.3.30–31). Reducing the poet to his labor, his poetry to verses, his body to paper, reduces the Sidneian golden world to rhyme and rhythm, intelligibility to sensibility—exactly what Antony had wanted. Moved by rhetorical energeia and *enargeia*, the plebs refuse—or are refused—the kind of engagement with the "dream, past the wit of man to say what dream it was," the "something of great constancy" that had dignified the experience of Bottom and his fellow mechanicals in *A Midsummer Night's Dream*.[75] As Sidney wrote in the *Defence*, poetry should move men not simply to well knowing but to well doing—to reasonable actions, in accord with recognized religious and moral values, that are definitive of a certain kind of humanist agency. In *Julius Caesar* rhetoric moves men to mischief, undertaken in response to an absence of reasons and an excess of feelings—and poetry is their victim.

And this brings us to the heart of the plebeian matter. Cinna's murder is indeed horrible, but it is no more horrible than Caesar's assassination, Mark Antony's "dogs of war" speech, or the murderous free-for-all encapsulated in the chilling proscription scene, where forceful rhetoric is replaced by the simple expedient of damning someone with a spot—a grotesque parody of Antony's interpellation of the plebs in 3.2, as well as of their subsequent murder of a man whose only guilt is his name. Neither the ephemeral subjectivation of democratic politics evident in 1.1 nor a more traditional, republican, patrician agency (action undertaken in service to communally recognized values) survive the carnage occasioned by the reduction of spirit and character to bloody marks. So why are the plebs so often singled out for critical judgment? One cannot, of course, know with any certainty; and it would be simplistic to blame conscious or unconscious class prejudice. But that long-standing critical problem—who is *Julius Caesar*'s tragic protagonist?—may indicate how the reading practices encouraged by generic distinctions betray a representational regime that affords a degree of cognitive and affective privilege to tragic protagonists whose bitter fates provoke understanding and sympathy. For *Julius Caesar*'s near-universal breakdown of agency (as an intelligible conceptual totality), both individual (patrician) and collective (plebeian), challenges more traditional understandings of tragedy. Raymond Williams has written, "The idea of tragedy, in its ordinary form, excludes especially that tragic experience which is social."[76] But a tragic experience that is social is just what is on display, precisely because Shakespeare so cogently depicts the breakdown of communal order, as well as the mimetic structures, the distribution of the sensible, that had informed and maintained that order. And with it goes the conception of human action fundamental to quasi-republican politics.

The Emancipated Spectator

For Rancière politics happens in the most unusual of places and unexpected of times. But it clearly does not happen in act 3's marketplace. For both Brutus and Antony are on the side of the police, their task (the securing of the plebeians' assent) a process of interpellation that pays only rhetorical lip service to an "agency" whose forms are limited. The plebs end up infected, not emancipated, reduced to vengeful "dogs of war." But their interpellation purchases the spectator's emancipation, which is necessary for Shakespeare's tragedy to do its work: the deconstruction of the various categories of thought, feeling, and action that underlay the Ciceronian republicanism of the early Elizabethan period. Liebler has argued that Shakespeare's spectators "are always present in the plays' representations, and are always implicated in the actions and behaviors performed onstage."[77] The events of 3.2 fundamentally change this dynamic: though it is, of course, impossible to predict audience response, Shakespeare's staging of an extrajudicial lynching for no (good) reason bespeaks an effort to disrupt that identification and alienate his spectators from the plebeians.[78] Whereas Antony's spectators are overwhelmed by his appeal to the speaking picture, Shakespeare's spectators are treated to a lesson about the divergence between image and sound, sensibility and intelligibility, in Antony's competing claims about the relationship between sweet Caesar's wounds and his own tongue.[79] Our judgment is freed from the discipline of mimetic processes that abet either the corporate sacrifice or all-encompassing expansion of sensibility that "Rome" demands.

Julius Caesar thus anticipates one of Rancière's most important contributions to aesthetics: his focus not on the purported autonomy of the object but of the subject—what he calls in one work the emancipated spectator: "There is aesthetics when the place of the receiver is empty, when the aim of poiesis is accomplished completely in what it produces."[80] In other words, the aesthetic artifact is neither created for nor expected to find a specific receptive context or an identifiable spectator—which obviously disrupts any regime that would align production with reception, the intelligible idea with the sensible object, an affective response with a preferred interpretation.[81] In this context, the relationship between sensibility and intelligibility becomes far less normative and predictable. The spectator's anonymity procures her emancipation, insofar as she cannot necessarily be disciplined to respond in particular ways. No longer can one predict or assume how a work will be received or used, or what ethics or politics it might support. In contrast to certain highly normative communitarianisms (including the view of Elizabethan public theaters as a popular and carnivalesque experience), for Rancière aesthetic community is a form of "being apart together," "a community structured by disconnection"—in other words, marked by a temporal disjointedness between the reality of social bonds in the present and the promise of "a people to come."[82] The equality of speaking *with* underwrites an often ephemeral universality in which the subject of the statement (as opposed to the subject of the enunciation) speaks *for*. But speaks for what? Not for some idealized but nevertheless closed community such as Rome, but for a provisional mode of sociality whose proleptic identifications license the unpredictably witty sympathies that would allow a cobbler to meddle with an all.

Aesthetic emancipation does not necessarily entail political emancipation—and some scholars have criticized Rancière's alleged failure to clarify the relationship between the two.[83] But this is less a theoretical weakness than a principled refusal to reinstate philosophically—and at the level of textual interpretation—that division between intellectual and manual labor, between intelligibility and feeling, that so often turns theory into yet another normativity. That his work provides no guidance on what is to be done might be seen as a casualty of this hesitation. But that hesitation is why his work is so useful in reading a play that has generated a remarkably divergent series of readings that have sought over the decades to translate Shakespeare's represented content, and spectators' purported reactions, into some programmatic message about monarchy or republicanism. In dividing feeling from morality, in conjoining horror with the politically desirable, Shakespeare actually refuses to dictate anything programmatic. Hence the play's sometimes horrifying depictions of judgments made in the name of, but also in the willful ignorance of, an intelligible reason that is clearly losing its purchase on a disintegrating community. As Cicero says to Caska, "Indeed it is a strange-disposed time. / But men may construe things after their fashion / Clean from the purpose of the things themselves" (1.3.33–35)—a description of a general interpretive disorder affecting both the weather and the climate. But *Julius Caesar*'s emergent model of aesthetic judgment is even more distinctive, insofar as that "purpose of the things themselves" is increasingly held in abeyance. The play is indeed a (public) thing, but as a thing, as an entity distinct from both author and spectator/reader, it cannot capture anyone's conscience.

Notes

1. Plutarch, *The Lives of the Noble Grecians and Romans Compared*, trans. Sir Thomas North (London: Thomas Vautroullier, 1579), 1071.
2. William Shakespeare, *Julius Caesar*, ed. David Daniell (London: Bloomsbury, 1998), 4.3.129–30; hereafter cited parenthetically.
3. Garry Wills, *Rome and Rhetoric: Shakespeare's "Julius Caesar"* (New Haven, Conn.: Yale University Press, 2011), 37–111.
4. Steve Sohmer, *Shakespeare's Mystery Play: The Opening of the Globe Theatre, 1599* (Manchester, U.K.: Manchester University Press, 1999).
5. Hannah Arendt, *Lectures on Kant's Political Philosophy*, ed. Ronald Beiner (Chicago: University of Chicago Press, 1992), 9, 39–46.
6. Terry Pinkard, *German Philosophy 1760–1860: The Legacy of Idealism* (Cambridge: Cambridge University Press, 2002), 82–85.
7. Paul Guyer, *Kant and the Claims of Taste* (Cambridge, Mass.: Harvard University Press, 1979), 77–78; J. Colin McQuillan, *Early Modern Aesthetics* (London: Rowman and Littlefield, 2016), 114.
8. Immanuel Kant, *Critique of the Power of Judgment*, ed. Paul Guyer, trans. Paul Guyer and Eric Matthews (Cambridge: Cambridge University Press, 2000), 173–74.
9. J. M. Bernstein, *The Fate of Art: Aesthetic Alienation from Kant to Derrida and Adorno* (University Park: Pennsylvania State University Press, 1992),

60–61, 65; Hannah Arendt, *The Human Condition* (Garden City, N.Y.: Doubleday, 1959), 23–63; Hannah Arendt, *On Revolution* (London: Penguin Books, 2006), 99–105; Jean-François Lyotard, *Lessons on the Analytic of the Sublime*, trans. Elizabeth Rottenberg (Stanford, Calif.: Stanford University Press, 2004), 149, 239.

10. Kant, *Critique*, 174.

11. Paul Guyer, *A History of Modern Aesthetics*, 3 vols. (Cambridge: Cambridge University Press, 2014), 1:4–7, 318–40.

12. Jacques Rancière, *The Politics of Aesthetics: The Distribution of the Sensible*, ed. and trans. Gabriel Rockhill (London: Bloomsbury, 2004), chap. 2, loc. 262 of 2656, Kindle.

13. Davide Panagia, "'*Partage du sensible*': The Distribution of the Sensible," in *Jacques Rancière: Key Concepts*, ed. Jean-Philippe Deranty (London: Routledge, 2010), 95.

14. These preoccupations were evident in Rancière's earliest published work: an interrogation of Althusser's dismissal of May '68, and the integrity of a Marxist-Leninist tradition in which "the competence of the masses" was forever denigrated in order to articulate and maintain a position that could represent the masses' interests to themselves in the form of a vanguard, a party, or a philosophy. See Jacques Rancière, *Althusser's Lesson*, trans. Emiliano Battista (London: Continuum, 2011), 14; 11–16.

15. Lack of space prevents my addressing the complex relationship between philosophical aesthetics and literary history. For cogent refutations of a naive historicism's occlusion of the possibility of an early modern aesthetic discourse, see Christopher Pye, *The Storm at Sea: Political Aesthetics in the Time of Shakespeare* (New York: Fordham University Press, 2015); John J. Joughin and Simon Malpas, "The New Aestheticism: An Introduction," in *The New Aestheticism*, ed. John J. Joughin and Simon Malpas, 1–19 (Manchester, U.K.: Manchester University Press, 2003); Clark Hulse, "Tudor Aesthetics," in *The Cambridge Companion to English Literature, 1500–1600*, ed. Arthur F. Kinney, 29–63 (Cambridge: Cambridge University Press, 2000); Mark Robson, "Defending Poetry, or, Is There an Early Modern Aesthetic?," in Joughin and Malpas, *The New Aestheticism*, 119–30.

16. Mark Goldie, "The Unacknowledged Republic: Officeholding in Early Modern England," in *The Politics of the Excluded, c. 1500–1850*, ed. Tim Harris, 125–52 (Houndmills, Basingstoke, Hampshire, U.K.: Palgrave, 2001).

17. Cynthia Marshall, "Shakespeare, Crossing the Rubicon," *Shakespeare Survey* 53 (2000): 80.

18. T. E. Baldwin, *William Shakspere's Small Latine and Lesse Greeke*, 2 vols. (Urbana: University of Illinois Press, 1944), 2:1–238; Patrick Collinson, "The Monarchical Republic of Queen Elizabeth," *Bulletin of the John Rylands University Library of Manchester* 69 (1987): 394–424.

19. Cicero, *De Oratore*, trans. E. W. Sutton and H. Rackham, 2 vols. (Cambridge, Mass.: Harvard University Press; London: Heinemann, 1959), 1:23; Cicero, *De Re Publica*, in *De Re Publica and De Legibus*, trans. Clinton Walker Keyes (Cambridge, Mass.: Harvard University Press; London: Heinemann, 1970), 75.

20. Cicero, *Brutus*, in *Brutus and Orator*, trans. G. L. Hendrickson (Cambridge, Mass.: Harvard University Press; London: Heinemann, 1988), 54, 289–91.

21. Andrew Hadfield, *Shakespeare and Republicanism* (Cambridge: Cambridge University Press, 2005), 168.

22. Cicero, *De Officiis*, trans. Walter Miller (Cambridge, Mass.: Harvard University Press, 1997), 355–57; Howard Jones, *Master Tully: Cicero in Tudor England* (Nieuwkoop, Neth.: De Graaf, 1998), 132–42. In *Julius Caesar*, when Cassius urges that Cicero be invited to join the conspiracy, Brutus objects: "Let us not break with him, / For he will never follow anything / That other men begin" (2.1.149–51)—an attribution of arrogance in keeping neither with their historical friendship nor with Plutarch's account in the *Life of Cicero*, where the conspirators exclude Cicero because of his age and timorousness (*Lives,* 933).

23. Victor Skretkowicz, *European Erotic Romance: Philhellene Protestantism, Renaissance Translation and English Literary Politics* (Manchester, U.K.: Manchester University Press, 2010), 233; Alexander Leggatt, *Shakespeare's Political Drama: The History Plays and the Roman Plays* (London: Routledge, 1988), 153–54.

24. Ros King, "'A lean and hungry look': Sight, Ekphrasis, Irony in *Julius Caesar* and *Henry V,*" *Shakespeare Survey* 69 (2016): 164.

25. Cicero, *De Oratore*, 1:15. In *Brutus*, Cicero compares the people's ear to a kind of flute (a metaphor also present in *De Oratore*), or to a horse in the process of being harnessed; response is crucial, yet it is clear that the people (*populo*) play a passive role in the rhetorical relationship.

26. Cicero, *De Oratore*, 1:325.

27. Elaine Fantham, *The Roman World of Cicero's "De Oratore"* (Oxford: Oxford University Press, 2004), 49–77. John Dugan points out that "Cicero uses an analogy of the body of a refined and polished Roman aristocrat" in describing how rhetoric aims at the truth ("Cicero's Rhetorical Theory," in *The Cambridge Companion to Cicero*, ed. Catherine Steel, 25–40 [Cambridge: Cambridge University Press, 2013], 34). See also Joy Connolly, *The State of Speech: Rhetoric and Political Thought in Ancient Rome* (Princeton, N.J.: Princeton University Press, 2007), 126–27.

28. Connolly, *The State of Speech*, 41–47; Andrew Lintott, *The Constitution of the Roman Republic* (Oxford: Clarendon Press, 1999), 220–25. As Patrick Sinclair has argued, even Cicero's Latinity reflected this preference, articulated as it was against Caesar's more populist emphasis on a rational approach to language that could be taught to all comers; "Political Declensions in Latin Grammar and Oratory, 55 B.C.E.–C.E. 39," *Ramus* 23, no. 1-2 (1994): 92–109.

29. Sir Philip Sidney, "A Defence of Poetry," in *Miscellaneous Prose of Sir Philip Sidney*, ed. Katherine Duncan-Jones and Jan van Dorsten (Oxford: Clarendon Press, 1973), 82–83.

30. Sidney, "Defence," 81.

31. George Puttenham, *The Art of English Poesy: A Critical Edition*, ed. Frank Whigham and Wayne A. Rebhorn (Ithaca, N.Y.: Cornell University Press, 2007), 227.

32. Philip Stubbes, *The Anatomie of Abuses* (London: Jones, 1583), L3r.

33. Sidney, "Defence," 96.

34. Sidney, "Defence," 96.

35. Plutarch, *Moralia*, trans. Frank Cole Babbitt, 15 vols. (Cambridge, Mass.: Harvard University Press; London: Heinemann, 1962), 4:425. As Plutarch wrote

in his *Life of Pelopidas*, Alexander continued his career in oppression, conquest, extortion, and rapine and was later murdered by his wife and her brothers for his cruelty (*Lives*, 329).

36. Sidney, "Defence," 114.

37. The episode is notorious for the detached "humor" with which the violence is presented, not least of which is the "behanding" of a poor painter who had accompanied the commoners so that he could see what a wound looks like. See Sir Philip Sidney, *The Countess of Pembroke's Arcadia (The New Arcadia)*, ed. Victor Skretkowicz (Oxford: Clarendon Press, 1987), 282. Despite the rhetorical trivialization of the violent deaths that the clowns seemingly deserve, David Katz argues that the entire episode indicts the rhetoric that moved them as morally deficient, especially given the status disparity between orators and auditors; "Counterfeiting Rhetoric: Poetics, Violence, and *Ekphrasis* in Sidney's *Arcadia* and the *Defence of Poesy*," *Sidney Journal* 34, no. 2 (2016): 69. What makes poetry superior to rhetoric is "that *idea* or fore-conceit of the work" (Sidney, "Defence," 79), which combines both the intelligible and the sensible; it appeals to, and is informed by, the senses, and yet it also lifts the erected wit above our fleshly weakness and "the too much loved earth" (78). Robert Stillman, *Philip Sidney and the Poetics of Renaissance Cosmopolitanism* (Aldershot, Hampshire, U.K.: Ashgate Publishing, 2008), 63–64, 109–22, provides an account of Sidney's indebtedness to Philip Melancthon for a Christian concept of Aristotelian scope in which the poetic end (its function and its teleology) shapes the totality of both writing and reading practices.

38. Thomas Heywood, *An Apology for Actors* (London: Okes, 1612), B4r.

39. Heywood B3v.

40. Heywood E3v.

41. Maria Wyke, *Caesar: A Life in Western Culture* (Chicago: University of Chicago Press, 2008); Robert S. Miola, "*Julius Caesar* and the Tyrannicide Debate," *Renaissance Quarterly* 38, no. 2 (Summer 1985): 271–89; Warren Chernaik, *The Myth of Rome in Shakespeare and His Contemporaries* (Cambridge: Cambridge University Press, 2011), 84–92; Martin Jehne, "History's Alternative Caesars: *Julius Caesar* and Current Historiography," in *Julius Caesar: New Critical Essays*, ed. Horst Zander, 59–70 (New York: Routledge, 2005).

42. Sianne Ngai, *Ugly Feelings* (Cambridge, Mass.: Harvard University Press, 2004), 5; emphasis added.

43. Robert S. Miola, *Shakespeare's Rome* (Cambridge: Cambridge University Press, 1983), 106; Leggatt, *Shakespeare's Political Drama*, 157; Robin Headlam Wells, "*Julius Caesar*, Machiavelli, and the Uses of History," *Shakespeare Survey* 55 (2002): 215; John Roe, "'Character' in Plutarch and Shakespeare: Brutus, Julius Caesar, and Mark Antony," in *Shakespeare and the Classics*, ed. Charles Martindale and A. B. Taylor (Cambridge: Cambridge University Press, 2004), 181; Chernaik, *Myth of Rome*, 104–5; Martha Nussbaum, "'Romans, Countrymen, and Lovers': Political Love and the Rule of Law in *Julius Caesar*," in *Shakespeare and the Law: A Conversation among Disciplines and Professions*, ed. Bradin Cormack, Martha C. Nussbaum, and Richard Strier (Chicago: University of Chicago Press, 2013), 266; David Hawkes, "Shakespeare's *Julius Caesar*: Marxist and Post-Marxist Approaches," in *Julius Caesar: New Critical Essays*, ed. Horst Zander (New York: Routledge, 2005), 206–7. Exceptions include Oliver

Arnold, *The Third Citizen: Shakespeare's Theater and the Early Modern House of Commons* (Baltimore: Johns Hopkins University Press, 2007); Nicholas Royle, "*Julius Caesar* and the Democracy to Come," in *Julius Caesar in Western Culture*, ed. Maria Wyke, 205–27 (Malden, Mass.: Blackwell Publishing, 2006).

44. Brents Stirling, *The Populace in Shakespeare* (New York: Columbia University Press, 1949), 149; Jerald W. Spotswood, "'We are undone already': Disarming the Multitude in *Julius Caesar* and *Coriolanus*," *Texas Studies in Literature and Language* 42, no. 1 (Spring 2000): 63.

45. Plato, *The Republic*, trans. Robin Waterfield (Oxford: Oxford University Press, 1993), 65–66.

46. Jacques Rancière, *The Philosopher and His Poor*, trans. John Drury, Corinne Oster, and Andrew Parker (Durham, N.C.: Duke University Press, 2003), chap. 1, sec. 1, loc. 431–49 of 4851, Kindle.

47. William Shakespeare, "The Rape of Lucrece," in *Shakespeare's Poems*, ed. Katherine Duncan-Jones and H. R. Woudhuysen (London: Thomson Learning, 2007), ll. 302–7; hereafter cited parenthetically by line number.

48. Rancière drew one of his most significant examples in *Disagreement: Politics and Philosophy* from book 2 of Livy's *Ab urbe condita*, one of Shakespeare's sources for *Coriolanus*. When the plebs demand liberty from debt so that they can fight for the city as free men, the patricians refuse to recognize them, therefore prompting the former to withdraw from the city to one of the sacred hills. The Senate sends Menenius Agrippa to negotiate, where he delivers his famed fable of the belly. Despite Agrippa's organic imagery (which naturalizes social hierarchy), the very fact that he addresses the plebs presumes that they are worth speaking with—which is why they return to the city and gain their own representatives, the tribunes, therefore becoming a recognized part of the republic. See Livy, *History of Rome, Books I–II*, trans. B. O. Foster (Cambridge, Mass.: Harvard University Press, 1919), 1:323–35; Anne Barton, "Livy, Machiavelli, and Shakespeare's *Coriolanus*," in *Shakespeare and Politics*, ed. Catherine Alexander and John Joughin, 67–90 (Cambridge: Cambridge University Press, 2004).

49. Jacques Rancière, "Politics, Identification, and Subjectivization," *October* 61 (Summer 1992): 59.

50. Jacques Rancière, *Disagreement: Politics and Philosophy*, trans. Julie Rose (Minneapolis: University of Minnesota Press, 1999), 22–27; Jacques Rancière, "The Thinking of Dissensus: Politics and Aesthetics," in *Reading Rancière*, ed. Paul Bowman and Richard Stamp (London: Continuum, 2011), 3–5.

51. Gabriel Rockhill, "The Politics of Aesthetics: Political History and the Hermeneutics of Art," in *Jacques Rancière: History, Politics, Aesthetics*, ed. Gabriel Rockhill and Philip Watts, 195–215 (Durham, N.C.: Duke University Press, 2009), 202–4. For a more sympathetic account of Rancière's effort to evade historicism, see Oliver Davis, *Jacques Rancière* (Cambridge: Polity Press, 2010), 36–73, 126–38; Alex Thomson, "On the Shores of History," in Bowman and Stamp, *Reading Rancière*, 200–16. In amplifying Kant's sensus communis as a political community, Rancière suggests that it possible for there to be a political aesthetic more affirming than the melancholy that J. M. Bernstein's powerful reading installs at the heart of philosophical aesthetics. And his very evasion of historicism via such quasi-historical concepts as the aesthetic regime makes it possible to interrogate aestheticism where the aesthetic might be said not to exist.

For aesthetics is less about the nature of the work itself and more about its reception—a reception whose very individuality and ephemerality can make finding those physical or institutional traces difficult, especially in eras addicted neither to tweets nor to selfies.

52. In Plutarch's account, the tribunes commit some of the celebrants to prison for calling Caesar king; other plebeians, however, follow them and call them *Brutes*, an allusion to Lucius Junius Brutus (Plutarch, *Lives,* 792).

53. Jacques Rancière, *The Emancipated Spectator*, trans. Gregory Elliott (London: Verso, 2011), 59.

54. Plutarch, *Lives*, 792.

55. Caska's narrative conflates two separate events in Plutarch's *Life of Caesar*, importing into the account of the coronet an earlier episode in which Caesar, after refusing to stand before the Senate, offered his throat to be cut for his folly (Plutarch, *Lives,* 791).

56. Arnold, *The Third Citizen*, 161.

57. In Plutarch's and Appian's accounts, the Senate is more significant than the plebeians in the postassassination machinations. Moreover, the events leading from Caesar's murder to Antony's funeral oration and the death of Cinna the poet take place over a period of at least three days.

58. In Plutarch's *Lives* Brutus, even in exile, organized the spectacular entertainments that were his responsibility as praetor.

59. Plutarch, *Lives*, 1055.

60. Richard Strier, "Against the Rule of Reason: Praise of Passion from Petrarch to Luther to Shakespeare to Herbert," in *Reading the Early Modern Passions: Essays in the Cultural History of Emotion*, ed. Gail Kern Paster, Katherine Rowe, and Mary Floyd-Wilson, 23–42 (Philadelphia: University of Pennsylvania Press, 2004); William J. Bouwsma, "The Two Faces of Humanism: Stoicism and Augustinianism in Renaissance Thought," in *Itinerarium Italicum: The Profile of the Italian Renaissance in the Mirror of Its European Transformations*, ed. Heiko A. Oberman with Thomas A. Brady Jr. (Leiden: Brill, 1975), 10–11, 38–39.

61. Geoffrey Miles, *Shakespeare and the Constant Romans* (Oxford: Clarendon Press, 1996), 123–48. In his dedication to a constancy that puts him at odds with the plebeians, Shakespeare's Brutus owes much to the *Life of Dion*, Plutarch's Greek parallel for the *Life of Brutus*. Dion (408–354 B.C.E.) was initially a trusted adviser to Dionysius I and Dionysius II, tyrants of Sicily; when the latter exiled him and later confiscated his property (and his wife), Dion returned to Sicily from Athens and deposed him. Both Dion and Brutus were followers of Plato and dedicated to the creation or restoration of a polity based on reason, not passion, which motivated, at least in part, their resistance to tyrants, real (in Dion's case) or imaginary (Plutarch is somewhat equivocal in his estimation of Julius Caesar's tyranny). Though Plutarch admired both Dion and Brutus for their constancy, he criticized the former's adoption of an explicitly aristocratic virtue that not only satisfied his self-interest but also prompted him to clash with the Syracusans' more democratic aspirations, as represented by Heracleides, whom he (Plutarch) vilified for "currying favor" with a common people who "would be flattered (as commonly the people be in free cities, where they onely be Lordes, and doe rule)" (Plutarch, *Lives,* 1043; see also Roe, "'Character' in Plutarch," 178). And like the Gracchi and Julius Caesar, Heracleides played his populist cards by proposing

land reform. Eventually, Dion had Heracleides murdered, an action that, when coupled with his efforts to establish a form of government more in keeping with Plato's *Republic*, led to his assassination (*Lives,* 1052). Dion thus out-Platoed Plato, his own constancy a kind of antisocial tyranny that neglected the sensibility not only of the Syracusan people but also of his erstwhile allies.

62. For Brutus's capacity for friendship, see Jennifer Feather, "'To tempt the rheumy and unpurg'd air': Contagion and Agency in *Julius Caesar*," in *Shakespeare and Moral Agency*, ed. Michael D. Bristol, 240–63 (New York: Continuum Books, 2010), 95.

63. Sidney, "Defence," 80.

64. René Girard, "Collective Violence and Sacrifice in Shakespeare's *Julius Caesar*," *Salmagundi* 88–89 (Fall 1990–Winter 91): 399–419; Naomi Conn Liebler, "Buying and Selling So(u)les: Marketing Strategies and the Politics of Performance in *Julius Caesar*," in Zander, *Julius Caesar*, 165–79.

65. As any number of critics have noted, Shakespeare—in a singular departure from his sources—chose to emphasize Caesar's age and debility, in opposition to the youth and vigor of the conspirators.

66. Liebler, "Buying and Selling So(u)les," 170; Nicholas Visser, "Plebeian Politics in *Julius Caesar*," *Shakespeare in Southern Africa* 7 (1994): 22–31.

67. In 1.1, Flavius and Murellus initially speak in verse, while the cobbler responds in prose. After his promise to mend them, they respond in prose (1.1.18–21) and then return to verse (1.1.28). Most of 1.2 is in verse, until Caska remains behind Caesar's exit to tell Brutus and Cassius what had transpired to inspire the cheers they had remarked earlier (1.2.214). The longest speech—Caska's description of the "rabblement"—is entirely in prose; when he leaves, Brutus and Cassius return to verse. Prose is strongly associated with plebeian status in the play, when the plebs are speaking, are spoken to, or are spoken about. In 3.2, though Mark Antony addresses the plebs in verse, it is unclear whether their responses are in prose or verse. Though Daniell has rendered their interjections of pity and anger as verse, the First Folio's layout doesn't necessarily support that editorial choice.

68. Puttenham, *Art of English Poesy*, 98.

69. Connolly, *The State of Speech*, 48.

70. Both Appian and Plutarch agree that it was less the will than Antony's display of Caesar's corpse, his bloody and mangled robe, and a wax effigy that had the most powerful effect on the Roman people; Appian, *Roman History*, trans. Horace White, 4 vols. (London: Heinemann; New York: Putnam's, 1933), 3:499; Plutarch, *Lives,* 976.

71. Though in modern criticism ekphrasis is often limited to the description of art objects, neither its etymology nor its history support that restriction. See Richard A. Lanham, *A Handbook of Rhetorical Terms*, 2nd ed. (Berkeley: University of California Press, 1991), 61; King, "'Lean and hungry look,'" 154. At its most basic, ekphrasis is "verbal pictorialism," the "thin" or "thick" description of objects or persons in order to promote *enargeia*, or "vividness," and therefore move one's auditor the more. See Claire Preston, "Ekphrasis: Painting in Words," in *Renaissance Figures of Speech*, ed. Sylvia Adamson, Gavin Alexander, and Katrin Ettenhuber, 115–29 (Cambridge: Cambridge University Press, 2007), 116–17.

72. James Heffernan writes of a "genealogical link between ekphrasis and sepulchral epigrams," a relationship to death that continues to inhabit verbal

pictorialism ("Ekphrasis and Representation," *New Literary History* 22, no. 2 [Spring 1991]: 302).

73. Though Plutarch and Appian recorded a number of violent episodes after the assassination, Shakespeare chose to dramatize only the murder of Cinna the poet.

74. Norman Holland, "The 'Cinna' and 'Cynicke' Episodes in *Julius Caesar*," *Shakespeare Quarterly* 11, no. 4 (Autumn 1960): 439–44.

75. I am here indebted to Hugh Grady's discussion of *A Midsummer Night's Dream* in *Shakespeare and Impure Aesthetics* (Cambridge: Cambridge University Press, 2009), 47–89.

76. Raymond Williams, *Modern Tragedy* (Stanford, Calif.: Stanford University Press, 1966), 64.

77. Liebler, "Buying and Selling So(u)les," 171.

78. King, "'Lean and hungry look,'" 165.

79. On Shakespeare's active spectators, see Andrew Gurr, *Playgoing in Shakespeare's London*, 3rd ed. (Cambridge: Cambridge University Press, 2004), 93; Dennis Kezar, "*Julius Caesar*'s Analogue Clock and the Accents of History," in Zander, *Julius Caesar*, 246–48; Pye, *The Storm at Sea*, 16–21.

80. Jacques Rancière, "What Aesthetics Can Mean," in *From an Aesthetic Point of View: Philosophy, Art and the Senses*, ed. Peter Osborne (London: Serpent's Tail, 2000), 21. For Rancière, art is never (fully) autonomous, as certain aesthetic ideologies hold (as Whitney describes); it is constantly engaged with the more prosaic world of "nonart"; see Jacques Rancière, *Aisthesis: Scenes from the Aesthetic Regime of Art*, trans. Zakir Paul (London: Verso, 2013), x–xi; Charles Whitney, "Ante-aesthetics: Towards a Theory of Early Modern Audience Response," in *Shakespeare and Modernity: Early Modern to Millennium*, ed. Hugh Grady, 40–60 (London: Routledge, 2000).

81. Gavin Arnall, Laura Gandolfi, and Enea Zaramella, "Aesthetics and Politics Revisited: An Interview with Jacques Rancière," *Critical Inquiry* 38, no. 2 (Winter 2012): 292; Rancière, *Emancipated Spectator*, 60.

82. Rancière, *Emancipated Spectator*, 59.

83. Richard Halpern, "Theater and Democratic Thought: Arendt to Rancière," *Critical Inquiry* 37, no. 3 (Spring 2011): 545–72.

Timon's Hunger in the Forest

Toward a Political Aesthetics of Being beside Oneself

Joan Pong Linton

In their coauthored play *Timon of Athens*, Shakespeare and Middleton give the legendary hater a backstory as a lover of mankind. The result is to reframe the legend's tradition from accounts of his misanthropic behaviors to the making of the misanthrope as a subjectivity tied to gold, the medium and agent of power within a social world of commerce and greed. The play further reinvents Timon for its time by locating its protagonist in contemporary England's mercantile networks of credit.[1] It is from this historical standpoint that the play engages with classical thought on topics that resonated with contemporary writers and audiences, in particular, the influence of money-based dealings like usury on society. By reinventing Timon as one who inhabits the limits of the social imaginary, loving and hating to the extreme, the play asserts its prerogative as fiction to theorize the implications that a changing economy has for the social ecology, that is, the modes of knowing and of being vital to the production of selves and society.

As a lover of mankind, Timon envisions an ideal community of friends sharing in one another's wealth. With the failure of his social vision and his subsequent turn to misanthropy, the play can be said to anticipate what Derrida points to in the "politics of friendship" as the "crime against the possibility of politics," even as the setting of Athens, where democracy had its beginnings, anticipates Derrida's sense of such "crime" as crucially the problem of democracy.[2] Through Timon, I argue, the play stages the fragility of political friendship, as Aristotle conceives it, based on likeness in virtue between friends. Where Timon embodies the telos-driven perfection that paradoxically transforms him from lover to hater, the play redefines friendship in the character of Alcibiades, Timon's true and imperfect friend. Friendship thus redefined renders a political aesthetics of theater, political in its engagement of a coproductive audience both through their awareness of genre and convention and through the staging of Timon's hunger as visceral grounding of an aesthetic in common. My analysis focuses on Timon's hunger in the woods as an embodied index to vital if hidden connections between economy and ecology in diverse registers of exchange, inviting the audience to coproduce a theater experience that is, in effect, a thought experiment on their own social world.

To begin, Timon's hunger has its precondition in his banqueting, that scene of plenitude associated with his "magic of bounty" that proves illusory. As Jowett points out, Timon's "bounty flows, not due to some miraculous access to the infinite, as though bounty really were magic, but thanks to the sleight of hand of credit."[3] In his self-imposed exile, Timon experiences hunger as a natural need that translates across psychological and social registers as hate and revenge, unleashed by his finding gold while digging for roots and his entry into money-based exchange as the self-identified *Misanthropos*. Remarkably, it is through Timon's hunger and hate that the play presents its most trenchant analysis of economy and ecology, including his speeches on the power of gold that Marx so admired. The exposition of Timon's hate-filled hunger makes room for crucial exchanges with his friend Alcibiades, his steward Flavius, and Apemantus, the play's Cynic philosopher.[4] In these exchanges, I argue, the play provides openings for redefining friendship, from its grounding in the centered self, for whom the ideal friend is ultimately reducible to oneself, to a relational self for whom friends are selves in their own rights and reciprocal beings beside oneself. This redisposition of friends as *beings beside* one another constitutes an ecology of coproduction in which friendship may yet render possible the political. In staging the coproductive practices that constitute theater, the play offers a political aesthetics that also unfolds as an apology for theater, an elaboration of what theater is for as a commercial institution within a commercial culture, how theater, in its practice of imperfection, can promise and perform in its attempt to repurpose ethos.

From Lover to Hater of All Mankind: Timon as the Centering Self

From the start, Timon's social vision is riddled with ambiguity in his speech to banquet guests he addresses as "my good friends": "We are born to do benefits; and what better or properer can we call our own than the riches of our friends? O, what a precious comfort 'tis to have so many like brothers commanding one another's fortunes!"[5] The speech can be taken both to advocate for a community based on shared use of wealth among friends as "so many like brothers" and to justify the appropriation of others' wealth in the name of friendship. It is unclear whether Timon is aware of his amphibious logic, but the reference to friends "doing benefits" for one another as "like brothers" indicates the play's philosophical engagement as it echoes Aristotle's discussion of friendship in relation to the political economy. Timon's speech hinges on two kinds of friendship predicated on two divergent senses of use, as shared use and appropriation. That such divergent logics should coexist in the same speech suggests the challenges of putting political friendship into practice.

In *Nicomachean Ethics*, Aristotle states that "complete friendship is the friendship of those who are good and alike in point of virtue," and that the exercise of "complete virtue" is "justice . . . in relation to another person." For Aristotle justice is a political virtue because "justice alone of the virtues is held to be another's good," as it goes beyond "members of [one's] household" to benefit "someone who shares in the community."[6] In the *Politics*, Aristotle goes on to say that "it is better for possessions to be privately owned, but to make them common property in use; and to train the citizens to this is the special task of the legislator."[7] The word "use" here connects the political friendship of "so many like brothers" with the *oikos*, or household, whose members share in the use of its wealth and resources within the natural limits of self-sufficiency. As such, the *oikos* is the basic unit of society that finds completion in the good life of the *polis*. Justice as a political virtue is vulnerable, however, in the face of exchange mediated by money. For Aristotle, commerce is "justly discredited" because it "involves men's taking things from each other." He especially condemns usury: "for money was brought into existence for the purpose of exchange, but interest increases the amount of the money itself."[8] Instead of the shared use of wealth, money-based exchange yields a relationship of utility, the use one can make of another. Such gain is a powerful inducement for one to be selfish, "to love oneself more than one ought," to take more than one's fair share—to be ruled by *pleonexia*, the desire to satisfy appetite, which "is in its nature unlimited."[9] Not surprisingly, Aristotle notes, "friendship [of virtue] is likely to be rare, since people of this sort are few," and "it is also not possible to be a friend to many, at least not when it comes to complete friendship."[10]

Eric Spencer points to a "philosophical double bind disclosed in . . . the Aristotelian analysis of money: namely, that the symbolic mediation money performs is at once . . . a necessary mechanism of community and an inevitable source of injustice."[11] Peter Remien further notes Aristotle's "assumption that the economy is a zero-sum game—wealth gained somewhere is elsewhere lost."[12] We may also wonder whether a zero-sum game isn't also implicit in the idea of friendship based on likeness between friends, especially the telos-driven friendship of virtue that finds completion in justice. The condition of likeness is crucial to Aristotle's notion of altruistic self-love as the basis for love of one's friend. In *Nicomachean Ethics*, he says that "the decent person" (read just person) "stands in relation to a friend as he is to himself—for a friend is another self." Where likeness between friends facilitates the self's tendency to relate to another, the centering self remains privileged in self-love. Aristotle goes on to differentiate between the just and the self-seeking, but he places both in the same category of self-love, specifying that one should cultivate the former and avoid the latter.[13] Michael Pakuluk finds it "especially interesting . . . that Aristotle thinks that a twofold prescription is required here. This suggests that he does not regard self-love as a single motive shared by all human beings, but rather as something acquired and as much an artefact of education and upbringing as virtue and vice."[14] The double prescription also underscores the problem democratic society faces when a few just men must struggle to uphold the public good against a self-seeking majority.

Shakespeare and Middleton would seem to contemplate the problem of democracy at its institutional limits by inventing a Timon who inhabits both the classical double bind of money and early modern culture in which usury as a practice was becoming normalized as a system of credit, with the government regulating the interest rate. In presuming the friendship of his guests as "so many like brothers," Timon seems to channel the pastoral ideal of *oikos* alive in the era's pastoral romances like Sidney's *Arcadia*.[15] In taking on a credit system already in place, Timon would disrupt the very logic of credit driving commerce and usury, whether it is by lavishing gifts upon others out of all proportion to the worth of gifts received or by hosting sumptuous banquets and entertainments.[16] In paying off Ventidius's debt, Timon refuses the latter's repayment "doubled with thanks and service": "I gave it freely ever, and there's none / Can truly say he gives, if he receives." Timon would undo the reciprocity that structures exchange itself, but in doing so he also undoes the reciprocity inherent in friendship (1.2.6, 9–10). By going to the extreme in "doing benefits," Timon paradoxically brings out the opposite in his beneficiaries. He succeeds only too well in incentivizing their greed, inviting them to make his wealth their own, even as he falls into debt financing his giving. As Flavius reports, "What he speaks is all in debt; he owes for every word. / He is so kind that he now pays interest for't; / His land's put to their books" (1.2.193–95).

Timon is thus caught in a system to which he is utterly unable, or refuses, to be accountable, pleading "indisposition" and "unaptness" when finally forced to confront his mounting debts (2.2.125, 126). Not surprisingly, this translates into divergent public images of Timon. To his followers, he is the charismatic figure "whom this beneath world doth embrace and hug / With amplest entertainment" (1.1.44–45). At the same time, speculation about the source of his wealth leads one Senator to suspect Timon of coining—"If I want gold, steal but a beggar's dog, / And give it Timon—why the dog coins gold"—and prostitution: "No porter at his gate, / But rather one that smiles and invites / All that pass by." Timon can embrace his charismatic image by remaining blind to his dependence on credit. But his image crumbles when the same Senator, for fear that Timon's "raging waste . . . cannot hold," calls in his loan and brings on the flood of creditors (2.1.4, 5–6, 10–12).

In voicing his suspicions about Timon, the Senator invokes urban vices and moneymaking schemes sensationalized in the rogue pamphlets and satirized in the city comedies. However, the fact that Timon is not guilty yet not above suspicion signals a different authorial intention, one that aligns his negative image with the parallel perception of theater in contemporary attacks on theater for promoting "whoredom," among other vices. In this light, Timon is not above suspicion because theater is not above suspicion: Timon is in effect a figure for the antitheatrical stereotype of theater, around which the play refigures a political aesthetics of theater in its defense. With this in mind, other aspects of Timon as figure also fall into place. He is the noble patron caught in the crosscurrents of socioeconomic change and in theater's transition to commercial patronage. His generosity and lavish living, the hallmarks of feudal liberality, are perceived as profligacy from the mercantile perspective.[17] At the same time, Timon's lavish living also connects the character with the image of stage players as idlers dressing above their social station and living beyond their means.[18] Since the audience learns from the start that Timon is living on borrowed wealth, his bounty is not so different from an actor's performance of wealth onstage.

As Tanya Pollard has shown, the early modern attacks on theater were often motivated by public theater's popularity as a commercial institution.[19] A salient issue in contention concerns theater's moral influence on spectators. In noting the "medical, bodily, and pharmacy-steeped vocabulary of early modern plays and contemporary writings about the theater," Pollard also argues that "drugs, with their ambivalent tension between curative promise and uncertain threat, offered a powerful vocabulary through which to imagine the effects of theatrical performance on spectators" (3). Rebecca Lemon further compares such effects to addiction (in the sense of devotion to, and losing oneself in, a higher power): "Early modern actors were imagined to release and transform themselves, not only through affect and gesture, but also through bodily comportment. In the process, they also transform the audience and the theater space, the scene of connection between the one and the many."[20] In this connection, *Timon of Athens* can be seen to complicate both theater's perceived immorality and the assumed hold that actors had over spectators. The play signals from the start this metatheatrical dimension through the Poet's running commentary, which constitutes a kind of doublespeak.

The opening scene, in which Timon opens his house to banquet guests, registers a self-conscious moment of theater's popularity. The poet's comment to the Painter, "You see this confluence, this great flood of visitors," gestures toward the theater audience arriving at the playhouse. Timon's charisma, the poet continues, "subdues and properties to his love and tendance / all sorts of hearts"; his "present grace to present slaves and servants / Translates his rivals" (1.1.42, 58–59, 72–73). The claim recalls the power of actors to spellbind beholders by their performance—but also dispels the binding, the modifier "present" suggesting not simply Timon's forceful presence but also the fleeting nature of his charisma, "his large fortune" being the favor of a fickle goddess. Again, the phrase "magic of bounty," while identifiable with Timon's charismatic generosity, is predicated to the Painter's power to draw the world into his work: "See, / Magic of bounty, all these spirits thy power / Hath conjured to attend" (5–7). A familiar trope emerges here: the pictorial framing of the play's action signals theater's claim of holding a mirror up to society, even as the Poet's speech doubles as an alternative account of how theater engages its audiences. Elsewhere I have explored the play's ambivalence toward the workings of charisma. Specifically, the hearts and minds Timon supposedly subdues and enslaves are disposed neither to embrace his social vision nor to imitate his generosity. It is rather their desire for wealth projected onto Timon as its source that produces his charisma, charisma that holds up as long as the desirers misrecognize his performance of wealth as bounty. Especially in the case of the "glass-faced flatterer," the Poet suggests that influence can go both ways, with the flatterer mirroring to Timon what he wants to see (1.1.59). Timon's charisma is thus not entirely his own but largely of the public's making.[21] By extension, even as Timon's charisma invokes the addictive power attributed to the actor, this addiction is shown to be actively coproduced on both sides. Indeed, Timon's charisma, maintained by his performance of wealth, embodies the logic of credit that underwrites a general performance of wealth, the practice of financing business deals through loans within the culture of credit. Through Timon, theater holds a mirror to the theatricality of credit itself, and the addiction to theater reflects a culture's addiction to credit, both operating on the promise to perform, a logic that reproduces itself systemically.

The question that arises, then, is how theater can render an experience that is critically and morally *responsive* to society. Within commercial culture, I would suggest, theater operates like charisma in that it offers a consumable "reality," a commodity that is realized in coproduction with, and consumed by, members of the audience, onstage or on the page. The difference is that by tracking the fate of Timon's bounty, the play also tracks the fate of charisma in an economy of consumption. In doing so, theater invites a different kind of coproduction from its audience. By showing that while Timon can draw a public he does not captivate all hearts and minds, the play asserts theater's prerogative to take a critical stance with respect to what it represents. Apart from Poet and Painter, other characters too, especially servants and strangers already socially distanced from Timon's circle, enact critical dispositions in conversation, as when one servant remarks to other servants of usurers how strange it is that "Timon in this should pay more than he owes." Critical commentary continues even in Flavius, one disposed to empathize with his master: "For bounty, that makes gods, still do mar men" (3.4.26, 4.2.41). In moments like these, the play prompts a range of critical responses toward the power of charisma. Of course, audience members may respond differently or not at all, but the potential for the critical among diverse dispositions crucially defines theater's practice in countering antitheatrical perceptions: in undoing the addictive power of charisma, it invites audience members to coproduce critical awareness.

We can further characterize the play's critical stance by noting how it differs from the satiric vein of the city comedy. In Jonson's *Alchemist*, for example, Face, Doll, and Subtle are seasoned users preying on their gulls' desires for wealth, sex, and power by promising without performing illegal acts such as prostitution and coining. By contrast, Timon falls prey to a legal system of promise and perform. Here, then, is tragedy with a difference: when "doing benefits" invites others to take advantage at one's own expense, when the desire for wealth turns "friends" into users, when such relational *use/usury* is distributed through a system of credit and debt bondage in which a public is implicated but for which no one is alone accountable, when injury is impersonally inflicted yet so personally felt in the undoing of Timon's reputation and social vision, then perhaps the only revenge possible is generalized hatred of mankind, to which Timon finally gives his name. In thus playing at the limits of both city comedy and revenge tragedy, *Timon of Athens* marks out a metatheatrical space in which the question of justice informs a political aesthetics of theater, engaging audience members ever alert to trespasses of genres and, especially in the latter half of the play, through a visceral aesthetics of hunger.

Gold, Roots, and the Aesthetics of Hunger

In his self-imposed exile in the woods, Timon finds gold while digging for roots to satisfy his hunger. Immediately after, coming upon Alcibiades, he declares himself Misanthropos to the friend he once loved, although the pastoral setting of his exile also brings to him the goodwill of several interlocutors, of whom more later. It is not without irony that Timon in his misanthropy should find a receptive ear with Marx, whose reading of Timon's speeches on gold informed the development of his own "alienation theory of money."[22] "Marx can cite Timon as a sort of expert witness on money," Crystal Bartolovich notes, "because the money form precedes capitalism."[23] Chris Fitter further aligns that expertise with "political economy . . . a legacy of political analysis born . . . in sixteenth-century England itself."[24] While Marx was writing mainly for his own time, some of his economic and ecological insights can shed light on the play, taking into account differences in historical contexts. Reading with Marx enables us to find in Timon, hateful as he is, an economy/ecology of hunger that provides grounding for a political aesthetic of theater.

In the first place, Timon's encounter with gold effects not only his turn to misanthropy but also his entry into exchange, engaging in the very activity he has so far managed to avoid. If finding gold enables him to resume the old habit of giving away his wealth, his intent is no longer to do benefits but to destroy society. Thus in funding Alcibiades's campaign against Athens, Timon singles out the captain's martial skill "with men's blood to paint the ground gules, gules," even as he pays Phrynia and Timandra to "whore still" and "consumption sow" (4.3.59, 146, 150). In paying others to do what he himself cannot, Timon activates the power of money, in Marx's phrase, as "the alienated capacity of mankind." Indeed, money is not just "alienated" but also "alienating": here Marx takes his cue from Timon when he calls gold the "touch[stone] of hearts" that "by thy virtue / Set them into confounding odds" (4.3.381–83). As the universal equivalent money "exchanges every quality for every other quality and object, even if it is contradictory."[25] Money thus builds into exchange a contradiction: it binds the parties involved to the economic system while undermining existing social relationships and communal bonds. There is, of course, some distance between economic exchange as a normalized activity and Timon's misanthropy: persons engaged in exchange are not all, like Timon, out for revenge. From a systemic view, as Marx notes, reciprocity is "presupposed" between parties in exchanges mediated by money, so that each is free to pursue his or her "self-seeking interest."[26] Such reciprocity Timon the philanthropist did once forgo in his bid to disrupt exchange, unleashing self-seeking interest in others. In pursuing revenge through exchange, Timon now takes self-seeking to the extreme in misanthropy—his hate running on an empty stomach.

For an early modern audience, then, Timon's misanthropic rant on gold as "the common whore of mankind" points to the power of money in "touching" hearts to effect systemic change within society. It is this mysterious power of money that Marx explicates in volume 1 of *Capital*, quoting Timon (in a footnote) by way of illustration: "Everything becomes saleable and purchaseable. Circulation becomes the great social retort into which everything is thrown, to come out again as the money crystal. Nothing is immune from this alchemy . . . Just as in money every qualitative difference between commodities is extinguished, so too for its part, as a radical leveler, it extinguishes all distinctions.

> Gold? Yellow, glittering, precious gold? . . .
> Thus much of this will make black, white; foul, fair;
> Wrong, right; base, noble; old, young; coward, valiant.
> . . . What this, you gods? Why, this
> Will lug your priests and servants from your sides,
> Pluck out men's pillows from below their heads;
> This yellow slave
> Will knit and break religions, bless the accursed,
> Make the hoar leprosy adored, place thieves
> And give them title, knee and approbation
> With senators on the bench: this is it,
> That makes the wappen'd widow wed again:
> . . . Come damned earth,
> Thou common whore of mankind (Shakespeare, *Timon of Athens*, act 4, scene 3)"[27]

These juxtaposed passages capture in contrast two historical perspectives of political economy. Where Marx describes the abstractive power of money in circulation, Timon renders "yellow, glittering, precious gold" in its sensuous materiality and evokes through images of persons, places, things, and actions a social world touched by gold. These images provide concrete particulars to the "qualitative differences" and "social distinctions" that money levels. In describing circulation as the "great social retort" from which emerges the "money crystal," Marx's language resonates with the play's alchemical imagination. His tendency, however, is to rationalize the "alchemy" as the social mechanism through which the "money crystal" emerges as the medium of exchange. Even as Marx sees in Timon premonitions of capitalist indifference, he overlooks one detail: Timon's hunger, the immediate provocation of his tirade on gold.

In staging Timon's hunger, the play effectively dramatizes the moment before use values are occulted in the great social retort of exchange in circulation. With this in mind, we return to the woods, where a famished Timon cries out for roots and digs up gold *first*:

> . . . Earth, yield me roots.
> [*Digs.*]
> Who seeks for better of thee, sauce his palate
> With thy most operant poison. What is here?
> Gold? Yellow, glittering, precious gold? (4.3.23–26)

The appearance of gold signals the presence of an alchemical world in which nature is alive and agential, perverse even, in responding to Timon's hunger. Gold appears unbidden, it would seem, when Timon cries out for roots. By appearing first gold preempts his efforts to relieve his hunger, and the effect is a double alienation. Timon thereafter loses the ability to relate to his own needs and, with it, the ability to relate to others—the sociability that is, for Marx, the essence of being human. As he explains, hunger is both a "natural need" most immediately satisfied by nature's productions[28] and the basis for human relationships in coproducing communal subsistence.[29] In the play, by coming between Timon and nature as the source of his sustenance, gold not only prevents him from meeting a natural need but also forecloses his basis for being communal.

The play's alchemical imagination thus locates Timon's encounter with gold at the heart of the human interaction with nature. Such interaction is fraught with ambivalence within the Renaissance conception of alchemy as a scientific and social experiment, summed up in the proposition that the process of producing gold can corrupt as well as ennoble human nature.[30] In Timon's perception, the gold that grows in the earth, transmuted by nature from baser metals, already bears the symbolic weight of cupidity, the root of evil. What's more, gold would seem to have appeared preemptively to "sauce his palate" and his disposition with earth's "most operant poison." To be clear, finding gold first does not prevent Timon from finding and eating roots later, but it does condition all his transactions thereafter through a poisoned hunger that is at once biological, psychological, and social. Timon's talk of "poison" (in five of the seven instances in the play) projects an imagined social and natural environment already latent with poison. In cursing Athens, he would have "breath infect breath," so "that their society, as their friendship, may / Be merely poison." In urging Alcibiades to "be as a planetary plague," Timon invokes the miasmic scourge, "when Jove / will o'er some high-viced city hang poison / In the sick air." Within this poisoned ecology/economy, even the physician's "antidotes are poisons" (4.1.30–32, 4.3.108–9, 425). In oversimplifying Paracelsian medical theory in which "nothing is without poison," Timon locates humans at the center of a cosmos "that was intensely integrated, unified, and activated through spirit."[31] For him, that spirit is "thievery," appropriating what belongs to others (4.3.428), reflecting the grievance of a centered self and selfhood based on property.

Timon's extended commentary on gold and poison unfolds along with, and builds upon his growing hunger. Some 170 lines will have elapsed after his first plea for roots before Timon finds one, and another 90 lines more before he actually "[*eats a root*]" (4.3.23, 192, 284). The staging of his prolonged hunger ensures ample opportunity for the audience to engage cocreatively with Timon in his predicament. The pivotal example occurs in an anguished speech leading up to his finding "one poor root":

> TIMON: That nature, being sick of man's unkindness,
> Should yet be hungry! Common mother, thou, [*Digging*]
> Whose womb unmeasurable and infinite breast
> Teems and feeds all . . .
> Yield him, who all the human sons do hate,
> From forth thy plenteous bosom, one poor root. (4.3.176–79,
> 185–86)

Timon's diffused hatred is here constricted by hunger into a half line, "Should yet be hungry." His plea to earth as "common mother" captures a trace of the sociability foreclosed to Timon that once might have informed his vision of a community of "like brothers." And yet the "common mother" does yield a root upon Timon's plea. And insofar as hunger is a natural experience familiar to audience members, theater engages their "fellow feeling," their connectedness to other beings at the level of animal sentience and affect. Bypassing moral judgment, this visceral aesthetics offers hunger as a natural need common to all: it renders Timon relatable despite his utter inability to relate to himself and others.

In engaging the audience, the aesthetic of hunger both centers the self viscerally and orients it in relation to others. Marx provides crucial insight here in his insistence on the aesthetic nature of human development as sensuous beings, from meeting natural needs to attaining creative expression. Along this trajectory, the self realizes its relational potential through passion: "To be sensuous is to suffer (to be subjected to the actions of another). Man as an objective sensuous being is therefore a suffering being, and because he feels his suffering [*Leiden*], he is a passionate [*leidenschaftliches*] being. Passion is the essential power of man energetically bent on its object."[32] This "energetically" relational self is what the play calls for in the audience, especially through Timon's frantic digging in the ground for roots. The gesture transforms a part of the physical stage, possibly the cellarage, into earth's womb, the "plenteous bosom" from which a root emerges. Timon's plea to the "common mother" thus figures the stage as a heterotopia or space of autonomy—a theatrical architecture for what is possible, cocreatively sustained by the audience's relational energy. Even as hunger draws Timon into himself, audience members can relate as *beings beside* him *com*passionate with his suffering, without necessarily being hungry themselves or assenting to his hate.

At the same time, an attentive ear may catch in the phrase "plenteous bosom" an echo from an earlier scene featuring a theatrical entertainment that presents a different appeal to, and aesthetic of, the senses. The phrase first occurs in the Masque of Ladies following the banquet feast, when Cupid the presenter greets Timon as follows: "The five best senses / Acknowledge thee their patron, and come freely / To gratulate thy plenteous bosom (1.2.116–18). As Jowett astutely observes, "The striking phrase 'plenteous bosom' is not found elsewhere . . . in the literature of the period. It is all the more remarkable that it should occur twice in *Timon of Athens*." This unusual linkage brings into sharp contrast the urban and pastoral scenes of the senses. As Jowett further points out, in Cupid's speech "the alienation of the phrase 'plenteous bosom' from earth and nature is extreme."[33] A similar alienation attends Cupid's "five best senses," which levels the traditional moralized hierarchy of the senses, inviting indiscriminate consumption of the masque's sensual surfeit. All this is suggestive of the unnatural addictive power that theater is supposed to have over passive consumers. Against such urban commerce of the senses, then, the play's alternative aesthetic finds its grounding in the pastoral moment, reclaiming the senses by staking its claim to the visceral that the experience of hunger awakens.

These highlighted moments of contrastive aesthetics can further be seen to operate as provocation to the play's larger question concerning theater's role in commercial society. How might a play engage an audience's relational energies cocreatively in breaking the inertia of passive consumption? In addressing this question, let us first note that Marx's idea of human development aligns well with Renaissance psychology, specifically the physiological basis of character predicated on the continuity of the senses, affects, and reason. Derived from Aristotle, this psychic continuity posits the senses as the matrix for both the ethical and political. In the *Nicomachean Ethics*, Aristotle writes that the senses provide the basis for perception, a relational activity necessary to the development of *phronesis*, the practical wisdom of prudence that is "bound up with action, accompanied by reason, and concerned with things good and bad for a human being." Centering and relational tendencies cooperate in the prudent, "because they are able to observe the good things for themselves and those for human beings," a quality one can find in "skilled household managers and politicians."[34]

Where Aristotle finds practical wisdom in some, theater purports to activate its relational potential in many through what Henry Pickford calls the "artistic cultivation of phronetic perception." Pickford finds the influence of Aristotle's thought in this "model of Marxist aesthetics" in "artworks that attempt to activate the recipient's capacity for situational, kairotic perception and reaction."[35] The situational and kairotic are integral to theater's ensemble practices of being beside oneself, whether this involves an actor relating to his character, or prompter cueing actors into character, or character materializing as interface in the coproduction between actor and audience, or the collaboration of playwrights, and so on. Beyond this embodied practice, the play would seem to engage in the artistic cultivation of the audience's phronetic perception from its grounding in the visceral sense by staging Timon's hunger in the woods and the modes of relational care undertaken by his pastoral interlocutors.

'I'll take . . . /Not all thy counsel': Political Aesthetics of Being Beside

A recurring phonetic cue—the words "eat" and "hate" being pronounced alike in early modern English—links Timon's hunger and hatred with consumption in several senses. The wordplay, recurring mainly in his pastoral exchanges, is most striking in Timon's declaration, "I am Misanthropos, and hate mankind," having just found gold while digging for roots. By the time he finally eats a root, his hatred has become all-consuming, driving him to wish "that the whole life of Athens were in this! / Thus would I eat it" (4.3.283–84). Implicitly, hunger is the physiological basis for the misanthrope's *poiesis*, or self-making, under the influence of gold. The wordplay becomes explicit in the conversation between Timon and Apemantus:

> APEMANTUS: . . . There's a medlar for thee: eat it.
> TIMON: On what I hate, I feed not (4.3.304–5)

Several possible meanings coexist in this exchange: in refusing to eat, Timon may hate the fruit, the meddler (punning on "medlar") who offers it, or, metaphorically, the counsel offered by that meddler. To early modern ears, moments of verbal dueling around a pun may be comical in distancing the audience from the characters, but the very offer of a medlar/meddler constitutes a gesture that channels the audience's relating impulses toward Timon.

It is not coincidental that Apemantus should be the interlocutor here: at the banquet, he was the one to implore the gods—and the audience, by extension—to witness "what a number of men eats Timon, and he sees 'em not" (1.2.38–39). Not only does he point to the societal context of hate in Athenian eating but also, importantly, his chosen diet of "honest water" and "a little oil and root" bespeaks his commitment to the Cynic way of life, living in accordance with nature and in contempt of society's corruptions (1.2.58, 127).[36] In this sense, his verbal dueling with Timon constitutes a moment of "distraction," in Christopher Pye's complex sense of the term,[37] catching Timon in his frenzy of hate and hunger and also opening the possibility of self-care. Specifically, Apemantus's comic meddling suggests the practice of Cynic self-care, the practice through which one cultivates a "relationship of self to self" as the crucial first step in relating to others. As Foucault explains, this "relational mode of knowledge" is ethopoetic, or knowledge that "provides or forms ethos"; it is "useful knowledge" in that "it asserts and prescribes at the same time and is capable of producing a change in the subject's mode of being." Such knowledge also equips one as *parrhesiastes*, or truth teller, to guide another with knowledge "that is relevant for the subject's transformation."[38] Like the Cynic, Apemantus can be said to offer ethopoetic guidance to Timon by pointing to the toxic social milieu that has shaped his mode of being: "The middle of humanity thou never knewest, but the extremity of both ends. When thou wast in thy gilt and thy perfume, they mocked thee for too much curiosity; in thy rags thou know'st none, but art despised for the contrary" (4.3.300–303). Apemantus fails, however, when Timon dispatches him instead to recruit "hirèd harm" by spreading word in Athens of his found gold. The move shows how fully Timon is possessed of and by the alienating power of gold, the "yellow slave" that in the course of his transformation has grown into a "visible god" (3.4.34, 391). Timon may have taken to the woods, but as Apemantus says, "the commonwealth of Athens is become a forest of beasts," and the forest materializes where Timon finds gold. Timon's hunger has always been in and of the forest.[39] Apemantus's parting shot is ironic in its resignation: "Eat, Timon, and *abhor* them," referring to bandits, "more things like men" (4.3.292, 342–43, 390–91). Some have surmised that Timon ends by suicide;[40] I suggest that Timon's turn to misanthropy tracks the self-seeking exile of addiction: that protracted detour to suicide that gold (as money) systemically enables.

My analysis here rejoins the discussion of addiction (see p. 126) with respect to a popular audience's devotion to theater and the spellbinding power of actors, or, in a positive vein, religious devotion. Lemon notes, "What unites these apparently opposed discourses is a shared emphasis, both rhetorical and experiential, on addiction as an overthrow of the will."[41] The will's overthrow is implicit in Timon's instruction to the bandits, dispatching them with gold to "go, suck the subtle blood o' th' grape, / Till high fever seethe your blood to froth" (4.3.422–43). This description aligns remarkably well with our perception today of addicts seeking to replicate an initial high they can never again attain from a substance that poisons them. Projected onto others, the description befits him: in his hunger, he recalls a past self "that never knew but better" (4.2.267), the charismatic high he once enjoyed giving his wealth away. In putting his found gold into circulation, however, the joy of giving gives way to vindictive calculation, even as gold the agent of addiction has become "most operant poison," the innermost betrayal of friendship, the promise without satisfaction that keeps the addict coming back for more. In his hunger Timon the hater becomes the ultimate consumer, the user who uses others for a self-seeking fix, consuming human labors and human bodies and the relational bonds of society.

The fact remains that Apemantus, Flavius, and Alcibiades do not come under the spell of gold as money, and this suggests that while misanthropy is a universal potential that can be actualized, and often is, in individuals, actualization is not inevitable. In their exchanges with Timon as the figure of addiction, each interlocutor performs an alternative mode of being and knowing grounded in the relating self that cultivates the audience's capacity for *phronesis* as part of theater's political aesthetic. In the case of Apemantus's comic meddling, the play offers a version of Cynic parrhesia, public performance aimed at "chang[ing] the value of the currency"; that is, by criticizing social convention and metaphorically erasing the authority stamped on coinage with one that will "enable it to circulate with its true value."[42] Apemantus's failed performance does not undercut the value of Cynic self-care; rather, it underscores the hold that gold as money has on Timon—and beyond him, in its systemic reach of a political economy.

In Flavius, the play presents the "skillful household manager" who remains virtuous in negotiating the world of commerce. In discharging his fellow servants with his own savings, he exemplifies what Elizabeth Rivlin calls "aesthetic service," both "acting for" and "acting as" his master, performing what Timon no longer can.[43] Michael Noschka relates Flavius's kindness to the root sense of ethos as "dwelling-with,"[44] to which we may add his capacity for suffering-with another when he weeps to find his master in the woods "so full of decay and failing" (4.3.453). Given instructions along with gold to set up house as a misanthropic hoarder, Flavius chooses instead to bring the Senators to Timon in hopes of effecting reconciliation. Early modern writers on service caution that a servant "should have 'no will of his owne, nor power over him selfe, but wholly to resign himselfe to the will of his Master, and this is to obey.' "[45] By this measure Flavius's devotion to his master is hardly obedient, unlike Timon's devotion to gold. Returning to Pye, it is in acknowledging Flavius's kindness that Timon gains a sense of himself as an aesthetic subject of tragedy.[46] The hater is not immune to Flavius's tears when he calls his steward a woman, exempting this "singly honest man" from his hatred of all men. This momentary distraction also expels any trace of trust that would render Timon vulnerable: "For I must ever doubt, though ne'er so sure," that any offer of kindness is "subtle, covetous, / A usuring kindness, . . . / Expecting in return twenty to one" (4.3.500–502, 515).

While Apemantus and Flavius engage Timon through performances of virtue, Alcibiades redefines the basis for a political friendship addressed to justice, virtue's political counterpart. In comparing his story with Timon's, initial likenesses set up for telling departures. Both men act in the interest of friendship,[47] and in so doing both test the limits of their social system. If Timon leaves Athens in rejection of its credit system, Alcibiades is banished for the challenge he poses to the Senate. Notably, the two are linked by their use of the word "usuring," which in its present-participle form suggests an ongoing relational usury, a behavioral addiction, if you will, in which the user takes advantage of the used through an existing relationship, whether personal as in friendship or institutional as in official authority. While Timon hates all men in general for the "usuring kindness" of some, his hatred forecloses the political. By contrast, Alcibiades in his campaign against Athens targets the "usuring Senate" for abuse of power in the name of law (3.6.108). His purposeful action returns to social relationships, including friendship, the possibility of politics. It is in light of this possibility that I read Alcibiades's response to Timon's instructions to destroy all the people of Athens: "I'll take the gold thou givest me, / Not all thy counsel" (4.3.129–30). In accepting the gold but declining to deliver as instructed, Alcibiades not only disrupts the logic of exchange that would have commodified his political action as hired labor but also makes room for redefining friendship. Couched in the friendly intimacy of the word "counsel" and the pronoun "thy," Alcibiades's "not all" marks his refusal to be drawn into Timon's all-or-none proposition.

The full significance of Alcibiades's "not all" emerges against Timon's prior demand of Alcibiades to "promise me friendship, but perform none" (4.3.73). In refusing Timon's demand, Alcibiades reframes the terms of friendship, asserting his autonomy as a friend at once different from Timon and worthy of his trust. After all, trust can never be predicated: it can be proved only in the performance. In his reading of the play, Derrida notes that Timon means "to make the other promise not to keep his promise, that is, not to promise, even as he pretends to promise: to perjure or to abjure in the very moment of the oath." For Derrida, Timon is "addressing himself to prostitution or the cult of money," prostitutes being, in Timon's word, "unoathable."[48] But then neither is a true friend like Alcibiades oathable on Timon's terms. In asserting his difference as a friend, Alcibiades undoes the logic of likeness—that presumption of the centering self—and, with this, he refuses the impossible oath meant to conjure trust in the temporal lag between promise and performance. Alcibiades is thus poised to redefine the politics of friendship on his return to Athens, not to avenge (as Timon wishes and the Senators fear) but to negotiate peace on his own terms.

When the First Senator pleads with Alcibiades "to wipe out our ingratitude with loves / Above their quantity," and the Second offers him the option of indiscriminate revenge, "by decimation and a tithèd death, / . . . take thou the destined tenth," Alcibiades asks only that "those enemies of Timon's and mine own / Whom you yourselves shall set out for reproof, / Fall, and no more." He has in mind to "atone their [Athenians'] fears with [his] more noble meaning" (5.5.17–18, 31–33, 56–58, 58–59). One might wonder if Alcibiades effects political change at all, since he only enforces existing laws in prosecuting offenders of justice. Yet victory cuts a fine line between vindication and vindictiveness, and this is where Alcibiades's crucial intervention reimagines the possibility of friendship as the basis for the political. While the Senators deal in quantity and division, Alcibiades atones by rejecting the logic of exchange—and systemic injustice—underwriting the sacrifice of innocent common lives. In doing so, he reopens within calculation a horizon of peace beyond calculation, beyond the nascent capitalist groundings of the political status quo. Here the condition for democracy emerges, when commoners are valued as citizens and coproducers of political decisions, atonement implying the coproduction of oneness out of (potentially violent) differences. The political change Alcibiades aims for is thus radical in its relational and coproductive emphasis and, for this reason, fraught with uncertainty in its Cynic bid to "change the value of the [social] currency."

In reading Timon's epitaph, Alcibiades translates his friend's misanthropy into the impetus for his own revised politics of friendship, noting Timon's "rich conceit" in "mak[ing] vast Neptune weep for aye / On thy low grave, on faults forgiven." Just whose faults, and forgiven by whom, he leaves ambiguous—perhaps because forgiveness, contingent on everyone, belongs to no one. But the imperative to forgive is clear. Including his friend by name, Alcibiades reintegrates Timon Misanthropos posthumously into Athenian society: "Dead / Is noble Timon: of whose memory / Hereafter more." Moving forward, Alcibiades promises, "I will use the olive with my sword. / Make war breed peace, make peace stint war, make each / Prescribe to other as each other's leech" (5.5.82, 83–84, 84–86, 87–89). Nor can he specify just how war and peace would each prescribe to the other, but the goal of breeding peace and stinting war is unambiguous. Already begun in his measures of atonement, his performance recognizes that peace requires forgiveness, which is not just love but also a condition from which hate cannot be entirely exorcised, against which each person must be ever vigilant. With the politics of friendship thus repurposed, Timon becomes a collective memory—a being-beside-ourselves for Athenians—of hate and money's addictive potential. Alcibiades calls it a temporary stay, a "stint" against war, because democracy was, still is, the struggle that has only just begun.

Within the political theater Alcibiades calls into operation, then, his immediate audience is made to recognize that misanthropy is, always has been, a part of business as usual, a systemic poison that can make users out of persons so predisposed. Timon's hunger in the forest becomes, in retrospect, the originary moment of misanthropy's emergence, anachronistic and displaced, which is already built into the cyclic continuity of the Athenian political economy. Insofar as Alcibiades stakes his political theater on friendship and redefines friendship away from the centering to the relational and coproductive self, the horizon of peace he establishes extends beyond the ruling body of Athens not only to its citizens but also to audiences both in and outside the play. As the play would have it, Alcibiades's performance is brilliant political theater, something even a common soldier would know: "Our captain hath in every figure skill," being "an aged interpreter, though young in days" (5.4.5–6). One may wonder whether this staging of political theater doesn't simply substitute one charismatic figure for the other, marking his emergence of yet another consumable "reality." But what the play offers goes beyond passive consumption in dramatizing through its linkage of hate with consumption in its diverse senses, from the physical activity of eating and economic activity of consumers, to the biopolitics of revenge, and the biopsychosocial cycle of the addict, the consumer who is ultimately consumed by hate, by addiction's inflexive desire for more of the same.

If we further consider Alcibiades's politics of remembrance and atonement as a bid for democracy, then, it is possible that the play reinvents him and Timon in order to "potentialize the past that never was" in devising a means to a viable future.[49] In this sense, Alcibiades stands beside Timon as another figure for theater, and his relational politics of friendship affords a rich vantage point from which to explore theater's coproductive fictions. Inhabiting modes of being beside ourselves, theater's aesthetic is political because it is neither totalizing nor totalizable.[50] In representational and performative terms, the closeness of theater's fiction to everyday life has always been an invitation for some and a source of discomfit and even threat for others. To the extent that *Timon of Athens* successfully engages an audience to participate in its fiction through the aesthetic commoning of hunger, theater has found a means to motivate the audience's sensuous, passionate, and cocreative energies in its socially responsive endeavor. As such, theater is never more relevant than now in our culture of late capitalism, with its information technologies, social media, and their power in the production of consumable realities that strain our far from perfect institutions of democracy.

Notes

1. Scholars have established the play's relevance to contemporary socioeconomic developments, specifically, to the emerging networks of credit at a time when there were no banks in London, building on Craig Muldrew's *The Economy of Obligation: The Culture of Credit and Social Relations in Early Modern England* (New York: Palgrave Macmillan, 1998). Even as credit entailed a new

institutional sense of trust, it raised questions as to how this would redefine social relationships that are likewise based on trust. Addressing the crisis of debt in early modern London (as a cash-poor economy), Amanda Bailey, in *Of Bondage: Debt, Property, and Personhood in Early Modern England* (Philadelphia: University of Pennsylvania Press, 2013), attends to the harsher side of debt bondage, in which a debtor who defaulted on a loan would come under a legal ban and be abandoned by the law to the discretion of the creditor.

2. Jacques Derrida, *The Politics of Friendship*, trans. George Collins (London: Verso, 1997), ix.

3. John Jowett, "Middleton and Debt in *Timon of Athens*," in *Money and the Age of Shakespeare: Essays in New Economic Criticism*, ed. Linda Woodbridge (New York: Palgrave Macmillan, 2003), 228.

4. Both Alcibiades and Apemantus are reinvented figures drawn from accounts of Timon in Plutarch's *Lives*.

5. William Shakespeare [and Thomas Middleton], *The Life of Timon of Athens*, in *The Norton Shakespeare*, ed. Stephen Greenblatt, Walter Cohen, Jean E. Howard, and Katharine Eisaman Maus (New York: Norton, 1997), 1.2.84, 95–98. References to the play are to this edition and hereafter cited parenthetically.

6. Aristotle, *Nicomachean Ethics*, trans. Robert C. Bartlett and Susan D. Collins (Chicago: University of Chicago Press, 2011), VIII.3, 1156^{b}7; V.1, 1129^{b}27, 1130^{a}4–5.

7. Aristotle, *Politics*, trans. H. Rackman (Cambridge, Mass.: Harvard University Press, 1990), II.2.6, 1263^{a}40.

8. *Politics* I.iii.23, p. 51.

9. *Politics* II.ii.6, II.iv.12, pp. 89, 119.

10. *Nicomachean Ethics*, VIII.iii.25, VIII.vi.11, pp. 168, 172.

11. Eric Spencer, "Taking Excess, Exceeding Account: Aristotle Meets *The Merchant of Venice*," in Woodbridge, *Money*, 143.

12. Peter Remien, "Oeconomy and Ecology in Early Modern England," *PMLA* 132, no. 5 (October 2017): 1123.

13. Aristotle, *Nicomachean Ethics*, IX.iv.30–32, p. 194, IX.viii.6–18, pp. 201–2.

14. Aristotle, *Nicomachean Ethics: Books VIII and IX*, trans. Michael Pakaluk (Oxford: Clarendon Press, 1998), 94.

15. Remien, "Oeconomy and Ecology," 1122.

16. Critics have compared Timon's bounty to a precapitalist form of political contest: the potlatch. In this case, the rival he takes on would not be another Athenian leader but the system of credit itself. John Jowett provides an overview in *Timon of Athens* (Oxford: Oxford University Press, 2011), 32.

17. Laurence Fontaine, *The Moral Economy: Poverty, Culture, and Trust in Early Modern Europe* (Cambridge: Cambridge University Press, 2008), 220–22.

18. See Glynn Wickham, "The Popular Image of the Stage Player," in *English Professional Theatre, 1530–1660*, ed. Glynne Wickham, Herbert Berry, and William Ingram (Cambridge: Cambridge University Press, 2000), 166, 167, 170, 179.

19. References to whoredom abound in antitheatrical tracts of the time, as documented in Tanya Pollard, ed., *Shakespeare's Theater: A Sourcebook* (Malden, Mass.: Blackwell Publishing, 2004). Attacks were fueled by the fact that "theaters were regularly situated near brothels, drinking houses, and other places of ill repute, and shared the stigmas of their neighbors" (xii).

20. Rebecca Lemon, *Addiction and Devotion in Early Modern England* (Philadelphia: University of Pennsylvania Press, 2018), xiii.

21. I discuss the "topology of enchantments and disenchantments" and the coproduction of charisma in "Charisma and the Making of the Misanthrope in *Timon of Athens*," in *Enchantment and Dis-enchantment in Shakespearean and Early Modern Drama*, ed. Nandini Das and Nick Davis (New York: Routledge, 2017), 124, 126.

22. Anitra Nelson, *Marx's Concept of Money: The God of Commodities* (London: Routledge, 1999), 17, 20.

23. Crystal Bartolovich, "Marx's Shakespeare," in *Great Shakespeareans, Volume 10: Marx and Freud*, by Crystal Bartolovich, Jean E. Howard, and David Hillman (London: Continuum, 2012), 28.

24. Chris Fitter, *Radical Shakespeare: Politics and Stagecraft in the Early Career* (New York: Routledge, 2012), 27.

25. Karl Marx, "Economic and Philosophical Manuscripts (1844)," in *Early Writings*, trans. Rodney Livingstone and Gregor Benton (New York: Vintage Books, 1975), 377, 379.

26. Karl Marx, *Grundrisse: Foundations of the Critique of Political Economy*, trans. Martin Nicolaus (London: Penguin Classics, 1973), 244.

27. Karl Marx, *Capital: A Critique of Political Economy*, vol. 1, trans. Ben Fowkes (New York: Penguin Books, 1990), 229–30.

28. Marx, "Economic and Philosophical Manuscripts," 390.

29. Marx, *Grundrisse*, 485.

30. Addressing more broadly alchemical ambivalence in Renaissance discourse, Karen Pinkus, *Alchemical Mercury: A Theory of Ambivalence* (Stanford, Calif.: Stanford University Press, 2010), 58–60, relates such ambivalence back to Aristotle's and Thomas Aquinas's and forward to Marx's conceptions of value and political economy.

31. Margaret Healy, *Shakespeare, Alchemy, and the Creative Imagination: The Sonnets and "A Lover's Complaint"* (Cambridge: Cambridge University Press, 201), 33.

32. Marx, "Economic and Philosophical Manuscripts," 390.

33. Jowett, "Middleton and Debt," 229.

34. *Nicomachean Ethics*, VI.v.5, 9, pp. 120–21.

35. Henry W. Pickford, "Poiêsis, Praxis, Aisthesis: Remarks on Aristotle and Marx," in *Aesthetic Marx*, edited by Samir Gandesha and Johan F. Hartle (London: Bloomsbury Academic Press, 2017), 39–41.

36. Frances Barasch, "Performing Apemantus in Shakespeare's *Timon of Athens*," in *Acts of Criticism: Performance Matters in Shakespeare and His Contemporaries*, ed. Paul Nelson and June Schlueter, 111–25 (Madison, N.J.: Fairleigh Dickinson University Press, 2006), observes that "Apemantus' role helps to clarify Shakespeare's intention to distinguish misanthropy from Cynic philosophy." Specifically, "although Timon has learned to hate flattery and hypocrisy, he has demeaned himself by excessive hatred" (122). See also Jowett's introduction to the Oxford edition of *Timon of Athens*, in which he sums up critical opinion on Apemantus as the figure of the Cynic philosopher in the play, associating the character through multiple "dog" references with the Cynic Diogenes (75–77).

37. Christopher Pye, *The Storm at Sea: Political Aesthetics in the Time of Shakespeare* (New York: Fordham University Press, 2015), 107.

38. Michel Foucault, *Hermeneutics of the Subject: Lectures at the Collège de France, 1981—1982*, ed. Frédéric Gros, trans. Graham Burchell (New York: Palgrave Macmillan, 2005), 230, 235, 237, 238, 242.

39. While Apemantus agrees to spread word about Timon's gold, "I'll say th'hast gold" (4.3.398), the play does not show him doing so. The words "wood" and "woods" occur six times in the play, while "forest" occurs only once. Apemantus is the only character to use both words, and he does so, I believe, to connote a difference. Where "woods" connotes wilderness and lack of cultivation, "forest" is "a tract of wooded land in England formerly owned by the sovereign and used for game" (Merriam-Webster, https://www.merriam-webster.com/dictionary/forest).

40. Richard D. Fly, "The Ending of 'Timon of Athens,'" *Criticism* 15, no. 3 (Summer 1973): 251, cites the following lines in presenting the suicide possibility: "My long sickness / Of health and living now begins to mend, / And nothing brings me all things" (5.1.184–86). D. Douglas Waters, "Shakespeare's *Timon of Athens* and Catharsis," *Upstart Crow* 8 (1988): 102, finds the textual evidence to be more ambiguous.

41. Lemon, *Addiction and Devotion in Early Modern England*, x.

42. Michel Foucault, *The Courage of the Truth: The Government of Self and Others II; Lectures at the Collège de France, 1983–1984*, ed. Frédéric Gros, trans. Graham Burchell (New York: Palgrave Macmillan, 2011), 227. According to Diogenes Laertes, the principle originated from a Delphic oracle given to Diogenes the Cynic.

43. As Elizabeth Rivlin, *The Aesthetics of Service in Early Modern England* (Evanston, Ill.: Northwestern University Press, 2012), 3, explains, the early modern conception of service is "fundamentally a representational practice."

44. Michael Noschka, "Thinking Hospitality with *Timon of Athens*: Towards an Ethics of Stewardship," in *Shakespeare and Hospitality: Ethics, Politics, and Exchange*, ed. David B. Goldstein and Julia Reinhard Lupton (New York: Routledge, 2016), 243, 254–55.

45. Quoted in Rivlin, *Aesthetics*, 15. As a representational practice, aesthetic service "exposes [servants'] potential to substitute for, and even supplant, their masters," a "license" didactic texts like Thomas Fosert's *The Servants Dutie* (1613) guard against (3, 15).

46. Pye, *The Storm at Sea*, discusses Shakespearean distraction in relation to aesthetic subjectivity: "that knowing distraction, a knowledge of the fact of one's inevitable inscription, is the psychic correlative of the emerging condition of aesthetic subjectivity" (107).

47. My analysis of Alcibiades in this and subsequent paragraphs revises and extends some points from a previous essay, "Charisma and the Making of the Misanthrope," in Das and Davis, *Enchantment and Dis-enchantment*, 129–30.

48. Jacques Derrida, *Specters of Marx: The State of the Debt, the Work of Mourning, and the New International*, trans. Peggy Kamuf (New York: Routledge, 1994), 43, 44.

49. Leonard Goldstein, "Alcibiades' Revolt in *Timon of Athens*," *Zeitschrift für Anglistik und Amerikanistik* 15 (1967): 257–78, recapitulates the critical

reception of Alcibiades as a positive counterpart to Timon in the sense that the former can adjust to the socioeconomic changes while the latter cannot. Goldstein sees Alcibiades's reformatory role as a conservative move that shows the play rationalizing "bourgeois progress" as development "in the interests of society and hence 'the people,'" thus giving the impression that "the contradictions of society at that stage of the development of capitalism are solvable" (276–77). My divergent reading builds on Giorgio Agamben's discussion of remembrance in *Potentialities: Collected Essays in Philosophy*, trans. and ed. Daniel Heller-Roazen (Stanford, Calif.: Stanford University Press, 1999): "Remembrance restores possibility to the past, making what happened incomplete and completing what never was. Remembrance is neither what happened nor what did not happen, but, rather, their potentialization, their becoming possible once again" (267).

50. This grounding of theater's political aesthetic approaches the challenge of "thinking 'democracy'" in Jean-Luc Nancy, "Is Everything Political," in *The Truth of Democracy*, trans. Pascale-Anne Brault and Michael Naas (New York: Fordham University Press, 2010), 51.

From Political Theology to Political Aesthetics in *A Midsummer Night's Dream*

Jennifer R. Rust

"Bottom's Dream" at the end of act 4 of Shakespeare's *A Midsummer Night's Dream* has long been recognized as an extended allusion to Saint Paul's First Letter to the Corinthians. This passage also develops a complex version of political aesthetics. In this essay, I trace how the peculiar aesthetics of Bottom's discourse are intertwined with the theological and political concerns of the Pauline text. The aesthetics of "Bottom's Dream" are intrinsically linked to the way that Paul's epistle composes the mystical body, a major trope for religious and social order in premodern Europe.[1] Paul's text develops the incarnational and eschatological elements of the mystical body that will form the foundation for a liturgical tradition that remained resonant into the sixteenth century. This tradition was closely linked to the paraliturgical practices of mystery plays, practices clearly referenced in the theatrical activities of Bottom and his companions.[2] The Pauline mystical body incarnates the Christian community as members of a larger body of Christ; this communal body also exists in multiple temporal dimensions, as it fulfills past prophecies and looks forward to a final future fulfillment at the end of history. Bottom's allusive vision maintains an essential relation to the eschatological aspects of the Pauline original even as its synesthetic elements reimagine the incarnational dimensions of Paul's text. "Bottom's Dream" merges aesthetics with politics and theology, but this aesthetics cannot be reduced to either pure politics or theology. Ultimately, the multifaceted character of this aesthetic vision resists becoming assimilated to the instrumental politics of the Athenian elite at the end of the play.

In order to appreciate how Bottom's aesthetic vision reconfigures Pauline concepts, it is helpful to begin with a brief review of the original scriptural text to which Bottom alludes: 1 Corinthians 2:6–10. The precise translation that Shakespeare adapts in Bottom's speech is still uncertain, with several variant sources evidently in play. However, one of the relevant variants is clearly the text of the Bishops' Bible of 1573:

> And we speak of wisdom among them that are perfect: not the wisdom of this world, neither of the princes of this world, which come to nought.
> But we speak the wisdom of God in a mystery, even the hid wisdom, which God ordained before the world, unto our glory.
> Which none of the princes of this world know: for had they known it, they would not have crucified the Lord of glory.
> But as it is written, The eye hath not seen, and the ear hath not heard, neither have entered into the heart of man, the things which God hath prepared for them that love him.
> But God hath revealed them unto us by his spirit: for the spirit searcheth all things, yea, the deep things of God.[3]

Critics have noted that Shakespeare also seems to draw upon the 1557 Geneva translation, a clear source of biblical allusions in his other plays. The Geneva text preserves Tyndale's original translation of "depths" as "bottom," a detail that strengthens the allusive resonance of this passage for *A Midsummer Night's Dream*.[4] The 1557 Geneva New Testament reads as follows:

> And we speak wisdom among them that are perfect: not the wisdom of this world, neither of the chiefest of this world which come to nought.
> But we speak of the wisdom of God, *which is hid* in a mystery, *to wit*, the secret *wisdom*, which God ordained before the world, unto our glory.
> Which wisdom none of the heads of this world knew: for had they known it, they would not have crucified the Lord of glory.
> But *we preach* as it is written, Things which eye hath not seen, and ear hath not heard, neither have entered into man's mind, which things God hath prepared for them that love him.
> But God hath opened *them* unto us by his Spirit, for the Spirit searcheth all things, yea, the bottom of God's secrets.[5]

From the perspective of the 1557 text, the eponymous "Bottom" is an absurd signifier of God's providence. The play's eclectic combination of variant translations of 1 Corinthians 2 into Bottom's discourse accords with the spirit of his larger aesthetic scheme: the authority of received understandings of Scripture is destabilized, deconstructed, and rearranged, along with the traditional metaphorics of the body they convey.

These iterations of 1 Corinthians 2 highlight an eschatological dimension in the convergence of aesthetics, politics, and theology in Bottom's speech. Bottom is the most appropriate figure to articulate this convergence as the absurd yet also peculiarly charismatic representative of art, as such, in the play. Bottom embodies art in its lower, artisanal sense—insofar as he is a weaver by profession—and in an aspirational higher sense insofar as he is a would-be tragic actor and poet. As he is released from the eroticized phantasmagoria of his interlude as the ass-headed lover of Titania, Bottom struggles to articulate his experience and its possible implications for art:

> When my cue comes, call me, and I will answer. My next is "Most fair Pyramus." Heigh-ho! Peter Quince! Flute, the bellows mender! Snout, the tinker! Starveling! God's my life, stolen hence and left me asleep! I have had a most rare vision. I have had a dream, past the wit of man to say what dream it was. Man is but an ass if he go about to expound this dream. Methought I was—there is no man can tell what. Methought I was—and methought I had—but man is but a patched fool if he will offer to say what methought I had. The eye of man hath not heard, the ear of man hath not seen, man's hand is not able to taste, his tongue to conceive, nor his heart to report what my dream was. I will get Peter Quince to write a ballad of this dream. It shall be called "Bottom's Dream," because it hath no bottom; and I will sing it in the latter end of a play, before the Duke. Peradventure, to make it the more gracious, I shall sing it at her death. (4.1.195–209)

The beginning and end of Bottom's speech are framed in metatheatrical terms, foreshadowing his role as the star actor in *Pyramus and Thisbe* and heightening the association between his visionary experience and the realm of artistic production. Bottom speaks at first as if he were still in the midst of the rehearsal with his fellow artisan-actors, as if the intervening acts had never happened: "When my cue comes, call me, and I will answer. My next is . . ." Already, the temporality of Bottom's experience is awry: in his captivation, he has been removed from the flow of linear time, cut out of the plot of ordinary events. This temporal confusion continues more subtly as Bottom recounts his dream and the artistic work it inspires: at one moment, Bottom asserts that the experience of the dream is something that man "is not able" to grasp or convey; in the next moment, the presence of the dream itself has slipped into the past ("what my dream was"), only to be immediately resurrected as a prospective form of art ("I will sing it . . . I shall sing it at her death"). The dream maintains a form of abyssal presence ("it hath no bottom"), yet it demands a creative recapitulation in the future ("it shall be called 'Bottom's Dream'"). The dream wavers between contradictory temporal modes.

The asynchronous character of Bottom's "most rare vision" correlates to the sensory derangement of his famously disordered allusion to Paul's epistle. While Bottom's name may be derived from the Geneva version of Paul's text, his precise phrasing more clearly echoes the syntax of the Bishops' translation ("the eye of man hath not heard, the ear of man hath not seen . . ."), although in Bottom's rendition, the sensory organs are confused to produce a synesthetic effect, and the passage pushes hyperbolically beyond the original to include many other parts of the body ("man's hand is not able to taste, his tongue to conceive, nor his heart to report"). Bottom's aesthetic, the vision he seeks to translate into the "ballad" of "Bottom's Dream," pairs synesthetic experience with eschatological temporality. This aesthetic is as much a matter of time as of sensation. Both time and sensation are processed through a theological paradigm, but they also diverge from it, a divergence marked by Bottom's obvious garbling of the Pauline text. It is this simultaneous proximity and difference from theology that is the unique feature of this aesthetics. This dynamic implicitly opens a way to reimagine the body as a trope of social order. It also sets the stage for a later collision between Bottom's aesthetics and a political hierarchy that strives to instrumentalize any aesthetic articulation.

The synesthetic qualities of Bottom's allusive vision warp the incarnational and eschatological dimensions of the Pauline text, without ever fully effacing it. Through this distortion of the scriptural text, Bottom's vision generates a peculiar aesthetic with a relative degree of autonomy. Yet at the same time, insofar as the allusive text remains legible within Bottom's speech, this aesthetic cannot be considered a secularization of the Pauline trope in any coherent sense: Bottom's vision distorts, but it neither empties out nor rationalizes the theological tradition to which it alludes. As a kind of paraliturgy, it persists alongside and in relation to—not in place of—a theological tradition that grants it greater depth and resonance. Insofar as it maintains a relation to the idea of the mystical body, the scriptural allusion affiliates Bottom's aesthetic with larger social and political questions, particularly since the allusion is part of a larger elaboration on the nature of Christian community. Previous critics have highlighted the potential political edge that the Pauline context lends to Bottom's reflection, particularly insofar as it enhances the sense of class tensions between the Athenian ruling class and the "rude mechanicals," tensions that mirror the conflicts that Paul attempted to negotiate among the Corinthians.[6] In contrast to some of these critics, however, I want to emphasize that the social, political, and religious tensions embedded in Bottom's allusive discourse cannot be separated from its aesthetic character, even if this aesthetic is neither a fully discrete sphere nor a coherently realized form of secularity.[7]

To develop a more precise understanding of what is at stake in this aesthetic vision, I draw upon Jacques Rancière's capacious definition of aesthetics as originary politics. Rancière's claim that the aesthetic is a "distribution of the sensible" that is the condition of possibility of any politics is particularly apt for capturing the aesthetic dynamic in Shakespeare's play.[8] The political aesthetics and political theology implicit in Bottom's visionary discourse emerge more explicitly through the dialogic response that frames them in the final act of the play as Theseus and Hippolyta stake out divergent positions on the status of the aesthetic, its relative autonomy, and the possibility of instrumentalizing it to serve the purposes of political hierarchy.

The synesthetic ecstasy of Bottom's speech conjoins the incarnational and eschatological into a distinctive aesthetic, and Rancière's reflections on affinities between incarnational theology and literary aesthetics bring the political and theological implications of this conjunction into sharper focus. Rancière's concepts help to highlight the social and political significance of Bottom's speech and its intertexts, which include not only the allusion to Paul's First Letter to the Corinthians but also a less-frequently recognized intertext, Erasmus's *The Praise of Folly*. Both of these allusive contexts reinforce the sense that Bottom's speech aesthetically refigures the Christian mystical body.

Rancière is better known for his claims about political aesthetics than for his engagement with theology, but his elaboration on incarnational theology and novelistic discourse offers some insights into the political and aesthetic stakes of Bottom's allusive dream, despite differences in genre and historical context. A brief review of both interventions is relevant in this context. In *The Politics of Aesthetics*, Rancière claims, "There is an 'aesthetics' at the core of politics."[9] The aesthetic is essentially political for Rancière because it "discloses the existence of something in common and the delimitations that define the respective parts and positions within it."[10] A "primary aesthetics" determines what can be seen and said, and who can speak and participate in a given community at any historical moment; the experience of the "possibilities of time" is also a component of "primary aesthetics."[11] The arts are fundamentally political insofar as they play a vital role in forming these determinations of communal experience. Rancière's concept of "primary aesthetics" offers a way of understanding how the aesthetic can be a meaningful category even prior to its explicit theorization in the eighteenth century. This concept also illuminates how shifts in the manifestation of the aesthetic, such as those conveyed in Bottom's speech, can have profound political implications.

While Rancière does not address the theology of incarnation as such in relation to the "distribution of the sensible," he does explore the aesthetic implications of theological discourse in a work of literary criticism, *The Flesh of Words*, in terms that are significant for understanding Bottom's moment in *A Midsummer Night's Dream*.[12] In an essay that begins as a critique of Auerbach's interpretation of Peter's denial of Christ in the Gospel of Mark, Rancière outlines "two theologies" of the novel that may be derived from this sequence; these are also two theologies of incarnation: "two relationships of the written to the body, two relationships of presence to absence, two theologies of the body of truth of Scripture" that produce "two ideas of the relationship between the body of writing and the body of fiction."[13] The first "theology" emphasizes a logic of typological fulfillment—in which one body calls forth another: "The figure is the bearer of a double reality: the *figurative* reality of its material production and the *figural* reality of its relationship with the body-to-come of its truth."[14] This version of incarnational theology is structured around the need for prophetic fulfillment; its prototype is the demand that the Old Testament be read in light of the New Testament. In this incarnational aesthetic, "the figural, present/absent in the figurative, makes the figurative an infinite reserve, an infinite capacity of the mind to produce at the same time images, consonances, fables and exegeses, to produce meaning in images."[15] Rancière associates this theology with Augustine, and, in the longer term, with a modern fictional tradition that includes the "hermeneutic intrigue" of writers such as Henry James, Joyce, and Borges.[16] The second theology involves the incarnation of the work as it is affirmed by the material suffering body, a theology originally associated with Tertullian: "There must always be the sacrifice of a new body to make the truth of a body of writing come."[17] In this conception, the ascetic suffering body guarantees the truth of Scripture. The sacrifice of the body reduces writing to materiality, which is the original aspiration of monastic copying, "a pure labor of mortification."[18] The literary heir of this second incarnational theology is Cervantes's Don Quixote: "Don Quixote presents his madness as equivalent of the madness of mystics, offering their bodies for the verification of the message, all the way to the limit of non-meaning."[19] Don Quixote's madness is driven by the desire to incarnate the fictional worlds of romance. Rancière ultimately claims that these two opposed incarnational models of aesthetic discourse are perpetually "intermingled" in the modern fictional tradition; these incarnational strategies turn out to be intertwined in the aesthetic regime of modernity.[20]

Rancière applies his insights specifically to the realm of modern novelistic discourse, but we can see similar tensions between these two incarnational concepts in Bottom's speech and its invocation of the Pauline mystical body; the "intermingling" of these incarnational theologies generates Bottom's unique aesthetic discourse. In Bottom's soliloquy, a figural, prophetic theology of incarnation is conflated with the embodied material experience of Bottom's absurd, if not exactly suffering, body. The prophetic strain enters in Bottom's botched rendition of Paul's eschatological discourse: "The eye of man hath not heard, the ear of man hath not seen, man's hand is not able to taste, his tongue to conceive, nor his heart to report what my dream was." The original Pauline text of 1 Corinthians 2 incorporates a citation of an Old Testament text—"they have not heard nor understand with the eare, nether hathe the eye sene *another* God beside thee, which doeth *so* to him that waiteth for him" (Isaiah 64:4)—and anticipates the fulfillment of its vision.[21] This detail emphasizes the typological dimension of Paul's discourse—a "prophetic" mode of incarnation, as Rancière would put it—embedded in the admonition of the Corinthians and, by extension, into Bottom's vision, which seeks to fulfill itself as a "ballad." However, Bottom's sensory confusion also draws attention to the materiality of the body in this allusion; the misalignment of the body parts and their senses makes the body more prominent in Bottom's variation, anticipating Bottom's later "palpable-gross play" (5.1.343). The prophetic elements of Bottom's discourse collide with his perhaps unwitting reference to the late transformations of his own body: "Man is but an ass if he go about to expound this dream." While Bottom is no longer literally an ass, his lines conjure his recently translated state. And since he goes on to "expound" the dream anyway, in garbled prophetic language, he figuratively becomes an ass yet again. The incarnational tensions that Bottom confronts in his awakening speech are neither canceled nor resolved—they have "no bottom" after all. Instead, they are ultimately channeled into an aesthetic creation—the "ballad" of "Bottom's Dream" that Quince will write. Bottom's speech highlights how tensions between two forms of incarnation may form a primary aesthetic without being fully evacuated of their theological content. This aesthetic has the potential to distribute its version of sensibility insofar as it unfolds into a ballad intended for communal performance; that this performance is finally thwarted at the end of the play by the authority of the Duke—who commands, "Let your epilogue alone" (5.1.337–38)—underscores the politically destabilizing potential of Bottom's artistic vision.

This destabilization is already implicit in the way that Bottom's speech deranges the larger concept of the mystical body as articulated in Paul's discourse. The passage from 1 Corinthians to which Bottom alludes is part of a longer sequence of the epistle in which Paul addresses the social disarray of the Corinthians by developing the metaphor of the community as "one body" of Christ: "For as the body is one, and hath many members and all members of one body, though they be many, yet are but one body: even so is Christ" (1 Cor. 12:12). This conception evolves into the performative tradition of the liturgical mystical body in the medieval and early modern eras.[22] Previous critics have found several elements of this larger Pauline context relevant to analyzing the underlying social tensions in *A Midsummer Night's Dream*. Specifically, they have observed that Paul's attempts to mediate class tensions in Corinth through the concept of the body of Christ and a reversal of values that privileges the "foolishness" of the godly over the wisdom of "this world" (1 Cor. 3:18–19) resonate with efforts to negotiate similar tensions in Shakespeare's comedy.[23] As these critics have emphasized, Paul's theological concepts are suffused with a political significance that carries over into Shakespeare's allusive text.

In this context, I want to stress that recognizing the aesthetic dimensions of Bottom's speech enhances rather than effaces the political theological elements derived from the Pauline context.[24] Bottom aestheticizes Paul's text by rearranging its body; Bottom's vision does not dissolve the bodily figure for community as such but suggests that it might be assembled (or, to use Rancière's term, "distributed") differently. Bottom echoes not only 1 Corinthians 2 but also a later passage in the epistle where Paul explicitly evokes an image of bodily confusion to heighten his call for social unity:

> If all the body *were* an eye, where were the hearing? If all were hearing: where were the smelling?
> But now hath God disposed the members every one of them a part in the body, at his own pleasure.
> If they were all one member, where *were* the body?
> But now are there many members, yet but one body.
> And the eye cannot say unto the hand, I have no need of thee: nor the head also to the feet, I have no need of you. (1 Cor. 12:17–21)

On one level, Paul imagines a collapse of the sensorium that bears a passing resemblance to Bottom's synesthetic confusion. This might suggest that Bottom's synesthesia is a disruption of divine government—the "disposition" or economy of the body that God has determined "at his own pleasure" beyond human wisdom. However, Paul is actually arguing against a static, overdetermined notion of the body that would collapse all the senses into one organ, all the organs into one sense; his argument presents a model of the human and social body as dynamic and interdependent ("many members, yet but one body"), a body in which even the lowest "member" may be seen as "necessary" (1 Cor. 12:22) and possessing "beauty" (1 Cor. 12:23). It is this paradoxical inversion of expectations about the body to which Bottom's incarnational vision remains faithful. Bottom challenges the common understanding of how the body functions, but this disorientation is actually consistent with the Pauline message. Jennifer Waldron emphasizes this aspect of Bottom's allusion, which "redirects the Pauline epistles towards a post-Reformation performance theory that is centered on the body even as it is strikingly decentered by the body's distributed functions and collective properties."[25] Waldron discusses Bottom's Pauline context in phenomenological and performative terms, but I want to emphasize that this "de-centering" can also be understood in terms of political aesthetics. The body—with all its theological, political, and social resonances—remains the organizing metaphor, but its essential organs and functions are redistributed, and its sensorium is rewired: eyes can see, ears can hear, tongues can "conceive." In its mutation of the body metaphor, Bottom's vision proposes a reconfiguration of the sociopolitical order that is consistent with the sprit, if not the letter, of the Pauline text. The eschatological overtones of Bottom's speech reinforce the continuity with the Pauline context as the body that is spatially reconfigured maintains the temporal complexity of the original conception of the mystical body.

The eschatological dimension of the incarnational theology underlying "Bottom's Dream" further emerges when a secondary allusive context is recognized: Erasmus's *The Praise of Folly*. Several critics have suggested that *A Midsummer Night's Dream* alludes to Erasmus's *Folly*, making the connection through the two texts' citations of 1 Corinthians 2:9 at a crucial moment.[26] The synesthetic apprehension of the mystical body in Bottom's soliloquy amplifies an eschatological dimension already present in the original Pauline text and in the Erasmian intertext. The context of the citation of 1 Corinthians 2:9 in *The Praise of Folly* is the supposedly serious concluding exploration of the state of the "holy fool," a state that persuasively approximates Bottom's ecstasy in 4.1. Erasmus recapitulates and extends Paul's paradoxical insistence on the weakest and most foolish as the most privileged to spiritual insight—"God hath chosen the foolish things of the world, to confound the wise" (1 Cor. 1:27)—a trope that also anticipates Bottom's position in the final acts of Shakespeare's play. Erasmus further highlights how the visionary reveries of holy Christian fools are essentially eschatological in nature. The mediation of the "spiritual" fool is an anticipation, a "taste or savor," of the "highest reward."[27] It is striking that "taste" is the persistent metaphor for this temporal anticipation: in this formulation, the temporal is translated into the sensory in a way that is reminiscent of synesthesia. A future spiritual state would seem immaterial, yet throughout this passage it is cast as something to be "tasted." In this way, the passage presents a merging of the eschatological and the synesthetic later echoed in Bottom's aesthetic vision. Erasmus's *The Praise of Folly* also emphasizes the inherent excess of this visionary state as an experience that "exceedeth all bodily pleasures" in the same passage where the direct citation of 1 Corinthians 2:9 occurs:

> For this undoubtedly is even the very guerdon that the Prophet promiseth, saying, *was never man's eye saw, nor ear heard, nor thought of heart yet compassed, what, and how great felicity god hath prepared unto such as do love him*.[28]

The Praise of Folly further elaborates on this condition:

> Who so ever therefore have such grace . . . by their life time to taste of this said felicity, they are subject to a certain passion much like unto madness . . . when ravished so in the spirit, or being in a trance then do speak certain things not hanging one with another, nor after any earthly fashion, but rather do put forth a voice they wot never what, much less to be understood of others.[29]

A bit later, this state is compared to a confusion of "waking or sleeping": "it is certain that they are wholly distraught and rapt out of themselves."[30] And, again, it is reinforced that such a state is inherently eschatological, the result of achieving a "thin taste of their bliss to come," the reference to "taste" again highlighting a synesthetic experience.[31] Folly's account of the prophetic "trance" of the holy fool has significant parallels to Bottom's discourse in 4.1. This intertext invites us to understand Bottom's linguistic lapses as expressions of temporal as much as of sensory confusion: "things not hanging one with another." Insofar as Bottom is like the holy fools caught between "waking and sleeping," he is out of synch with his present being, already inhabiting a "bliss to come." For an aesthetic reading, it is important that Bottom wants to encompass the eschatological ecstasy that Erasmus describes within the writing of a "ballad" that would be able to transmit this dislocated sensory and temporal experience to a larger audience. In envisioning his ballad, Bottom aestheticizes the eschatological. This aestheticization is further layered onto the sociopolitical-theological construct of the Pauline mystical body, which itself already contains eschatological impulses.

Both these intertexts demonstrate that Bottom's synesthetic discourse reconfigures the sociopolitical concept and eschatological dimensions of the mystical body. However, Bottom's aesthetic reconfiguration of the Pauline mystical body resists being categorized as a kind of secularization, if the secular is understood as a form of linear progression or a rationalization of irrational prior traditions. In this claim, I differ from Hugh Grady's otherwise perspicacious account of the aesthetic in *A Midsummer Night's Dream*. Drawing on Adorno, Grady claims, "Bottom's parodic allusions to Paul's Epistle by no means suggest a literal claim for divine insight . . . Bottom is being secular and true to aesthetics, rather than theological . . . the veiled allusions to the divine serve as metaphors for an experience that is otherwise coded secular and natural, if marvelous: the concept-without-a-name, the aesthetic."[32] But it is precisely the temporal complexity of this allusive moment that marks it as aesthetic beyond any opposition between secular and sacred. Such an understanding of the aesthetic is actually made available in Adorno's theory, particularly insofar as it acknowledges that the aesthetic incorporates an element of eschatology. This dynamic is visible at key moments in Adorno's *Aesthetic Theory*. For example, Adorno claims,

> In their relation to empirical reality, artworks recall the theologumenon that in the redeemed world everything would be as it is and yet wholly other. There is no mistaking the analogy with the tendency of the profane to secularize the realm of the sacred to the point that only as secularized does the latter endure; the realm of the sacred is objectified, effectively staked off, because its own element of untruth at once awaits secularization and through conjuration wards off the secular.[33]

Adorno uses the dynamic of secularization as an analogy to emphasize that the aesthetic cannot be contained within its own present moment; it is enclosed within its phenomenal manifestation and also simultaneously outside or in excess of it. Interestingly, in this analogy, the work of art occupies an eschatological space: it is the "redeemed world" in which nothing—and everything—has changed. Because it is essentially dialectical, the aesthetic work both invites the work of secularization and also continually thwarts it, failing to settle into a final "objective" form. While we need not understand Adorno to be making theological or religious claims for art, his insistence on the dialectical dynamic of the aesthetic work should not be collapsed into an understanding that the aesthetic is equivalent to the secular. Maura Nolan also stresses this aspect of Adorno's theory, which she finds particularly valuable for the way in which it disrupts conventional historicist perspectives: Adorno's aesthetic theory refuses to be confined to any "singular thesis of secularization," and any claim it appears to make about the secularity of art "takes its place . . . as part of an endless contradictory process of development and change."[34] We can see further examples of this dynamic elsewhere in Adorno's text as he continues to draw upon theological language to characterize the inherent instability of the aesthetic: "In the incineration of appearance, artworks break away in a glare from the empirical world and become the counterfigure of what lives there; art today is scarcely conceivable except as a form of reaction that anticipates the apocalypse."[35] The aesthetic perpetually oscillates between the secular and the sacred; this instability is its condition of possibility. The aesthetic is disjoined from the coordinates of secular temporality, which are instrumentalizing insofar as they impose a scheme of linear progress, in contrast to the "apocalyptic" temporality of art, which ruptures such linear schemes. Adorno thus recognizes that an eschatological quality may be essential to the aesthetic, a view that finds unexpected support in Bottom's visionary interlude.

While Adorno's aesthetic theory is helpful for articulating how an eschatological dynamic may be enclosed within the aesthetic event, Rancière's work more overtly focuses on the aesthetic as the condition of possibility for any political community. It is helpful, therefore, to return to Rancière's concept of the "distribution of the sensible" to develop how Bottom's vision takes on a political as well as theological dimension in the remainder of the play. Bottom's unstable aesthetic cannot be confined to the present of its articulation; just so, it escapes from the confines of the scene of Bottom's awakening to infuse the subsequent metatheatrical interlude of act 5. The "tedious brief" performance of "tragical mirth" (5.1.56–57) is reminiscent of the paradoxical concepts and experiences conveyed by Paul and Erasmus, but only insofar as these paradoxes have been rearticulated in terms of Bottom's own visionary aesthetic. This aesthetic transgresses the bounds of Bottom's discrete soliloquy and begins to contaminate the common space of Athens in the production of *Pyramus and Thisbe*. In this regard, it threatens to "distribute the sensible" in ways that may be disruptive to the extant political order. This threat of dissensus is countered by a sovereign discourse that ostensibly marginalizes, but also ultimately emphasizes, the political potential of this aesthetic work.

In the scene immediately after Bottom's awakening, his vision is counterpointed by the rationalizing discourse of the sovereign, Theseus. In a sense, Bottom and Theseus are mirroring sovereign figures. At the beginning of the play, Bottom claims that his "chief humor is for a tyrant" (1.2.21)—echoing the paraliturgical mystery-play figure of Herod the tyrant, even as he accepts his assigned role as a lover.[36] Theseus also enters the play in the dual role of tyrant and lover, underscored by his relationship to Hippolyta, whom he "wooed . . . with [his] sword" (1.1.16). Through this doubling structure, the play invites the audience to understand its characters as articulating competing positions on art and visions.[37] As Grady suggests, rather than presuming that Theseus functions as the final authoritative voice in the play, we should understand his "rationalism" as standing "in dialogic relation" to the positions articulated by other characters, including Bottom and Hippolyta.[38] The "dialogic" structure at the beginning of act 5 models two distinct modes of sovereign response to the possibility of aesthetic autonomy as a socially constitutive dimension of experience. Both Theseus and Hippolyta recognize the political and social capacity of the aesthetic to generate both consensus and dissensus, but they convey divergent sovereign receptions of this revelation.

In this context, Theseus, as a figure of political authority, goes beyond an effort to contain manifestations of the aesthetic; he seeks to instrumentalize them, for the aesthetic is essential to his polity.[39] In this sequence, Theseus discloses that his polis—Athens—is itself an aesthetically derived consensual reality. When it is recognized that political community (which Theseus identifies as a "compact") is inherently aesthetic, the potential political stakes of Bottom's alternative aesthetic political theology comes into greater focus. While he is ostensibly reflecting on the tale of the lovers—a tale that is fantastic but, in itself, not necessarily an artistic production—Theseus himself interjects an overtly aesthetic dimension that, from the perspective of the larger audience, refers the subject of his speech back to the aesthetic vision of "Bottom's Dream":

> The lunatic, the lover, and the poet
> Are of imagination all compact.
> One sees more devils than vast hell can hold;
> That is the madman. The lover, all as frantic,
> Sees Helen's beauty in a brow of Egypt.

The poet's eye, in a fine frenzy rolling,
Doth glance from heaven to earth, from earth to heaven;
And as imagination bodies forth
The forms of things unknown, the poet's pen
Turns them to shapes and gives to airy nothing
A local habitation and a name. (5.1.7–17)

In Theseus's recounting, the merging of erotic desire, divine madness, and poetic creation implicitly forms a kind of counterpolity: "The lunatic, the lover, and the poet / Are of imagination all compact." In these lines, "compact" is frequently glossed as "formed, composed": all three figures are bound together as forms of "imagination" or formed by "imagination."[40] But "compact" has an obvious political meaning as well; in this sense, common in the sixteenth century, including in other works by Shakespeare, "compact" signifies a social contract: "a covenant or contract made between two or more persons or parties."[41] A compact may be political—formed among towns or territories, rulers and subjects—or religious; the "body of Christ" was often cast as a "compact" (for instance, Richard Hooker writes of "Christs owne compact solemnely made with his Church").[42] Theseus's syntax is ambiguous; it hovers between the nominal and adjectival. Is he making a claim simply about how these figures are composed, in a way that allows them to be classified together? Or is he suggesting that they form a countercontract, the cornerstone of a countersociety that shadows and obliquely threatens the order of his Athens? The suggestion that "imagination" can be a "compact" lends a political edge to Theseus's musings on these seemingly marginal figures.

If there is a political dimension to the "compact" that Theseus evokes, the poet, as the figure who materially "bodies forth" the projections of "imagination," emerges as a particularly potent political agent. According to Theseus's account, the poet can create new forms of the "distribution of the sensible": he can disrupt the established consensus and potentially establish new forms of consensus by creating unforeseen discourses. The "poet's pen" gives substantial "shapes" to the "form of things unknown": in this formulation, aesthetic creation is also an inherently political act. The "fine frenzy" of his "eye," which roves between immanence and transcendence—"heaven and earth"—has the ability to generate autonomous forms with political implications: a "local habitation" and a "name." While Theseus attempts to marginalize such poetic creations, to assign them to the realm of the absurd ("how easy is a bush supposed a bear!" [5.1.22]), he inadvertently testifies to the political potential of the aesthetic act. Even in Theseus's discourse of diminishment, the aesthetic has the ability to form "compacts" that range beyond the realm of sovereign control. His language also implies that there is an aesthetic dimension to the "compacts" to which the sovereign himself is indebted. In this sense, Theseus's speech forms a clear prelude to his subsequent efforts to instrumentalize the aesthetic activity of the wedding-night entertainment, to bend it toward reflecting his own sovereign glory, rather than allowing it to establish an autonomous zone of alternative political potentiality. The "compact" as an aesthetic consensus is double-edged from this sovereign perspective; it may be an opportunity to reinforce his authority, but it may also undermine the political order that he rules.

However, even within the realm of sovereign Athens, Theseus's efforts to marginalize and implicitly instrumentalize aesthetic creation do not go uncontested; Hippolyta offers a further counterpoint to his reflections. She emphasizes the social content of aesthetic visions, respecting not only their autonomy but also their potential to assemble collectivity. Her interpretation is distinctly noninstrumentalizing; it highlights what Rancière would call the political core of the play's visionary aesthetic. Her resistance furthers the notion that the sovereign order of Athens always depends upon some version of aesthetics even as it seeks to deny this dependence.[43] Hippolyta challenges Theseus's rationalization:

> But all the story of the night told over,
> And all their minds transfigured so together,
> More witnesseth than fancy's images
> And grows to something of great constancy;
> But, howsoever, strange and admirable. (5.1.23–27)

Like Theseus, Hippolyta turns the lovers' experience into an aesthetic work; if not exactly a poem, it is a "story" that has been "told over," revealing a curious integrity. Hippolyta echoes Theseus's notion of a visionary "compact," but she insists it is an even more substantial form of community: in this "story," the lovers' "minds" are "transfigured so together" into "something of great constancy." Hippolyta refuses to banish such a collective "constancy" to the margins of the political order; such a story is not merely "fancy" but possesses an autonomous reality, whatever its "strange" origins. Hippolyta respects the emergence of an alternative "distribution of the sensible" in the community of the lovers. She is willing to admit this "strange and admirable" consensus into the social reality of Athens.

Although they appear to embrace opposing accounts of the lovers' experience, Theseus and Hippolyta actually share an acknowledgment of this story as an autonomous aesthetic event. They differ in how they attempt to incorporate this aesthetic into their existing consensual reality: Theseus favors a strategy of marginalizing and instrumentalizing aesthetic phenomena, while Hippolyta welcomes instead the intrusion of a "strange" new consensus in their midst, without attempting to assimilate it to an existing hierarchy. She allows an autonomy that Theseus constantly seeks to defer or to master. Hippolyta actually radicalizes Theseus's earlier hints of an aesthetic "compact" in the speech on the "poet, madman, and lover." Taken together, despite their divergence, Theseus and Hippolyta raise the idea that any political consensus, including that of Athens itself, may be an inherently aesthetic production. They set the stage for interpreting the aesthetics of Bottom's play in political terms.

Both Theseus and Hippolyta recast the lovers' tale as an aesthetic artifact, which strengthens the associative link to the aesthetic vision Bottom articulates at the end of 4.1. Furthermore, Theseus and Hippolyta's exchange comprehends the aesthetic as also constitutive of social and political order; this revelation also links back to Bottom's vision, which, as we have seen, reconfigures the Pauline concept of the mystical body in an aesthetic discourse that mingles incarnational and eschatological theologies. Theseus and Hippolyta reinforce the implicit suggestion of Bottom's speech: that aesthetic productions have the potential to reconfigure existing modes of social and political consensus. At the outset of act 5, this dialogic framing of the political stakes of the aesthetic takes place in relatively philosophical terms, as a reflection on the strangeness of the lovers' experience: the links to Bottom's performance are associative rather than direct. However, the play soon stages a direct encounter between the sovereign couple and Bottom's destabilizing aesthetic discourse. While this encounter is played to great comic effect, it also continues to develop a more serious underlying reflection on the political implications of the aesthetic, even as it emerges in the unlikely form of Bottom's performance.

The problem of the relationship between sovereignty and the aesthetic is further developed in Theseus and Hippolyta's subsequent debate over the evening's entertainment. Here again, a tension arises between the desire to instrumentalize aesthetic expression and a willingness to acknowledge (if not exactly respect) its relative autonomy. Theseus calls for "masques" and "dances" in order to "wear away this long age of three hours" (5.1.32–33). In this request, Theseus treats aesthetic experience as a time-management device. Theseus's linear notion of temporality conveys an instrumental view of the aesthetic; his understanding of time is in accord with a secular progression of moments, implicitly contradicting the apocalyptic temporality of Bottom's aesthetic ecstasy. Theseus's instrumental approach to the aesthetic is further developed in his efforts to manage the entertainment options with which he is presented. As Louis Montrose has observed, all of these options imply some form of political threat: "the battle with the Centaurs" and the "riot of the tipsy Bacchanals" indirectly challenge Theseus's "patriarchal" control, while the "satire, keen and critical" seems to "smack of social protest" (5.1.44–54).[44] The play that he chooses to hear would seem, on the surface, to be the least politically charged option. However, the "tragical mirth" of *Pyramus and Thisbe* immediately recalls the temporal and sensory disorientation of Bottom's earlier aesthetic vision, which poses a deeper challenge to the sovereign "distribution of the sensible" that Theseus seeks to maintain. At the same time, it is telling that Theseus is drawn to the mechanicals' play precisely because of its oxymoronic derangement: "Merry and tragical? Tedious and brief? That is, hot ice and wondrous strange snow. How shall we find the concord of this discord?" (5.1.57–60). The contradictory aesthetics of the play's abstract entice Theseus, who adds his own paradoxical formulations as he extemporizes in the mechanicals' mode of discourse. From one angle, Theseus may be striving to fit the nonsensical language of the play into a classic rhetorical trope—*concordia discours*—seeking a harmony of opposites that will allow him to impose some higher order.[45] However, Theseus's attraction to this play also betrays the sovereign order's own dependence on aesthetics, a dependence that has already been suggested in his earlier exchange with Hippolyta, including his reflections on the "compact" of imagination and Hippolyta's emphasis on the "constancy" of the lovers' story. In this light, the appearance of the mechanicals' anomalous aesthetic discourse is both a challenge and an opportunity: its autonomy from the realm of ordinary sensibility provokes an assertion of Theseus's own autonomy as he proceeds to appropriate it in his own terms to burnish his hierarchical authority. However, as Hippolyta's immediate objection shows, this appropriation is never fully accomplished or entirely persuasive. Mirroring the paradoxical character of the play's presentation, Theseus's own sovereign integrity is cast into a contradictory position: it is both strengthened and undermined by its encounter with Bottom's aesthetic chaos.

Hippolyta highlights this contradiction through her questioning of Theseus's judgment. Theseus insists on having the play performed despite warnings that the players will be pushed beyond their limits by the demands of the production. He asserts: "For never anything can be amiss / When simpleness and duty tender it" (5.1.82–83). Theseus seeks to collapse the players into an instrumentalized hierarchy that confines them to a "simple" class. In this rhetorical move, any eccentricity is deprived of serious consequence; order is externally imposed by projecting the deference expected from the lower classes. The supposed "simpleness" of the mechanicals' play is a highlight for Theseus; its disorder will be a foil for his higher order. But Hippolyta objects: "I love not to see wretchedness o'ercharged, / And duty in his service perishing" (5.1.85–86). Here again, Hippolyta defends a version of aesthetic autonomy; she protests the ideological baggage that Theseus seeks to impose on the players. They will be "o'ercharged," overburdened, excessively invested, with Theseus's political needs, his drive to turn their art into "service" (however inept). To be sure, she also doubts the quality of the "wretched" players. But her repudiation of Theseus's instrumental imperative can be read more broadly as a larger disavowal of his sovereign agenda toward the aesthetic; in this sense, it is consistent with her earlier emphasis on the "great constancy" of the lovers' story. This rhetorical struggle between Theseus and Hippolyta is doubtless part of a larger pattern of gender tensions in the play, tensions that have been perceptively analyzed by Montrose: "Although *A Midsummer Night's Dream* reaffirms essential elements of patriarchal ideology, it continues to call that affirmation into question, thus intermittently undermining its own comic propositions."[46] I want to add that this pattern applies not only to the play's representation of struggles over gender ideology but also to its metacritical discourse about political aesthetics. Theseus's instrumental assertions of control over the meaning of aesthetic experiences and events frequently fail to cohere; these assertions may even appear altogether self-thwarting when they are subject to the pressure of dissent.

The agonistic dialogue between Theseus and Hippolyta throughout this metatheatrical sequence demonstrates that the sociopolitical status of the aesthetic is never settled in the play, even among the Athenian elite. Indeed, the very terms that Theseus uses to close this round of debate both invert and echo the Pauline paradox of weakness over strength, foolishness over wisdom, that underlies Bottom's earlier aesthetic interlude: "Love, therefore, and tongue-tied simplicity / In least speak most, to my capacity" (5.1.104–5). Theseus appears to restore the expected worldly order of things in these lines, guiding the audience's interpretation in advance of the performance. However, insofar as he distinctly echoes Bottom's Pauline source text, he remains within the force field of the peculiar political-theological aesthetic that has been established prior to this scene. In this context, Theseus says more than he appears to mean, as the "least" turn out to speak "most" in ways that are perpetually beyond his "capacity" as sovereign. Even as he seeks to assert his dominance over a set of discursive resources affiliated with Bottom's aesthetic, he undermines his own authority by using a discourse that he does not fully control.

While Theseus expresses a desire for a "simple" play that reaffirms the sovereign status quo, the play he is drawn to and actually gets is not only absurd but also suffused with an aesthetics of eschatological and incarnational excess as Bottom's aesthetic vision is performed in real time before the Athenian elite. These characteristics are already on display in the prologue to *Pyramus and Thisbe*. As previous commentators have noted, as it struggles to maintain a discursive decorum appropriate to its audience, Quince's maladroit prologue can be read as conveying a sense of political threat. Montrose refers to the prologue as "a potential act of impudent effrontery."[47] Andrew Barnaby adds that the prologue continues to echo the previously established Pauline context, particularly in its reference to repentance: "All for your delight / We are not here. That you should here repent you, / The actors are at hand" (5.1.114–16). Barnaby suggests an instrumental reading of these lines: "Theatre . . . like a Pauline letter, might be a tool of ethical and spiritual correction."[48] However, in light of the preceding analysis, it is perhaps the discordant *form* of Quince's discourse, its oxymoronic echo of Bottom's earlier aesthetic interlude, that is most politically disconcerting. The opening of the prologue is exemplary in this regard:

> If we offend, it is with our good will.
> That you should think, we come not to offend,
> But with good will. To show our simple skill,
> That is the true beginning of our end. (5.1.108–11)

While "good will" and "offend" would normally be opposed, they instead seem to be allied in Quince's mangled syntax, establishing a rhetorical pattern of collapsing oppositions that continues throughout the speech.

The political implications of Quince's aesthetic disorientation of social norms are emphasized in Hippolyta's immediate response to the prologue: "he hath played on his prologue like a child on a recorder: a sound, but not in government" (5.1.122–23). Hippolyta critiques Quince's lack of skill, but she also more subtly posits an intrinsic link between the aesthetic and the political. A "recorder"—a musical instrument—is imagined in political terms as something to be governed; playing the notes appropriately is a form of "government." If we take her critique in the most literal terms, she does not say Quince performs badly per se but that his performance transgresses the bounds of expected order—it lacks "government." Her commentary suggests that this kind of aesthetic expression has the capacity to challenge existing forms of governance or to propose alternative ways of governing or being governed.[49]

Hippolyta's comments suggest higher stakes than might be expected for the "simple skill" advertised in this prologue, and a closer examination of Quince's opening lines reveals a theological as well as a political dimension. To "show" such "skill" is the "beginning of our end": this is a vexing phrase that challenges Theseus's prior appeal to "tongue-tied simplicity," which he imagined would "end" in an affirmation of his worldly sovereign authority. Instead, Quince's "beginning of our end" suggests a larger, if somewhat inchoate, ambition. The showing of "simple skill" is cast as the first step in a larger, albeit undetermined, process. The "beginning" and "end" juxtaposed so closely introduce an eschatological note as they recall the "alpha" and "omega" of the opening of the book of Revelation ("I am α and ω, *that is* the beginning and the ending, sayeth the Lord" [Rev. 1.8]).[50] In this regard, Quince's prologue resonates with the apocalyptic elements of Bottom's earlier aesthetic vision. Far from resting with a demonstration of "simple skill," the allusiveness of Quince's language implies that the performance might herald the total overthrow of all existing worldly order. The notes of political disturbance in this speech are reinforced by hints of apocalyptic temporality.

The subsequent play is, of course, far from apocalyptic in its consequence; however, it continues to introduce a synesthetic aesthetic that has become politically and theologically charged by the prior contexts that frame it: "Bottom's Dream," Theseus and Hippolyta's debate, and Quince's prologue. Bottom's synesthesia appears harmless enough when it intrudes into his hero's romantic exertions: "I see a voice . . . I can hear my Thisbe's face" (5.1.186–87). Even here, though, the synesthetic effect challenges the impermeability of the supposed "Wall"; Bottom projects a dislocated sensibility that has the ability to thwart socially constructed barriers (he can "see" Thisbe in her voice, defying the sensory impasse demanded by the plot of parental opposition). The politics of Bottom's aesthetics may take on a somewhat sharper edge for an Elizabethan audience when he addresses the Moon in terms that disrupt and possibly critique conventional sixteenth-century political symbolism:

> Sweet Moon, I thank thee for thy sunny beams;
> I thank thee, Moon, for shining now so bright;
> For, by thy gracious, golden, glittering gleams,
> I trust to take of truest Thisbe sight. (5.1.254–57)

Bottom refers to the "Moon" as "sunny," confusing the established properties of these essential planets; the moon's "gleams" are "golden" rather than the expected silver. These celestial objects are, of course, freighted with a great deal of emblematic value in an early modern context: the sun was a long-standing symbol of regal, usually masculine, authority; the moon, its feminine opposite, was adopted in Shakespeare's era as a symbol by the reigning Virgin Queen, who sought to affiliate herself with classical precedents, such as the moon goddess Diana.[51] Bottom's confused discourse potentially embeds a political joke: the sovereign sun is really the feminine moon, a play on the ongoing awkwardness of female rule in a patriarchal culture (a problem that preoccupies the play at large, as Montrose and others have persuasively demonstrated). But beyond this possible topical reference, Bottom's disorientation of the established symbols of sovereign authority highlights the significant political consequences of unbridled aesthetic play. It underscores how such symbols are themselves arbitrary aesthetic constructs, which may be reconfigured to signify in other, dissonant ways by unprecedented aesthetic interventions.

The political implications of Bottom's discursive distortions explain Theseus's curious hostility at the end of *Pyramus and Thisbe* as he blocks Bottom's promised "epilogue." Theseus's effort to foreclose any further performance of Bottom's aesthetic vision suggests that the play's absurdity is not merely comically inexpert but also threatening on some level. At the end of his play, Bottom persists in speaking in synesthetic terms, transgressing the boundaries between the aesthetic space of the performance and the hierarchy of the court as he offers his long-envisioned epilogue: "Will it please you to see the epilogue, or to hear a Bergomask dance between two of our company?" (5.1.331–32). Bottom continues to reconfigure the faculties of seeing and hearing in counterintuitive ways, harking back to the political aesthetics introduced at his awakening in 4.1. While the moment for his ballad has arrived, the Duke abruptly prevents its performance: "No epilogue, I pray you; for your play needs no excuse. Never excuse; for when the players are all dead, there need none to be blamed . . . But, come, your Bergomask. Let your epilogue alone" (5.1.333–39). Theseus interprets the epilogue, which Bottom has earlier imagined as enhancing the conclusion of the play (making the death scene "more gracious" [4.1.208]), as an effort to "excuse" the play. His earlier posture of benign if condescending indulgence has dissipated; his new attitude suggests that he has beheld something more disturbing than merely a bad play. Theseus's rhetoric turns violent and threatening as he projects a scenario in which "the players are all dead." If Bottom's aesthetic challenges conventional political symbolism and established forms of social order, Theseus's retort threatens to annihilate both the aesthetic and the social. Taken literally, Theseus proposes to destroy the mystical body of the polity altogether. While these lines may be performed in a spirit of mocking jocularity, the contrast with Theseus's earlier whimsical evocation of "the lunatic, the lover, and the poet" (5.1.7) is striking and highlights political and aesthetic tensions that cannot be readily resolved.

These tensions are further heightened after the anticlimactic "Bergomask dance" and the wordless departure of the players. As Bottom is deprived of his final aesthetic epilogue (or any other form of meaningful closure), Theseus takes over as the poetic voice, switching from prose to verse to assert the inevitable reign of linear time: "The iron tongue of midnight hath told twelve. / Lovers, to bed . . ." (5.1.339–40). Theseus evacuates Bottom's role as the aestheticized tyrant-lover and assumes his rightful place, marginalizing the play yet again as a mere pastime: "This palpable-gross play hath well-beguiled / The heavy gait of night" (5.1.343–44). Theseus casts the play as brute matter, devoid of any higher sensibility, a foil or background against which the more advanced aspirations of the newly married lovers may shine more brightly. Theseus attempts to overwrite the visionary and eschatological aspects of Bottom's aesthetic with his own assertion of a sovereign aesthetic order. However, even here, the note struck by "beguiled" suggests that a more wayward visionary aesthetics lingers, complicating efforts to reduce the play to base matter.

Glimmers of Bottom's play nonetheless immediately return once the elite Athenians leave the stage as Puck enters to re-create certain motifs of the mechanicals' performance. Most strikingly, two familiar characters reappear: the "hungry lion" who "roars" and the "moon," which is now "behowl[ed]" by the wolf (5.1.347–48). The faeries reconstitute Bottom's aesthetics almost as soon as the worldly sovereign leaves. Furthermore, intimations of eschatology also return as Puck collapses the witching hour of midnight into an image of the Final Judgment: "Now it is the time of night / That the graves, all gaping wide, / Every one lets forth his sprite" (5.1.355–57). Puck casts this fictional Athens into a larger eschatological frame, a move anticipated by the visionary elements of "Bottom's Dream" and its allusive relation to Paul's epistle. This incarnational and eschatological aesthetic significantly appears beyond the sphere of sovereign control, particularly insofar as this sphere is defined in terms of the fiction of a pre-Christian pagan Athens. In this regard, it heightens the sense of a potentially reconfigured community. Puck provides the epilogue that Theseus had sought to forestall, emphasizing the limits of his sovereignty and its instrumental logic, which cannot contain or overrule the political and theological excess of the aesthetic. This excess represents a new "distribution of the sensible," a political and theological potential that glimmers at the end of the play without being fully absorbed into established fictions of authority and order.

Notes

1. See Jennifer R. Rust, *The Body in Mystery: The Political Theology of the Corpus Mysticum in the Literature of Reformation England* (Evanston: Northwestern University Press, 2014): "[T]his communitarian paradigm is the very medium in and through which early modern people conceive of social and political order" (xiv).

2. On the connection between *Midsummer Night's Dream* and the mystery play tradition, see Louis Montrose, *The Purpose of Playing: Shakespeare and the Cultural Politics of the Elizabethan Theatre* (Chicago: University of Chicago Press, 1996), esp. 179–90. On the York Corpus Christi plays as "a complex kind of para-liturgy," see Sarah Beckwith, *Signifying God: Social Relation and Symbolic Act in the York Corpus Christi Plays* (Chicago: University of Chicago Press, 2001), 135. On paraliturgical performances (including mystery plays) and the tradition of the mystical body, see Rust, *Body in Mystery*, xv; 55–56.

3. 1 Cor. 2:6–10 in the Bishops' Bible (London, 1573), in *A Midsummer Night's Dream: Texts and Contexts*, ed. Gail Kern Paster and Skiles Howard (New York: Bedford/St. Martin's, 1999), 323–24. Unless otherwise noted, all citations of *A Midsummer Night's Dream* are from the Paster and Howard edition.

4. For the larger critical discussion, see Hannibal Hamlin, *The Bible in Shakespeare* (Oxford: Oxford University Press, 2013), 109. Andrew Barnaby, "'The Botome of Goddes Secretes': I Corinthians and *A Midsummer Night's Dream*," *Renaissance Drama* 43, no. 1 (2015): 4, assumes that the 1557 Geneva translation is Shakespeare's main reference point.

5. 1 Cor. 2:6–10 in *The New Testament of Our Lord Jesus Christ* (Geneva, 1557). The spelling has been modernized; subsequent citations of 1 Corinthians are from this edition, with modernized spelling. Italicized words follow the original text.

6. For readings of Bottom and the mechanicals that emphasize the class tensions raised by the Pauline allusion in Bottom's dream, see Montrose, *The Purpose of Playing*, 192–94; Annabel Patterson, *Shakespeare and the Common Voice* (Cambridge: Blackwell Publishing, 1989), 68–70; and, most recently, Barnaby, "'Botome of Goddes Secretes,'" 1–26.

7. In this sense, my essay builds on Hugh Grady, *Shakespeare and Impure Aesthetics* (Cambridge: Cambridge University Press, 2009). I agree with Grady's insistence that the aesthetic is a crucial aspect of the play and that it is "possible . . . to pursue ideology-critique and aesthetic analysis simultaneously" (54), although I differ in my assessment of how far the aesthetic is secularized in the case of Bottom.

8. See Jacques Rancière, *The Politics of Aesthetics: The Distribution of the Sensible*, trans. Gabriel Rockhill (London: Continuum, 2004), especially "The Distribution of the Sensible: Politics and Aesthetics," 12–19.

9. Rancière, *The Politics of Aesthetics*, 13.

10. Rancière, *The Politics of Aesthetics*, 12.
11. Rancière, *The Politics of Aesthetics*, 13.
12. Jacques Rancière, *The Flesh of Words: The Politics of Writing*, trans. Charlotte Mandell (Stanford, Calif.: Stanford University Press, 2004). See especially "The Body of the Letter: Bible, Epic, Novel," 71–93.
13. Rancière, *The Flesh of Words*, 79.
14. Rancière, *The Flesh of Words*, 81; emphasis in original.
15. Rancière, *The Flesh of Words*, 83–84.
16. Rancière, *The Flesh of Words*, 77–78.
17. Rancière, *The Flesh of Words*, 84.
18. Rancière, *The Flesh of Words*, 85.
19. Rancière, *The Flesh of Words*, 86.
20. Rancière, *The Politics of Aesthetics*, 59–60.
21. The verse from Isaiah is quoted in Jennifer Waldron, "'The Eye of Man Hath Not Heard': Shakespeare, Synaesthesia, and Post-Reformation Phenomenology," *Criticism* 54, no. 3 (2012): 414; emphasis in original. Waldron addresses how the history of Christian typological interpretation of this Old Testament verse emerges in Bottom's allusion, in terms that resonate with Rancière's analysis: "It is this very claim [of Christian commentators] for universal and equal access that Bottom's 'rare vision' exploits, rendering in common, theatrical and bodily terms the act of exegesis itself" (414).
22. On this link, see Rust, *The Body in Mystery*, 7.
23. See Montrose, *The Purpose of Playing*, 193; Patterson, *Shakespeare*, 68–69; and Barnaby, "'Botome of Goddes Secretes,'" 16–17.
24. Thus, my argument departs from the claims of both Montrose and Patterson, insofar as they tend to oppose aesthetic and political readings; see Montrose, *The Purpose of Playing*, 204–5, and Patterson, *Shakespeare*, 60.
25. Waldron, "'Eye of Man,'" 413. Patterson also associates 1 Cor. 12 with Bottom's vision, although her analysis is more explicitly political: "In the *Dream* . . . the 'unrepresentable parts' of the social body are invested with greater honor by their momentary affinity with a utopian vision" (*Shakespeare*, 68).
26. See Thelma N. Greenfield, "*A Midsummer Night's Dream* and *The Praise of Folly*," *Comparative Literature* 20, no. 3 (Summer 1968): 236–44, and Hamlin, *The Bible and Shakespeare*, 110–11.
27. Erasmus, *The Praise of Folie*, trans. Thomas Chaloner (1549), sig. T2v. Spelling modernized here and in all subsequent citations of this text. A modern translation, *The Praise of Folly*, trans. Clarence H. Miller (New Haven, Conn.: Yale University Press, 1979), has also been consulted.
28. Chaloner, *The Praise of Folie*, sig. T3r.
29. Chaloner, *The Praise of Folie*, sig. T3r.
30. Chaloner, *The Praise of Folie*, sig. T3r.
31. Chaloner, *The Praise of Folie*, sig. T3v.
32. Grady, *Shakespeare and Impure Aesthetics*, 79–80.
33. Theodor W. Adorno, *Aesthetic Theory*, ed. and trans. Robert Hullot-Kentor (Minneapolis: University of Minnesota Press, 1997), 6.
34. Maura B. Nolan, "Making the Aesthetic Turn: Adorno, the Medieval, and the Future of the Past," *Journal of Medieval and Early Modern Studies* 34, no. 3 (Fall 2004): 569.

35. Adorno, *Aesthetic Theory*, 85.

36. On Bottom's potential affiliation with the Herod of the "Nativity pageants," see Montrose, *The Purpose of Playing*, 194.

37. On "double vision" in *A Midsummer Night's Dream*, see David Marshall, "Exchanging Visions: Reading *A Midsummer Night's Dream*," *ELH* 49, no. 3 (Autumn 1982): 543–75.

38. Grady, *Shakespeare and Impure Aesthetics*, 85.

39. For the classic New Historicist account of Theseus as a mirror of Renaissance authority, see Montrose, *The Purpose of Playing*: "The social order of Theseus's Athens depends upon his authority to name the forms of mental disorder and his power to control its subjects . . . For Theseus no less than for the Elizabethan Privy Council, the ruler's task is to *comprehend*—to understand and to contain—the energies and motives, the diverse, unstable and potentially seditious apprehensions of the ruled" (191–92). But Montrose also notes a corresponding "*apprehension*" in tension with this comprehension: "For he himself and the fictional society over which he rules have been shaped by the fantasy of a poet" (192). This ironic apprehension may simply be the acknowledgment of the "limits" (192) of his own authority, which is where Montrose leaves it, but a fuller account of the political and social stakes of the play's engagement with the aesthetic as such lends a potentially sharper edge to Theseus's "apprehension." The aesthetic must be controlled because it is politically constitutive.

40. See gloss in Paster and Howard, *A Midsummer Night's Dream*, 72n8.

41. See "compact n.1 a." in the *OED Online*, http://www.oed.com/view/Entry/37366.

42. *Of Lawes Eccl. Politie* v. lxii. 146, quoted in the *OED Online*.

43. René Girard's classic essay about *A Midsummer Night's Dream* makes an analogous point about the Theseus and Hippolyta dynamic, although his focus is myth and mimetic desire rather than the aesthetic as such: "Myth and Ritual in Shakespeare: *A Midsummer Night's Dream*," in *Textual Strategies: Perspectives in Post-Structuralist Criticism*, ed. Josué V. Harari, 189–212 (Ithaca, N.Y.: Cornell University Press, 1979). In Girard's argument, Hippolyta recognizes a "common structure of mythical meaning" to which Theseus is blind: "Hippolyta clearly perceives Theseus's failure to come up with the holistic interpretation that is necessary" (211). I agree with Girard that the play invites us to take Hippolyta's intervention seriously, but I believe that a close reading of the text shows that both Theseus and Hippolyta actually do recognize the aesthetic as a "holistic" structure; they diverge in their strategies for addressing this recognition.

44. Montrose, *The Purpose of Playing*, 187.

45. On *concordia discours* in *A Midsummer Night's Dream*, see Grady, *Shakespeare and Impure Aesthetics*, 76–77.

46. Montrose, *The Purpose of Playing*, 145.

47. Montrose, *The Purpose of Playing*, 195.

48. Barnaby, "'Botome of Goddes Secretes,'" 22.

49. On the early modern preoccupation with "government," which has multifarious applications throughout the period, see Jennifer R. Rust, "Forms of Governmentality in *The Alchemist*," *SEL: Studies in English Literature 1500–1900* 58, no. 1 (Winter 2018): 95–121. This essay draws on Michel Foucault's genealogy of government in *Security, Territory, Population: Lectures at the*

Collège de France, 1977–1978, ed. Michel Senellart, trans. Graham Burchell (New York: Picador, 2007).

50. *New Testament* (Geneva, 1557); spelling modernized.

51. This association arguably begins at the very opening of this play, with Theseus's complaint about the "old moon" that "lingers . . . like to a stepdame or a dowager" (1.1.4–5), a line that seems to echo sentiments about the old queen in the mid-1590s. On the pervasive moon imagery in the play as an "oblique refraction of Elizabeth" and the "dangers and difficulty of representing power to the powerful" in early modern theater, see Richard Wilson, *Shakespeare and French Theory: King of Shadows* (New York: Routledge, 2007), 152–53.

"Need Makes Good Schollers"

Spenser and the Poverty of Aesthetics

Joel M. Dodson

In *The Philosopher and His Poor* (1983), Jacques Rancière retells the history of Western mimetic thought through the lens of a single figure, the poor cobbler. In this essay, I propose to examine another poverty lurking at the origins of Tudor humanism—the figure not of the poor craftsman but of the poor scholar. Ever since the Greek painter Apelles scolded his shoemaker-critic to stick to what he knew best, poverty has been an essential part of a social and political distribution (*partage*) that reveals—as other contributions to this volume have explored—the contours of those who have the free time for art and those who do not.[1] In his preface to *The Benefits of a Liberal Education* (1517), however, the English humanist Richard Pace recounted for John Colet the remarkably different tale of a drunk nobleman at a recent banquet in Rome who regarded that freedom as impoverished itself:

> When he heard us praise learning, he became wild, overwhelmed with an uncontrollable rage, and burst out, To hell with your stupid scholars. Scholars are a bunch of beggars [*omnis docti sunt mendici*]. Even Erasmus is a pauper [*etiam Erasmus ille doctissimus (ut audio) pauper est*], and I hear he's the smartest of them all. In one of his letters he calls *ten kataraton penian*, that is, goddamn poverty, his wife and complains bitterly that he's not able to get her off his back and throw her in the ocean, *bathyketea ponton*. God damn it, I'd rather see my son hanged than be a student.[2]

Pace's anecdote was of course a fabrication, though one that works precisely because its satirical target was the author of *De Copia*, who extolled the Quintilian model of rhetoric as rich furnishing and attire and excoriated those who "having professed *copia* (abundance) . . . have betrayed their poverty."[3] It also works because Pace seems to have recognized how such poverty always attends the claim to humanist abundance itself. In a 1518 letter to Thomas More, Erasmus confessed that Pace's "drivel" had irritated him greatly. It impoverished, he urged, not just the paper it was written on; it risked impoverishing the riches of England's literary future.[4]

Given the precarity and increasingly real poverty confronting liberal arts education in the twenty-first century, it's an impoverishment that—despite Erasmus's best efforts—continues to bear on academic criticism and on the question of political aesthetics in particular. On the one hand, Pace's conceit of the beggar-scholar neatly captures what Rancière in his 1983 book began calling the "part of those who have no part": an art of learning that does something other than its allotted craft; a sensibility that clings forever to the back of literary humanism and its "golden world" legacy, like a wife it might throw into the sea.[5] This extra or supernumerary part assumes in *The Philosopher and His Poor* the promise and conflictual shape that Rancière later identifies in his work with the aesthetic. Poverty is both the unstated assumption of an intellectual regime—from Plato to Bourdieu—that equates art with knowledge and aesthetics with leisure (Gr. *skholé*) and its democratic potential. For the shoemaker who exercises the liberty to think, or the joiner who writes poetry at night, or the specialist who delights in the rags of his own learning, together disclose what Rancière calls a shared *aisthesis*: the capacity of a people (demos) always to be at once more and less than they appear to be.[6]

On the other hand, the very idea of a beggar-*scholar* suggests the confusion of parts by which the humanities, since early modernity, has struggled to convert that shared sensibility into political cause. Bourdieu's influential critique of *skholé* as a sphere of privilege does not, for example, take into account that intellectuals might themselves be poor.[7] Yet in a rare reference to Rancière's work, Giorgio Agamben notes how even that apparent democratization points to a deeper confusion, long perceived by those committed to the solidarity of academy and labor: whether the vicissitudes of need are merely the site of struggle or the means to equality.[8] Long before the current concern over the academic precariate, this confusion about the size and shape of "poverty" in relation to the arts was being felt in the sixteenth century. Beginning with the Act Concerning Punishment of Beggars and Vagabonds (1531) and continued with the Elizabethan statutes of 1576 and 1597, Tudor poor laws routinely grouped "Scollers of the Univ[er]sityes of Oxford and Cambrydge that goe about begginge" and "all persons calling themselves Schollers going about begging" with those unlicensed men subject to whipping and banishment.[9] Writers in the Age of Shakespeare, meanwhile, could look to another tradition, from Boccaccio to du Bellay and from Marlowe to John Taylor (the Water Poet), in which poverty might be conceived as the condition of poetic invention and wit, even its source.[10] In book 3, canto 3 of the 1590 *Faerie Queene*, Edmund Spenser captures something of that creative and political tension when he has the nurse Glauce advise the knight Britomart, at the start of her heroic quest, with a seemingly minor proverb that places Pace's conceit at the very heart of his narrative poem: "Need makes good schollers" (3.3.53).[11]

This essay follows Spenser's lead by asking how we might consider the aesthetic as a space of need, rather than a forestalled or foreshadowed Enlightenment potential, in nondramatic verse outside the works of Shakespeare. A variant of Erasmus's *Necessitas magistra* and its modern counterpart, "Necessity is the mother of invention," adages like Glauce's have virtually nothing to say about the real or imagined conditions of the poor in early modern England. They are an expression of humanist sententiae rather than of the human subject; of rhetoric, poetry, and the school rather than "the thing itself" (*King Lear* 3.4.104) Lear famously imagines himself to see in the face of poor Tom on the heath.[12] Such fantasies of the visible and invisible poor have been the subject of important historicist and cultural studies work by William Carroll, Linda Woodbridge, Patricia Fumerton, and others, detailing how representations of rogues, vagabonds, and the homeless in Tudor England often contested the bounds of representation itself.[13] The question of poverty has thus usually been a question of *popular* aesthetics—or, at the very least, of the "impurity" of pre-Enlightenment aesthetics, famously figured in Shakespeare's own masterless men.[14]

Equally compelling, I believe, are those poverties so internal to elite literary humanism's self-conception that they complicate the proleptic discourse of a pure or impure aesthetic in the first place. Situated within Glauce's and Britomart's return from Merlin's cave in canto 3, "need makes good schollers" expresses one such structuring need. The nurse's "bold devise" that the two women "in feigned armes our selues disguize" and teach "our weak hands . . . / The dreadful speare and shield to exercise" (3.3.53) marks, in effect, the zero moment of the Legend of Chastity. It initiates Britomart's decision to don men's armor, her quest for Artegall, and what critics have generally acknowledged—from the Garden of Adonis to Busirane's tapestries—to be Spenser's most aesthetically engaged narrative sequence. That engagement has typically been regarded from the standpoint of allegory's ironic or irresolvable excess.[15] Spenser's interest in the poor scholar, I argue, signals an alternative trajectory within the English new poetry that began, in *The Shepheardes Calender* (1579), with the antinomies of "plenty" and "poverty." Rather than an aesthetics of poverty, Spenser helps us examine in *The Faerie Queene* the poverty of aesthetics.

The two sections that follow seek to take that inversion of the genitive seriously. By the "poverty of the aesthetic," I mean to suggest something other than a latent or negative aesthetic sensibility in early modern England. Rather, I mean to suggest an explicit instance of what Christopher Pye has called the "breach or division" that marks its foundation as a delimitable concept.[16] In the first section, I trace that breach through the figure of the poor scholar in the humanist tradition and its immediate context in book 3, canto 3 of *The Faerie Queene*, identifying a "beggarly," if not fully autonomous, notion of creative freedom disclosed within the hierarchical body of Tudor allegorical and political thought. In the second, I consider what part, exactly, this impoverished aesthetic represents through a comparison of Britomart's experience before Malecasta's tapestries in canto 1 with one of the most needy, if unremarkable, characters of *The Faerie Queene*—the idle "churl" of canto 7, whose pursuit of Florimell Spenser bookends with the two other uses of Glauce's conceit in book 3.

Taken together these varying, and often elusive, needs complicate the recuperative prospect of an *aisthesis* that is both "part" and "not a part" of early modern studies. In a recent essay on poverty and Tudor humanism, Crystal Bartolovich has argued—in a direct challenge to Rancière's critique of Bourdieu—that our part as early modern critics in the face of such need is to universalize the conditions of intellectual privilege.[17] Rancière, by contrast, has increasingly spoken of poverty as an injunction to the shared space of "aesthetic ignorance." Spenser's conceit of the poor scholar forces us to reckon, I suggest, with what Agamben identifies as another, more difficult part—the poverty that endures within, even as it proves resistant or unrecoverable to, scholarship itself. In this respect, the "Age of Spenser" may afford an alternative history of political aesthetics in the time of Shakespeare: a time based not on a more abundant notion of the aesthetic to come but on its persistent and lasting exigency.

The Aphoristic Cut, or Remembering the Poor Scholar

Glauce's aphorism serves as a particularly useful device for thinking about such questions of aesthetic history as it embodies, in miniature, what Agamben calls the *aphorismenos* (separation, division), or cut, that divides and exposes our expectations of a pre-Enlightenment aesthetic. As recounted by Pliny in *Naturalis Historia* 35, Apelles's retort to the shoemaker, *Sutor, ne ultra crepidam* (Shoemaker, stick to thy last), seems forever to divide premodern art along the lines of inclusion and exclusion, privilege and unprivilege, artistic freedom and its lack.[18] "Need makes good schollers," I suggest in this section, requires us to observe two, more complex lines in the sixteenth century: a surprisingly cohesive line running through Tudor mimetic thought, in which poverty forms an enabling, rather than disabling, condition of English poetry; and the corresponding lines that define the aesthetic and political limits of *The Faerie Queene* not only by the needs its allegorical verse chooses to represent but by those that remain within it.

In *The Time That Remains*, Agamben proposes the term "exigency," drawn from Walter Benjamin, as one way of expressing that sense of historical need. In his early essay on Dostoevsky, Benjamin refers to *The Idiot*'s Prince Mishkin as a life that had remained unforgettable, even as it was forgotten.[19] Agamben, tracing that life from the monastic poor to the Marxian concept of a people, finds in it a language of poverty, class, and aesthetic life that resists the weak or subtle Messianism by which the needs of premodernity anticipate the coming, in Kant, of a more disinterested form of aesthetic judgment.[20] In exigency, Agamben imagines, need instead constitutes a form of life itself:

> Exigency does not properly concern that which has not been remembered; it concerns that which remains unforgettable. It refers to all in individual or collective life that is forgotten with each instant and to the infinite mass that will be forgotten by both . . . In every instant, the measure of forgetting and ruin, the ontological squandering that we bear within ourselves far exceeds the piety of our memories and consciences. But the shapeless chaos of the forgotten is neither inert nor ineffective.[21]

Forgotten yet unforgettable has historically been the lot of the impoverished mind and pen in the "aesthetic of society," as the historian Peter Brown notes.[22] While Tudor homilists exhorted believers to "remember the poor" (Galatians 2:10)—in the sense of the deserving poor, or objects of charity—the needs of scholars and poets prove at once more ephemeral and (im)memorable in the period. Poverty, in the famous words of Marlowe's *Hero and Leander*, will "always kiss" the descendants of Mercury, while Nashe's *The Unfortunate Traveller* imagines the university students fawning before the Elector of Saxony as "a companie of beggers," whose learning amounted to "ragges gathered up from the dunghill."[23] In the disciplinary idiom of state and society that has guided criticism over the past three decades, these metaphorical rags and kisses constitute a seemingly indiscernible mass. Poverty is the fractured "image of authority," according to Lear, and humanism's "negative exception," according to Laurie Shannon: it is the forgotten or "shapeless" form out of which the exceptional body of Tudor mimetic and political form defines itself.[24]

A more unforgettable version of need nevertheless appears in *The Faerie Queene* when we consider the aphoristic lines that divide and delineate that mimetic body as a shaping entity in the first place. If Benjamin's example of the exigent life is Prince Mishkin, Spenser's is Britomart, a character whose allegorical fate as progenitor of the Tudor myth remains unforgettable in *The Faerie Queene* precisely insofar as she exists to be forgotten.[25] That exigency is announced in book 3, canto 3 with a famously interrupted prophecy:

> Thenceforth eternall union shall be made
> Betweene the nations different afore,
> And sacred Peace shall louingly persuade
> The warlike minds, to learne her goodly lore,
> And ciuile armes to exercise no more:
> Then shall a royall Virgin raine, which shall
> Stretch her white rod ouer the *Belgicke* shore,
> And the great Castle smite so sore with all,
> That it shall make him shake, and shortly learn to fall.
>
> But yet the end is not. There *Merlin* stayd,
> As ouercomen of the spirites powre,
> Or other ghastly spectacle dismayd,
> That secretly he saw, yet note discoure:
> Which suddein fitt, and halfe extatick stoure
> When the two fearefull wemen saw, they grew
> Greatly confused in behaueoure; (3.3.49–50)

In the space of Merlin's "not" (50.1), Ernst Kantorowicz's classic image of the king's two bodies hovers over the allegory of *The Faerie Queene*. The image of Elizabeth, heir to Britomart and Artegall's foretold union, persuades the body politic to "sacred Peace" (49.3); yet the controlling arm by which that royal image shapes the political body is consigned to a Messianic time that "yet . . . is not" (50.1). In *The Poem's Two Bodies*, David Lee Miller draws on Kantorowicz's founding articulation of political theology to argue that Spenser's poem thus works to mystify questions of *aisthesis*. The "poem's vision of its incorruptible aesthetic body rests on a pervasively internalized principle of self-renunciation," Miller writes, and what it renounces are the sensible workings out of which that poetic operation is constituted.[26]

Cutting across that theo-political vision, however, is Glauce's and Britomart's response, as their "confused . . . behaueoure" at Merlin's "suddein fitt" (50.5–8) suggests a corresponding political affect within the governing image of the poem's two bodies defined not by exception or lack but by need:

> At last the Nourse in her foolhardy wit
>   Conceived a bold deuise, and thus bespake;
>   Daughter, I deeme that counsel aye most fit,
>   That of the time doth dew advantage take;
>
> . . . .
>
> That therefore nought our passage may empeach,
>   Let us in feigned armes our selues disguize,
>   And our weake hands (need makes good schollers) teach
>   The dreadfull speare and shield to exercize: (3.3.52–53)

In *The Storm at Sea*, Christopher Pye describes a similar moment of affect in act 2 of *Hamlet* when the player's moving rendition of "Pyrrhus' pause" re-creates, for actor and for audience, the distraction of the "painted tyrant" (2.2.418, 425). Such distractions, Pye argues, have less to do with a particular political form than with the ground of autonomous form itself: "[It] bears on the groundless betwixt-and-between status of the work itself—the work as representational go-between between world and subject. In that sense, distraction indexes the appearance of an explicitly aesthetic subjectivity."[27] For Pye, the name of that aesthetic subjectivity is "Shakespeare," a name whose aphoristic quality fills the absent space outside the body of the painted sovereign with all the received cultural markers of autonomy and indeterminacy. For Spenser, it is a much smaller aphorism that, in Glauce's "foolhardy wit," fills the space of *The Faerie Queene* in the lines directly following Merlin's pause not with an indeterminate potential but with a more pressing "need" that "makes" and "teach[es]" what to do with the time that remains (52.4).

How seriously ought we to take the scholar's need as itself a kind of political and aesthetic ground? Spenser, for one, seems to have done so. In the 1596 *Faerie Queene*, Spenser altered line 3 of stanza 53 to read, "And oure weake hands (whom need new strength shall teach)," a labored revision that changes Glauce's advice from the theme of making to edification, and "improved the sense but not the syntax," according to A. C. Hamilton.[28] Improvement aside, we might say the revision draws our attention to "need" as a kind of sense itself. In the immediate context of canto 3, the "need" Glauce refers to is not the "hidden hooke" of "loves cruell law" implanted in Britomart's heart by the romantic image of Artegall (3.2.38). The surrounding stanzas detailing the women's return from Merlin's cave describe a Britain that "now . . . doth burne" (52.9) amid the armed conflict of Uther and Paynim princes "Beside *Cayr Verolame*" (52.8). This is the same Roman "Verlame" that Spenser elsewhere recalls in *The Ruines of Time* as "Wasted . . . as if it never were" (l. 120), meaning that Glauce's advice is situated within the yawning waste of humanist *imitatio* and its attempted bridge with the classical past.[29] It is also thereby situated within an earlier image of British freedom, as Graham Hammill notes, a sensus communis—prior to the divided image of sovereign and people—whose "historical situation neither Spenser nor the poem entirely comprehends."[30]

These links between need and a more liberated form can nevertheless be comprehended if we consider the broader English proverb tradition from which Glauce's aphorism is derived. While Chaucer provides perhaps the most famous image of a "poure scholar" in English literature in the figure of "hende" Nicholas—whose "sleigh" and "privee" ways forgo the strictures of scholastic arts in favor of licentious "fantasye" (ll. 3190–99)[31]—by the sixteenth century, "poverty" and "need" begin appearing as key terms within the humanist curriculum for intellectual achievement itself. Handlists like Horman's *Vulgaria* and Erasmus's *Adagia* encouraged rote memorization of the Latin device "Necessity is a teacher" (*Necessitas magistra*) and "Nede taught him wytte" (*Necessitats ingenium dedit*), valences of "need" and "necessity" that do not—in their subsequent iteration in English print—fall neatly along ethical, religious, or pedagogical lines.[32] Grafton's *Preceptes of Cato* (1553), for example, credits Publius with the observation that "Extreme nede and wretched pouerte" are the cause of "aventure and great jeoardie"; Thomas Pritchard's handbook for "pettie Schollers," meanwhile, lists numerous exempla from Seneca to Cicero that "Povertie impareth not Virtue," including Apuleius, who "boldely blazeth this commendacion of Pouertie, that in those dayes, it was the builder of Citties, the maintainer of Equitie and Science" (14). As a spur to invention, poverty thus assumes a kind of architectonic quality over the course of the sixteenth century. *Englands Parnassus* (1600) features multiple encomia to the poetic powers of poverty, from Fairfax's "povertie, chiefe of the heavenly brood" to Silvester's "Powerful need (arts auncient dame, and keeper)"; the Cambridge Parnassus plays (1598–1602) make it the condition of academic pilgrimage; and Nashe, in his introduction to *Pierce Penniless*, extols the toil and pain of the "Scholler" as the (ironic) legacy of Sidney.[33]

As even this hasty survey of English sententiae shows, the cut of Glauce's aphorism can thus be extended back, from the indeterminate affect of Merlin's "not" to a cluster of ideas surrounding learning, invention, and *poiesis* in the sixteenth century. More important, it shows poverty to be an actively shaping—rather than shapeless—principle within the representative regime on which Spenser's governing image of the poem's two bodies rests. Not unlike Merlin, Rancière frequently imagines that regime as a hierarchical body, a conception of the liberal and servile arts that would not be set free until the eighteenth century, when Winckelmann discerned in the broken body of the *Belvedere Torso* "the beautiful inactivity of the god of stone . . . the product of the free activity of the people."[34] Aesthetic autonomy, or art for art's sake, thus emerges in the Enlightenment as a kind of rupture or division within the political body. Yet in stark contrast to the "not" that separates the twofold body of early modern state and society, Rancière's *Aisthesis* describes that division—in a reference to Ruskin's moving account of the poor artisan in *The Stones of Venice* (1851)—in generative terms: "the art of an imperfect being, thus constantly in progress, always capable of renouncing initial plans to better respond to the difficulties of the enterprise."[35]

Rancière's perennial target here is Bourdieu, whose account of aesthetics as the elite taste of *skholé* (free time, leisure, the school) versus the popular taste of necessity (*a-scholia*) serves to render such imperfect art—and the prospect of a generative relationship between need and aesthetic life—an apparent contradiction in terms. In the name of challenging intellectual hierarchy, Rancière argues, Bourdieu's account of aesthetic autonomy as the "fallacy" of social and scholastic privilege merely reinstates another: "the simple alternative laid down by the sociologist that claims you are either ignorant and subjugated or have knowledge and are free."[36] Social constructivist method (and by extension, the models of historicism and cultural studies drawn from it) presumes the very distribution of the sensible (*le partage du sensible*) it sets out to critique.[37] Winckelmann and Ruskin, in blurring that simple alternative, show us how it might be redistributed.

Long before Winckelmann and Ruskin, however, that redistribution was already being imagined in the sixteenth century in the body of the poor scholar. *Paupertatem summis ingeniis obesse, ne provehantur*

Fig. 1. Detail from Andrea Alciati, *Emblematum Liber* (Augsburg, April 6, 1531). The Huntington Library, San Marino, California, RB 150511.

(Poverty hinders the greatest talents from advancing) provides a striking example, an emblem that serves as a fitting counterpoint both to the mystified, outstretched arm of *The Faerie Queene*'s sovereign and the purportedly liberated arms of the *Belvedere Torso*. Featured in each edition of the *Emblematum liber* printed in the sixteenth century, Alciati's emblem portrays poverty as the heavy stone (*onus*) in the left hand of the man of talents (*ingenium*) whose winged right hand reaches up to the heavens. Corresponding woodcuts in the period's Latin and vernacular editions reveal important variations in that conceit. While the Augsburg edition of 1531 portrays a scholastic figure who weighs with apparent soberness and equanimity heavenly aspiration against the burden of earthly obligation (fig. 1), later French, Italian, German, and English versions depict a sinewy body in rags reaching up to Jove only to be thrust back under the visibly heavier weight of a real *paupertas* (fig. 2).[38] Taken together, these images of the poor scholar imagine the refinement and emerging independence of the arts as an increasing, rather than decreasing, impoverishment in sixteenth-century humanism. More important, they imagine a body that complicates both Bourdieu and Rancière's critique of Bourdieu. In the body of the poor scholar, the heiarchical image of *skholé* is not only blurred or redistributed within a body broken by need (*a-skholia*); those needs have become the artist's enduring and defining form. This latter

Fig. 2. Detail from Andrea Alciati, *Emblematum Liber* (Lyon, 1550). The Huntington Library, San Marino, California, RB 111026.

sense is captured in Geffrey Whitney's accompanying verse to the English *Choice of Emblems*:

> My wishe, and will are still to mounte aloft.
> My wante, and woe, denie me my desire:
> I shew theire state, whose witte, and learninge, ofte
> Excell, and woulde to highe estate aspire:
>   But povertie, with heavie clogge of care,
>   Still pulles them downe, when they ascending are.[39]

Whitney's play on "want" as need versus desire both complements and contrasts what is surely the most famous "poesie" on poverty, Spenser's "Plenty made me poor" (*Inopem me copia fecit*; see Ovid, *Metamorphoses*

3.466), itself a rendering of Alciati's *Philautia* emblem and a refrain Spenser would recycle in *The Shepheardes Calender*, the 1590 *Faerie Queene*, and the sonnets. In the "September" eclogue, poverty is Diggon's punishment for wandering into Romish pride; in the Narcissistic gaze of *Amoretti* 35, it is the result of "hungry eyes [that] through greedy covetize" yearn "to behold the object of their paine" (ll 1, 5–8). In Whitney, Alciati, and the aphoristic tradition evoked by Glauce, poverty refuses to be reduced to the punitive or misspent plenty of mimetic desire; poverty is its intellectual source.

This genetic relationship between poverty and poetry, I suggest, illuminates a parallel trajectory in English new poetry to that which is commonly identified in Spenser as the emergence of a bourgeois style. Writing of Spenser's "plenty made me poor," Christopher Warley notes that "it's hard to imagine a more succinct description of nascent capitalism . . . Whatever possession and stability—both social and epistemological—the speaker achieves in [the *Amoretti*] is continually situated within and against the material and physical dispossession he suffers."[40] In *The Poetics of Primitive Accumulation*, Richard Halpern traces that dialectic of poverty and plenty to the Tudor educational system. An autonomous "style" becomes visible in early modernity through institutions like the Merchant Taylors' School, Halpern argues, as a form of primitive capital, dividing working-class boys from the medieval guild culture through a culture of aspiration. In such a context, to speak of poverty and aesthetics is merely to speak of what Halpern defines as the latent core of all mimetic education: "By *imitation*, I mean a set of practices that places the subject in an imaginary relation with a governing model; it is the imaginary grasped *as* practice . . . It thus produces the ideological effect that Louis Althusser has dubbed 'interpellation,' or 'hailing,' wherein the subject comes both to recognize himself within and to depend upon a dominant specular image."[41]

On purely biographical grounds, Spenser, we know, had a direct education in this process. Having matriculated as a sizar at Pembroke College, Cambridge, in 1569, Spenser participated in a system where poverty served not only as a symbolic social marker but as a tool for negotiating its academic status.[42] Yet in telling that story primarily as one of increasing plenty or accumulation, studies like Halpern's or Warley's also leave unexplained what proves most remarkable about images like Alciati's pauper or its structural equivalent in *The Faerie Queene*'s dynastic vision: what happens when poverty becomes poetry's explicit, rather than latent, form; what happens, that is, when it becomes the "governing model" itself?

In a fascinating study of "scholarly abjection" and the Tudor university, Linda Shenk traces this explicit relationship between poverty, governance, and mimetic form to what the Latin dramatist William Gager, in his 1592 letter to John Rainolds, called the scholar's "beggerly . . . style."[43] Writing against Rainolds's attack on the scurrilous effects of student dramatic and poetic performance, Gager appeals to the creative freedom of "poore Schollers" as its own kind of "magnificence."[44] For Aristotle, magnificence refers to the outward splendor that promotes the public good and, in its medieval manifestation, the sanctity of the body politic. Such doing or making good (*magnum facere*), Gager notes, was originally modeled by those Roman citizens who, in times of great need or plague, sponsored public performances on behalf of the state out of their private largesse. Yet in a colorful, if counterintuitive, passage, Gager goes on to explain how the arts of the poor scholar in the Tudor university can themselves be considered "magnificent towards the peeple," if by less-abundant means:

> Next I deny that we are to be termed *scenici* or *histriones* for cumminge on the Stage once in a yeere, or twoe yeere, sevne, ten, or somtyme twenty yeeres. As he is not a wrastler, that sometyme to prove his strencthe tyrieth for a fall or twoe; nor he a fencer, that sometyme takethe up the cudgells to play a vennye; nor he a danser, that sometyme leadeth the measures or dansethe a galliarde; . . . And yet if a man shoulde doe these thinges usually and in evry place, I think he might be noted to be a wrastler, a ffencer, a danser, an a ffidler. Besyde, we differ from [professional players] in the manner of owre playinge . . . Thay did it with excessyve charge; we thriftely, warely, and allmost beggerly . . .[45]

Gager's defense of the scholar's beggarly style, or "manner," here literalizes the bodily confusion of Alciati's *Paupertatem summis*, anticipating one of the most well-known passages of Marx. In *The German Ideology*, Marx imagines a future day in communist society when one might "hunt in the morning, fish in the afternoon, rear cattle in the evening, criticize after dinner . . . without ever becoming hunter, fisherman, shepherd, or critic."[46] For Marx, it's the freedom of a day to come. For Gager, it's a freedom that exists precisely in the fact one can't *quite* fit it all in in a single day. Scholars and students might imitate wrestlers, fencers, or dancers, like professional actors, without ever becoming a wrestler, a fencer, a dancer. But because they do so "thriftely, warely, . . . beggerly"—once a year, once every two, or even less—their "magnificence" lies not in their ability to reflect the established hierarchy of the Tudor state, or the masterless freedoms of the people. Rather, their "beggerly . . . style" discloses the limits between the two: the bodily, temporal, and material needs by which the English body politic imagines itself to be otherwise.

In a spirit evocative of Schiller, the arts of the poor scholar might thus be understood as a kind of structured free play.[47] For Gager, such limits on recreative art make it a fitting preparatory for future state service. Yet in her own "feigned armes" (3.3.53), Britomart's embodiment of the poor scholar in book 3 reveals something even more "beggerly" about that educational path. Her disguise as a knight, her cross-dressing as a man, affords a series of lessons that may never rise to the allegorical magnificence of an Arthur or Merlin's messianic image of the "royall Virgin," of which she is the progenitor. Yet it is precisely in that exigency that Britomart's "need" makes visible another kind of *skholé*—an aesthetic autonomy that becomes visible in *The Faerie Queene* precisely insofar as it is poetically impoverished.

Not Seeing the Poor: Britomart and the Exigencies of Art

What aesthetic part, exactly, is this? When we turn to the afterlife of Glauce's aphorism in the surrounding cantos of *The Faerie Queene*, it is tempting to see in the needs of Tudor humanism I have been examining thus far the vaguely democratic part of a poetry that celebrates its own ambiguity or "dark conceit." In "The Aesthetic Dimension," Rancière reframes the part of the poor he began tracing in his 1983 book as a larger "aesthetic ignorance," constitutive of any creative act that assumes the part, or perspective, of the anyone (demos).[48] Something of that shared sensibility is apparent in book 3, canto 1, when in the sumptuously adorned Castle Joyeous, Britomart evades Malecasta's amorous gaze by "dissembl[ing] it with ignoraunce" (3.1.50), suggesting the subversive potential of women's mutual "self-feeling"(54.2). It is also apparent in the much more dire conditions of book 2, canto 7, when Guyon's encounter with the laborers of Mammon's mine evokes an equally mutual scene of "wonder" (2.7.37) prompted by the sight of "open-mouthed" fiends "unable to understand their situation."[49] These instances of the ignorant or disconnected gaze, as Rancière calls them, not only anticipate the disconnected gaze that Kant will later identify with those disinterested judgments indicative of the aesthetic. They suggest the fundamentally democratic ignorance whenever we see the needs and sensibility of a particular part, or group, as representative of the larger whole.

One problem, of course, with such synecdochal moments of aesthetic wonder in didactic verse like Spenser's is that they typically exist, as Tracey Sedinger notes, "to be administered."[50] The other problem, as we have seen, is that the needs of sixteenth-century poetry are not always those of the unwitting gaze but those that elude our gaze, because—as Pace first suggested in the image of Erasmus the beggar—English humanism knew them all too well. In his dedicatory sonnet "To all the gratious and beautifull Ladies in the Court," appended to the 1590 *Faerie Queene*, Spenser imagines his own verse a space of inevitable need:

> The Chian Peincter, when he was requirde
> To pourtraict Venus in her perfect hew,
> To make his worke more absolute, desird
> Of all the fairest Maides to haue the vew.
> Much more me needs to draw the semblant trew,
> Of beauties Queene, the worlds sole wonderment,
> To sharpe my sence with sundry beauties vew,
> And steale from each some part of ornament. (DS 17, ll. 1–8)

In a textual confusion well noted by Spenser's editors, Spenser's sonnet seems to set up a contest of mimetic abundance with the wealthy Greek painter Zeuxis (to whom Pliny attributes the tale of the fair maids), while the "Chian" painter referred to in line 1 is in fact Apelles of Chios. Apelles's aphoristic trace (*Ne sutor ultra crepidam*,) returns us to the problem with which this essay began: the relation between poor shoemakers and poor poets, or between the real poverty excluded from the arts and that which is internal to it—and what "need," if any, they might share. As Clark Hulse notes in his wonderful essay on the visual arts and teaching *The Faerie Queene*, such questions are mitigated in Spenser's dedicatory sonnet by a peculiarly generative sense of "need."[51] "Much more me needs to draw the semblant true" (l. 5) implies either that the poet *needs* to view more of the world's beauties to draw the greater wonder of his Queen or that her beauty creates a *need* no artistic semblance, however "absolute," could fill. Waylaid by need, Spenser resolves in the closing couplet, in an appeal to Elizabeth's ladies-in-waiting, to embrace a different part, defined by its negligibility: "Of each a part I stole by cunning theft : / Forgive it me faire Dames, sith lesse ye have not lefte" (13–14).

"[Since] lesse ye have not lefte": like Gager's scholars or Alciati's pauper, Spenser accords to *The Faerie Queene* the freedom of what is "lefte" at the limits of court and world, the body of his sovereign and the body of the people, since it is so little that it neither takes nor leaves anything "lesse" behind. Rather than the latent potential of an ignorant or unwitting aesthetic, Spenser draws our attention to the historicity of an aesthetic that assumes, in Christopher Pye's words, "the form of a breach or division that takes place neither within nor beyond the structure, an effect neither immanent within nor transcendent to it."[52] In *The Time That Remains*, Agamben identifies this historicity as the lingering part implicit in Rancière's expansive notion of "the part that is not a part," which Agamben claims Rancière derived from a 1977 interview with Michel Foucault:

> The pleb does not exist in all probability, but there is something of the pleb, nevertheless (*il y a de la plèbe*). Something of the pleb is in bodies, in spirits, in individuals, in the proletariat, but, with each dimension, form, energy, and irreducibility, differs in each and every instance. *This part of the pleb does not represent some exteriority with regard to power relationships as much as it represents their limit*, their ruin, their consequence.[53]

The thematic problem of the "pleb"—discussed elsewhere in this volume—lies outside the scope of the present essay. Yet Foucault's words are equally notable for an aphoristic cut that divides political life along less-visible lines than the line between cobblers and artists. Rather than a part that evokes the wonder of a larger whole, Foucault, like Spenser's dedicatory sonnet, imagines a political part made meaningful because it is forever being lost within the whole.

As Agamben reminds us, such exigencies are properly the work of scholars, whose job is "to remain faithful to that which having perpetually been forgotten, must remain unforgettable."[54] But if so, then they are also the work of readers, for what I want to suggest in the final pages remaining is that this same sense of exigency—of losing one's self within the poem and the need for the aesthetic it creates—marks the part of "Need makes good schollers" in *The Faerie Queene*. Interestingly, that part is clearest in book 3 in the aesthetic experience of two characters linked by the repetition of Glauce's aphorism yet who *never* see each other: Britomart and the witch's son, or "poor" churl, of canto 7.

Spenser in fact repeats Glauce's aphorism twice in the canto 7. Following the encounter with Malecasta at Castle Joyeous, Britomart continues her quest with a seaside lament that will ultimately lead her to the House of Busirane and the rescue of Amoret. As the narrative splits, Florimell encounters her own set of needs when, having fled the forester in canto 1 (and Arthur in between), she is forced to dismount her tired horse and walk on foot: "A traveiler unwonted to such way: / *Need teacheth her this lesson hard and rare*, / That fortune all in equall launce doth sway" (3.7.4; emphasis added). The "equall launce" of Florimell's "lesson" recalls Merlin's response to Glauce earlier in the poem. When asked, "What needes [Britomart] to toyle, sith fates can make / Way for themselves" (3.3.25), Merlin tells the nurse that divine necessity is not the same as the needs and toils of mortal endeavor. Spenser reinforces the lessons of exigency twenty-two stanzas later when, having taken refuge in the crude lodgings of a witch and her son, Florimell is forced again to flee on foot: "fear gave her wings, and *need her corage taught*" (3.7.26; emphasis added). In between these two iterations of Glauce's earlier trope, however, we are introduced to a figure whose needs would seem to have nothing to do with either scholars or the travails of beauty: a "laesy loord, for nothing good to doone" (12.3), whose laziness makes him "lewd and poore" (l. 9).

Thomas Roche has called the witch's son an idiot, but although he is guilty of lethargy, this minor character is not so easily discarded.[55] Unlike the metaphorical poverty of the emblem to the "September" eclogue or of *Amoretti 35*, the churl's poverty is real and legally recognized: he is idle, he will not work, and he refuses to "ply him selfe to any honest trade" (3.7.12). This idleness is consistent with the "sturdy" poor of Elizabethan statute law who "beyng whole and mightye in Body and able to labour . . . can gyve no reckninge howe hee or shee dothe lawfully get his or her Lyvinge."[56] Yet it also places him in a unique relationship to the Spenserian hero. At first sight of Florimell, the churl feels what Redcross felt on the Mount of Contemplation: "his feeble eyne, with too much brightnes daz'd, / So stared he on her, and stood long while amaz'd" (3.7.13).[57] At the girl's flight several stanzas later, he is reduced to a "frenzy" and "sore plight" (20.6–9) that directly echoes both Britomart's own romantic ardor for Artegall and Glauce's attempts to cure her lovesick charge in cantos 2 and 3.[58] Spenser, in this respect, links a story of failed magic to one that is properly magical, in the prophetic sense suggested by Merlin, but also raises a further a question: to what degree the churl's poverty is not merely an object of representation but representative of a formal principle within the poem.

Spenser, interestingly, answers that question by aestheticizing it. Quite literally, Spenser links Britomart and the poor churl through the shared experience of a work of art, distinguished by how much it remains, even as it is easily lost, within *The Faerie Queene*.

Traces of that aesthetic experience can be seen in the poor churl himself. As Florimell "grew familiare in that desert place," the witch's idle son, we are told, begins to perceive her kind courtesy as "affection bace"

(15.5–7). Driven by lust, he seeks to communicate "his desire" (16.4); lacking the requisite eloquence, he resorts to "lovely semblaunces" and "resemblances," so that the girl might read "his affection entire" (16.5–9). Spenser, as he is prone to do, implicates his own allegory or "false semblaunt" (Puttenham) in the unlettered deeds of the idle poor, suggesting what Evan Gurney has called a certain vagrancy or roguish element at the heart of Spenser's poetics.[59] But the poverty goes beyond the waywardness of word and image; for Spenser's poem indicates that the poor churl has at his disposal a more diverse sensibility in the arts and crafts of love:

> Oft from the forrest wildlings he did bring,
> Whose sides empurpled were with smyling red,
> And oft young birds, which he had taught to sing
> His maistresse praises, sweetly caroled,
> Girlonds of flowres sometimes for her faire hed
> He fine would dight; sometimes the squirrell wild
> He brought to her in bands, as conquered
> To be her thrall, his fellow servant vild;
> All which, she of him tooke with countenance meeke and mild. (3.7.17)

Rather than the excluded part or Marx's future day of many parts, clearly this is a man of multiple, if limited, parts. Between hunting, floral arrangement, and the teaching of birdsong, his efforts resemble the rude pastoral gifts of a Hobbinol or Coridon, as well as the native arts of "making-do" Patricia Fumerton notes constituted the majority of England's underclass in the sixteenth and seventeenth centuries.[60]

We seem, that is, to be in the realm of a spontaneous, hitherto unaccounted *aisthesis*—were it not that this aesthetic part appears unaccounted only insofar as the elaborate artifice of *The Faerie Queene* encourages us to forget another, more unforgettable instance of garlands being woven for an unwilling lover that we have already seen in book 3: the extended ekphrasis of Malecasta's sumptuous tapestries (3.1.33–39), where Britomart stares mutely at Venus weaving garlands for Adonis.

> The wals were round about appareiled
> With costly clothes of *Arras* and of *Toure*,
> In which with cunning hand was pourtrahed
> The love of *Venus* and her Paramoure,
> The fayre *Adonis*, turned to a flowre,
> A worke of rare device, and wondrous wit

First did it shew the bitter balefull stowre,
Which her assayd with many a fervent fit,
When first her tender hart was with his beautie smit.

Then with what sleights and sweet allurements she
Entyst the Boy, as well that art she knew,
And wooed him her Paramoure to bee;
Now making girlonds of each flowre that grew,
To crowne his golden lockes with honour dew; (3.1.34–35)

In form and content, the tapestry's artistry makes us keenly aware, like Spenser's dedicatory sonnet, of what is both left and lost in his poem. Venus's "allurement" anticipates that of the poor churl as she proffers floral garlands, the forest shade (35.6), the starry skies (36.1), fragrant violets (36.8), and sweet Nectar (36.9) to woo the reluctant Adonis. Spenser's narrator subsequently re-creates those wordless sensations for us as Britomart passes through the chamber, as Rachel Eisendrath notes, with a series of deictic gestures, telling us "'now' this happened 'now' that happened," so that our eyes move across the visual scene with her.[61] The ekphrastic verse suggests the sense and "semblaunce" we will later encounter with the churl. Yet it also re-creates what neither a tapestry nor a rude boor could *ever* communicate through sense or semblance alone, as indicated in its final lines: "But when she saw no helpe might him restore, / Him to a dainty flowre she did transmew, / *Which in that cloth was wrought, as if it lively grew*" (38.9; emphasis added).

Since the churl cannot transform his beloved into the thing he most wants, he must content himself with the False Florimell of his mother's creation; since a tapestry cannot in fact show a lively flower growing, Spenser reveals in these lines, as Eisendrath argues, something else—a reified art object. In *Poetry in a World of Things*, Eisendrath argues that Spenser's verse separates the art of humanist self-fashioning from art for art's sake by taking us "outside" the mimetic work of art. Spenser's anticipation of the Kantian "as if" (*als ob*) invites us to see what the tapestry is *not*—a living flower, a speaking picture, the thing itself—in order to see it for what it *is*, a "costly Arras."[62] An autonomous aesthetic thus appears, for Eisendrath, at the point of its commodification or plenty. Yet I would add that Spenser also pulls us back "inside" the mimetic encounter, to an aesthetic experience made possible not by a more abundant, aesthetic modernism to come but by the poverty we have already seen internal to the sixteenth-century humanist tradition. For in canto 1, stanzas 33–40, the very thing that makes possible the fragile autonomy of the "as if"—Britomart's mute or suspended judgment—is the very thing that makes her most like the poor churl. As Jeff Dolven puts it, Britomart tends to "idle at that threshold [of learning], feeding herself continuously without digesting anything."[63]

This curiously needy version of *skholé* for viewer and reader alike is dictated, in part, by Spenser's word choice, which describes Malecasta's tapestries as cladding the chamber in a "stately manner" and "goodly wize" (*OED*: manner; style, mode). Like the beggarly style or "manner" of Gager's scholars, we are left to wander at the limits of possible aesthetic experiences: though Britomart's fellow knights disdain the lascivious behavior of the chamber's courtly inhabitants (stanzas 39–41), the tapestry's description over the space of four stanzas leaves the relationship between the magnificence of that "stately" work and the "goodly wize" it effects (or not) on Britomart herself unclear. In his 1590 treatise on learning and fame, the Elizabethan pedagogue Thomas Fenne portrays this liminal position as the aesthetic provocation needed for all poor or "pettie schollers":

> Is it not reported, that *Aeneas* coming to *Carthage* (there viewing and perusing the destruction of *Troy*, being painted on the wall of *Didoes* pallaice) with his faithfull companion *Achates*, to haue more imaginations and thoughts in his minde concerning the effect and substaunce, than the wall by painting could signifie, yet notwithstanding the picture first caused those thoughts (by representing the matter) to reuolue in his experienced minde : so that the setting downe of a part, causeth the wise to conceiue the whole : and by penning a briefe, the learned coniectureth a volume.[64]

What Fenne calls the relation of part to whole is here experienced in *The Faerie Queene* as a kind of aesthetic cause ("more imaginations and thoughts in his minde") without corresponding, allegorical effect ("than the wall by painting could signifie"). In canto 9, Britomart will articulate the political allegory that the episode of Malecasta's tapestries is clearly meant to evoke—her own parallels to the myth of Aeneas and the coming of a new Troy, or third "wonder of the world" (3.9.45), in England. In canto 1, that conflation of synecdoche and causation is ruptured by an autonomous aesthetic experience that is, itself, impoverished by the very thing we know separates that future wonder from its classical, humanist past: the waste and "need," according to Glauce, through which both we and Britomart must journey for the remainder of the poem.

The Faerie Queene, in this sense, locates the aesthetic in the space of the needy, if not quite good, scholar. For Britomart and the poor churl, the shared *aisthesis* conferred by that shared need is, of course, not distributed equally throughout book 3. In canto 8, the poor churl will be bereft of his (false) Florimell, a "trembling" (3.8.13) minor character who remains only to be forgotten. In books 4 and 5, Britomart will linger on the threshold of love, driven by a projection of Artegall and a dynastic union from which she must, unforgettably, exit stage left. As Crystal Bartolovich argues, early modern political aesthetics in this way fails to achieve the liberal expansion of aesthetic and intellectual privilege called for by Bourdieu; the conceit of the poor scholar does nothing to universalize the material conditions of such privilege. At the same time, its life within *The Faerie Queene* yields something more and less than privilege. It yields an aesthetic whose exigency makes it neither an object of future Enlightenment abundance nor of indeterminate lack in the sixteenth century but a part of the quest.

In *The Second Part of the Return to Parnassus* (1602)—performed at St. John's College, Cambridge, three years after Spenser's death—Spenser was remembered in the play's pantheon of contemporary English wits as the gentle shepherd and author of *The Faerie Queene* whose verse is to be celebrated above Shakespeare, Drayton, Jonson, and others for its sweet song and "melting tong." To this remembrance, the play's speaking characters added a further epithet that, as we have seen, clung even to the preceding century's most eminent authors:

> And yet for all, this unregarding soile
> Unlac't the line of his desired life,
> Denying mayntenance for his deare releife:
> Carelesse ere to prevent his exequy,
> Scarce deigning to shut up his dying eye.
> *Ingenioso* Pity it is that gentler witts should breed,
> Where thick-skin chuffes laugh at a schollers neede.[65]

For decades now, the old historicist question of whether Spenser died in poverty has been dispatched by critical attention to the religious, political, and ideological abundance his allegorical verse enables. Spenser, on these grounds, did not as Jonson claimed "die for lack of bread."[66] Yet as the persistent trope of "schollers need" suggests in Ingenioso's refrain, there are, perhaps, other poverties at work in Spenser's poetry that "unlac[e] the line" of these desired biographical and literary lives: the idea of a poetry that both creates in and out of its "need" in the sixteenth century and that lingers, like Britomart and the churl, at the threshold of a more liberated aesthetic sensibility. As Richard McCabe writes in *Ungainefull Arte*, the legend of Spenser's impoverished death was thus not incidental, for "it was amidst the debris of [Spenser's] patronal hopes that the Prince of Poets was finally crowned."[67] This essay has argued that the conceit of the poor scholar in Tudor humanism offers a means not only to historicize that emerging aesthetic sensibility in early modern England. As the anonymous student authors of the Parnassus Plays recognized, poverty discloses the aesthetic life as a kind of remainder or loss to be historicized in the first place.

Just as a seemingly inconsequential aphorism like Glauce's may prove consequential for *The Faerie Queene*, it is worth asking, in this respect, how the often-invisible forms of poverty in the academy today might inform how we approach early modern political aesthetics. In 2018, the University of Wisconsin HOPE Lab reported that approximately 36 percent of American undergraduates had experienced unstable housing in the previous academic year, 36 percent were food insecure, and 9 percent were officially homeless. (For students at public colleges and universities in my own state of Connecticut, the latter number is as high as 17 percent.)[68] In his original preface to *The Philosopher and His Poor*, Rancière noted that his own interest in the relationship between poverty and aesthetics sprang from an attempt to understand why, since the nineteenth century, "when proletarians . . . invaded the territory of the literati, the literati answered evasively by celebrating work as the true culture of the poor and the future of the world."[69] Rancière's point is that even the most socially engaged criticism often works to preserve and protect itself from the "split personality" of an aesthetic history written, informed, and shaped by the needs closest to it. Further inspection of the poetic tradition in the Age of Spenser and Shakespeare, I have suggested, shows how this split personality was in fact always part of England's literary consciousness, and one to which early modern criticism remains indebted.

Notes

1. Pliny the Elder, *Natural History*, volume IX, books 33–35, trans. H. Rackham (Cambridge, Mass.: Harvard University Press, 1952), 35.84–87 (pp. 322–25).

2. Richard Pace, *De fructu qui ex doctrina percipitur* (*The Benefit of a Liberal Education*), ed. and trans. Frank Manley and Richard S. Sylvester (New York: Renaissance Society of America / Ungar, 1967), 23. On Pace and changing class attitudes toward sixteenth-century education, see Fritz Caspari, *Humanism and the Social Order in Tudor England* (Chicago: University of Chicago Press, 1954), 136–37.

3. Desiderius Erasmus, *On Copia of Words and Ideas* (*De utraque verborum ac rerum copia*), trans. Donald B. King and H. David Rix (Milwaukee: Marquette University Press, 1999), 11.

4. Erasmus to More, February 22, 1518, in *The Correspondence of Erasmus: Letters 594 to 841 (1517–1518)*, trans. R. A. B. Mynors and D. F. S. Thomson (Toronto: University of Toronto Press, 1979), 776–77.

5. Jacques Rancière, *The Philosopher and His Poor*, trans. Andrew Parker (Durham, N.C.: Duke University Press, 2003), 3–8.

6. Jacques Rancière, "The Aesthetic Dimension: Aesthetics, Politics, Knowledge," *Critical Inquiry* 36, no. 1 (Autumn 2009): 7–11; Jacques Rancière, "Ten Theses on Politics," *Theory and Event* 5, no. 3 (2001): para. 23.

7. The Old English word *scole*, meaning "place of instruction," is derived from Latin *schola* and Greek *skholé*, which encompass the intermission, free time, leisure, ease, and idleness necessary for learning and, by extension, its space of otiose discussion (see "school, n.1," *OED Online*, Oxford University Press, September 2019, www.oed.com/view/Entry/172522; accessed October 13, 2019.). For Bourdieu's account, see Pierre Bourdieu, *Pascalian Meditations*, trans. Richard Nice (Stanford, Calif.: Stanford University Press, 2000), 12–28, and Pierre Bourdieu, "The Scholastic Point of View," *Cultural Anthropology* 5, no. 4 (November 1990): 380–91.

8. Giorgio Agamben, *The Time That Remains: A Commentary on the Letter to the Romans*, trans. Patricia Dailey (Stanford, Calif.: Stanford University Press, 2005), 58. "Years later, Rancière himself returned to this Foucauldian concept so as to develop it into the concept of a people, understood as 'the part of those who have no part,' meaning a supernumerary party, the bearer of a wrong which establishes democracy as a 'community of dispute.' But everything here depends on how one interprets 'wrong' and 'dispute.' If democratic dispute is understood for what it truly is, that is, the possibility of *stasis* or of civil war, then this definition is pertinent. If, however, following what Rancière seems to think, the wrong for whom the people are the cipher . . . can be 'processed,' then the line between democracy and its consensual, or postdemocratic, counterfeit (which Rancière goes so far as to overtly critique) tends to dissolve." Agamben refers here to Foucault's 1977 interview with Rancière and the editors of *Les révoltes logiques*, which I quote on page 186.

9. A. L. Beier, *Masterless Men: The Vagrancy Problem in England 1560–1640* (London: Methuen, 1985), 102–3.

10. See Giovanni Boccaccio, *Genealogia Deorum Gentilium* (book 14), in *Boccaccio on Poetry: Being the Preface and the Fourteenth and Fifteenth Books of Boccaccio's "Genealogia Deorum Gentilium,"* ed. Charles G. Osgood (New York: Bobbs-Merrill, 1956), 21–32; Joachim du Bellay, *The Regrets, with The Antiquities of Rome, Three Latin Elegies, and The Defense and Enrichment of the French Language*, ed. and trans. Richard Helgerson (Philadelphia: University of Pennsylvania Press, 2006), 55–56; Christopher Marlowe, *Hero and Leander*, in *The Complete Poems of Christopher Marlowe*, ed. Patrick Cheney and Brian J. Striar (New York: Oxford University Press, 2006), ll. 465–84; John Taylor, *The Praise, Antiquity, and commodity, of Beggery, Beggers, and Begging* (London, 1621), sig. B2r–B3r.

11. Edmund Spenser, *The Faerie Queene*, ed. A. C. Hamilton, text ed. Hiroshi Yamashita and Toshiyuki Suzuki (London: Longman, 2001); references are to this edition and hereafter cited parenthetically.

12. William Shakespeare, *King Lear*, ed. R. A. Foakes (London: Arden Shakespeare, 1997).

13. William Carroll, *Fat King, Lean Beggar: Representations of Poverty in the Age of Shakespeare* (Ithaca, N.Y.: Cornell University Press, 1996); Linda Woodbridge, *Vagrancy, Homelessness, and English Renaissance Literature* (Champaign: University of Illinois Press, 2011); Patricia Fumerton, *Unsettled: The Culture of Mobility and the Working Poor in Early Modern England* (Chicago: University of Chicago Press, 2006).

14. Hugh Grady, *Shakespeare and Impure Aesthetics* (Cambridge: Cambridge University Press, 2009).

15. See Genevieve Guenther, "Spenser's Magic, or Instrumental Aesthetics in the 1590 *Faerie Queene*," *English Literary Renaissance* 36, no. 2 (Spring 2006): 194–226; Rachel Eisendrath, "Art and Objectivity in the House of Busirane," *Spenser Studies* 27 (2012): 133–61; and Rachel Eisendrath, "Going Outside: Human Subjectivity and the Aesthetic Object, *The Faerie Queene*, Book III," *Spenser Studies* 30 (2015): 343–68.

16. Christopher Pye, *The Storm at Sea: Political Aesthetics in the Time of Shakespeare* (New York: Fordham University Press, 2015), 15.

17. Crystal Bartolovich, "Utopia and Its Enemies: Intellectuals, Elitism, and the Commonwealth of Learning," *Journal for Early Modern Cultural Studies* 13, no. 3 (Summer 2013): 35.

18. Pliny, *Natural History,* 324. On the "cut of Apelles"—a phrase that Agamben derives from Pliny's parallel aphoristic tale of Apelles's contest with Protogenes—see Agamben, *The Time That Remains*, 44–51.

19. Agamben, *The Time That Remains*, 39–40. See also Walter Benjamin, "Dostoevsky's *The Idiot*," in *Selected Writings, Volume 1: 1913–1926*, ed. Marcus Bullock and Michael W. Jennings (Cambridge, Mass.: Harvard University Press, 1996), 80.

20. On the role of need and compulsion as essential to Kant's conception of universal aesthetic judgment and the "as if" (*als ob*), see Gregg M. Horowitz, *Sustaining Loss: Art as Mournful Life* (Stanford, Calif.: Stanford University Press, 2001), 28–37.

21. Horowitz, *Sustaining Loss*, 39. For an expanded account of exigency and poverty as "form of life," see also Giorgio Agamben, *The Use of Bodies: Homo Sacer IV, 2*, trans. Adam Kotsko (Stanford, Calif.: Stanford University Press, 2015), 81–87.

22. Peter Brown, "Remembering the Poor and the Aesthetic of Society," *Journal of Interdisciplinary History* 35, no. 3 (Winter 2005): 520–22.

23. Marlowe, *Hero and Leander*, l. 470; Thomas Nashe, *The Unfortunate Traveller and Other Works*, ed. J. B. Steane (New York: Penguin Books, 2006), 265–66.

24. See Laurie Shannon, "Poor, Bare, Forked: Animal Sovereignty, Human Negative Exceptionalism, and the Natural History of *King Lear*," *Shakespeare Quarterly* 60, no. 2 (Summer 2009): 175; see also Carroll, *Fat King, Lean Beggar*, 8.

25. See Judith H. Anderson, "'Nor Man It Is': The Knight of Justice in Book V of Spenser's *Faerie Queene*," *PMLA* 85, no. 1 (January 1970): 72: "The problem remains that Britomart herself has eventually to be transcended. If she improves as a person, she becomes irrelevant as one."

26. David Lee Miller, *The Poem's Two Bodies: The Poetics of the 1590 "Faerie Queene"* (Princeton, N.J.: Princeton University Press, 1988), 81.

27. Pye, *The Storm at Sea*, 98–99.

28. See Hamilton, *The Faerie Queene*, 319–20n, and *The Works of Edmund Spenser: A Variorum Edition*, ed. Edwin Greenlaw, Charles Grosvenor Osgood, and Frederick Morgan Padelford (Baltimore: Johns Hopkins University Press, 1966), 3:423. Ralph Church, in his 1758 edition, expressed the opposite sentiment: "But I prefer the reading given. The [1596] alteration is so much for the worse, that I dare be confident it is not Spenser's" (*The Faerie Queene, by Edmund Spenser. A New Edition, with notes critical and explanatory, by Ralph Church, M.A.* [London: William Faden, 1758], 73).

29. *The Yale Edition of the Shorter Poems of Edmund Spenser*, ed. William A. Oram et al. (New Haven, Conn.: Yale University Press, 1989); references to Spenser's shorter verse are to this edition and hereafter cited parenthetically.

30. Graham Hammill, "'The thing / Which never was': Republicanism and *The Ruines of Time*," *Spenser Studies* 18, no. 1 (2003): 171, 177. As Hammill notes, William Harrison records Verlamium as *municipium Romanorum*, or that which enjoyed "the whole freedom of the Romans."

31. Geoffrey Chaucer, *The Riverside Chaucer*, ed. Larry D. Benson (Oxford: Oxford University Press, 1987).

32. William Horman, *Vulgaria uiri doctissimi* (London: Pynson, 1519), 54; Erasmus, *Adagia*. For a partial list, see also Morris Palmer Tilley, *The Proverbs in England in the Sixteenth and Seventeenth Centuries* (Ann Arbor: University of Michigan Press, 1950), 492; G. L. Apperson, *English Proverbs and Proverbial Phrases: A Historical Dictionary* (Detroit: Gale Research, 1969), 439; and *The Oxford Dictionary of English Proverbs*, 3rd ed., rev. F. P. Wilson (Oxford: Clarendon Press, 1970), 558.

33. Thomas Pritchard, *The Schoole of honest and vertuous lyfe: Profitable and necessary for all estates and degrees, to be trayned in but (chefely) for the pettie Schollers* (London: Jones, 1579?), 14; *Englands Parnassus; or, The choysest Flowers of our Moderne Poets, with their Poeticall comparisons* (London, 1600), 241–42; J. B. Leishman, ed., *The Three Parnassus Plays* (London: Nicholson and Watson, 1949); Thomas Nashe, *Pierce Penniless His Supplication to the Devil*, in Steane, *The Unfortunate Traveller*, 50–51.

34. Jacques Rancière, *Aisthesis: Scenes from the Aesthetic Regime of Art*, trans. Zakir Paul (New York: Verso, 2013), 18.

35. Rancière, *Aisthesis*, 141.

36. Rancière, "The Aesthetic Dimension," 8.

37. Bourdieu, *Pascalian Meditations*, 20–21. Writing of the Renaissance, for example, Bourdieu describes the liberalization of the arts beginning in the sixteenth century as a repression of material determinants.

38. Andrea Alciati, *Emblematum Liber (Viri clarissimi D. Andree Alciati . . .)* (Augsburg: Heinrich Steyner, 6 April 1531), sig. A8r; and Andrea Alciati, *Emblemata* (Lyon: Guillaume Rouille, 1550), sig. I2v (p. 132). For an overview of the Latin and vernacular versions of the emblem, see the online facsimiles at *Alciato at Glasgow*, www.emblems.arts.gla.ac.uk/alciato/index.php (accessed 13 October 2019).

39. Geffrey Whitney, *A Choice of Emblemes* (1586), in *The English Emblem Tradition*, ed. Peter Daly (Toronto: University of Toronto Press, 1988), 247.

40. Christopher Warley, "'So Plenty Makes Me Poore': Ireland, Capitalism, and Class in Spenser's *Amoretti and Epithalamion*," *ELH* 69, no. 3 (Fall 2002): 584.

41. Richard Halpern, *The Poetics of Primitive Accumulation: English Renaissance Culture and the Genealogy of Capital* (Ithaca, N.Y.: Cornell University Press, 1991), 29.

42. See Andrew Hadfield, *Edmund Spenser: A Life* (New York: Oxford University Press, 2012), 51–52, 55–57. Hadfield notes that Spenser's receipt of a small behest from Robert Nowell upon leaving the Merchant Taylors' School for Cambridge does not support the image of Spenser as a lower-class student or son of the journeyman John Spenser. At the same time, his status as a sizar—a student granted board and lodging in exchange for menial service to fellows, possibly in Spenser's case to Gabriel Harvey—does point to Spenser's relative poverty and periodic absences from school in search of employment. On the often porous nature of these distinctions, and the ease with which gentlemen could be mistaken for "poor scholars" themselves, see Elizabeth Hanson, "Education, the University, and Marlowe," in *Christopher Marlowe in Context*, ed. Emily C. Bartels and Emma Smith (Cambridge: Cambridge University Press, 2013), 184–86.

43. Linda Shenk, "Gown Before Crown: Scholarly Abjection and Academic Entertainment Under Queen Elizabeth I," in *Early Modern Academic Drama*, ed. Jonathan Walker and Paul D. Streufert (Burlington, Vt.: Ashgate Publishing, 2008), 34–35.

44. William Gager, "Letter to Dr. John Rainolds of July 31, 1592," in *William Gager: The Complete Works*, ed. Dana F. Sutton, rev. ed. (Birmingham, U.K.: Philological Museum, 2005), accessed August 23, 2017, http://www.philological.bham.ac.uk/gager/prose/rainolds/index.html, para. 8.

45. Gager, "Letter."

46. Karl Marx and Friedrich Engels, *The German Ideology*, in *The Marx-Engels Reader*, ed. Robert C. Tucker, 2nd ed. (New York: Norton, 1978), 160.

47. See Friedrich Schiller, *On the Aesthetic Education of Man*, trans. Keith Tribe (London: Penguin Books, 2016), 17–23, 53–63 (letters 6 and 15).

48. Rancière, "The Aesthetic Dimension," 8. "This ignorance is by no means the illusion that conceals the reality of possession," Rancière writes. "Rather, it is the means for building a new sensible world, which is a world of equality within the world of possession and inequality."

49. Russ Leo, "The Species-Life of Worldlings," *Spenser Studies* 30 (2015): 208–9. As Leo argues, though Guyon ultimately tempers and transcends this scene of unthinking wonder, the encounter "expose[s] an abiding continuity" of human need within capitalism, "integrating the fiendish laborers . . . into the thoughtless irrational activity of men and markets above" (220).

50. Tracey Sedinger, "Women's Friendship and the Refusal of Lesbian Desire in *The Faerie Queene*," *Criticism* 42, no. 1 (Winter 2000): 97.

51. Clark Hulse, "'Painted Forgery': Visual Approaches to *The Faerie Queene*," in *Approaches to Teaching Spenser's "Faerie Queene,"* ed. David Lee Miller and Alexander Dunlop (New York: Modern Language Association of America, 1994), 95.

52. Pye, *The Storm at Sea*, 15.

53. Quoted in Agamben, *The Time That Remains*, 60; emphasis in original. For the sake of continuity, I adopt Kotsko's translation of Agamben's citation of Foucault; for the original interview with Rancière and the editors of *Les révoltes logiques*, as well as Foucault's wider response to the problem of neoliberalism this idea of the "pleb" entails, see Michel Foucault, "Power and Strategies," trans. Colin Gordon, in *Power/Knowledge: Selected Interviews and Other Writings, 1972–1977*, ed. Colin Gordon (New York: Pantheon Books, 1980), 139.

54. Agamben, *The Time That Remains*, 40.

55. Thomas Roche, "*The Faerie Queene*, Book III," in *The Spenser Encyclopedia*, ed. A. C. Hamilton et al. (Toronto: University of Toronto Press, 1990), 271; on the role of Spenser's minor characters, see Harry Berger Jr., "The Discarding of Malbecco: Conspicuous Allusion and Cultural Exhaustion in *The Faerie Queene* III," *Studies in Philology* 66, no. 2 (April 1969): 135–54.

56. "An Acte for the Punishment of Vacabondes, and for Releif of the Poore and Impotent" (1572; 14.Eliz.c.5), in *The Statutes of the Realm* (1819), vol. 4, part 1, p. 591.

57. See Redcross, book 1, canto 10: ". . . but dazed were his eyne, / Through passing brightnes, which did quite confound / His feeble sence, and too exceeding shine" (1.10.676–78).

58. Compare Glauce's failed cure in canto 3, "Full many waies she sought, but none could find, / Nor herbes, nor charmes, nor counsel that is chiefe" (3.3.5), with the witch's in canto 7: "All wayes she sought, him to restore to plight, / With herbs, with charms, with counsel, and with teares, / But tears, nor charms, nor herbs, nor counsell might" assuage the young man's passion (3.7.21.1–3).

59. Evan Gurney, "Going Rogue: Spenser and the Vagrants," *Studies in Philology* 113, no. 3 (Summer 2016): 546–76.

60. Patricia Fumerton, "Making Vagrancy (In)visible: The Economics of Disguise in Early Modern Rogue Pamphlets," in *Rogues in Early Modern English Culture*, ed. Craig Dionne and Steve Mentz (Ann Arbor: University of Michigan Press, 2004), 195–96.

61. Eisendrath, "Going Outside," 350–51.

62. Rachel Eisendrath, *Poetry in a World of Things: Aesthetics and Empiricism in Renaissance Ekphrasis* (Chicago: University of Chicago Press, 2018), 49–60; see also Eisendrath, "Going Outside," 350–51.

63. Jeff Dolven, *Scenes of Instruction in Renaissance Romance* (Chicago: University of Chicago Press, 2007), 169.

64. Thomas Fenne, *Fennes Frutes: Which Worke is devided into three severall parts; The first, A Dialogue between Fame and the Schollers . . .* (London: Richard Oliffe, 1590), sig. A4v.

65. Anon., *The Second Part of the Return from Parnassus*, ll. 220–27, in Leishman, *The Three Parnassus Plays*, 236–37.

66. Quoted in Hadfield, *Edmund Spenser*, 391. Spenser was indeed still receiving his pension and was owed eight pounds from the Privy Council at the time of his death; the inference of his poverty, however, was widespread. Camden, for example, writes, "But by a Fate which still follows Poets, he always wrastled with poverty . . . and returned into *England* a poor man, where he shortly after died" (393–94).

67. Richard A. McCabe, *'Ungainefull Arte': Poetry, Patronage, and Print in the Early Modern Era* (Oxford: Oxford University Press, 2016), 252.

68. Sara Goldrick-Rab et al., "Still Hungry and Homeless in College," Wisconsin Hope Lab, April 2018, https://hope4college.com/wp-content/uploads/2018/09/Wisconsin-HOPE-Lab-Still-Hungry-and-Homeless.pdf; "Homelessness and Housing Instability in Connecticut Colleges and Universities," Connecticut Coalition to End Homelessness, July 9, 2018, http://www.cceh.org/wp-content/uploads/2018/07/FINAL-FINAL-CSCU-Youth-Count-Data-Report-July-9-2018.pdf.

69. Jacques Rancière, "A Personal Itinerary," in *Philosopher and His Poor*, xxvi.

Part Three

Island Voices

“I . . . Will Cry It O’er Again”

Virgil, *The Tempest*, and the Aesthetics of Imitation

Lydia C. Heinrichs

Early in *The Politics of Aesthetics*, Jacques Rancière, challenging the traditional literary critical and art historical equation of modernist art with the avant-garde, numbers among the constitutive features of the “aesthetic regime of the arts” a refusal to acknowledge historical dichotomies such as old and new, tradition and avant-garde. “The aesthetic regime of the arts did not begin with decisions to initiate an artistic rupture,” he writes. “It began with decisions to reinterpret what makes art or what art makes . . . The aesthetic regime of the arts is first of all a new regime for relating to the past.”[1] The aesthetic regime, he continues, originates in the writings of certain eighteenth-century philosophers who, refuting the idea that artistic beauty is transhistorical, instead thought of canonical works of art as immanent manifestations of the forms of expression of particular historical communities. Citing Mendelssohn’s recuperation of the works of Bach as an example, Rancière further insists that this reinterpretation of what and how art means, achieved in the reinterpretation of canonical works of art, is not merely the accomplishment of the philosophical and critical writings of Vico, Hegel, Hölderlin, and others, but also of the period’s art. If, as Rancière writes, the aesthetic regime is characterized by “a form of thought that has become foreign to itself,” that estrangement of thought springs first from the defamiliarization of the canonical that occurred, not when artists and philosophers initiated a break from the past but when they used its historical difference to overturn the mimetic regime’s assumptions about the nature of art and beauty.[2] The aesthetic regime of the arts, he remarks, “devotes itself to the invention of new forms of life on the basis of an idea of what art *was*, an idea of what art *would have been*.”[3] In this sense, the revisitation of canonical works of art that occurred in the late

Enlightenment and Romantic periods both initiated and participated in the dislocation of familiar modes of organizing the sensible and the creation of new sensible forms that characterize the aesthetic regime as a whole.

If "the temporality specific to the aesthetic regime of the arts is a co-presence of heterogeneous temporalities," that temporality appears in Rancière's writings to be a primarily post–eighteenth century phenomenon, breaking from the Aristotelian "poetic regime of the arts," in which works of art are evaluated in terms of their obedience to certain hierarchical formal standards.[4] This chapter reconsiders a Renaissance practice that would seem to be the paradigmatic expression of such a regime's rigid adherence to neoclassical rules: *imitatio*. In particular, I examine the use of the early modern period's single most admired classical poem, Virgil's *Aeneid*, in Shakespeare's late play *The Tempest*. *The Tempest*'s many Virgilian echoes, in addition to its unusually unified dramatic structure, have long been understood to represent Shakespeare's most extended engagement with the emergent neoclassicism of the early seventeenth century, manifested particularly in the works of Ben Jonson.[5] Yet *The Tempest*'s imitation of *The Aeneid*, which informs its apparently Aristotelian plot structure as much as more-local allusions, implies no mere reverential obedience to a classical ideal or artistic norm. The play does not historicize *The Aeneid*, but it is deeply aware of the consequences of that poem for the phenomenalization of history itself, one that serves as the basis for Roman, and subsequently early modern, political identity. *The Tempest*, in other words, is highly conscious of the classical poem's investment in the formation of a hierarchical vision of history and of the community that history produces. In particular, it reflects on the paradoxically central place of the Virgilian model of history in the nascent emergence of autonomous subjectivity in the early modern period.

The play's exceptional clarity about the ideological stakes of Virgilian *imitatio*, artistic or political, is, nevertheless, most evident not in the play's absolute break from or rejection of *imitatio* but rather in the very process of imitating Virgil, through which it instantiates the contradictions in the fantasy of absolutely transcending reiterative convention. Prospero's own dream of subjective autonomy is foiled throughout the play by his attempt to legitimate that autonomy with reference to Virgil's poem, an attempt that merely refers the play to *The Aeneid*'s own anxieties about the tensions between the desire for historical novelty and the need for the legitimation bestowed by patriarchal inheritance. Rather than either conforming entirely to the practice of imitation or attempting to break the shackles of convention, the play alienates the classical exemplar from its own exemplarity. Throughout this chapter, then, I attempt to think

Rancière's aesthetic regime and Shakespearean imitation together, despite the received history that might contrast the aesthetic regime's estrangement of thought with earlier periods' apparently more normative artistic practices. I thus both join Rancière's critique of the conceptualization of modern history as the progressive advancement and realization of pure novelty and extend the implication of that critique to practices that, even within Rancière's revision of the history of aesthetics, would seem entirely opposed to the new forms of historical consciousness and aesthetic thought emergent in and after the Enlightenment.

No classical poem more obviously claims to break history from the hold of reiterative historical consciousness than does *The Aeneid*. Tracing Aeneas's errant journey from Troy to Rome, where he will establish Rome's prophesied *imperium sine fine* on the shores of the Tiber, the epic's first six books attempt to wrest imperial history away from the individual's tendency to wander aimlessly over landscapes haunted by the past, even as they seek on a stylistic and formal level to displace a Homeric idiom with a distinctively Roman one. The contrast between the reiteration of Trojan defeat and progressive history proper emerges in book 4's juxtaposition of its two empire builders, the Trojan Aeneas and the Carthaginian Dido, who each strive to bury the wounds inflicted by the past and to construct new empires unfazed by the legacy of failed precursors. Dido's incapacity to establish psychological and emotional independence from the traumatic fall of Troy, however, dooms the imperial aspirations of her city.[6] Though she is not Trojan and bears no memory of Troy or its incineration, the poem elides her with the fallen city when, in book 4, Aeneas's tale of its downfall inflicts her with the "wound" and "blind fire" (*volnus*, *caeco igni*; 4.2) of desire for Aeneas—a fire that recalls the burning of Troy and transfers to Dido Aeneas's debilitating memory of the event.[7] Aeneas, instead, succeeds in burying the obstructive memory of Troy in order to carry on its legacy in Rome, or so the epic hopes. When Aeneas, persuaded by the warnings of Mercury, finally departs from Dido for Italy, leaving Dido to spew futile curses at him from her flaming deathbed, the poem condemns all forms of resistance to imperial narrative to a phantasmic existence as iterations and reiterations of Dido's avenging spirit, and thus reiterations of Troy's own ghost—a recursive model of history Rome only narrowly escaped:

> Then, O my Tyrians, besiege with hate
> His progeny and all his race to come:
> Make this your offering to my dust. No love,

> No pact must be between our peoples; No,
> But rise up from my bones, avenging spirit!
> Harry with fire and sword the Dardan countrymen
> Now, or hereafter, at whatever time
> The strength will be afforded. Coast with coast
> In conflict, I implore, and sea with sea,
> And arms with arms: may they contend in war,
> Themselves and all the children of their children! (4.621–28)[8]

Here alluding specifically to Hannibal and the Carthaginians, who are Dido's direct descendants, Dido's ghost will reappear later in the poem in Cleopatra and Mark Antony, depicted on the shield of Aeneas, carried away from the tide of history by the winds and waves of fickle fortune, and in the Latin Turnus, sent at the end of the poem to a restless, vengeful, and inconclusive afterlife in Hades.[9] Unifying the disparate threads of anti-imperial rebellion under the shadow of Dido's curse permits the poem, similarly, to set every subversion of the Roman imperial narrative adrift from its claim to a historical truth external to itself. All resistance can take the form only of self-replicating historical phantasms originating in Dido's "wound," the unnarratable memory of Troy—a nightmare of conventionality indeed. Against this groundless self-replication the poem poses the Romans' sublimation of repetition and their inauguration of a progressive history rooted in the truth of divine fiat as they conclusively set sail for Italy.

Yet the dichotomy of progression and regression, as well as the direct correspondence of poetic fiction and cosmic truth, imperial narrative and divine history, may very well, the poem suggests, be phantasmic.[10] The aim of the poem is to dispel by reconjuring the historical ghosts against which it saw the Roman Empire defining itself, and the poem is, consequently, haunted by the possibility that imperial success is no more substantial than that ever-repeated gesture of emancipation from historical precedents. At the end of book 4, Dido's dying curse commits Aeneas to a death eerily similar to her own:

> If by necessity that impious wretch
> Must find his haven and come safe to land,
> If so Jove's destinies require, and this,
> His end in view, must stand, yet all the same
> When hard beset in war by a brave people,
> Forced to go outside his boundaries
> And torn from Iulus, let him beg assistance,

Let him see the unmerited deaths of those
Around and with him, and accepting peace
On unjust terms, let him not, even so,
Enjoy his kingdom or the life he longs for,
But fall in battle before his time and lie
Unburied on the sand! (4.612–20)

The curse vividly captures Rome's nightmare, a nightmare not of the failure of empire but of the failure of the Roman ideology of progress to secure empire's historical inevitability by sealing its distinction from its precursors, particularly the curse's speaker, Dido. Torn from his son, deprived of the filial *pietas* Aeneas represented in life, lingering above the ground and outside the protection of Rome, Aeneas's forlorn body transforms the very representative of empire's emancipation from its historical predecessors into another of the series of ghosts that pervade the poem's first half, denying Rome the psychic closure, dependent on a substantial and embodied manifestation of the legitimate transfer of power, on which its ideology of progress hinges. In the nightmare of Dido's curse, the circular, reiterative time of empire's challengers is not an alternative to epic narrative but is its very structural principle, which achieves success only by repeatedly raising and abandoning the specter of a past that eludes burial—even when that past is the very source and representative of Rome's historical novelty. Underneath *The Aeneid*'s ostensible historical optimism lurks a more troubling vision of historical progress: a history that is nothing more than the reiterated break from the perpetual reiteration of convention.

The Tempest begins in both the New World and the Old. With one foot in William Strachey's account of the 1609 shipwreck of Sir Thomas Gates off the coast of Bermuda and the other in the squall raised by Aeolus against Aeneas in *The Aeneid* 1, the play's opening storm immediately situates it in a tangled web of allusions to classical poetry as well as to the most recent journeys to the Americas.[11] This is no accident. For it is in *The Aeneid* that history understood as the sequential unfolding of novelty paradigmatically confronts its mirror image in the mere reiteration of socially reflexive convention. The play's conflation of Bermuda and *The Aeneid*, the most admired exemplum of Latin texts, must, then, navigate the troubled waters that lie between Troy's innumerable phantoms and the imperial dream of virgin territory.

Isolated from the Old World, seemingly "uninhabitable and almost inaccessible" (2.1.40),[12] surrounded by the metamorphic seas that leave nothing unchanged, the play's island sows dreams of the complete burial of the past and the inscription of the absolutely novel in the imaginations of all who set foot on it.[13] "I'th' commonwealth I would by contraries / Execute all things, for no kind of traffic / Would I admit; no name of magistrate; / Letters should not be known" (2.1.148–51), begins Gonzalo's close paraphrase of Montaigne's essay *Of the Canniballes*. Gonzalo envisions an island that lacks letters, communication with the Old World, and also the letters of words, the power of language to reinstate wearied convention. The island is self-sustaining ("nature should bring forth / Of its own kind all foison, all abundance / To feed my innocent people" [2.1.163–65]); untainted by sexuality ("And women, too, but innocent and pure" [2.1.156]); and seemingly egalitarian ("No sovereignty" [2.1.157]), although, as Sebastian reminds him acerbically, Gonzalo "would be king on't" (2.1.157). When they plot the murder of Alonso, Antonio and Sebastian also fall for the temptation of the new: the latter, Antonio claims, is destined by the shipwreck "to perform an act / Whereof what's past is prologue, what to come / In yours and my discharge!" (2.1.252–54). The island's carte blanche beguilingly offers the chance to realize complete reorganization of the political status quo. The play's most successful attempt to do so is, of course, Prospero's. "Now does my project gather to a head . . . [Time] / Goes upright with his carriage" (5.1.1–3), Prospero will proclaim shortly before he reinstates himself as Duke of Milan. A newly erect and directed force of historical reckoning dispenses with the effeminate supinity and homogeneity forced upon him by his exile.

As is all too clearly indicated by the oddly bitter argument about "widow Dido" that immediately precedes Gonzalo's utopian fiction, the attempt to sublimate bygone trauma, or indeed to obliterate the memory of the past completely and replace it with an entirely new signifying order unhampered by historical constraints, is foiled by the inherent Virgilianism of any such attempt to consolidate historical identity as against a historical other understood to be inherently errant, recursive, and traumatized by the burden of failure. The paradoxical claim to simultaneous novelty and conventionalism points to a broader tension in early Jacobean political culture. Though James VI and I touted his reign as the inception of a new *pax Augustana*, and invested heavily in an iconographic program that depicted him as a new Augustus, he was no less interested than Gonzalo, Antonio, and Prospero in breaking from historical convention in order to establish a regime that would be completely divorced from historical grounding. Over the course of a quarrel with Parliament not long after his coronation regarding the monarch's subjection to the common law, James resorted to an argument that monarchical authority exceeded the legitimacy bestowed by right of inheritance and that, indeed, authority as such in the commonwealth derived from the king: "it lyes in the power of no Parliament," he wrote in *True Law of Free Monarchies*,

> to make any kinde of lawe or statute, without [the king's] Scepter bee to it, for giuing it the force of a law . . . when the Bastard of *Normandie* came into *England*, & made himselfe King, was it not by force, and with a mighty army? Where he gaue the law, & tooke none, changed the laws, inuerted the order of gouernment . . .[14]

This is not *The Aeneid*'s *translatio imperii*, despite James's pretensions to Augustanism and his attempt to consolidate his image as dynasty founder: here, the derivation of the king's authority by right of conquest, rather than by hereditary right, demonstrates the grounds of monarchical authority within the pure, autogenic force of the monarch himself. A similar argument implicitly justifies Prospero's claim to the Mediterranean isle against Caliban's claim by inheritance: "This island's mine by Sycorax, my mother, / Which thou tak'st from me" (1.2.332–33), Caliban reminds Prospero, though Prospero's "art is of such power / It would control my dam's god Setebos, / And make a vassal of him" (1.2.373–75). The island, to which he had no hereditary right, provides the former duke an opportunity to reverse history and establish himself as the absolute source of his own authority and the sole authority on the island, much as William the Conqueror conjured his own extralegal authority in the mere act of conquest. The monstrous offspring of the isle's former ruler, however, stubbornly retains the trace of its other history.

Eliding the play's pervasive Virgilian allusions with a "master discourse"[15] of absolutist Virgilian politics and poetics, critical attention to *The Tempest*'s deployment of *The Aeneid* has tended to assume that those allusions work in favor of Prospero's own absolute authority, even if the play as a whole undermines that "master discourse." Despite her desire to "disfigure" Shakespeare and Virgil, Margaret Tudeau-Clayton sees the play's Virgilian allusions to represent the voice of consolidated authority in the play—a "Virgilian grammar of Nature"[16]—which the play seeks, in the "original, contestatory and usurping difference of the imitation," to disrupt.[17] The tendency to associate allusions to *The Aeneid* with Prospero's struggle for dominance over the play, and by extension with Jacobean absolutism and New World colonialism, however, itself superimposes on the play a totalized origin of classical legitimacy that the play seeks to undermine. *The Tempest*'s allusions to *The Aeneid* do not merely reinstate the poem's cultural prominence as a coherent and totalizing master signifier that must be either supported or resisted. Instead, it extracts from *The Aeneid* the poem's own representation of the—only partially suppressed—historical other that both impels and haunts its claim to a self-originating and absolutist regime. *The Tempest*, then, does not merely confront the totalized origin with its other—James with representational democracy, colonizer with New World indigenous, Virgil's grammar of nature with the "confused noise" of empirical nature—but also unravels the poem's dominant tone of imperial triumphalism from within.

The other of Virgilian history is, of course, Dido, whose necessarily ghostly presence in the play extends far beyond the obvious allusion to "widow Dido" in 2.1. Dido is the thread of Virgil that Prospero attempts, and fails, both to obliterate and remember: "Dost thou forget / From what a torment I did free thee?" (1.2.250–51), Prospero demands of Ariel; ". . . hast thou forgot / The foul witch Sycorax, who with age and envy / Was grown into a hoop?" (1.2.257–59). Brought, like Prospero, with child from a Mediterranean country to an island in the middle of nowhere in order to establish a new life freed from the trace of past failures, Sycorax immediately recalls Dido, the exile whose history eerily parallels the European's and from whom the latter must distinguish himself. Sycorax's aged and envious hoop embodies recursive history and imports into the play *The Aeneid*'s anxieties about the groundlessness of its own claim to legitimacy.[18] The witch's subsequent association with confinement and eternal pregnancy integrates that circular image into a broader network of associations with demonized classical women and their failure to adequately articulate essential distinctions between birth and death, past and future, parent and child, much like the hoop's own fusion of beginning and end: ". . . she did confine thee," Prospero reminds Ariel,

> By help of her more potent ministers
> And in her most unmitigable rage,
> Into a cloven pine, within which rift
> Imprisoned thou didst painfully remain
> A dozen years, within which space she died
> And left thee there, where thou didst vent thy groans
> As fast as millwheels strike. (1.2.274–81)

The anaphoric "within which" phrases constrict spatial and temporal extension into an arboreal vagina, the cleft of the pine, which impregnates itself with a being already alive. The cloven pine is notably reminiscent of Ovid's Myrrha, who, after being impregnated by her own father, transforms into a tree and cannot give birth to her child, Adonis, without divine aid.[19] Even as Myrrha, in bearing her father's issue, also takes within herself her own origin, Sycorax, or at least the imprecisely defined arboreal space with which her power is associated, absorbs the island's only prior inhabitant, the only being that might present an alternative claim to dominion. She thus appears to become mother to her own predecessor. Young and old, folding in upon herself the linear chronology of masculine inheritance, eluding both absolute life and absolute death—"For one thing she did / They would not take her life" (1.2.266–67)—the impregnated witch circumscribes the island's prehistory within a recursive narrative that lacks any constitutive relation to a patriarchal signifier.[20] Prospero claims to set in motion—through what is itself a reversal—Sycorax's apparent stagnation of spatiotemporal reality: "It was mine art, / When I arrived and heard thee, that made gape / The pine and let thee out" (1.2.291–93). Yet lacking a point of referentiality outside itself, Sycorax's circle also refuses that attempt to open her to masculine time and authority. The memory of the witch long outlives any power she had on the island.

"If thou more murmur'st," Prospero tells a recalcitrant Ariel, "I will rend an oak / And peg thee in his knotty entrails till / Thou hast howled away twelve winters" (1.2.294–6). Prospero's threatened punishment precisely repeats Ariel's earlier punishment at the hands of Sycorax, though the masculine oak has replaced the feminine pine tree. The witch's powers of confinement mirror Prospero's own restriction of the movements of other characters in the play: in 5.1, for example, Prospero conjures a circle around the Italians before he wakes them from their dream state in order to set history on its forward path. The same unmooring from external referent that inspired *The Aeneid*'s anxieties about the reiterativity of history equally inspires *The Tempest*'s, and James's, vision of a fully novel—because self-originating, self-legitimating, and completely ungrounded—sociohistorical order. It is thus also in Sycorax's hoop that *The Tempest* most explicitly confronts the paradoxical relation between the desire for autonomy and the early modern search for the legitimacy bestowed by the imitation of convention.[21]

Though its appearance in the play is only occasionally made explicit—for example, when Prospero conjures one around the Italians in act 5—the circle is deeply rooted in the play's structure: it is implicit in the play's isolated setting on an island surrounded by water; in the fantasies of containment and isolation imposed on the island by its visitors; in Prospero's own obsession with confining and circumscribing the movements of others in the play; in the geographical thrust of Prospero's narrative from Milan to the island and back again; and, despite the play's internalization of Aristotelian poetic theory, in the play's return in its epilogue to the very vessel with which it began. The paradoxical mobility and stasis of circumscription above all torques and torments Prospero's narrative of exile in 1.2, and in this narrative we begin to see more clearly the coincidence of the desire for absolute reflexivity and the desire for absolute novelty. As Stephen Orgel notes, wives and mothers are notably absent from the play, and Prospero's relation of his fall in Milan and subsequent exile partly reflects his desire to excise any source of origination in the play other than himself.[22] His insistence that he incorporate any external sources of narrative action into himself is manifested even on the grammatical level: "My brother and thy uncle, called Antonio . . ." (1.2.66), he begins, and nine lines later arrives at the predicate of the sentence, attached to a new nominative: "The government I cast upon my brother . . ." (1.2.75). When a seeming slip of the tongue indicates a fear of the godlike powers of his brother—Sebastian "new created / The creatures that were mine, I say, or changed 'em, / Or else new formed 'em" (1.2.81–83), he rapidly reattributes that seeming divinity to his own paternity: "my trust, / Like a good parent, did beget of him / A falsehood in its contrary as great / As my trust was, which had indeed no limit, / A confidence sans bound" (1.2.93–97). Such paternity necessarily presages the image of the mother, who absorbs all external entities into her own womb, who will make her elusive entrance only one hundred lines later in the scene.

Because Prospero must therefore make himself the agent of his own passivity, however, his attempts to locate in himself the historical force that drives his narrative is doomed by its own logical structure. His interweaving of limitlessness and confinement, stasis and mobility, pinpoints that faulty, but nevertheless productive, logic. Prospero's parenthood "sans bound" originates in the "closeness" of his isolated library, a "dukedom large enough" (1.2.110), wherein, "neglecting worldly ends, all dedicated / To closeness and the bettering of my mind / With that which, but by being so retired, / O'er-prized all popular rate" (1.2.89–92), he withdraws the external referent—the worldly end—into the close self; that is, into the end that is endless confinement. Within the stability of his paternal library, Prospero collapses the Virgilian poles of Carthaginian stasis and imperial translation, self-reference and reference to the world: the liberal arts "being all my study, / The government I cast upon my brother / And to my state grew stranger, being transported / And rapt in secret studies" (1.2.74–77). Prospero is unable to choose between competing desires to achieve absolute self-consonance—closeness—and the necessary self-difference of limitless agency, between the secret isolation of fantasy and extension into the strangeness of empirical reality. Rapt—or raped, for the two were homonymous in the period—by himself, traveling inside the infinite expanse of his own walls, stranger to his own Milan, Prospero withdraws into a prison sans bound, not unlike the infinite circumscription of Sycorax's impregnated hoop. In the very narration of the event, too, Prospero reenacts the paradoxical dynamic of extension and introversion, in a story that reiterates as it progresses, loses itself even as it seeks self-return ("Dost thou attend me?" [1.2.78]; "Thou attend'st not!" [1.2.87]). Though Prospero locates in himself an origin self-contained and apparently completely self-referential, he also finds that very origin to be that which, stranger to itself, transported from itself, is least capable of complete internalization. Dido's groundless self-reiteration, which he finds in himself at the very height of his power, thus both elicits Prospero's attempt to incorporate the other, the transportation, of Virgilian tradition into a coherent, self-driven narrative, and renders that attempt futile when incorporation merely estranges the self from the self.

Prospero's increasingly desperate attempts to anchor himself as the subject of his own story reach a climax when he narrates his sea journey to the island that so temptingly invites the illusion of self-creation. "There," Prospero tells his daughter, the usurpers

> hoist us
> To cry to th' sea that roared to us, to sigh
> To th' winds, whose pity, sighing back again,
> Did us but loving wrong.
> MIRANDA: Alack, what trouble
> Was I then to you?
> PROSPERO: O, a cherubin
> Thou wast that did preserve me. Thou didst smile,
> Infused with a fortitude from heaven,
> When I have decked the sea with drops full salt,
> Under my burden groaned, which raised in me
> An undergoing stomach to bear up
> Against what should ensue (1.2.148–58)

Stephen Orgel was, again, the first to note Prospero's appropriation of motherhood in this scene: Prospero "groans" under his "burden" as if he were giving birth.[23] Jonathan Goldberg has subsequently argued that this passage reasserts the play's predominant masculinity in the phallic image of the stomach "bearing up"; Prospero's self-birth, for him, enables him to shed the femininity of the past in which he was "transported" and "rapt" in favor of a masculine "upright Time," directed by and originating from himself.[24] In this reading, the scene merely reiterates Ariel's release from confinement in the pine tree. Yet if we read the "undergoing stomach" "raised" in Prospero as an image of the womb swelling with child, the passage also might enact a birth in reverse: Prospero sees his child, goes into labor, and then finds himself impregnated with the burden of himself, as well as of the same celestial daughter who aided his delivery. In seeking in himself the autochthonous origin of his own authority, the mage tangles himself within the chronological loop of Sycorax's perpetual confinement. Further, his self-birth relies for its fruition not only on himself but also on the smiling "cherubin" to whom he should be giving birth, who nevertheless precedes him. Prospero's internalization of subjective agency simultaneously asserts the novelty of the self and undermines its own break from its reiteration of convention. It also, paradoxically, reveals, in Virgil's fruitless search for a referential grounding in a patriarchal legitimacy outside the self, the constitutive dynamic of the innermost self—thereby ensuring that self's failure to achieve the absolute inwardness it seeks.

At this odd moment, when Prospero's narrative seems most inward facing, most tangled within its own self-absorption, it refers itself to the very scene of its narration. "There, they hoist us / To cry to th' sea that roared to us, to sigh / To th' winds, whose pity, sighing back again, / Did us but loving wrong" (1.2.148–51), Prospero relates to Miranda immediately preceding the description of his self-birth. The father-daughter couple and the tempestuous seas mirror one another in their reciprocated exhalations, and those exhalations themselves are reflected in the sighs of the listening Miranda: "Alack, for pity. / I, not rememb'ring how I cried out then, / Will cry it o'er again" (1.2.132–34), Miranda tells her father. And later: "still 'tis beating in my mind, your reason / For raising this sea-storm" (1.2.176–77).

Prospero's narration of his exile and arrival on the island is apparently intended to be cathartic for Prospero and Miranda, to structure, circumscribe, and free them from the "dark backward and abysm of time" (1.2.50) that continually threatens to suck them into the chaos of unnarrated memory. Miranda's "Alack, for pity" recalls the pity of the spectator of Aristotelian tragedy, a pity that should ease the burden of historical error. Yet the closure and release expected within the Aristotelian paradigm is foiled by the scene's unmistakable echo of Virgil. A future monarch relates a tragic tale of political upheaval to an all-too-eager female audience, who is almost physically wounded by the relation: "O, my heart bleeds," Miranda tells her father, "To think o'th' teen that I have turned you to, / Which is from my remembrance" (1.2.63–65). Prospero inflicts Miranda with a scar from which she previously never suffered and passes to her the flames of Troy.

As the story progresses, Prospero demands from Miranda an ever more exacting imitation of Dido. As if soliciting from her a sufficiently piteous response—or as if unsure that his story was engaging to anyone other than himself—Prospero repeatedly and unnecessarily asks for her attention: "The very minute bids thee ope thine ear. / Obey and be attentive" (1.2.37–8); "I pray thee mark me, that a brother should / Be so perfidious" (1.2.67–68); "Dost thou attend me?" (1.2.78); "Thou attend'st not!" (1.2.87); "I pray thee, mark me" (1.2.88). These requests for her attention in turn elicit Miranda's insistence on the validity of her Dido-like compassion: "It is a hint," she assures him, "That wrings mine eyes to't" (1.2.134–35). In the process of narrating his absolute assimilation of all external sources of legitimacy, then, Prospero continues to require the assurance of an external audience, Miranda, that that assimilation has taken place. And yet that "external" source of affirmation is merely the Virgilian intertext his narrative intended to internalize in the first place; the gesture of assimilation, then, renders the intertext all the more elusive. The ghosts of *The Aeneid*'s own failure to achieve novelty remain, denying Prospero any assurance of autonomy and his historical narrative any form of closure, merely by the fact of his own obsession with it. Imitation both elicits the desire for the incorporation of the origin and eludes its achievement.

For the mirroring effect of the winds and seas render any attempted absorption reciprocal. "There they hoist us / To cry to th' sea that roared to us, to sigh / To th' winds, whose pity, sighing back again, / Did us but loving wrong": imitation is deprived of referent, even as Miranda's sighs, "cried o'er again," both respond to and perform the winds' "pity, sighing back again." Miranda's tears are, further, not only imitative but mimetic—that is, they replicate not only the famed sighs of Dido but also, proleptically, the pity of *The Tempest*'s own spectators, thus inserting the London theater into Virgil's intertext. Mimesis mirrors *imitatio*. And Aristotelian narrative trajectory, shaped into a beginning, middle, and end by the demands of tragic catharsis as well as of apparent naturalism, opens into a spiral of ungrounded *imitatio*, the Virgilian nightmare of the endlessly imitative and endlessly unfulfilled narrative into which imperial time inserts itself even in the process of extracting itself.

The Tempest's allusions to *The Aeneid*, then, occur when the play confronts and attempts to overcome the boundary between outside and inside, between mimesis and *aesthesis*.[25] Though I have focused on the play's prehistory, the same struggle resurfaces when Ferdinand, believing himself alone, stranded, and hopeless, first meets Miranda, who is both Virgil's Venus, an otherworldly and exotic presence—"Most sure the goddess / On whom these airs attend!" (1.2.422–23), he wonders to himself, translating Aeneas's "O dea certe" address to his mother in book 1 of *The Aeneid*—and merely a young maid who even speaks "My language" (1.2.429). And it surfaces again in the Virgilian harpy scene—when the Italians, stranded on the island of seeming novelty, are confronted by ministers of fate who know their darkest secrets. Each time, the wonderful and traumatic encounter with the new resolves in an unsettling resurgence of a long-buried past, even as the island with no letters reveals itself to be imprinted, already, with Ferdinand's language. Mimesis—representation of the world as such—meets *imitatio*—the representation of representation, of language's contentless reiteration.

The startling proximity between the untainted, the self-reflexive, and the wound and blind fire of tradition is shatteringly realized in the masque Prospero orchestrates to celebrate the betrothal of his daughter. Miranda has, throughout the play, hovered menacingly between the admired goddess of love and the Ovidian witch Medea, who threatens patrilineal dynastic ambitions, and Prospero intends the masque to translate her "virgin-knot" (4.1.15) safely into the knot of marriage, in part by excising the very goddess of love, Venus, whom, for Ferdinand, Miranda had represented. The masque alludes both to Jacobean masques, such as those written by Ben Jonson and Samuel Daniel, and to the scene of Dido's mock wedding in book 4 of *The Aeneid*, to which Ferdinand perhaps obliquely refers when he assures Prospero that "the murkiest den" "shall never melt / Mine honour into lust" (4.1.25, 27–28). Prospero's plan appears to succeed: "So rare a wondered father and a wise," Ferdinand marvels, omitting mention of his betrothed, "Makes this place paradise" (4.1.123–24).

Yet the masque does not quite have its intended effect. Prospero suddenly remembers the petty plot of Caliban, Trinculo, and Stephano and is so upset that the spirits directing the masque vanish. "Never till this day / Saw I him touched with anger so distempered" (4.1.144–45), Miranda tells Ferdinand. Prospero is touched, angered, vexed, upset. His anger is, also, not tempered, inclement, indeed tempestuous,[26] repeating, that is, winds and sighs of pity that first tossed Prospero's rotten barque to the island, repeating his own "drops full salt" that joined the sighs of the wind.

"A turn or two I'll walk / To still my beating mind" (4.1.162–63), Prospero alliteratively assures them, beating again Miranda's question about the play's inaugural tempest. The masque has rendered Prospero the passive, piteous spectator of its dream of unstained order, the spectator who both negates and completes its fiction and who, ultimately, beholds the spectacle of his own potential usurpation. To "still" himself—to anchor himself again against his tendency to self-transport—Prospero takes a turn, or two, or perhaps three or four, turning endlessly merely in order to stop himself.

In these embedded reminders of the Virgilian storm—reminders of the Virgil that Virgil himself tried to bury—the play's simultaneous desire for progress beyond itself and for absolute internal consonance repeatedly finds itself preceded and reflected by *The Aeneid*'s own worries about the proximity of empirical history, the history grounded in cosmic truth, and Dido's phantasmic reiteration, a reiteration both of herself and of a past she never experienced. By conflating its unstable absorption of a highly familiar classical fiction with the proliferating pity of its internal and external spectators, *The Tempest* vividly figures the capacity for aged fictions—and the ever-reiterated attempt to break from those fictions—to realize themselves endlessly in the realm of the apparently modern, the apparently empirical. Mimesis imitates Virgil as much as it does seventeenth-century London. Yet the play also undermines the perceived systematic coherence of those fictions, a coherence on which the claim to historical legitimacy is based. Not only does the superposition of play, theater, and classical poem disclose in the claim to historical progress the reiterativity of the convention-bound system but it also confronts the aesthetic thirst for self-systematicity with the condition of its possibility, that is, its assimilated and inassimilable original. At the moment when the tempest finds itself most isolated from empirical reference, it also finds itself distempered, in the face of the otherness of what should be familiar: tradition.

When, in the epilogue, a disrobed Prospero reminds the audience that its "Gentle breath . . . my sails / Must fill, or else my project fails" (epilogue, 11–12), he does not only bring the play back to its beginning in a gesture of apparent self-completion. He also brings it back to its beginning in the tempest of *The Aeneid* book 1. He may call for Christian "mercy" (epilogue, 18) or he may once again beg for the pity that Aeneas's story elicited in Dido, which reinscribed the flame of Troy in the passion of the queen. In a final gesture of historical progression beyond the "bands" (epilogue, 9) by which the audience has "confined" (epilogue, 4) Prospero—much as Sycorax confined Ariel, and Prospero confined himself in his "dukedom large enough"—the play reopens Dido's wound. And as it infinitely unfolds the space of reiteration, it also engenders an early modern aesthetic of imitation.

If we can speak of the early modern aesthetic of imitation—at least as instantiated by Shakespeare's imitation of Virgil—it might present itself as "a regime of the sensible that has become foreign to itself, the locus for a form of thought that has become foreign to itself" not in a modernist repudiation of imitation or mimesis but rather in an enactment of imitative thought's inescapable foreignness to itself and to the conventions that it imitates.[27] If the Shakespearean aesthetic that plays out that foreignness can be called political, it is so not by making its poetry the spokesman of early English republicanism in direct resistance to the totalizing structures of absolutist monarchy and its fantasies of legitimacy, Augustan or otherwise.[28] For any such assertion of the absolute primacy of the law only reinstates the impossible claim to a prior origination. Rather, that aesthetic would be political insofar as, in denying the Virgilian narrative of progress its claim to logical systematicity, it reveals the contingency, the lack of historical inevitability, of that political narrative, one that continues to structure conceptualizations of modernity. It thus opens an alternative distribution of the sensible that no longer reinscribes the absolute opposition between the conventional and the foreign, imitation and aesthetic, formal imitation and the political.

Notes

1. Jacques Rancière, *The Politics of Aesthetics: The Distribution of the Sensible*, trans. Gabriel Rockhill (London: Bloomsbury Academic, 2013), 20.
2. Rancière, *The Politics of Aesthetics*, 18.
3. Rancière, *The Politics of Aesthetics*, 20.
4. Rancière, *The Politics of Aesthetics*, 21.
5. See, for example, Donna B. Hamilton, *Virgil and "The Tempest": The Politics of Imitation* (Columbus: Ohio State University Press, 1990).
6. For a Freudian reading of the repetition compulsion exemplified by Dido and any who resist empire, see David Quint, *Epic and Empire: Politics and Generic Form from Virgil to Milton* (Princeton, N.J.: Princeton University Press, 1993), 50–83. A similar reading of the relationship between Virgilian narrative and Freudian repetition is Duncan Kennedy, "Virgilian Epic," in *The Cambridge Companion to Virgil*, ed. Charles Martindale (Cambridge: Cambridge University Press, 1997), 145–54.
7. Elizabeth Bellamy, *Translations of Power: Narcissism and the Unconscious in Epic History* (Ithaca, N.Y.: Cornell University Press, 1992), 79, makes the connection between Dido's wound and the wound inflicted by the memory of the burning city of Troy in Rome's cultural unconscious. My analysis here is indebted to her Lacanian reading of secondary epic and the *translatio imperii* as repetition compulsion.

8. I use Robert Fitzgerald's translation, Virgil, *The Aeneid* (London: Harvill, 1983).

9. On the iconography of the shield of Aeneas and the contrast it poses between the reiterative romance narrative of those conquered by Rome and the teleological and epic-historical narrative of Roman imperialism, see Quint, *Epic and Empire*, 21–31.

10. Bellamy, *Translations of Power*, 75–77, makes a similar point in arguing that the *translatio imperii* does not forget or sublimate the memory of Troy but rather enacts a negation of it, an apparent easing of repression that merely inscribes that repression more permanently in the cultural unconscious.

11. The most prominent treatments of Virgil's presence in *The Tempest* include Hamilton, *Virgil and "The Tempest"*; Margaret Tudeau-Clayton, *Jonson, Shakespeare and Early Modern Virgil* (Cambridge: Cambridge University Press, 1998); David Scott Wilson-Okamura, "Virgilian Models of Colonization in Shakespeare's Tempest," *ELH* 70, no. 3 (Fall 2003): 709–37, https://doi.org/10.1353/elh.2003.0030; and Leah Whittington, "Shakespeare's Vergil: Empathy and *The Tempest*," in *Shakespeare and Renaissance Ethics*, ed. John Cox and Patrick Gray, 98–120 (Cambridge: Cambridge University Press, 2014). For the most recent argument suggesting *The Tempest*'s direct use of and response to Strachey's *Reportory*, see Alden T. Vaughan, "William Strachey's 'True Reportory' and Shakespeare: A Closer Look at the Evidence," *Shakespeare Quarterly* 59, no. 3 (September 2008): 245–73, https://doi.org/10.1353/shq.0.0017. For Shakespeare's engagement with *The Aeneid* in other plays, see Heather James, *Shakespeare's Troy: Drama, Politics, and the Translation of Empire* (Cambridge: Cambridge University Press, 1997), and Colin Burrow, *Shakespeare and Classical Antiquity* (Oxford: Oxford University Press, 2013).

12. References in this essay are to William Shakespeare, *The Tempest*, ed. Virginia Mason Vaughan and Alden T. Vaughan (London: Arden Shakespeare, 1999).

13. On the island and its inhabitants as a carte blanche onto which European humanist culture can be inscribed, see Jonathan Goldberg, *Tempest in the Caribbean* (Minneapolis: University of Minnesota Press, 2004), 124–41.

14. King James VI and I, *The True Lawe of Free Monarchies: Or The Reciprock and Mutuall Dutie Betwixt a Free King, and His Naturall Subiectes* (Edinburgh, 1598), fol. C4^{v}.

15. Hamilton, *Virgil and "The Tempest,"* xi.

16. Tudeau-Clayton, *Jonson, Shakespeare*, 199.

17. Tudeau-Clayton, *Jonson, Shakespeare*, 211.

18. The name Sycorax recalls that of the Odyssean witch and island dweller Circe, which in turn recalls the Greek word for "circle." On Sycorax's Homeric prototype, see Maria Warner, "Circean Mutations in the New World," in *"The Tempest" and Its Travels*, ed. Peter Hulme and William H. Sherman, 97–113 (London: Reaktion, 2000).

19. Ovid, *Metamorphoses*, ed. R. J. Tarrant (Oxford: Clarendon Press, 2004), 10.298–518.

20. I draw here partly on Janet Adelman's psychoanalytic reading of the male fear of absorption and loss of identity in the maternal body in *Suffocating Mothers: Fantasies of Maternal Origin in Shakespeare's Plays, Hamlet to The Tempest* (New York: Routledge, 1992).

21. In an argument similar to mine, Christopher Pye has argued that reiterativity is the necessary consequence of the dream of autonomy, because autonomy attempts to constitute both its own beginning and its own end; yet reiterativity also marks a continual return to the moment of self-loss, where autonomy's self-recuperation encounters its nonrelation to what it has excluded. *The Storm at Sea: Political Aesthetics in the Time of Shakespeare* (New York: Fordham University Press, 2015), 148–49.

22. See, for example, Stephen Orgel, "Prospero's Wife," *Representations*, no. 8 (Fall 1984): 1–13, https://doi.org/10.2307/2928555.

23. Orgel, "Prospero's Wife," 4.

24. Goldberg, *Tempest in the Caribbean*, 44–45.

25. On the play's attempt to incorporate its external grounds, an attempt that corresponds to the emergent early modern aesthetic question of the possibility of self-referentiality, see Christopher Pye, *The Storm at Sea: Political Aesthetics in the Time of Shakespeare* (New York: Fordham University Press, 2015), 150–52.

26. I paraphrase here the *OED*'s first definition of "distempered": "Of the weather, air, etc.: Not temperate; inclement; = distemperate adj. 1.": *OED Online*, "distempered, adj.1," accessed February 5, 2018, http://www.oed.com/view/Entry/55617?rskey=MTABjv&result=3&isAdvanced=false.

27. Rancière, *The Politics of Aesthetics*, 18.

28. For the latter argument, see Hamilton, *Virgil and "The Tempest,"* 105–32.

The Political, the Aesthetic, and the Utopian in *The Tempest*

A Shakespearean Dialectic Unfolded

Hugh Grady

The central terms of this collection of essays—the political and the aesthetic—are complex and protean and have been much discussed in recent years from a number of different points of view. In this essay I want to bring them together and probe into issues of how they relate to each other in one of Shakespeare's masterpieces, the late play *The Tempest*. I will argue that the relation between them is one defined in the tradition of Frankfurt School/Marxist theories of the aesthetic and the utopian developed by Ernst Bloch, Walter Benjamin, Theodor Adorno, and others. From this point of view, politics in *The Tempest* is seen as instrumental and corrupt, while the aesthetic functions in the play as a vehicle through which to envision the fulfillment of the human needs and desires negated in the operations of instrumentalized power. That is, in this play, the aesthetic operates in a utopian mode as theorized by Bloch and others. The utopian in this sense, Bloch wrote, "makes no peace with the world already given." "Utopian consciousness," he states, "remains wholly without deception inasmuch as the moment of its fulfillment is still outstanding."[1]

A related view was enunciated by Theodor Adorno, using somewhat different language (influenced by his late friend Walter Benjamin) in a passage Adorno composed in 1946–47: "The only philosophy which can be responsibly practised in face of despair is the attempt to contemplate all things as they would present themselves from the standpoint of redemption . . . Perspectives must be fashioned that displace and estrange the world, reveal it to be, with its rifts and crevices, as indigent and distorted as it will appear one day in the messianic light."[2]

Politics in *The Tempest*

Shakespeare embodies political ideas in his plays through a representation of political dynamics in the story lines and in the speeches and acts of the various characters. In *The Tempest*, as in most of Shakespeare's political or partially political plays, a specific version of the political is in question—rather than, say, any attempt to define the political as such as several theorists and critics have attempted. Rather, at issue in the plays is an instrumentalized, "Machiavellian" politics of the sort I have discussed in previous works.[3]

Machiavellian politics in the sense I am using the term were first clearly delineated in Shakespeare's oeuvre in the series of plays beginning with *King Richard II* in 1595 through *King Henry V* and *Julius Caesar* in 1599.[4] Whether Shakespeare had come across one of the many transcripts and translations of *The Prince* circulating in London in his lifetime[5] or perhaps had merely absorbed Christopher Marlowe's embodiment of Machiavellian political logic in plays like *Tamburlaine* and *The Jew of Malta*, he had clearly interiorized the idea that political success followed rules that were only partially compatible with the values of traditional morality, that "truth" in politics was a hotly contested and ideological issue, and that the image projected by a political agent was far more important than the "reality" (if indeed, such a privileged epistemological category has any relevance in this context at all) of the prince's character.[6]

In doing so, as recent criticism has shown, Shakespeare was involved in a larger historical project, leading ultimately to a transformation of political thinking across Europe. In the terms developed by the conservative Catholic (and later Nazi) German political theorist Carl Schmitt in the 1920s—a Schmitt revival across several disciplines has been a major influence in recent critical theory—the early modern saw the waning of the medieval, organic, ontological view of political authority that conceived of the king as a "natural" lynchpin of a wholly hierarchical cosmos and the development of a secular, pragmatic approach to politics that in most of Europe led to the figure of the sovereign, absolutist monarch. A theorist like Machiavelli was crucial in the intellectual evolution of this development, but so were defenders of monarchy such as Jean Bodin (whom Schmitt emphasizes in his discussion in *Political Theology* and elsewhere).[7] Within this framework (as in so many others), Shakespeare is seen as inhabiting a politically transitional period between the medieval and absolutism—with different plays emphasizing different constellations of the complex development.[8]

The Aesthetic in Recent Criticism

Recent years have seen not only a renewal of thinking about the political through the discussion of political theology but also a similar (and at times related) development of ideas of the aesthetic, one largely separate from the Frankfurt School–influenced tradition of the New Aestheticism in Shakespeare studies that appeared in the late 1990s and in the following decade, and of which my own work was a part.[9] The crucial figure here is Jacques Rancière, who in the decades since his break with his former teacher, the Marxist philosopher Louis Althusser, has developed across several works a complex theory that connects the production of two related concepts, the political and the aesthetic. Both are linked to the history of modernity through a process he calls the distribution of the visible (*le partage du visible*). This "distribution" or differentiation is similar to that brought about through language, culture, and myth in the various structuralist epistemologies (and thus to Althusser's much-criticized concept of ideology), but Rancière's argumentation has been informed by many critiques of structuralism and Althusser—and is a subtler version of what remains a familiar approach to epistemology. He writes, for example, of the particular version of *partage* that constitutes the aesthetic: "If the reader is fond of analogy, aesthetics can be understood in a Kantian sense—re-examined perhaps by Foucault—as the system of *a priori* forms determining what presents itself to sense experience. It is a delimitation of spaces and times, of the visible and the invisible, of speech and noise, that simultaneously determines the place and stakes of politics as a form of experience." That is, for Rancière politics depends on these same delineations.[10] This central formulation is a good example of what is bracing and what is disappointing in Rancière's theory of aesthetics and politics.

There is much to admire in Rancière's writing—most especially his hard-won attachment to democracy, his thorough going antielitism, and his defense of a concept of the aesthetic as a crucial component of modernity that should not be dissolved into its merely status-conferring functions à la Bourdieu. Works like Rancière's *Aisthesis*, *The Politics of Aesthetics*, and *Aesthetics and Its Discontents* are valuable and welcome contributions to the contemporary discussion of both aesthetics and politics.

However, I find some of the specifics of Rancière's elaborate theory problematic. In particular, I think that Rancière's approach to aesthetics is in many ways more properly a theory of epistemology than of the aesthetic per se and that it is deficient in its treatment of such classic aesthetic concerns as the concepts of beauty, affect, meaning, and desire—among others. The *partage du sensible* is a primal epistemological act that is basic not just to art and politics but also to all of human knowledge and culture. As such, it seems to me mislabeled as "the aesthetic," in that in Kant and the line of aesthetic theory he founded, aesthetic perception is a specialized faculty of the human subject independent of cognition. For Rancière, it is the very basis of knowledge and cognition. It seems to me (as I suggested above) to be a version of structuralist epistemology, akin to Foucault's (later abandoned) concept of the *episteme*, that common framework of intellectual disciplines that Foucault posited as underlying the erection of knowledge in the various changing epochs or periods of Western thought.[11] The resemblance is particularly clear in Rancière's attempt to define aesthetic-intellectual periods (analogous to Foucault's epistemic epochs), which Rancière calls "historical regimes of art."[12] The first of the two such "regimes" relevant to Shakespeare's time is the seventeenth- and eighteenth-century "representative regime," essentially recapitulating the neo-Aristotelian ideas of the French *Âge classique* of art as an imitation of nature. As intimated by Christopher Pye in the introduction to this volume, however, the dynamics of this era are not those of Shakespeare. Somehow, his (and those of other poets of his culture) seem more comfortably situated in the second era, for Rancière more or less coterminus with romanticism, modernism, and postmodernism: that of "the aesthetic regime," in which artworks are autonomous and self-constituting.

There are interesting ideas here, especially in the descriptions of the structure of art in the aesthetic regime. But as period concepts they are as incomplete and arbitrary and Francocentric as Foucault's earlier argument for a succession of epistemic regimes—and similarly suggest that there is something wrong in the premises that underlie them. Both theories are subject to the criticism that their attempts to posit and concretely define epoch-defining epistemological frameworks inevitably fail to account for all the diversities, exceptions, and anomalies characteristic of human cultural production. The complex, "modern" art of Shakespeare is a big problem for this theory. Of course, it is possible to identify commonalities within aesthetic periods, I would argue, but not through monolithic categories like these.

The relation between the political and the aesthetic that I am working with here, then, is one of dialectical or dialogical antagonism rather than of cogeneration as in Rancière. In both accounts, to be sure, the two categories are generated in the series of differentiations constituent of the crystallization of modernity; and in this I am in agreement with both Rancière and Christopher Pye.[13] But the relation I want to explore here is one in which the aesthetic works in its utopian mode to dialectically negate the workings of instrumental politics rather than to complement them. This is one of the central ideas of both Adorno's and Benjamin's aesthetic writings, inspired in part by Schiller's celebrated historicizing of Kantian aesthetics in his *Letters on the Aesthetic Education of Man*; and it is one about which Rancière has complex thoughts but about which he has expressed skepticism on more than one occasion.[14] In my view the Frankfurt theorists provide a more adequate theoretical apparatus for understanding the utopian aesthetic in Shakespeare. In a sense, for Rancière, every work of art in the aesthetic regime is in itself a utopian space. In his *Aisthesis* he credits Winckelmann as the first to make this discovery, in his idealizing depiction of a culturally harmonious ancient Greece: "This German Greece, sister to the Rome dreamt of by French revolutionaries, nourished the utopia of art's destiny, which destined it to negate itself in order to become what it used to be once again: the fabric of sensible forms of a people's life."[15] In Shakespeare, however, this idea is itself incorporated into a work that represents that self-creation within a larger world in an epoch well before the constitution of Rancière's aesthetic regime.

Shakespeare's Evolving Representation of Politics

In order to understand the dynamic in question between political power and the utopian, we should return momentarily to Shakespeare's Machiavellian moment, when the form of politics he critiques in the later plays was first defined.

Shakespeare's approach to history in 1595–1600 displayed a different approach to politics than that of his earlier histories and tragedies. In these midcareer plays the earlier villainous Machiavels, such as *Titus Andronicus*'s Aaron or Richard III, were replaced by characters of much "grayer" moral qualities. Aaron and Richard are immensely entertaining and psychologically interesting, but they are self-declaring evildoers. But in the newer plays the political intriguers are much more morally ambiguous. Bolingbroke of *Richard II* and Cassius of *Julius Caesar* are both masterful intriguers, but Shakespeare closes off their interiority to us, so that while they are skilled interlocutors and highly successful in achieving their political aims, they are silent on how they see themselves morally, and they lack emotional appeal, striking most audiences as cold at best. In addition, unlike the later plays, the aesthetic as a theme is largely absent from these political plays.

In the "tragic period" that follows the political plays of 1595–99, Shakespeare continues his exploration of the political/instrumental, in *Hamlet*, *Othello*, *King Lear*, and *Macbeth*. In these great plays there are only incidental references to the aesthetic as a theme. In two later tragedies, however, he brings in notions of the aesthetic first developed in *Romeo and Juliet* and *A Midsummer Night's Dream*. I've discussed this dynamic in *Timon of Athens* previously,[16] but the discussion of aesthetic ideas there is largely sui generis. It is *Antony and Cleopatra* that seems to chart the way to the use of the concept of the aesthetic in relation to politics that will inform all the late plays or tragicomedies. In that play, after an initial depiction of Roman power politics that seems intertextual with that of the 1599 *Julius Caesar*, the drama turns in its spectacular conclusion to the aesthetically heightened deaths of the two principals, drawing on the aesthetic potentials of mourning to idealize memory and create an aura of beauty surrounding the departed.

This is a pattern that not only looks back to *Romeo and Juliet* (and to the other plays of 1595–1600) but seems clearly transitional to the late tragicomedies as well. In both *The Winter's Tale* and *The Tempest*, a political world following broadly Machiavellian rules is depicted—as (crucial) background in *The Tempest* and as intermixed with personal jealousy even to madness in *The Winter's Tale*. Each play develops a utopian response to unjust power in highly stylized conclusions that produce fairy-tale endings powered by rich and evocative poetry and drama. In both the aesthetic appears in the form of an unlikely Providence.

The Case of *The Tempest*

In *The Tempest*, the relation between the political and the aesthetic is similar to that of *Antony and Cleopatra* and *The Winter's Tale*. The realm of the political described in the background story is a Machiavellian one, inscribed in the tale of Antonio's treacherous usurpation of his brother's position as Duke of Milan, and then (in the play itself) in the attempted murder and usurpations planned by Sebastian and Alonso (echoed in a parodic comic way by the plan to assassinate Prospero launched by Caliban). Ordinary moral norms are suspended and power is pursued for its own sake. But the interaction between the political and the aesthetic is at first decentered and dispersed, including such ways of representing the aesthetic as Ariel's songs, Prospero's masque, and Caliban's dreams. This changes in the conclusion, when the aesthetic seems to overpower the political rather than coexist with it as political injustice produces its own negating utopian compensation in the artifice of the ending.

The play has become widely interpreted in our multicultural world as an analysis of the dynamics of colonialism, and this indeed is a powerfully revelatory interpretive schema to make sense of much of its thematic armature. This reading sees Prospero as figuring a European colonizer who enslaves his island's native inhabitants Ariel and Caliban, claims the land as his own, and harnesses magical powers (suggestive of European technology) to subdue the land and its inhabitants. Caliban has been appropriated by any number of third world writers and artists as a representation of colonialized subjects in a post-Columbian world, his mixture of partial acculturation, grudging submission, abiding grief, and violent resistance all evocative of the situation of many colonized subjects[17]: "You taught me language, and my profit on't / Is I know how to curse."[18] All this is, in its own way, also an example of instrumentalized, Machiavellian politics too.

But *The Tempest* is an exceedingly complex play and contains material for other interpretations, supplemental to the much-discussed postcolonial one—or to the "European politics" reading developed by David Kastan.[19] Given this situation, I propose taking a leaf from Walter Benjamin's idea of a double hermeneutic interpretive strategy. Benjamin in his 1928 *The Origin of German Tragic Drama* and in *The Arcades Project* often spoke of baroque images that simultaneously figured dialectically opposite meanings—"dialectics at a standstill," he later said of this structure. I want to argue that *The Tempest*, speaking very broadly, can be read this way as well. I want to investigate the play's utopian meanings, but without at the same time obscuring its colonialist qualities. We are dealing with two different, but dialectically connected, meanings.

The utopian vector of the play is initiated, as many critics have noted, as the opening storm scene stages the existence of class privilege and political inequality in the form of reverence for the king and prince from his party. But the storm demonstrates the upper class's uselessness in the emergency of the storm ("What care these roarers for the name of King") and dissolves the hierarchy in the wreck of the ship on Prospero's enchanted island. More dramatically than in other "green woods comedies," *The Tempest* enacts the transition from a hierarchical first world to a liberated and fluid second world as a sudden, even catastrophic, metamorphosis. However, the island otherwise functions like the woods outside Athens in *A Midsummer Night's Dream* and like the Forest of Arden in *As You Like It*: as a space of refuge for outcasts to experiment in new social forms and modes of life.

In fact, the utopian qualities of the play were recently on display in a well-publicized outdoor, all-female, and selectively nude production held in Central Park in New York on May 19 and 20, 2016. The troupe explained its interpretation of the play as follows:

> This Tempest focuses on the contrast between the harsh restrictions of "civilization"—where political maneuvering costs thrones and lives—and the Edenic, magic-suffused tropical island on which the sorcerer Prospero and his daughter Miranda have lived in exile for twelve years. The contrast will be dramatized not only through performance and staging but also through inventive and integral use of costuming, with the harrowed, conspiring shipwreck victims initially forced to navigate the play's island setting in constricting outfits suggestive of European aristocracy.[20]

As noted, however, we need to keep in mind that, as Stephen Greenblatt and other postcolonialist critics demonstrated, the island, while in a heightened and privileged relation to the play's "real world," is no paradise. It has already been sullied by coercive power politics. Prospero has enslaved the half-human Caliban and the spirit Ariel, subordinating them and coercively controlling them through his magic. And as the shipwreck survivors wander through the island, they reproduce the ills of the European society they had left behind, in high political and low comical modes, as two different political murders are contemplated and planned.

The Utopian in *The Tempest*

When I speak of the utopian here, I am drawing from a tradition within Western Marxism. The roots of the idea are in Marx (and some of his sources), but the concept of the utopian in art was substantially developed by Ernst Bloch and Walter Benjamin in the early twentieth century, with each influenced by the other and by Jewish traditions of what Benjamin called Messianic time. Their works and influence have led to a rich archive of theoretical work on the subject. In addition to the extensive writings of Bloch and Benjamin, the idea of the utopian in art has been developed by Horkheimer and Adorno, by Herbert Marcuse, and in several publications by Fredric Jameson.[21] And as both Benjamin and Bloch noted, it is possible to see psychoanalytic dimensions in the utopian as well. We can see it, for example, as implicated in and produced from a Lacanian play of desire within a reified "real."[22]

The utopian is that contradiction in terms, the place for the (imaginary) fulfillment of frustrated needs and desires that is also an index and reflex of the experienced deprivations of specific social locations. Over a very long career, Ernst Bloch at times coquetted with a language of "archetypes" and "timeless artworks" in a dialogue with the critics of his day, but he also consistently grounded specific utopian visions in specific socioeconomic situations, insisting on the open-endedness of all utopian constructions, but equally in their determinate relation to the material world of their creations. We can better formulate this through a paraphrase of Marx: people create utopias through imagination, but not just as they please; they do not make them under circumstances chosen by themselves but under circumstances directly encountered, given and transmitted from the past.[23]

In many ways *The Tempest* is an obvious choice. It is a play that incorporates a strong utopian vector in its array of aesthetic techniques, in particular its power to imaginatively overcome instrumental politics, death, and mourning and to counterpose eros to thanatos to provide a sense of completion to longing. The aesthetic has other modes than the utopian, to be sure, but the utopian is one of its most common ones.

We hear an evocation of the aesthetic utopian especially in Ariel's celebrated song "Full fathom five . . . ," with its description of the transformation of a drowned body into an aestheticized object symbolic of rebirth:

> Of his bones are coral made;
> Those are pearls that were his eyes;
> Nothing of him that doth fade,
> But doth suffer a sea-change
> Into something rich and strange. (1.2.398–402)

The "sea-change" announced here is both an aesthetic and a utopian transformation: death is transfigured into art, just as the logic of the plotting of this play enacts such a move from threatened and feared deaths to the fairy-tale happy ending. It is a self-conscious, meta-aesthetic assertion of how art can transform the givens of human experience into stylized, idealized, "utopian" representations in a relation of "other" to ordinary life—a technique that both defamiliarizes and allows for critical assessment. And the song echoes in its way Ferdinand's own testament to the transformative power of aesthetic experience when he exclaims, "This music crept by me upon the waters, / Allaying both their fury and my passion" (1.2.392–93).

Prospero's masque in the fourth act is another instance of meta-aesthetics at work, this time invoking, like *As You Like It* and *The Winter's Tale*, pastoral visions celebrating community, fertility, eros, and reproduction—strong counterpoint to the Machiavellian treachery, violence, and death lurking as unfulfilled potentialities throughout the play.

Walter Benjamin pointed out in his study of baroque allegory that in one sense Renaissance allegory came into being when the pagan gods were no longer considered (as they were in early Christian writings) to have been demons or fallen angels but rather were refunctioned for aesthetic uses as allegories representing their mythological qualities.[24] The inset masque of act 4 is a perfect example of this practice, with its invocation of the gods and goddesses associated with marriage, fertility, and beauty. It is also a good example of another aspect of the development of the aesthetic in that it removes a form that had ritual and political meanings—the court masque—into a radically different setting (the theater) that is at once an arena of commercialism, "entertainment," and art in the modern sense. But this transference is a complex one that deserves further exploration.

In his classic 1975 *The Illusion of Power* Stephen Orgel pointed out the extent to which Jacobean court masques were displays of power explicitly celebrating the centrality of the sovereign.[25] They were, however, written for the most part by professional playwrights, with Ben Jonson the most prolific and successful of them. They were designed to be visually spectacular and cleverly produced, with the talented Inigo Jones often called on to provide the set and visual effects. And they incorporated music, both instrumental and vocal. Thus, while they employed aesthetic techniques, they did so in the service of power and so lacked the quality of aesthetic autonomy that so many theorists, beginning with Kant, see as essential to the concept.

In Shakespeare's inset masque, in contrast, the entertainment is fully integrated into the play as a whole, and the sovereign authority it celebrates is fictional. In its depiction of a monarch reigning within an "uninhabited isle" (the words of the Folio dramatis personae) that nevertheless hosts a "dukedom" (consisting of father and daughter, innumerable spirits, and a fish-man of dubious provenance), we might even say it is ironized—and thus refunctioned for aesthetic-dramatic and thematic purposes. It is a diminution of the political wholly consistent with the play's critique of Machiavellian politics.

But the masque also relates to the theme of utopia. In his introduction to his edition of *The Tempest*, Steven Orgel states flatly that "Prospero the illusionist, moving his drama towards reconciliation and a new life, presents in the betrothal masque his own version of Gonzalo's Utopia, a vision of orderly nature and bountiful fruition."[26] The allegorical figures of Ceres and Juno, he goes on to argue, symbolically unite the fragmented world of the play. Juno figures forth the missing wife and mother whom Miranda never knew and, as a votive figure of matrimony and agriculture, represents a society in harmony with nature as Gonzalo had described. Ceres is also a figure associated with an agricultural civilization harmonizing nature and humanity. Iris, goddess of the rainbow, signifies a utopian divine providence through the biblical associations of the rainbow as the sign of God's future benevolence to humanity.[27]

The masque also, as Orgel goes on to argue, throws into relief two "anti-masques" within the play, the storm itself and Ariel's harpies' feast presented to the corrupt courtiers. In the wish-fulfilling vision of the central masque (and the play's utopian ending), these are both revealed as illusions of disharmony that were both temporary and preludes to the reconciliations of the end.[28]

Counterutopias

But as in other of Shakespeare's investigations of the utopian, *The Tempest* puts the category into interrogation as well as representing it in appealing heightened language and drama. And the play is unique in that it contains an explicit description of a utopian society in the political sense of the term. Famously, the description is lifted and only slightly reworked from Florio's translation of Montaigne's essay "On the Cannibals." The speech (2.1.145–62) is given to one of the play's relatively "good" characters, the old counselor Gonzago (who we learn had saved Prospero's and Miranda's lives by supplying the boat of exile with food, water, and Prospero's indispensable books). Gonzalo, inspired by the pristine environment of the island on which he is shipwrecked, announces a utopian plan, silently based on Montaigne's account of a coastal Brazilian native tribe, which Montaigne had derived from his talks with two tribe members visiting France. He is struck by the closeness to nature and by the honesty and simplicity of their way of life, for the group lacks many of the arts taken for granted by the Europeans. Shakespeare adopts this passage closely from Florio's translation but recontextualizes it in his drama:

> For no kind of traffic
> Would I admit; no name of magistrate;
> Letters should not be known; riches, poverty,
> And use of service, none; contract, succession,

Bourn, bound of land, tilth, vineyard, none;
No use of metal, corn, or wine, or oil;
No occupation, all men idle, all,
And women too, but innocent and pure;
No sovereignty. (2.1.146–54)

Because of this, Gonzalo asserts, the society would be free of numerous corruptions of civilization:

All things in common nature should produce
Without sweat or endeavour. Treason, felony,
Sword, pike, knife, gun, or need of any engine
Would I not have, but nature should bring forth
Of its own kind, all foison, all abundance
To feed my innocent people. (2.1.157–62)

While Gonzalo puts forward his Montaignean plan, he is met by a series of mocking criticisms from the "Machiavellian" characters Sebastian and Antonio. In the end, Gonzalo seems to laugh off his speculation as just idle chatter, but it resonates in a play very much given to interrogating the binary opposites wildness/civilization (otherwise known as nature/culture). And as Stephen Orgel pointed out and I discussed above, it is very much recapitulated in spectacular and symbolic form in Prospero's wedding masque in act 4.

The fabulous monster Caliban is at the center of the antiutopian strain of the play by those who see it as a "reply" to Montaigne's "On the Cannibals." His name, as noted, is an obvious anagram of "cannibal," but he is anything but the noble savages described by Montaigne—he is a resentful, violent, and gullible figure with a weakness for alcohol who seems in some ways a prescient example of notable stereotypes of Native Americans. It is not hard to read the play at one level as a reply to Montaigne's idealizing depiction of the South American Indian culture he conflates with accounts of the Golden Age from ancient Greece. Instead, Shakespeare's characterization of Caliban seems to draw from a number of pejorative accounts of Native American culture and life circulating in Renaissance Europe.[29]

The corrupt activities of the Europeans transported to this Edenic space also undercut the idea that it would be a simple matter to found a new human society untainted by inequality or guile. On the question posed by Gonzalo of the founding of a new Eden, the dialectic of the play in its middle is overweighed toward the skeptical.

But the counterutopian Caliban is a complex creation, with aesthetic and utopian dimensions as well as counterutopian ones. Like Bottom in *A Midsummer Night's Dream*, he participates in the play's utopian theme through his aesthetic sensibility ("Sometimes a thousand twangling instruments / Will hum about mine ears; and sometimes voices . . . that when I waked / I cried to dream again" [3.2.135–41]) and his unexpected ability to learn from his experience at the end.[30] Julia Lupton has recently written a strikingly original interpretation of Caliban, using some of the complexity of Walter Benjamin's idea of "the creaturely," an adjective that denotes the qualities and domain of a fallen nature. According to Benjamin scholar Beatrice Hanssen, the term evokes a "conception of the creaturely as the realm of the passions, mythical guilt, wanton melancholy, and animality—in short, a fallen nature on *this* side of transcendence and revelation."[31] At the same time, she argues, there is another—a "more positive, benign conception." She goes on to identify this as a more affirmative openness to nature, a stance that is derived from certain Judaic traditions and the idea of the "just man" (*der Gerechte*), who, "as the advocate of the creatural (*Fürsprech der Kreatur*), was also its highest embodiment."[32]

Lupton doesn't evoke this last meaning in her discussion explicitly, but she does come near it with her startling and eye-opening identification of Caliban with Adam. The connection is clearest when Caliban describes how at first Prospero had treated him well and educated him in a positive way:

> When thou cam'st first,
> Thou strok'st me and made much of me, wouldst give me
> Water with berries in't, and teach me how
> To name the bigger light, how the less. (1.2.332–35)

The allusion to the sky's two lights of course recalls Genesis 1:16 describing God's creation of the greater and lesser lights. And the act of naming links Caliban with Adam—with the important difference, as Lupton emphasizes, that Adam spoke naturally and generated his own (Adamic) language, while Caliban is taught language by Prospero and Miranda. "Caliban," Lupton writes, "not unlike Miranda is a *wonder who wonders*, a creature capable of an affective response to the world around him."[33] He is both a fallible creature and an aesthetic being, and thus he is essentially human. Despite Prospero's condemnations of him, he represents that degree zero of all true humanism that Ernst Bloch described when he wrote that the ultimate goal of utopian liberation must be "the overthrow (instead of the hypocritical new installation) of all conditions in which the human individual is a humiliated, enslaved, forsaken, and despised creature."[34] Caliban's liberation from Prospero's enslavement, while not directly staged, is another important facet of the play's overall utopian vision. His role in the play is dialogic, not merely subordinated to the discourse on order and hierarchy associated with Prospero.

Miranda and Ferdinand

Much of the play's dramatic vector from chaos and the threat of violence to the harmony of the moving happy ending is carried by the two young lovers, Miranda and Ferdinand. Shakespeare, as in many other plays, takes advantage of young love and marriage and their accompanying aura of renewal to help create the sense of rebirth and redemption that are important facets of the complex ending. Indeed, with the prominence of young daughter figures in the plays of the last half of his career, many have suspected that Shakespeare might be drawing from his own affections for his daughters Susanna and Judith. Susanna had married in 1607, four years before the first recorded performance of *The Tempest* in 1611; Judith married after the composition of the play. But whatever the purely personal resonances the figure of the young daughter may have carried for the author, Miranda herself is, among other things, a personification of the utopian, an uncorrupted, idealizing, desirous and desirable young woman revered by all who come in contact with her.

Her suitor, Ferdinand, is a straightforward earnest young man who dutifully mourns his presumed lost father, laments his isolation from his newly inherited kingdom—and he is highly sensitive to aesthetic stimulation, as indicated in one of the play's many famous passages (this one adapted by T. S. Eliot in *The Waste Land*), as he reacts to Ariel's singing:

> Where should this music be?—i'th' air or th' earth?
> It sounds no more; and sure it waits upon
> Some god o'th' island. Sitting on a bank,
> Weeping again the King my father's wreck,
> This music crept by me upon the waters,
> Allaying both their fury and my passion
> With its sweet air. Thence I have followed it,
> Or it hath drawn me rather; but 'tis gone.
> No it begins again. (1.2.388–96)

And this is the context for Ariel's great "Full fathom five" song discussed previously as a central enunciation of the aesthetic theme of the play. Ferdinand himself does not yet know that the song at its most personal level for him is a message that his father's death is not what it seems. And it is also an enunciation of one of the play's central themes: a utopian aesthetic trajectory that turns potential tragedy into bittersweet comedy.

Ferdinand carries forward the play's dissolution of the first world's social hierarchy when he accepts Prospero's charge that he perform hard physical labor to transport logs for several hours. This is, as we have learned, one of Caliban's chief tasks—Prospero mentions it, and he is carrying a log in the previous scene when he encounters Stephano and Trinculo. Miranda, her innocence notwithstanding, is very conscious of the insult to Ferdinand's princely status, as we learn in Ferdinand's report, "My sweet mistress / Weeps when she sees me work, and says such baseness / Had never like executor" (3.1.11–13). Ferdinand goes on to say he accepts the humiliation only for the sake of his new beloved, Miranda, and this prompts his first declaration of love to her. He thus enters into the role of the Petrarchan lover, a suppliant to an empowered mistress.

But Miranda refuses the role of Petrarchan lady and insists on her own willingness to servitude for love in the name of "plain and holy innocence" (3.1.82). She thus joins a number of other Shakespearean love heroines (Juliet, Rosalind, Viola, Desdemona, Cordelia, and others) who do likewise. Petrarchan love is dissolved on the island as much as the traditional social hierarchy that its form parodies. Equal mutual love is part of the utopian vision of this play—and others by this author.

More important, perhaps, is the reasoning behind her refusal, or rather what we might call her overall social vision: Miranda is a consummate "outsider" observer/narrator who sees everything in a new light. With a name meaning in Latin "wondered at, admired"—but also, as Julia Lupton suggested, "a *wonder who wonders*"—she comes to experience freshly and thus is the subject of what the Russian formalist Victor Shklovsky called defamiliarization or estrangement in his essay "Art as Technique."[35] She is an idealizer, seeing beauty and majesty in what she surveys as well as soliciting wonder at her beauty and demeanor from others. Hers is an inherently utopian vision.

All this comes to the fore in the play's last scene, with her famous lines

O wonder!
How many goodly creatures are there here!
How beauteous mankind is! O brave new world
That has such people in't! (5.1.181–84)

No character in the play, except perhaps for Caliban (to whom Prospero is linked in a complex master-slave dialectic), has had such a varied reception as its protagonist, Prospero. For much of critical history, to be sure, he was seen as a positive figure—in the eighteenth century a wise sage and mage, in the nineteenth a personification of Shakespeare himself as he bid farewell to the stage in what was then thought to be his last dramatic work.[36]

For a good deal of the twentieth century as well, Prospero was taken largely as positive, seen generally either as a consummate Renaissance man in a hierarchical world or as a humanist educator who is educated, achieving restoration, forgiveness, and renewal at the end. But since the advent of more political critical paradigms in the 1980s, that perception has shifted—though of course not unanimously. Steven Orgel, writing in 1987, summed up the range of then recent interpretations of Prospero this way: "In recent years we have seen Prospero as a noble ruler and mage, a tyrant and megalomaniac, a necromancer, a Neoplatonic scientist, a colonial imperialist, a civilizer.[37] And in the years since Orgel wrote this, feminist accounts of Prospero have also been largely critical, on top of what became the hegemonic view of him as a colonialist exploiter. Consequently, Prospero has become a much less admired character than he had been in the past—and Caliban has been seen as much more sympathetic than before.

As I stated earlier in the essay, I think the colonialist reading of the play is a powerful and needful one in our times, but it is clearly one-sided in that it tends to deemphasize the play's enactment of a story of wonder, of the potential harmony of nature and culture, and of the possibilities of more egalitarian societies—that is, its more utopian side. Here I want to complete such a reading and delineate how *The Tempest*'s comic ending concludes the dynamic interaction between the political and the aesthetic in the play and embodies the qualities of a utopian, happy ending—and to suggest what that means and does not mean. It does not, for example, presuppose an entirely noble Prospero.

The Tempest's Happy Ending

At the end of volume 1 of his monumental *The Principle of Hope*, Ernst Bloch discusses the phenomenon of literary happy endings in a short chapter that is crucial for an understanding of the utopian in question here. It is called "Happy End, Seen Through and Yet Still Defended."[38] The political message of the passage—written in the early days of the

East German regime in the late 1940s and 1950s from Bloch's exile in the United States—shows that Bloch had a misplaced faith in the future of socialism in the German Democratic Republic. But the literary meaning remains important nevertheless. Noting a human inclination both to be deceived and to pursue happiness and pleasure, Bloch discusses how easily happy endings can manipulate and mislead readers. "There is a lot to be said for condemning outright the illusion at the end," he writes ruefully, specifying the utopian's uses in commercial advertising and in political propaganda. But, he goes on, "this is only one side of illusion, which is itself false. An unmistakable drive is working in the direction of the good end, it is not only confined to gullibility . . . Hope is too indestructibly grounded in the human drive for happiness, and it has always been too clearly a motor of history."[39] The phrasing gives Marx's well-known idea of the class struggle as the motor of history a new interpretation.

In short, if we see it for what it is—a literary device based on art's status as other than reality, on its ability to create the golden world of aesthetic utopia—we can and should value artful happy endings as embodying both a critical sensibility and a genuine satisfaction of a real human need for pleasure. The ending of *The Tempest* is of this sort.

Importantly, it is complex. It balances the restoration of the presumed dead son Ferdinand to his grieving father (along with news of the forthcoming nuptials) with the noticeable if muted lack of any repentance on the part of the usurpers (or would-be usurpers) Antonio and Sebastian. There is instead a kind of willful strategic hushing up about these matters in Prospero's words, "Let us not burden our remembrances with / A heaviness that's gone" (5.1.198–99). Political justice is partially achieved in the form of the restoration of Prospero's dukedom, but this is belated, and we are led to believe Prospero expects an early death. Like the ending of the other late plays, this one is bittersweet, with weight given both to past sufferings and to the joy taken in the overcoming of them to create a present happiness. All accounts are not settled. Some of them are just allowed to slip by, in the spirit Prospero offers to Sebastian and Antonio concerning their contemplated but unperformed murder: "At this time / I will tell no tales" (5.1.128–29).

In short, the play proffers no political revolution; and Machiavellian politics, it seems, can be expected to continue upon the return of the characters to Italy—Prospero's sense of baroque *desengaño* (withdrawal from the world) notwithstanding. The play does, however, put the political in a new light, as there is a condemnation of the human costs of the treachery and the murders and would-be murders of power politics. It all seems, in light of the magical world of the island, to be simply petty. This, it appears, is the meaning of the enigmatic detail mentioned when Prospero climaxes his talk to the King of Naples by revealing his supposedly dead son from behind a curtain as he plays chess with his new love. Chess here is an emblem of political struggle reduced to a lovers' game, very much in the spirit of John Donne's great utopian love poem "The Sunne Rising," with its famous lines,

> She'is all States, and all Princes, I,
> Nothing else is.
> Princes doe but play us; compar'd to this,
> All honor's mimique; All wealthe alchimie.[40]

In the inverted, utopian world of the island, politics becomes a game while nature, sexuality, family, and a certain pragmatic justice come to the fore. The egalitarian vision suggested in the dissolution of traditional hierarchy into an egalitarian community in the storm scene even survives in the drunken Stephano's exclamation, "Every man shift for all the rest, and let no man take care for himself, for all is but fortune" (5.1.256–57). But this is all part of an island whose subtleties "will not let you / Believe things certain" (5.1.124–25). The utopian is diagnostic, not prophetic. It discloses gaps in the fulfillment of our needs and desires but does not guarantee their satisfaction. One of the crucial qualities of the aesthetic is that it allows critical reflection on the political—and imaginings of how things might be different. *The Tempest* can still serve that function for us, even as it reveals the darker realities of politics and human existence as well.

Notes

1. Ernst Bloch, *A Philosophy of the Future*, excerpted in Maynard Solomon, ed., *Marxism and Art: Essays Classic and Contemporary* (New York: Vintage, 1974), 587, 585.
2. Theodor Adorno, *Minima Moralia: Reflections from Damaged Life*, trans. E. F. N. Jephcott (London: New Left Books, 1974), 274.
3. This essay is thus a work of synthesis, drawing from my earlier work on both the political and the aesthetic and the relationship between them—and trying to develop the ideas further. The works I am building on are noted below.
4. Hugh Grady, *Shakespeare, Machiavelli, and Montaigne: Power and Subjectivity from "Richard II" to "Hamlet"* (Oxford: Oxford University Press, 2002).
5. Alessandra Petrina, *Machiavelli in the British Isles: Two Early Modern Translations of "The Prince"* (New York: Ashgate Publishing, 2009), 1–45.
6. I make this case in Grady, *Shakespeare, Machiavelli, and Montaigne*, 26–57.
7. Carl Schmitt, *Political Theology: Four Chapters on the Concept of Sovereignty*, trans. George Schwab (Chicago: University of Chicago Press, 1985), 8–10, 16–17.

8. This specific view of Shakespeare's era—which, it should be noted, hardly represents all of Schmitt's controversial ideas, which I am far from endorsing—is essentially complementary to the position on the evolution of political ideas I assumed in *Shakespeare, Machiavelli, and Montaigne* for the period 1595–1600—a position I am further developing in this discussion of *The Tempest*. See also Christopher Pye, *The Storm at Sea: Political Aesthetics in the Time of Shakespeare* (New York: Fordham University Press, 2015), 1–36, for a summary and application of many of these ideas—and a linkage to a unique theory of the aesthetic.

9. See Hugh Grady, *Shakespeare and Impure Aesthetics* (Cambridge: Cambridge University Press, 2009), 4, 230–31; and John Joughin and Simon Malpas, eds., *The New Aestheticism* (Manchester, U.K.: Manchester University Press, 2003).

10. Jacques Rancière, *The Politics of Aesthetics: The Distribution of the Sensible*, trans. Gabriel Rockhill (New York: Continuum, 2004), 13.

11. Michel Foucault, *The Archaeology of Knowledge*, trans. A. M. Sheridan (New York: Harper Colophon, 1972), 191.

12. Rancière, *The Politics of Aesthetics*, 20–30.

13. Pye, *The Storm at Sea*, 190n71, critiques Rancière's approach to the aesthetic, claiming that the idea of a *partage du visible* implies a domain of the sensible prior to any division. In other ways, however, his approach to the aesthetic resembles Rancière's in its emphasis on the idea of aesthetic autonomy as its most important defining characteristic. For my dialogue with Pye on this point and others, see Hugh Grady, "Theory 'After Theory': Christopher Pye's Reading of *Othello*," *Shakespeare Quarterly* 60, no. 4 (Winter 2009): 453–59.

14. Rancière, *The Politics of Aesthetics*, 40–41; Jacques Rancière, *Aesthetics and Its Discontents*, trans. Steven Corcoran (Cambridge: Polity Press, 2009), 19–60.

15. Jaques Rancière, *Aisthesis: Scenes from the Aesthetic Regime of Art*, trans. Zakir Paul (London: Verso, 2013), 15.

16. Grady, *Shakespeare and Impure Aesthetics*, 90–129.

17. The number of studies along these lines is large. For a good account of several up to 1999, see Thomas Cartelli, *Repositioning Shakespeare: National Formations, Postcolonial Appropriations* (London: Routledge, 1999), 87–119.

18. William Shakespeare, *The Oxford Shakespeare: The Tempest*, ed. Stephen Orgel (Oxford: Oxford University Press, 1987), 1.2.362–63. Subsequent citations are to this edition and appear parenthetically in the main text.

19. David Kastan, *Shakespeare after Theory* (New York: Routledge, 1999), 183–97.

20. Quoted in Maddie Crum, "Nude, All-Women Production Of Shakespeare's 'The Tempest' Honors Free Expression: 'O, wonder! How many goodly creatures are there here!,'" May 20, 2016, *Huffington Post*, https://www.huffpost.com/entry/nude-all-women-shakespeare_n_573f78a1e4b045cc9a710e0c. See also https://coedtoplesspulpfiction.wordpress.com/ for a longer description by the troupe; accessed May 27, 2016.

21. The concept of the utopian has been interpreted and developed in a number of Frankfurt School works on the aesthetic; it permeates the work of the like-minded Walter Benjamin, who used his own terminology (like "Messianic time")

to convey concepts closely allied to Bloch's "utopian." It also permeates Herbert Marcuse, *An Essay on Liberation* (Boston: Beacon Press, 1969), and other works. Horkheimer and Adorno make use of the term or concept throughout their works; see particularly the ending of Theodor Adorno, *Minima Moralia: Reflections from Damaged Life*, trans. E. F. N. Jephcott (London: New Left Books, 1974), 247, and Adorno's posthumous *Aesthetic Theory*, trans. C. Lenhardt, ed. Gretel Adorno and Rolf Tiedemann (Boston: Routledge, 1984). The utopian has been a topic in several of Fredric Jameson's works. See his chapter on Bloch in *Marxism and Form: Twentieth-Century Dialectical Theories of Literature* (Princeton, N.J.: Princeton University Press, 1971), 116–59; as well as "Introduction/ Prospectus: To Reconsider the Relationship of Marxism to Utopian Thought," *Minnesota Review* 6 (Spring 1976): 53–58; "Reification and Utopia in Mass Culture," *Social Text* 1 (Winter 1979): 130–48; *The Political Unconscious: Narrative as a Socially Symbolic Act* (Ithaca, N.Y.: Cornell University Press, 1981), 281–99; and, more recently, *Archaeologies of the Future: The Desire Called Utopia and Other Science Fictions* (London: Verso, 2005).

22. See Hugh Grady, *Shakespeare's Universal Wolf: Studies in Early Modern Reification* (Oxford: Clarendon Press, 1996), 181–212.

23. This material is drawn from Grady, *Shakespeare's Universal Wolf*, 192–93.

24. Walter Benjamin, *The Origin of German Tragic Drama*, trans. John Osborne (London: New Left Books, 1977), 223–28.

25. Stephen Orgel, *The Illusion of Power: Political Theater in the English Renaissance* (Berkeley: University of California Press, 1975), 38.

26. Stephen Orgel, introduction to Shakespeare, *The Oxford Shakespeare*, 47.

27. Orgel, introduction, 47–48.

28. Orgel, introduction, 47.

29. Orgel, introduction, 33–36.

30. Cf. Julia Reinhard Lupton, *Citizen-Saints: Shakespeare and Political Theology* (Chicago: University of Chicago Press, 2005), 170: "Yet there is a more positive dimension to Caliban's speech: the passion of wonder that characterizes the creature's reaction to Creation."

31. Beatrice Hanssen, *Walter Benjamin's Other History: Of Stones, Animals, Human Beings, and Angels* (Berkeley: University of California Press, 1998), 104; emphasis in original.

32. Hanssen, *Walter Benjamin's Other History*, 104, 105.

33. Lupton, *Citizen-Saints*, 165–71; emphasis in original.

34. Ernst Bloch, "Kann Hoffnung enttaüscht werden?" (Can hope be disappointed?), quoted and translated in Jack Zipes, "Introduction: Toward a Realization of Anticipatory Illumination," in *The Utopian Function of Art and Literature: Selected Essays*, by Ernst Bloch, trans. Jack Zipes and Frank Mecklenburg (Cambridge, Mass.: MIT Press, 1993).

35. Victor Shklovsky, "Art as Technique" (1916), in *Literary Theory: An Anthology*, 2nd ed., ed. Julie Rivkin and Michael Ryan, 15–21 (Malden, Mass.: Blackwell Publishing, 2004).

36. See Orgel, introduction, 5–18, for a useful summary of the play's critical history.

37. Orgel, introduction, 11.

38. Ernst Bloch, "Happy End, Seen Through and Yet Still Defended," in *The Principle of Hope, Volume 1*, trans. Neville Plaice, Stephen Plaice, and Paul Knight, 441–47 (Cambridge, Mass.: MIT Press, 1986).

39. Bloch, *The Principle of Hope*, 442–43.

40. John Donne, "The Sunne Rising," in *John Donne: Poetry and Prose*, ed. Frank J. Warnke (New York: Modern Library, 1967), 10–11.

"A Diversity of Sounds, All Horrible"

The Political Aesthetics of Soundscapes in *The Tempest*

Colby Gordon

> GONZALO: This Tunis, sir, was Carthage . . .
> ANTONIO: His word is more than the miraculous harp.
> SEBASTIAN: He hath raised the wall, and houses too.
> ANTONIO: What impossible matter will he make easy next?
> SEBASTIAN: I think he will carry this island home in his pocket and give it his son for an apple.

Still reeling from the shock of a shipwreck, Prospero's water-logged guests make an attempt at small-talk that drifts toward the topic of the foundation, destruction, and resurrection of a great city. In an empty pleasantry, Gonzalo compares Alonso's daughter Claribel, just wed to the king of Tunis, to the "widow Dido," leading to an argument about whether Tunis is the same city as the historical Carthage (2.1.77). Mocking Gonzalo's assertion that Tunis supplanted Carthage as an ahistorical fabrication, Antonio and Sebastian turn to an origin myth of Thebes, whose walls were built by stones cheerfully marching to the tune of Amphion's "miraculous harp" and settling themselves into position according to the sounds of his lyre.[1] In dredging up Thebes's enchanted stones, dancing their way toward the edges of a settlement on the cusp of becoming a city, the courtiers mean to be dismissive. Even so, this Ovidian B-side speaks with unusual clarity to the situation that obtains on *The Tempest*'s little island, raising crucial questions about the relation between aesthetics and politics and, more specifically, the foundations of the *polis* in song and sound. Prospero, like a colonial Amphion, builds his island regime through creating immersive soundscapes that variously schedule streams of action, direct movements, temper emotions, frame encounters, and terrorize his enemies. Put differently, his political mastery depends on his ability to control what Jacques Rancière calls the "distribution of the sensible," that is, the "apportionment of parts and positions" within the political order or "commons" through the "distribution of spaces, times, and forms of activity."[2] This essay offers a dual-track reading of *The Tempest*'s acoustic terrains, first attending to Prospero's manipulation of sound to establish a godlike authority, and then tapping the political possibilities of a resistant, nonhuman aesthetics embodied in *The Tempest*'s soundscapes.

The myth of Amphion served as a convenient topos for Renaissance humanists to trace the connections among music, architecture, rhetoric, politics, and poetry. George Puttenham, for instance, opens *The Arte of English Poesie* by binding poetry to music and architecture through the myth of Amphion, who "builded up cities, and reared walles with the stones that came in heapes to the sound of this harpe, figuring thereby the mollifying of hard and stonie hearts by his sweete and eloquent perswasion."[3] As hearts soften, the city hardens: in this explication, the architectural shell of the polis stands for the mass of subjects that constitute the body politic, their individual wills melded together through the aesthetic force of "sweete and eloquent" rhetorical strategies. The foundational role of aesthetics is given more depth and specificity in Horace's *Ars Poetica*, a text that also takes up Amphion's lyre in a passage that Ben Jonson Englished thus:

> Amphion too, that built the Theban towers,
> Was said to move the stones by his Lutes powers,
> And lead them with his soft songs, where he would:
> This was the wisedome that they had of old,
> Things sacred and prophane to separate;
> The publicke from the private; to abate
> Wild ranging lusts, prescribe the marriage good,
> Build townes, and carve the lawes in leaves of wood.
> And thus at first, an honour, and a name
> To divine Poets, and their verses came.[4]

These lines, which continued to resonate for Jonson, enumerate the foundational, even law-giving tasks achieved by the "divine Poets" whose aesthetic craft inscribes originary distinctions that, like the walls of the city, separate inside from outside, citizen from stranger. Amphion's harp institutes divisions that are simultaneously conceptual and spatial, generating multiple walls that traverse both the city and the life of the citizen-subject: the physical threshold that distinguishes the public realm of the polis from the private space of the *oikos*; the temple wall that splits the sacred realm from the "prophane" world of daily life; even the libidinal urges that "range" or wander (*concubitu uago*) outside their proper bounds in the home. In Horace's reckoning, Amphion builds out the political sphere through a practice that is simultaneously aesthetic, juridical, and religious. In this respect, the myth of Amphion invites inquiry into the passages and exchanges between politics, aesthetics, and theology, issues that animate *The Tempest* and exercise early modern studies more broadly.

The study of aesthetics, once central to the project of literary criticism, has recently made a return to the field, entering early modern studies in texts like Hugh Grady's *Impure Aesthetics*, which casts Shakespeare as a "proto-theorist of the aesthetic," and a recent special issue on "Cute Shakespeare," which seeks out the political dimensions of the "minor affects" threaded throughout Shakespeare's canon.[5] In another vein, a new volume curated by Paul Kottman explores the histories of Kant's and Hegel's aesthetic philosophy in early modern sources.[6] In a line of inquiry that resonates with Amphion's Shakespearean cameo, Christopher Pye's *The Storm at Sea* advances a powerful argument that, in the "post-theocratic" landscape of Reformed England, the aesthetic assumed a new potential to shape the foundations of political authority.[7] In the historical era between Henrician secularization and the emergence of the "rationalized" state, Pye asserts, aesthetics replaced the religious sources of the political sphere with a "creationist *poiesis*" that he glosses as "the work's world-creating capacity."[8] Although the specifically *creationist* bent of this world-building practice might suggest that aesthetics quietly carries forward lingering traces of the theological worldview it displaces, Pye argues that the early modern political aesthetic "reflects back on" and in this way "problematizes the analogy with divine creation."[9] In this respect, Pye inserts political aesthetics into debates in early modern studies concerning political theology and secularization, arguments that frequently revolve around the place of *poiesis* in the production of the political realm. In recent work, Julia Reinhard Lupton clears space for a "divine *poiesis*" that feeds into the autopoietic or self-organizing capacities of creaturely life in a project that seeks to "remain faithful to the potentialities and achievements of liberalism."[10] Conversely, in a robust defense of secularism, Victoria Kahn asserts that a concept of "aesthetics and poiesis" that emerged in early modernity came to ground "a locus of the genuinely political" that owes nothing to theological imaginaries of divine creation. Kahn opposes this "purely secular conception of poiesis" aligned with a "purely human realm of the symbolic" to Carl Schmitt's totalitarian state theory, in which all significant political concepts derive from religious sources.[11] Republican politics do not emerge from theological concepts but rather from the "interpretive activity of giving form," a practice with roots in Renaissance allegorical writing that anticipates Enlightenment aesthetics.[12] Thus, questions surrounding the ongoing legacies of political theology turn on differing interpretations of early modern aesthetics and their afterlives.

Carl Schmitt, who scoured early modern sources for models of state power, remained vigorously opposed to the convergence of politics and aesthetics, an argument he develops in his 1919 volume on *Political Romanticism*, which locates the shortcomings of liberalism in the aesthetic theory of Kant, Schlegel, and Müller.[13] Early modernity lent Schmitt a model for his preferred state form in the "political myth" of Hobbes's Leviathan, a figure embodying the "classical representative of the decisionist type": a personalist sovereign cast in the "image of the architect and master builder of the world."[14] In Schmitt's genealogy of modern governance, romantic aesthetics served as a crucial switch point between the properly political state theory of the seventeenth century and its replacement by the weaker state forms offered by liberalism in the nineteenth. Under the creeping influence of romanticism, the place once occupied by God as the "final, absolute authority" and "absolute center" grounding "every binding norm" is replaced by the private individual—or, rather, by the individual's "ironic, scheming ego."[15] Because "the romantic subject treats the world as an occasion . . . for subjective creativity," every potential point of contention is reduced to an opportunity for "aesthetic interest" and "romantic productivity."[16] Rather than confronting conflicts with aggressive action, the romantic retreats to an attitude of "subjective occasionalism," poeticizing and ironizing his individual experience to satisfy his "creative ego."[17] Schmitt reserves particular scorn for aesthetic autonomy, not only as an incentive to "snobbery and Bohemianism" but as a philosophical development that privatizes all domains of intellectual and political life.[18] The disaggregating properties promoted by aesthetic autonomy infiltrate the political sphere through the electoral procedure of voting by secret ballot, a practice Schmitt denounces in *Constitutional Theory*.[19] Schmitt maintains that if voters are "isolated at the decisive moment" when power is transferred, they do not constitute a real "political entity" or "public" or "common will" but merely a dispersed and scattered set of individuals, each of whom is led by their own personal interests.[20] Thus, any "genuine election" is frustratingly derailed by "the sphere of irresponsible private feeling" that obstructs unified action from the body politic.[21]

For Schmitt, then, the "subjective occasionalism" of the individual aesthete is mapped onto the political sphere of a romanticized liberal state that opts for endless dithering rather than decisive action. Worse yet, political romanticism's indecision can be exploited by "unromantic" political actors, since the romantic state will "unconsciously submit to the strongest and most proximate power," leaving "everything that is romantic at the disposal of other energies that are unromantic" until "the sublime elevation above definition and decision is transformed into a subservient attendance upon alien power and alien decision."[22] In strikingly gendered language, Schmitt cautions that the feminized aestheticism of political romanticism espoused by liberalism puts the state at risk of succumbing the virile authority of its "strongest" and "most proximate" neighbors, transforming the once decisive and autonomous nation into the mere handmaiden of foreign powers. In this way, "aesthetic-romantic" tendencies finally drain the "heathenish vitality" of the Hobbesian sovereign, not only accompanying but actively enabling the historical processes of depoliticization, neutralization, and secularization.[23]

Nevertheless, when Schmitt attempts to offer realist alternatives to political romanticism, he stumbles into a different, but equally emotive, aesthetic formation. For Schmitt, what constitutes properly political activity, as opposed to the occasionalist fancies of political romanticism, flows from an old ritual sourced from the deep histories of political theology: acclamation, which Schmitt dubs "the most authentic activity, capacity, and function of the people."[24] Indeed, the originary task of the people as such is to "proclaim a leader."[25] The "authenticity" (*Echtheit*) of this procedure is threatened by the electoral practices of liberal democracy, which renders "any acclamation . . . impossible."[26] The act of hailing seems to have no content in particular: the people merely express "consent or disapproval" or "honor the king or some other person" by way of a "simple calling out," or even coyly withhold the acclamation "by silence."[27] Any attempt to channel the acclamation into specific policy outcomes would both smack of bourgeois individualism and sap its spontaneity, since both the people and the acclamation exist only in an "unorganized form . . . uncontrolled" by government organs or social bodies like trade unions.[28] And yet, despite Schmitt's efforts to maintain a bright-line distinction between the "social reality" of acclamation and the abstractions of political romanticism, acclamation is equipped with its own heady aesthetics, serving as a sonic practice that lends an aura of religiosity to the act of hailing a new leader.[29] Ernst Kantorowicz, normally so hesitant to make explicitly political statements, caps his study of the *laudes regiae*, the liturgical acclamations that greeted imperial coronations from antiquity to early modernity, with a chapter on "The *Laudes* in Modern Times," noting that acclamations are "indispensable to the emotionalism of a Fascist regime."[30] The emotive outburst from the assembled people marks the moment of political foundation, a sonic supplement to the people's "vital energy and political unity" as they proclaim a representative.[31] The eruption of the crowd's roar lent a muscular punctuation to the political liturgies of the dictatorial leader cult, offering an acoustic complement to the well-documented visual aesthetics supporting the totalitarian regimes of the twentieth century.[32] The chilling soundscape of the *laudes* is the noise generated where political theology meets political aesthetics.

The Tempest is a particularly apt text to explore the political aesthetics of sound, to judge whether sonic spectacle tends to be channeled into Schmittian theo-political forms or instead to generate a secular *poiesis* that gives rise to resistant and egalitarian politics. The first reason is historical, since early modernity occupied a privileged but contested space within Schmitt's genealogy of the modern state. Schmitt considered the seventeenth century "the heroic age of occidental rationalism," and he turned to Hobbes and Shakespeare for political and aesthetic models as part of his larger project of resuscitating a charismatic absolutism in the juridical scaffolding of totalitarianism.[33] At the same time, both Schmitt and his critics locate the seeds of secularization, the emergence of liberal thought, and the origins of the aesthetic in the same historical moment, issues that shape *The Tempest*'s treatment of magic as an instrument of patriarchalism and imperialism.[34] *The Tempest* is also, as Christopher Pye demonstrates, "the most 'aestheticizing' of Shakespeare's plays," its island a zone where "sovereign authority, autonomy, and aesthetic formation" overlap.[35] More to the point, as its evocation of Amphion suggests, *The Tempest*'s political aesthetics are specifically sonic in nature, and not only because the play sports Shakespeare's most richly realized soundscapes: Prospero massages the "distribution of the sensible" through his resourceful manipulation of ambient sound to govern the behaviors and dispositions of his shipwrecked audience. Prospero understands his mastery over the sound world in patriarchal terms, a sign of his insertion at the top of an anthropocentric hierarchy according to which the created world exists for his instrumental use. From this perspective, the liveliness of the sonic spirits that do his bidding merely reflects the human intentions they channel. However, as Prospero's experiments with sound progress in ambition and complexity, the distinctions between artificed sound and environmental sonorities blur. The indeterminate nature of *The Tempest*'s soundscapes, which seem to belong both to the world and to the self, raises questions about aesthetic autonomy that are both theoretical and political.[36] The threshold moments in which soundscapes slip the grasp of human engineering gesture toward the possibility of an autonomous inhuman aesthetic. *The Tempest* is a play saturated in noise that the audience and the shipwrecked characters alike experience according to those audio cues dictated by displays of sonic virtuosity, sometimes on the part of Prospero, and sometimes through the agency of the island itself as personified in the network of spirits.

The aesthetic magic that Prospero employs to found his political regime is acoustic, beginning with the tempest itself, a study of bodies submerged in immersive ripples of sound. The tempestuous wall of sound progressively drowns out speech in a superabundance of noise: no one can speak clearly enough over the bellowing waves to make themselves heard properly, so the opening lines of the play must be delivered in barely decipherable screams. The master attempts to maintain a semblance of order by turning to his own instrument, a whistle whose pathetic chirping is barely audible above the crashing breakers: "Heigh, my hearts; cheerly, cheerly, my hearts! yare! Yare! Take in the topsail. Tend to the master's whistle!" (1.1.5–7). The cumulative effect of the storm's "dreadful thunderclaps," the "fire and cracks / Of sulphurous roaring" on the passengers reduces their voices from tools of speech to so much useless sound, shrieks of anguish and terror directed indiscriminately at one another and the storm as the passengers are rendered mere "insolent noise-makers" (1.1.43). The crew and cowering passengers are confronted by "roarers" that generate such substantial volumes of sound that they override and disable communication among the ship's passengers (1.1.17). After a point, individual voices become indistinguishable, blending together in a cluster of shrill dissonance that the stage directions render as a "*cry*" or "*confused noise within*" (1.2.202–4, 1.1.35, 60). With an ear to the door, listening to the passengers as they curse, or pray, or wail, or scream, the boatswain notes how their language has degenerated into a babbling that is ever more fully absorbed into the storm's sonic scene: "A plague upon this howling. They are louder than the weather or our office" (1.1.35–36). In this "tempestuous" or "confused" clamor, the desperate cries of the passengers are steadily drained of significance until their howls lose meaning entirely and bleed into a manifold of environmental noise compiled from human, oceanic, and meteorological sources.

The storm disables and reshuffles the political order that held sway over the ship, creating an opening for Prospero to assert his authority, a show of force that is all the more necessary given the contingency of his power. Although it is customary to speak of Prospero in the terms offered by absolutism or patriarchalism, to those on board the ship he is only a disappeared dissident, a stateless refugee, or at the very most a minor duke in the presence of a king.[37] The storm marks a moment of crisis or interregnum, in which one political regime is disabled and another emerges. As the boatswain informs a flustered Gonzalo in the midst of the tempest, the social order once ensured by the political sway of King Alonso no longer applies: "What cares these roarers for the name of the king?" (1.1.16). Given the brute fact of natural catastrophe, social hierarchies evaporate as Gonzalo witnesses the order underwritten by Alonso unspooling before his eyes. The swirling noise of the tempest, however, seems to speak, to name a new sovereign. While Gonzalo imagines the roaring sea as a cursing and ravenous mouth that seems to "swear" and "gape at widest to glut" itself, Alonso recalls that "the winds did sing it to me, and the thunder— / That deep and dreadful organpipe— pronounced / The name of Prosper" (3.3.97–99). Like the acclamatory cries in which the commons united in a resonant body to hail the prince, here meteorological systems and tectonic masses and oceans of sound offer up a screaming endorsement of their god-king. While this acclamation does not follow the liturgical pattern documented by Kantorowicz, it clings closely to the model described by Schmitt, in which the private desires and personal positions of each single subject merge together in a homogeneous clamor, a "simple calling out . . . celebrating a leader" or "honoring the king or some other person."[38] The sound field of the storm, which celebrates and honors Prospero by calling out his name, encompasses not only the environmental sounds whipped up in the climatic event of the tempest but the voices of the buffeted ship's passengers as well. The screams of the crew, the sound of the ruptured vessel, the bellowing winds, the crashing waves pour together in a confused din that, with the boatswain, we might describe as a nightmarish assemblage of "strange and several noises / Of roaring, shrieking, howling, jingling chains, / And more diversity of sounds, all horrible" (5.1.232–34). Just as Schmitt's acclamation empties the semantic content of speech acts and leaves only a remainder of pure sound, the rolling cacophony of the tempest's sound field overrides singular speech acts and reduces them to the undifferentiated noise of a "diversity of sounds," uniting them in the sonorous mass of a new body politic. The shock and awe of the tempest, a percussive torrent of waveforms that baptizes the newcomers in water and noise, literalizes the tropes of divine-right kingship as all creation joins in a thunderous, howling acclamation of Prospero's authority. In the acoustic ecology of Prospero's design, every element of the natural world reflects his power back to him, the god in the whirlwind, who swells the chorus of terrified cries with the prayers of drowning men, the shattering timber of a ship dashed to pieces, and roaring torrents of wind and water.

The sonic whirlwind composed of a "diversity" of horrible sounds aligns the tempest with the "aesthetics of horror" Richard Wolin unearths in Schmitt's fascination with the "semantics of rupture, discontinuity, and shock."[39] As Peter Bürger argues, this position aestheticizes the political realm by "assimilating the aesthetic categories of the 'new and strange' to the decision, which he conceives, following the model of the free act of the artistic genius, as an absolute act."[40] The tempest is precisely such a decisive moment, at once a political act and an aesthetic production crafted by a virtuoso indulging his "self-delighting recreative impulse," perfectly capturing the emergence of the "new and strange" that is everywhere at issue in *The Tempest*.[41] The vocal dynamics of the tempest's acclamatory soundscape stress the autonomy of the new political order instituted by Prospero, which owes nothing to the will of the new arrivals. The tedium of the norm that had obtained on the ship is burned to the ground as a new leader arises, cloaked in godlike authority and attended by a bombastic, muscular spectacle, a point of rupture whose shock value, carried on sound waves, ripples through the characters and audience alike. Following Wolin and Bürger, who are suspicious of Schmitt's skepticism toward the aesthetic, artistic and political autonomy overlap in the tempest, which signals the harmonic convergence of political aesthetics and political theology.

For Schmitt, by contrast, the self-constituted nature of the political order on Prospero's island would be precisely what marks his dominion as "unromantic," in the sense that his power is authoritarian and autonomous. This decisive power then allows him to exert his control over the "romantic" figures who wander about his island. The shipwrecked court, immersed in the thunderous coil, all exhibit signs of extreme physical, emotional, and psychological reactions as the acoustic dimensions of the storm enhance the simple fact of physical pain and target their mental stability. Prospero admits as much in a satisfied response to Ariel's account of the storm: "Who was so firm, so constant, that this coil / Would not infect his reason?" (1.2.207–8). Invasive and immersive, sound waves penetrate and stimulate the bodies of the sailors and passengers as they set the dense matter of bones vibrating, the softer stuff of flesh pulsing under swells of noise, muscles tensing and relaxing in response to the flow of sound. Prospero engages the abusive potentials of aural stimulation as he submerges his guests in the liquid ambience of his watery soundscape, bewildering and tenderizing his victims until they are passive, submissive, and open to suggestion. The bone-rattling coil of thunderous sound and flashing lights aggravates the physical threats of drowning and burning, complementing the fear of death and physical exhaustion with a sensory overload that induces psychological effects ranging from disorientation and skewed reality testing, in the case of Ferdinand, to Alonso's full-blown shock. After arriving safely onshore, Gonzalo desperately attempts to wrest his king out of his dazed and dissociated state of mind, reminding his lord that they have escaped death and found dry land: "Beseech you sir, be merry. You have cause / (So have we all) of joy" (2.1.1–3). Alonso will not, or cannot, respond, only begging again and again for silence, a respite for his overfull ears: "Prithee, peace" (2.1.9); "I prithee, spare" (2.1.27); "Prithee, no more. / Thou dost talk nothing to me" (2.1.171–72); "You cram these words into the mine ears, against / The stomach of my sense" (2.1.107–8). In the aftermath of the tempest, Alonso is sluggish and full of despair, describing himself as "attached with weariness / To th'dulling of my spirits," ready to "put off [his] hope" and give in to sleep rather than take any meaningful action (3.3.5–6). This indecisiveness extends to a passive embrace of death, evinced in his reluctance to eat. Finally, under duress, he begrudgingly consents, agreeing to "stand to and feed / Although my last; no matter, since I feel / The best is past" (3.3.49–51). This melancholic exhaustion, at once physiological and emotional, renders the old king pliant and impressionable, open to the musical sedative issued by Ariel, who plays "solemn music" to induce slumber: "I wish mine eyes / Would, with themselves, shut up my thoughts. I find / They are inclined to do so" (2.1.191–93). Prospero leverages the injurious and damaging affordances of sound against his old nemesis, corroding the old king's sense of self and eliminating his capacities to think, converse, plot, and act, effectively sidelining Alonso in the new distribution of the sensible.

The shipwreck is, in every sense, a crisis. At every turn on the island, Alonso confronts different opportunities to make decisions with real consequences for his sworn subjects. Where will they go? What will they eat? Should they search for Ferdinand? Should they construct shelter or rafts? Rather than assuming the responsibility and authority necessary to make those decisions, Alonso treats the entire experience as an occasion to feed his "creative ego" with reveries swirling around his son's worm-eaten corpse: "O thou mine heir / Of Naples and of Milan, what strange fish / Hath made his meal on thee?" (2.1.112–14). If Ferdinand as heir embodies the sovereign futurity of Alonso's line, the hallucinatory emblem of a "strange fish" fattening itself on the youth's body gestures toward the transformations undergone by sovereignty in the wake of the tempest.[42] Instead of acting like a sovereign by taking decisive action, concocting a plan for escape or survival, or issuing commands to his followers, Alonso indulges in poetic flights of fancy that offer nonresponses to the pressing realities at hand. As Schmitt has it, the old king may have found a "small island of free creativity" through aestheticizing his experience, but it does indeed leave him available to the instrumental uses of another, less romantic actor, who plies the king with soporific songs that guide and govern his activities.[43] In Alonso, the romantic subject and romantic state coincide: disarmed by the storm and then terrorized by Prospero's sonic spirits, Alonso has been neutralized, reduced to subservience to a foreign power and foreign decision.

If the tempest renders Alonso a "subjective occasionalist" in the Schmittian sense, the most committed romantic in the play is, fittingly, his son, who submits absolutely to Prospero's directives as issued by Ariel's song. In the aftermath of the storm, Ferdinand reflects on the enticing song that steered him toward land, an ambient web of sound that now envelops him fully:

> Where should this music be? I'th' air, or th'earth?
> It sounds no more; and sure it waits upon
> Some god o'th' island. Sitting on a bank,
> Weeping again the King my father's wrack,
> This music crept by me upon the waters,
> Allaying both their fury and my passion
> With its sweet air; thence I have followed it,
> or it hath drawn me, rather. But 'tis gone.
> No, it begins again . . .
> This is no mortal business, nor no sound
> That the earth owes. I hear it now above me. (1.2.388–96, 407–8)

Engaging in a kind of phenomenological description, Ferdinand recalls the orientating properties of sound as Ariel's song pulls him around the island and massages his mood. Like Alonso, Ferdinand is a figure of passivity in the face of crisis, immobile and weeping on a bank after suffering his own traumatic encounter with the storm when strange music "crept by [him] upon the waters" and tempered his grief, "allaying" his "passion" with a "sweet air." After first asserting that he "followed [the music]," Ferdinand corrects himself in a way that minimizes his own agency and emphasizes the song's agential capacities: "it hath drawn me, rather." Although Ferdinand recognizes that he is being acted upon, he cannot determine the source of the song that appears to be site specific, slyly piped in from the earth, air, and water, while also seeming to exceed the ambient noise of the environment. This time, Prospero does not employ sound to abuse and overwhelm, as he does for the sailors caught in the storm, nor does it fatigue, as it does with Alonso and company. Rather, this soundscape serves scenographic ends, directing young Ferdinand's movements and synchronizing them with Miranda's in a spatial and temporal choreography.

The erotic dominance Prospero exercises over Ferdinand and the others relies on his knack for selecting sound cues that drive his captive audience from one side of the island to another, setting the stage for romance or revenge and adjusting their moods. Sound is the instrument Prospero takes up to keep the sorry, shipwrecked sailors precisely where he wants them, both physically and psychologically. Happily for Prospero, the young prince is admittedly susceptible to acoustic persuasion:

> Full many a lady
> I have eyed with best regard, and many a time,
> Th'harmony of their tongues hath into bondage
> Brought my too diligent ear. (3.1.39–42)

Ferdinand is a sensitive boy, and, as he sheepishly confesses to his new mistress, he has a storied history of succumbing readily to audio bondage. An ear too diligent is receptive to sonorous spells that snake their way into his cavities, thrilling through his body and rendering him a bundle of excited flesh, a packet of enlivened, vibrating matter. The acoustically enriched landscape works on Ferdinand's mind and body together, weaving his fears and desires together in a dreamscape laced with fantasy and leaving him open to manipulation:

> My spirits, as in a dream, are all bound up.
> My father's loss, the weakness which I feel,
> The wreck of all my friends, nor this man's threats
> (To whom I am subdued) are but light to me,
> Might I but through my prison once a day
> Behold this maid. All corners else o'th'earth
> Let liberty make use of; space enough
> Have I in such a prison. (1.2.488–95)

Not merely disciplinary, the soundscape in which Ferdinand is moored actively contours his behavior, emotions, and mind-set through a somatic intervention. Or, as Prospero puts it to Ferdinand, "Come on, obey: / Thy nerves are in their infancy again / And have no vigour in them"

(1.2.484–86). By grinding down Ferdinand's defenses and exhausting his vitality, the rolling waves of sound have broken his resistance, not debilitating him precisely but uncluttering his mind of previous attachments, redirecting his attention and libido toward a new object. The weak point in his physical system, the prince's nerves are at once the focal point of an attack and the vehicle of Prospero's control. The patriarch plays Ferdinand like an instrument, plucking his sinews until he sings perfectly in harmony with his master.[44] Like a child or a captive, the prince gives himself over to Prospero's guardianship, exchanging obedience and labor for guidance and protection.

So far, the sound bath of *The Tempest* seems to accord harmoniously with the antiaesthetic schema of Schmitt's political realism. The storm, summoned up through sheer force of will and the prodigious capacities of Prospero's "beating mind," ruptures the preexisting political norm and subordinates every other character to his authority. The thunderous soundscape of the tempest, which combines the screams of the sailors with the roiling clamor of the laments in an acclamatory cry, lends a theological aura to Prospero's dominion. Henceforth, Prospero remains the only "decider" on the island, the one figure capable of taking purposeful and consequential action. Compare his careful scene setting in introducing Ferdinand to Miranda with the broad slapstick of Caliban, Stephano, and Trinculo's coup, or with the abortive regicide imagined by Sebastian and Antonio. Through his clever weaponization of sound, Prospero carefully orders the distribution of the sensible and organizes the phenomenal experience of the newcomers. Mastering the aesthetic in this way, Prospero effectively controls the activities, attitudes, and emotional states of his old and new subjects alike. By contrast, the romanticism or occasionalism of Ferdinand and Alonso renders them immobile, indecisive, and ineffective; under the influence of Prospero's sonic machinations, they are powerless to react to the crises they face. Finally, in what would be the most central point for Schmitt, Prospero's political power is utterly autonomous: it was produced through fiat, not election, and his regime owes nothing to any agent, collective, or institution outside himself. As such, it seems that *The Tempest* holds out little promise for an early modern aesthetics that might resist political theology, decisionism, and absolutism.

However, listening to *The Tempest* with an ear to the inhuman, ecological base of the island soundscapes might undermine the political autonomy of Prospero's little kingdom. The soundscapes do not emerge, pure and undiluted, from Prospero's mind or the books he imports to the isle but require the instrumentalization of Ariel, a fluid, flighty embodiment of the island's ambient sound. The faerie world of *A Midsummer*

Night's Dream was essentially floral and fungal, but the sprites of *The Tempest* are airy and ethereal, invisible yet material, and everywhere associated with song.[45] Before Prospero's arrival on the island, Ariel was a disembodied voice with just enough materiality to cleave within a pine tree, an obscure noise machine in the forest "vent[ing] [his] groans / As fast as millwheels strike" (1.2.280–81). Ariel's songs, half sound and half scream, feed him into the network of a broader sound world, stirring up currents of empathy or irritation profound enough to "make wolves howl and penetrate the breasts / Of ever-angry bears," which lend their calls to a rich acoustic ecology, the sonorous body of the landscape (1.2.288–89). Likewise, the elusive songs dissolve into distributed choruses, often with spirits voicing animal sounds. When Prospero subdues and marshals the island landscape by forcing Ariel into bondage, he taps the landscape for audio resources that he can remix and amplify to serve his purposes, releasing the sprite from his imprisonment in the tree to "tread the ooze / Of the salt deep, / To run upon the sharp wind of the north," and "To do . . . business in the veins o'th' earth" (1.2.252–55). In overpowering Ariel, Prospero enhances and extends his own power by tapping into the infrasounds of tectonic rumblings and low-frequency winds in a sound world that extends from earthy subterranea to stratospheric heights. Even so, when Ariel's screams have been remixed as song that activates geological resonances and meteorological overtones, he remains embedded in a complex acoustic landscape incorporating ecological and creaturely elements that can be exploited by Prospero but also exceed his directives.

Embodying the island's sound world in faeries who do the bidding of their human master might appear to be an instance of anthropomorphism in which we, like Prospero, ascribe our own desires to the nonhuman world. From this perspective, the aesthetic is the exclusive purview of human ingenuity and intentionality. The ostensible liveliness of the sonic sprites betrays a certain childish credulity in desperate need of ideology critique: the deceptive magic of the island, including its stable of supernatural creatures, merely disguises the aesthetic designs and stagecraft of a human agent. However, recent work falling under the rubrics of the posthuman turn, ecocriticism, animal studies, and object-oriented ontology has recuperated such moments by treating them not as instances of naiveté but rather as acknowledgments of the agentic qualities embedded in the nonhuman world.[46] As Jean Feerick and Vin Nardizzi note, recognizing that the web of objects, environments, and creatures that form the setting for human activity is invested with its own autopoietic capacities for action tends to "scatter the unity of the human actor" and render the category of the human indistinct from the "things" that "not only surround him, but also inhabit him."[47] In this respect, as Jane Bennett argues, "a touch of anthropomorphism" can be salutary in that it "catalyzes a sensibility that finds a world filled not with ontologically distinct categories of beings (subjects and objects) but with variously composed materialities that form confederations."[48] From this vantage, the personification of the island's sonic spirits is not reducible to the disguised machinations of human culture but serves as a sign of collaborative "confederations" of human and nonhuman actants. Far from serving as a sign of Prospero's anthropocentric ascendency, then, the vitality of the island's sound world exposes his deep dependency upon the affordances of his environment in a way that blurs the divisions between subject and object, human and nonhuman.

Unlike Prospero, whose arrogance leads him to assume that his sonic spells are an expression of his undiluted will, Caliban is keenly aware of the eerie vitality animating the island's acoustic ecology, which he catalogs in a multitrack reading of the island's ambient noise attentive to the sweet, soft, insidious pull of ambient sound that wraps together human agents with their environment:

> Be not afeard. The isle is full of noises,
> Sounds and sweet airs that give delight and hurt not.
> Sometimes a thousand twangling instruments
> Will hum about mine ears; and sometimes voices,
> That if I then had waked after long sleep,
> Will make me sleep again; and then in dreaming,
> The clouds, methought, would open and show riches
> Ready to drop upon me, that when I waked
> I cried to dream again. (3.2.135–43)

Like Ferdinand's musings after washing ashore, this reverie amounts to an attempt at phenomenological orientation. Unlike Ferdinand, however, Caliban does not automatically assume there is human engineering or something "more than the Earth owes" implicit in the tones that needle, tease, and invade him. What Caliban describes is an experience of *aisthesis* in which sensation does not belong exclusively to the self or to the world; the "sounds" and "sweet airs" of his environs surround him, wash over him, and rush through him, filling him with "delight" that is both somatic and conceptual. At the same time, Caliban experiences his enjoyment as exterior to himself, dangling above him in clouds that are perpetually on the verge of bursting. This receptivity to the texture of the sensible allows Caliban to linger in a boundary condition where he feels his sense of self emerge and recede, as if he were on the edge of a dream. The permeability of Caliban's subjectivity does not necessarily signal his essential childishness. Rather, Caliban embraces what Jane Bennett calls the "methodological naiveté" of the vital materialist who experiences a "strange" and "incomplete commonality" with an "out-side that is active, forceful, and (quasi)independent."[49] The stimulation of this environmental subtone, coursing through his ears in a low-level hum, is an agonizing and erotic experience that softens the borders separating inside from outside, mind from body, self from other. Unlike Ferdinand, whose aural sensitivity left him open to Prospero's "unromantic" machinations, Caliban is able to leverage his openness to the noise of the world against Stephano and Trinculo, who, enraptured by Caliban's strategic account of his sensuous experience, can be recruited for his regicidal stratagem.

What Caliban discovers in his commonality with his quasi-independent environs is the aesthetic autonomy of *The Tempest*'s soundscapes: the sprites are "vivid entities" that thread together the sonic fabric of the island in order to carry out their own self-directed designs.[50] Prospero is not the only figure on the island capable of manipulating sound, as Caliban and Ariel bend the sound world of the island to their own ends. Enchanted by Ariel's haunting music and Caliban's exegesis, Stephano and Trinculo are eventually persuaded to chase the noise wherever it leads. As Ariel recounts, a distant, bewitching song guides them across the island, by the most malodorous path possible:

> Then I beat my tabor,
> At which like unbacked colts they pricked their ears,
> Advanced their eyelids, lifted up their noses
> As they smelt music; so I charmed their ears
> That calf-like they my lowing followed, through
> Toothed briars, sharp furzes, pricking gorse and thorns,
> Which entered their frail shins. At last I left them
> I'th'filthy-mantled pool beyond your cell,
> There dancing up to th'chins, that the foul lake
> O'erstunk their feet. (4.1.175–84).

The haptic, tactile quality of the ambient music penetrates Stephano and Trinculo, who smell Ariel's music, absorbing it into their pores. The stimulus provided by the hum of background noise guides their actions, creating incentives for their movement. The sound world shaped by Ariel creates a scenographic sequence that guides its occupants through the landscape according to a strictly ordered progression. The drunken, uncritical sailors follow a predetermined path charted for them by sound, winding through the island's natural and artificial landforms, first traipsing through the prickly underbrush and finally stalled in a stinking, putrid pool doubling as a sewer. Stephano and Trinculo are trained to the tones of Ariel's tabor, as the environmental spirits tame, even domesticate the sailors like calves or colts. Like a good behaviorist, Ariel stimulates and punishes the pair until they are so receptive to his audio instructions that they follow his directions even at the cost of humiliation and physical pain. Although Prospero has ordered Ariel to distract and humiliate these would-be regicides, the spirits exceed Prospero's demands at every turn. Unlike the micromanaged sonic event of the tempest, here Ariel is given considerable freedom to play with his charges, guiding them and tormenting them according to his own desires, sharpening a set of tools that he will soon turn against Prospero. The scene also undercuts Prospero's easy assumption that the tempest is a sign of his unilateral command over nature. Rather, all acoustic events on the island are collaboratively constructed with distinct but complementary objectives in mind: Prospero wants an escape from his exile, and the island wants to be rid of Prospero. The very instruments Prospero employs to direct action prove capable of autonomously plotting, designing, and engineering a scene and contouring the distribution of the sensible. In this respect, *The Tempest*'s soundscapes are both human and inhuman, existing in a space between art conceived in intentionalist terms and an art that passes beyond the subject.

As the sonic spirits take ever greater initiative, Prospero's autonomous powers also appear to heighten, reaching a crescendo in the betrothal masque he assembles for Miranda and her fiancé. This performance, a "fantasy of patriarchal creation," crystallizes what Christopher Pye describes as the play's "preoccupation with autogenesis or self-constitution."[51] Prospero's creationist poetics are on full display in the masque, which conjures a host of goddesses on an untouched pastoral landscape whose contours are mapped by the all-powerful magician-king in his role, as Schmitt puts it, as the "image of the architect and master builder of the world."[52] The conjectural rewriting of the island landscape summons up "turfy mountains" dotted with "nippling sheep," "flat meads thatched with stover," "banks with pioned and twilled brims," and "broomgroves" and "seamarge" alongside "grass-plots" and "bosky acres" (4.1.62–69, 82). This alternative creation myth offers a spectacular form to the paternal injunction against sex, offering a vision of a beautiful world purged from the discord arising from sexuality. Romance is literally banished from this apparition: "Mars's hot minion" Venus has been dispatched to another island, "cutting the clouds" toward Cyprus, while her "waspish-headed son has broke his arrows" and promises henceforth to "be a boy right out" (4.1.93–101). In this strange Eden, "temperate" and "cold nymphs" weave "chaste crowns" while shadowy "broomgroves" are traversed by "dismissed" and "lass-lorn bachelors" (4.1.66–68, 132). The barrenness of bodies extends to the landscape composed of "pole-clipped" vines, pilled and pruned, which abut a "sterile and rocky-hard . . . sea-marge" (4.1.68–69). Where the tempest cast Prospero as the god of Job, emerging from the whirlwind to castigate and chasten in a show of spectacular force, the masque enlists Prospero as the creator God of Genesis, gently molding and ordering a world that is at once fertile and sterile, as yet untouched by the sin of sexuality.

However, if the masque embraces a creationist *poiesis* of political theology that mirrors the decisive character of Prospero's regime in a "free act of artistic genius," the performance simultaneously beats a retreat to the apolitical autonomy of the aesthetic sphere.[53] This "paradise" offers a depopulated world where the sprawling expanse of creation has contracted down to three spectators whom the performer-goddesses address directly with clumsy blessings and admonitions (4.1.124). No sign remains of the sinister dynamics that have pruned Prospero's family unit, whose "minor" members, Caliban and Ariel, have been neatly expunged along with all the broader geopolitical issues dragged onto stage by their presence, including discourses of sexual consent and political obligation, not to mention the long histories of colonialism and white supremacy.[54] Nor could the harmonious fantasy be maintained if it acknowledged the political context within the diegetic frame established by the play: Antonio's coup undertaken with Alonso's blessing, Prospero's subsequent exile, the brutal subjugation of Sycorax, Caliban's incarceration and servitude, and the escalating rebellion. Ariel understands this, later admitting that he "thought to have told" Prospero of the threat, but he "feared / lest [he] anger" his unpredictable and violent sovereign (4.1.168–69). In this moment, political autonomy, which Schmitt sharply distinguished from political romanticism, becomes so self-contained and elliptical that it merges with aesthetic autonomy, and Prospero is reduced to the ultimate subjective occasionalist. Rather than dispassionately treating the betrothal as an intermediate step in a plan to return to Milan and reestablish his authority, he seizes upon the romantic possibilities conjured up by his daughter's engagement to a shipwrecked prince and threads the fairy-tale happenstance of their encounter into themes from religion and mythology. An event that might have been passed over quickly in proper Schmittian fashion so that the plot would preserve the forward momentum of a revenge scheme becomes the occasion for mincing about, as the pathetic patriarch magics up a song-and-dance routine that impedes rather than facilitates action. Decision relaxes into indecision: charmed by his own cleverness, Prospero disregards the pressing crises that threaten his very life. The betrothal masque engineers an island within an island, an aesthetic bubble that temporarily shields the little family from political emergencies of their own making as well as the historical and contextual pressures that contour their relationships.

For Schmitt, this kind of aesthetic reverie was unsustainable, not only because it would leave the romantic open to the designs of unromantic powers. In his 1956 essay *Hamlet or Hecuba: The Intrusion of the Time into the Play*, Schmitt considered how political emergency would force its way into an aesthetic production, rupturing its self-contained structure in the face of "a reality externally given, imposed and unavoidable . . . around which the play timidly maneuvers."[55] What precipitates the destruction of Prospero's aesthetic interlude is not the weight of its own internal contradictions, nor is the dreamscape ruptured by the arrival of the political crisis constituted by the human agents of Caliban and company. Instead, sound literally intrudes into the play in the form of a "*strange hollow and confused noise*," a sonorous outburst that we might hear as the inversion of the "diversity of sounds, all horrible" that constituted the tempest's theo-political soundscape. No name of the king echoes through this hollow reverberance, which does not obviously reflect the designs of any particular human agent. Rather, the confused noise announces an inhuman aesthetic that tears through the "baseless fabric of this vision," destroying the edifice of his fantasy in an apocalyptic portent of the inevitable collapse of "the cloud-capped towers, the gorgeous palaces, / The solemn temples, the great globe itself" (4.1.151–53). This propulsive tone shivers through the sound world Prospero painstakingly constructs with a terrifying noise that suggests death and decay, a shock wave anticipating the inevitable deterioration of this, and every, political regime. The sonic spirits that, moments before, had enfleshed Prospero's most closely held fantasies turn on him, retreating to subtones and infrasounds, hovering in frequencies that can be felt but not heard, plying his body with ripples of unease. At the very peak of Prospero's powers and in the fullness of his command over the landscape, the shattered masque showcases the world-breaking as well as world-making properties of ambient sound from which he derived his acoustic sovereignty. Although, like a colonial overlord, Prospero had couched his authority in a technical mastery over nature, the acoustic ecology he so effectively instrumentalized rejects his final imposition, deserting him and leaving him in a state of impotent shock. Where the assaultive sound bath of the tempest quilts together a new body politic by tuning and adjusting the distribution of the sensible, this reprise marks the limits of Prospero's power to force new worlds into being.

Where does that leave us with regard to the encounter between aesthetics and political-theological modes of sovereignty? Certainly *The Tempest* showcases the potentialities of sound to contribute to oppressive, decisionist techniques of rule: the acoustic worlds woven together under Prospero's direction consistently and efficaciously massage the behaviors, attitudes, and emotions of his targets by managing their experience of the phenomenal realm. At the same time, as Prospero's regime becomes increasingly decisive, it finally transforms into a species of romantic occasionalism in which political autonomy deteriorates into aesthetic autonomy. In the aftermath of the betrothal masque's implosion, Pye discovers a more sophisticated and reflexive relationship to representation, a modernizing impulse that sets "the logic of the aesthetic" as the ground and sustenance of a contingent, not divinely authorized, theory of sovereignty.[56]

However, if *The Tempest* advances toward a posttheocratic political symbolics, it still would not offer the "purely secular" and "purely human" *poiesis* that Victoria Kahn locates in early modern aesthetics; the play remains too muddied with theological symbols and rituals to suggest a clean break with religion. Moreover, Shakespeare's sonic scenography turns on a nonhuman *poiesis*, a distribution of the sensible that exceeds the instrumentalization of environmental sound by human actors aiming at totalizing political power. In this way, *The Tempest* explores a political aesthetics of sound in a double sense: the play produces an aesthetics fashioned out of and also by environmental noise, a collaborative soundscape that wraps human and nonhuman agents in a sonic manifold. On *The Tempest*'s island, Amphion's stones do more than move in harmony with the master's lyre; they settle themselves into place according to their own designs.

In spite of Prospero's efforts to micromanage the island scene like a sound designer, the environment generates its own acoustic territories in which the landscape itself guides the actions, teases out the fantasies, and impedes the projects of the shipwrecked arrivals. The acoustic environs of *The Tempest* test the affordances of sound in the political sphere, plumbing the potentials of noise to map out scenes that explore the empowering dimensions of sounds without ever neglecting or minimizing its abusive potentials. Under the aesthetic magic of soundscape, the desolate domains of exile transform into inhabitable scenes of violent settlement, pastoral romance, and even grudging hospitality. *The Tempest* is Shakespeare's essay on sound and aesthetics, a multitrack meditation on noise as a place-making protocol, a scenographic device, an environmental phenomenon, and an agent of social engineering. While Prospero turns to the aesthetic affordances of sound to impose form on the sprawling mass of an unruly environment and its inhabitants, the soundscapes at play in *The Tempest* mark the limits of this model. The sound world of *The Tempest* is a vibrant, vibrational field of mutual, multidirectional influence. On the island, sound traverses bodies and binds together human, animal, plant, and meteorological actors in a sonorous ecology, a resonant body, a consonant—and dissonant—commons.

Notes

The chapter epigraph is from *The Tempest*, ed. Virginia Mason Vaughn and Alden T. Vaughan (London: Arden Shakespeare, 1999), 2.1.84–92. Subsequent parenthetical citations are to this edition.

1. Amphion appears in Apollodorus *Lib.* 3.3.5 and briefly in Ovid *Met.* 6. 220–270; Propertius 1.9 and 4.2; Horace *Odes* 3.11; and Apollonius of Rhodes *Argon.* 1.735–741.

2. Jacques Rancière, *The Politics of Aesthetics: The Distribution of the Sensible*, ed. and trans. Gabriel Rockhill (New York: Bloomsbury, 2004), 7.

3. George Puttenham, *The Arte of Englishe Poesie* (Menston, U.K.: Scolar Press, 1968), 4.

4. *Q. Horatius Flaccus: his Art of poetry. Englished by Ben: Jonson* (London: Printed by I. Okes, for Iohn Benson, 1640), 23.

5. Hugh Grady, *Shakespeare and Impure Aesthetics* (Cambridge: Cambridge University Press, 2009), 41; Julia Reinhard Lupton, "Cute Shakespeare?," *Journal for Early Modern Cultural Studies* 16, no. 3 (Summer 2016): 1–12.

6. Paul A. Kottman, ed., *The Insistence of Art: Aesthetic Philosophy after Early Modernity* (New York: Fordham University Press, 2017).

7. Christopher Pye, *The Storm at Sea: Political Aesthetics in the Time of Shakespeare* (New York: Fordham University Press, 2015), 3.

8. Pye, *The Storm at Sea*, 3, 30.

9. Pye, *The Storm at Sea*, 30.

10. Julia Reinhard Lupton, "Invitation to a Totem Meal: Hans Kelsen, Carl Schmitt, and Political Theology," in *The Return of Theory in Early Modern English Studies*, ed. Paul Cefalu and Bryan Reynolds (New York: Palgrave Macmillan, 2011), 123. On *poiesis*, political theology, and creaturely life, see Julia Reinhard Lupton, *Thinking with Shakespeare: Essays on Politics and Life* (Chicago: University of Chicago Press, 2011); and Julia Reinhard Lupton, *Shakespeare Dwelling: Designs for the Theater of Life* (Chicago: University of Chicago Press, 2018), esp. chap. 3, "Grace and Place in *Pericles*."

11. Victoria Kahn, *The Future of Illusion: Political Theology and Early Modern Texts* (Chicago: University of Chicago Press, 2014), 7, 30; Carl Schmitt, *Political Theology: Four Chapters on the Concept of Sovereignty*, trans. George Schwab (Chicago: University of Chicago Press, 1985), 36.

12. Victoria Kahn, "Allegory, Poetic Theology, and Enlightenment Aesthetics," in Kottman, *The Insistence of Art*, 33.

13. Carl Schmitt, *Political Romanticism*, trans. Guy Oakes (Cambridge, Mass.: MIT Press, 1996).

14. Carl Schmitt, *The Leviathan in the State Theory of Thomas Hobbes: Meaning and Failure of a Political Symbol*, trans. George Schwab and Erna Hilfstein (Westport, Conn.: Greenwood Press, 1996), 6; Schmitt, *Political Theology*, 48.

15. Schmitt, *Political Romanticism*, 16–17; Karl Löwith, "The Occasional Decisionism of Carl Schmitt," in *Martin Heidegger and European Nihilism*, ed. Richard Wolin (New York: Columbia University Press, 1995), 140.

16. Schmitt, *Political Romanticism*, 17, 160, 162.

17. Schmitt, *Political Romanticism*, 160.

18. Schmitt, *Political Romanticism*, 15.

19. Carl Schmitt, *Constitutional Theory*, trans. and ed. Jeffrey Seitzer (Durham, N.C.: Duke University Press, 2008).

20. Schmitt, *Constitutional Theory*, 273–74.

21. Schmitt, *Constitutional Theory*, 274; Schmitt, *Political Romanticism*, 15.

22. Schmitt, *Political Romanticism*, 162.

23. Carl Schmitt, "The Age of Neutralizations and Depoliticizations," in *The Concept of the Political*, trans. George Schwab (Chicago: University of Chicago Press, 2007), 84; Schmitt, *Leviathan*, 9; Schmitt, *Political Romanticism*, 107.

24. "Die eigentlichste Tätigkeit, Fähigkeit und Funktion des Volkes," Carl Schmitt, *Volksentscheid und Volksbegehren: Ein Beitrag zur Auslegung der Weimarer Verfassung und zur Lehre von der unmittelbaren Demokratie* (Berlin: de Gruyter, 1927), 34. Translations from this text are mine. On the political theology of the *laudes* and their contemporary biopolitical consequences, see Giorgio Agamben, *The Kingdom and the Glory: For a Theological Genealogy of Economy and Government*, trans. Lorenzo Chiesa (Stanford, Calif.: Stanford University Press, 2011), and Eric L. Santner, "Response," in "An Engagement with the Work of Eric Santner," special issue, *Journal for Cultural and Religious Theory* 12, no. 1 (Spring 2012): 44–52.

25. "Das Volk akklamiert einem Führer," Schmitt, *Volksentscheid und Volksbegehren*, 34.

26. "Die geheime Einzelabstimmung . . . vernichtet gerade die spezifischen Möglichkeiten des versammelten Volkes," Schmitt, *Volksentscheid und Volksbegehren*, 33–34; Schmitt, *Constitutional Theory*, 273.

27. Schmitt, *Constitutional Theory*, 272.

28. Schmitt, *Constitutional Theory*, 275.

29. Schmitt, *Volksentscheid und Volksbegehren*, 34.

30. Ernst H. Kantorowicz, *Laudes Regiae: A Study in Liturgical Acclamations and Mediaeval Ruler Worship* (Berkeley: University of California Press, 1958), 185.

31. Schmitt, *Leviathan*, 81.

32. On this visual culture, see Simonetta Falasca-Zamponi, *Fascist Spectacle: The Aesthetics of Power in Mussolini's Italy* (Berkeley: University of California Press, 1997); Emilio Gentile, *The Struggle for Modernity: Nationalism, Futurism, and Fascism* (Westport, Conn.: Praeger, 2003); and Emilio Gentile, *The Sacralization of Politics in Fascist Italy* (Cambridge, Mass.: Harvard University Press, 1996).

33. Schmitt, "Age of Neutralizations," 83. See also Carl Schmitt, *Hamlet or Hecuba: The Intrusion of the Time into the Play*, trans. and ed. David Pan and Jennifer R. Rust (New York: Telos Press, 2009).

34. On secularism, magic, and aesthetics in *The Tempest*, see Richard McCoy, *Faith in Shakespeare* (New York: Oxford University Press, 2013), 146–51, and Genevieve Guenther, *Magical Imaginations: Instrumental Aesthetics in the English Renaissance* (Toronto: University of Toronto Press, 2012), esp. chap. 4, "The End of Magic: Instrumental Aesthetics in *The Tempest*," 86–106. On the colonial implications of this, see Peggy Simonds Muñoz, "'Sweet Power of Music': The Political Magic of 'the Miraculous Harp' in Shakespeare's *The Tempest*," *Comparative Drama* 29, no. 1 (Spring 1995): 61–90.

35. Pye, *The Storm at Sea*, 142, 146.

36. Paul Oskar Kristeller's influential essay "The Modern System of the Arts," *Journal of the History of Ideas* 12, no. 4 (October 1951): 496–527, parses out distinctions between the instrumental function of premodern art, which does not rise to the level of the aesthetic because it is insufficiently "detached" from its "practical function or content" (506). While Prospero's instrumentalization of environmental sound would seem to belong to this merely "mechanical" register, the difficulties in establishing where artifice begins and ends anticipates later phenomenological conceptions of *aisthesis*. For a helpful overview of sensible experience in aesthetics, see Hans Rainer Sepp and Lester Embree, eds., *Handbook of Phenomenological Aesthetics* (New York: Springer, 2010).

37. According to Stephen Orgel, *The Illusion of Power: Political Theater in the English Renaissance* (Berkeley: University of California Press, 1975), 48–49, Prospero's "authority over elemental nature" renders him both divine and kingly, the theo-political inheritor of a divine right to order nature. On *The Tempest* and absolutism, see Donna B. Hamilton, *Virgil and "The Tempest": The Politics of Imitation* (Columbus: Ohio State University Press, 1990), and, more recently, Melissa E. Sanchez, *Erotic Subjects: The Sexuality of Politics in Early Modern English Literature* (New York: Oxford University Press, 2011).

38. Schmitt, *Constitutional Theory*, 272. On the historical evolution of the *laudes* cry of *Christus vincit*, *Christus regnat*, *Christus imperat* from the Gallo-Frankish context onward, see Kantorowicz, *Laudes Regiae*.

39. Richard Wolin, "Carl Schmitt: The Conservative Revolutionary and the Habitus of Horror," *Political Theory* 20, no. 3 (August 1992): 434. A range of scholars have argued that Schmitt succumbs to his own aestheticizing tendencies. Victoria Kahn discovers an "incarnational aesthetic" in the mythical figure of the sovereign representative, while Jürgen Habermas points to Schmitt's fascination with an "aesthetics of violence" and notes that Schmitt's denunciation of political Romanticism is designed to "conceal the aestheticizing oscillations of his own political thought" (*Future of Illusion*, 16; "The Horrors of Autonomy: Carl Schmitt in English," in *The New Conservatism: Cultural Criticism and the Historians' Debate*, ed. and trans. Shierry Weber Nicholsen [Cambridge, Mass.: MIT Press, 1989], 137). This last insight was developed at greater length by Karl Löwith, who classifies Schmitt's decisionism as another species of occasionalism ("The Occasional Decisionism of Carl Schmitt," in *Martin Heidegger and European Nihilism*, ed. Richard Wolin, trans. Gary Steiner, 137–69 [New York: Columbia University Press, 1995]).

40. Quoted in Wolin, "Carl Schmitt," 434.

41. Harry Berger Jr., "Miraculous Harp: A Reading of Shakespeare's *Tempest*," *Shakespeare Studies* 5 (1969): 256.

42. On the significance of Shakespeare's ghostly children for theories of sovereignty, see Joseph Campana, "The Child's Two Bodies: Shakespeare, Sovereignty, and the End of Succession," *ELH* 81, no. 3 (Fall 2014): 811–39.

43. Schmitt, *Political Romanticism*, 162.

44. Nerves, meaning here tendons and other connective tissues, were used as strings for stringed instruments. Tortured bodies rendering up either howls of anguish or confessions were often depicted as contorted instruments strummed by their torturers. See Bruce Holsinger, *Music, Body, and Desire in Medieval Culture: Hildegard of Bingen to Chaucer* (Chicago: University of Chicago Press, 2005).

45. On Shakespearean microbes, see Robert N. Watson, "The Ecology of Self in *Midsummer Night's Dream*," in *Ecocritical Shakespeare*, ed. Lynne Bruckner and Dan Brayton, 33–56 (Burlington, Vt.: Ashgate Publishing, 2011).

46. These theoretical schools have transformed medieval and early modern studies as well. On the early modern posthuman, see Julian Yates, *Of Sheep, Oranges, and Yeast: A Multispecies Impression* (Minneapolis: University of Minnesota Press, 2017), and Stefan Herbrechter and Ivan Callus, eds., *Posthumanist Shakespeares* (New York: Palgrave Macmillan, 2012). For the animal turn, see Laurie Shannon, *The Accommodated Animal: Cosmopolity in Shakespearean Locales* (Chicago: University of Chicago Press, 2013); Erica Fudge, *Brutal Reasoning: Animals, Rationality, and Humanity in Early Modern England* (Ithaca, N.Y.: Cornell University Press, 2006); and Bruce Boehrer, *Shakespeare among the Animals: Nature and Society in the Drama of Early Modern England* (New York: Palgrave Macmillan, 2002). Steve Mentz offers a view of Shakespeare's oceans as refracted through object-oriented ontology in *At the Bottom of Shakespeare's Ocean* (New York: Continuum, 2009), while Vin Nardizzi considers the trafficking between forests and theaters in *Wooden Os: Shakespeare's Theatres and England's Trees* (Toronto: University of Toronto Press, 2013). On objects, see Jonathan Gil Harris, *Untimely Matter in the Time of Shakespeare* (Philadelphia: University of Pennsylvania Press, 2010); for the vibrancy of the object world in light of affordance theory, see Lupton, *Thinking with Shakespeare*.

47. Jean E. Feerick and Vin Nardizzi, eds., *The Indistinct Human in Renaissance Literature* (New York: Palgrave Macmillan, 2012), 4.

48. Jane Bennett, *Vibrant Matter: A Political Ecology of Things* (Durham, N.C.: Duke University Press, 2009), 99.

49. Bennett, *Vibrant Matter*, 17.

50. Bennett, *Vibrant Matter*, 5.

51. Pye, *The Storm at Sea*, 148.

52. Schmitt, *Political Theology*, 48.

53. Burger, quoted in Wolin, "Carl Schmitt," 434.

54. On the legal status of Caliban's minority and its implications for liberal thought, see Lupton, *Thinking with Shakespeare*, chap. 6, "The Minority of Caliban," 187–218. On consent and political obligation, see Victoria Kahn, *Wayward Contracts: The Crisis of Political Obligation in England, 1640–1674* (Princeton, N.J.: Princeton University Press, 2004); on *The Tempest*'s engagement with

colonialism, see, among many others, Ania Loomba, *Gender, Race, and Renaissance Drama* (New York: Manchester University Press, 1989); Paul Brown, "'This Thing of Darkness I Acknowledge Mine': *The Tempest* and the Discourse of Colonialism," in *Political Shakespeare: New Essays in Cultural Materialism*, ed. Jonathan Dollimore and Alan Sinfield, 48–71 (Ithaca, N.Y.: Cornell University Press, 1985); and Kim F. Hall, *Things of Darkness: Economies of Race and Gender in Early Modern England* (Ithaca, N.Y.: Cornell University Press, 1995).

55. Schmitt, *Hamlet or Hecuba*, 44.

56. Pye, *The Storm at Sea*, 151.

Shakespeare's *Sturm*, Caliban's *Drang*

Walter Benjamin and *The Tempest*

Julia Reinhard Lupton

A Princely Caliban

In an early unpublished fragment, the German-Jewish philosopher and critic Walter Benjamin (1892–1940) presented *As You Like It* as a reverie on infinitude and as a prelude to *The Tempest*:

> [Shakespeare] suggests that this play should be viewed as a summer cloud which dissolves into the blue as its symbolic shapes are dissolved in infinity, where they are at the same time most profound and graceful. [*As You Like It*] must be considered in connection with *The Tempest*, for which it could, as it were, be seen as a prelude. There infinity is already approaching Being (*Dasein*), making us lose our breath. Prospero lets go of his magic staff; the storm is no longer blowing as you like it, or because this one time you may hear nothing more (*oder weil er es dieses eine Mal noch tat dürft Ihr nichts weiter hören*). Shakespeare's creation dies from immortality (*Shakespeares Schaffen stirbt an Unsterblichkeit*).[1]

Beginning with this fragment, Freddie Rokem argues that *The Tempest* was a foundational text for Benjamin. Hoping to someday write a commentary on the play, Benjamin identified with Prospero as an esoteric scholar who desired to "'make whole what has been smashed'" and to "restore his lost kingdom assisted by the books in his library and the magic they contain."[2] Whereas in history the storm blows perpetually from Paradise, as Benjamin writes in the ninth of his "Theses on History," in *The Tempest* the storm is in retreat, soliciting new forms of attention from those who enter its washed and brightened space. In the enigmatic final line, Benjamin suggests that the very perfection of *The*

Tempest is a mortal blow, bringing Shakespeare's writing to an end and perhaps closing off the very avenue of *poiesis* it had opened. The claim that "Shakespeare's creation dies from immortality" anticipates Benjamin's dictum in *The Origin of the German Tragic Drama*: "A major work will either establish the genre or abolish it; and the perfect work will do both."[3] *The Tempest*, standing at the top of the Folio, transforming the genres of tragedy and comedy, and often considered Shakespeare's farewell, might even be the text that Benjamin had in mind when he arrived at that formulation.

In *The Storm at Sea: Political Aesthetics in the Age of Shakespeare*, Christopher Pye draws on Benjamin's account of "the open, infinitized political space of the early modern period" to map the forms of boundlessness, dispersed and distracted vision, and floating anxiety convened by his book's governing metaphors, "the storm at sea" and "the view *from* the sea."[4] Pye's identification of distraction with aesthetic subjectivity comes very close to Benjamin's description of the conditions of a newly fluid spectatorship framed by *The Tempest* ("The storm is no longer blowing as you like it, or because this one time you may hear nothing more"). Pye argues that *The Tempest* works the interval or noncoincidence—the shifting sands—between the subject and the state as the zone in which new forms of political right and autonomy were imagined and tested in the seventeenth century, especially through the discourses of natural law (*ius naturale*) and international law (*ius gentium*).[5] Pye reads *The Tempest* as a mise-en-scène of *ius gentium*, in which the claims of European settlers confront the claims of indigenous inhabitants, leading to a new legal and spatial order, "at once a localization of what had been the universal community of Christendom and an abstraction of such a territorial conception into juridically fluid versions of *civitas* applicable beyond the physical limits of the city."[6] The space of the aesthetic, Pye argues, allowed the historical subject of these ventures to become "knowable to itself, if only as the effect of an artificial and inhuman gaze."[7] Caliban, at once the object of colonial exploitation and the subject of emergent rights, labors in the natural law tradition that infuses the landscapes of the romances with both the traces of intractable alterity and the dream of a common world. The poet-curator-DJ of the island's ambient music, as Colby Gordon argues in the preceding essay, Caliban translates that political process into a distinctively aesthetic form by giving voice to the sounds of the retreating storm as they trickle through a mind awakening to a new consciousness of its own powers.

Although Rokem rightly focuses on Prospero as Benjamin's esoteric alter ego, Caliban makes an appearance in Benjamin's 1925 review of

Hugo von Hofmannsthal's play *Der Turm* (*The Tower*), a rewriting of Calderón's *Life Is a Dream* and itself a modern instance of *Trauerspiel* in Benjamin's wary judgment.[8] In Calderón's play, Sigismundo is a prince whose father, King Basilio, tries to avoid a curse by imprisoning him in a tower, where he is dressed in animal skins and denied a proper education. When the sleeping youth is brought back to court and greeted upon awakening as the royal hero of his own courtly drama, the feral boy responds to his new privileges with acts of lust, anger, and envy. Declared unfit to rule, Sigismundo is taken back to the tower, where he is led to believe that his brief life as a royal was simply a dream (hence the play's title). When he is again recalled to court, Sigismundo manages his passions and exercises his virtues in a manner befitting the king he finally becomes. Hofmannsthal's version ends more darkly: Sigismund takes the throne from his father with help from a faction of nobles but is soon assassinated by a counterforce of peasants. For Calderón, the "perfect prince" (*der vollkommene Prinz*) is the keystone of the arch that connects the creature and the Christian; for Hofmannsthal, however, Benjamin writes, Christian optimism is already in decline (*Untergang*), manifesting a broken Baroque.

Benjamin calls Sigismundo a "princely Caliban" (*fürstlichen Caliban*). If Calderón's perfect prince is a kind of beast, Shakespeare's most abjected creature is also a prince: underlying Benjamin's association of Sigismundo with Caliban is the figure of Hamlet. All of them are deprived of their birthright and forced into a prolonged and debilitating minority by vindictive and suspicious father figures. They all bear tortured and transitional relationships to a sovereignty that borders on bare or creaturely life. Finally, each is associated with phenomenal and subjective states that test the limits of consciousness in order to probe the conditions of art.[9] The English "prince," like the German *Fürst*, comes from the Roman imperial nomination of the sovereign as the first among equals, which euphemized the transition from republic to empire. In *Hamlet*, the hero's princeliness names his anticipation of an accession that never arrives, replaced instead by circles of friendship and election that harbor liberal alternatives to monarchy.[10] Caliban, too, is a prince of transitions: removed from his natural kingship of the island (*ius naturale*), he had coexisted with Prospero and Miranda in a new form of civil society (*ius gentium*), before being abruptly enslaved by his new associates and stripped of all rights. He allies with the proletariats Trinculo and Stephano but fails to realize his political aims. At the end of the play, Caliban's future is indeterminate but likely involves a renewed relationship to the island and to his own expanded political and aesthetic capacities.

Hofmannsthal's *Turm* rhymes with Shakespeare's *Sturm*: in German, *The Tempest* is usually translated as *Der Sturm*, recalling the *Sturm und Drang* writers whose proponents canonized Shakespeare as a modern poet. Caliban has often been associated with the *Drang* of baser instincts, like the envy, lust, and anger exhibited by the untutored Sigismundo when he is brought back to his father's palace, yet Caliban is also the play's most compelling exponent of the dignity and rights that accrue to creatures bearing the image of God and to an aesthetic sensibility that relinquishes dominance in order to hear differently. In Shakespeare and Benjamin, the prince is a creature, his will infected by the *Drang* of original sin, but the creature is also a prince, possessing dignity and capable of seeking grace, a grace not devoid of violence and hence partaking in the drives it sublimates. Shakespeare shapes Caliban from Scriptural motifs that include the creation of Adam, God's Noahide covenanting with the drowned world after the Flood, and the musical melancholy of David and Jonah. In this chapter, I construe a "princely Caliban" who claims political autonomy, articulates a political project, and vocalizes a political aesthetics from within a messianic archaeology and a network of creaturely drives that affiliate him with Benjamin's Baroque.

Son of Adam: From Natural Law to Natural History

In the "Epistemo-Critical Prologue" to the *Trauerspiel* book, composed after the central philological portion had been submitted and rejected as a *Habilitationsschrift* in 1925, Benjamin somewhat defiantly declares that the *Trauerspiel* should be approached not as a genre at all but rather as an Idea: "In the sense in which it is treated in the philosophy of art the *Trauerspiel* is an Idea."[11] Whereas literary history aims to "demonstrate variety," relativizing "differences and extremes" in an evolutionary scheme, the Idea asserts a unity composed of extremes held in vibrant and visible tension. Because the Idea seeks out "the extreme example of a form or genre," it "does not enter into the history of literature."[12] Benjamin seeks the Platonic Idea within a creaturely sphere of history marked by the Scriptural events of creation, fall, prophesy, and redemption: "In philosophical contemplation, the idea is released from the heart of reality as the word, reclaiming its name-giving rights. Ultimately, however, this is not the attitude of Plato, but the attitude of Adam, the father of the human race and the father of philosophy."[13] Benjamin grafts Plato's Ideas onto Adam's naming of the world in Genesis in order to send ideas into time: the broken, heaving, yearning time of creation and creatureliness.

Benjamin famously compares ideas to constellations:

> Ideas are to objects as constellations are to stars [*Die Ideen verhalten sich zu den Dingen wie die Sternbilder zu den Sternen*] . . . Ideas are timeless constellations [*ewige Konstellationen*], and by virtue of the elements' being seen as points in such constellations, phenomena are subdivided and at the same time redeemed [*aufgeteilt und gerettet zugleich*] . . . Just as a mother is seen to begin to live in the fullness of her power only when the circle of her children, inspired by the feeling of her proximity, closes around her, so do ideas come to life only when extremes are assembled around them.[14]

The Idea divides the things of the world, holding them apart in relationships of agonized extremity, but also "redeems" or "rescues" (*rettet*) them by showering them with the promise of significance. The meaning of the things constellated by an idea, however, remains schematic and subliminal, requiring the work of the philosopher and the poet to draw the lines among isolated phenomena. Philosophy becomes philology, and the "Epistemo-Critical Prologue" gives way to the intricate historiography of the *Trauerspielbuch* itself. In Jane O. Newman's apt formulation, Benjamin "testified to the 'origin' of the German Baroque as the sum of its 'pre- and post-histories' in material form."[15]

Benjamin calls the creaturely temporalization of ideas and their collection in the Baroque spaces of contemplative observation "natural history":

> The past and the subsequent history of such essences is—as a token of their having been redeemed or gathered into the world of ideas—not pure history, but natural history. The life of the works and forms which need such protection in order to unfold clearly and unclouded by human life is a natural life. Once this redeemed state of being in the idea is established, then the presence of the inauthentic—that is to say natural-historical—past and subsequent history is virtual. It is no longer pragmatically real, but, as natural history, is to be inferred from the state of completion and rest, from the essence.[16]

Natural history is the phenomenal form that ideas take in the world as they gather meanings and become estranged from their transcendental home. Benjamin opposes "human life" to "natural life": human life belongs to res gestae, the record of public virtue that characterizes Roman historiography, whereas "natural life" submerges human life in the world of things and other animate beings, what Benjamin calls creaturely life. Baroque pastoral, to which Shakespeare's romances belong, exemplifies the natural-historical sensibility:

> What is peculiar about the baroque enthusiasm for landscape is particularly evident in the pastoral. For the decisive factor in the escapism of the baroque is not the antithesis of history and nature but the comprehensive secularization of the historical in the state of creation. It is not eternity that is opposed to the disconsolate chronicle of world-history, but the restoration of the timelessness of paradise. History merges into the setting [*Schauplatz*]. And in the pastoral plays above all, history is scattered like seeds over the ground.[17]

Benjamin's portrayal of history as scattered seeds recalls *The Tempest*'s pearls and coral, the image taken by Hannah Arendt as an image of Benjamin's own citational romance with the thought fragments of the past.[18] Benjamin warns that this merging with the setting risks becoming an "escapism" in which the mereness of life evacuated of meaning animates the illusory and dangerous dream of a restored paradise. The work of the critic, messianic rather than secular, is to reestablish points of significance and capacities for virtue within the collapsed temporal bubbles of natural history.[19] A messianic criticism does not leave the seeds of history lying on the ground but finds ways for them to grow in the cracks of the present.[20]

Adam is Benjamin's first and primary image of the creature and the first hero of posttragic drama, as Milton and others intuited:

> Fate, whatever guise it may wear in a pagan or mythological context, is meaningful only as a category of natural history in the spirit of the restoration-theology of the Counter-Reformation. It is the elemental force of nature in historical events, which are not themselves entirely nature, because the light of grace is still reflected from the state of creation. But it is mirrored in the swamp of Adam's guilt [*gespiegelt aber in dem Pfuhl der adamatischen Verschuldung*]. (129)

Fate in postclassical drama has passed through the defiles of monotheism, founding history as profane time and then spatializing profane time as natural history. The story of the Creation denies the eternity of the cosmos posited by Plato and Aristotle; creation renders nature historical by giving the world a beginning and immerses human history in the flora and fauna of creaturely life that Adam was born to name and thus to draw into significance. In a typically Benjaminian formulation, this sedimented landscape still "reflects the light of grace" from "the state of creation," an image that implies the pale transmission of energy across space (from heaven to earth) and time (from the moment of creation to the present), like the constellation of stars that charts elements from vastly different times and locales on one virtual plane. This reflected grace does not appear in pure form but is rather "mirrored in the swamp of Adam's guilt." This mirroring issues in anamorphic *Entstellungen* that turn man into monster but also suggest the abyssal birth of the aesthetic as a play of reflections. Muddy rather than transparent, the swamp of Adam's guilt is teeming with lower life forms, its dark viscosity sucking the creature's divine yearnings into the root rot of intrigue, envy, violence, and desire, which in turn spawn the image-making capacity of *poiesis*.

Shakespeare fashioned his most memorable creature, that "thing of earth" Caliban, from this wetland. Caliban's counternarrative to Prospero is replete with Adamic references:

> I must eat my dinner.
> This island's mine by Sycorax my mother,
> Which thou tak'st from me. When thou cam'st first,
> Thou strok'st me and made much of me, wouldst give me
> Water with berries in't, and teach me how
> To name the bigger light, and how the less,
> That burn by day and night; and then I loved thee
> And showed thee all the qualities o'th' isle,
> The fresh springs, brine-pits, barren place and fertile—
> Cursed be I that did so! All the charms
> Of Sycorax, toads, beetles, bats, light on you;
> For I am all the subjects that you have,
> Which first was mine own king, and here you sty me
> In this hard rock, whiles you do keep from me
> The rest o'th' island. (1.2.331–45)[21]

Princely Caliban begins by arguing that he inherited the island from his mother, Sycorax, and ends by asserting his original self-sufficiency: "For I am all the subjects that you have, / Which first was mine own king." To be one's own king is to discover a law within oneself and by oneself through the exercise of rational capacities shared with other human beings. As Benjamin notes, Baroque jurists traced the idea of an originary kingship to

Adam, whether in the patriarchal fiat favored by Filmer or in the contractual scenarios imagined by Hooker and Locke.[22] Hooker turned to Adam in the context of natural law, which posits that human beings can discover basic principles for self-governance from the resources of their own reason. The maxims of natural law include fear of god, honor for parents, love of neighbor, and the pursuit of human association; sociability, he suggests, affords both material well-being and its own source of dignity and happiness. All these natural law teachings are evident in Caliban's account of his early history with Prospero and Miranda.[23] Welcoming the Italians to the island, exchanging knowledge with them, learning their language, and expressing love and affection, Caliban's forms of governance blend the *ius naturale* of self-rule into the *ius gentium* of relating to another social group. In *ius gentium*, the law of nations, ancient laws of hospitality generate the unwritten principles for engaging with strangers in a manner designed to keep warfare at bay.[24]

What destroys this hospitable settlement is Caliban's advances on Miranda. Framed as an attempted rape by the two Italians, Caliban's desire to mate reflects natural law. Hooker writes that all creatures, human and nonhuman, "desire the continuance of their being" in order to be like God, who is eternal.[25] In a typically natural-historical formation, "eternity" functions as an Idea realized through creaturely copulation, through which finitude strives to participate in infinity without reconciling the gap between them. Hooker associates Adam's desire for a helpmeet with human sociability, not just human reproduction.[26] In Hooker's creaturely reading of natural law, the sexual act achieves its own dignity, which is shared with other forms of animate life, made into a cornerstone of human fellowship and offered up as an approximation of the Idea in time. Hooker also, however, places consent at the heart of civil society. By ignoring Miranda's consent, Caliban's move on Miranda constitutes his own fall, expressing at once an urge toward divine and human participation and an affront to such participation, a turning within his own being that obscures his rational capacities and gives his passions the upper hand. At the same time, consent implies a parity among the players that the Italians deny him: formal equality is undercut by structural domination. In the irresolvable battle over the meaning of Caliban's overtures on Miranda (just or unjust? naive or calculating? amorous or violent?), Shakespeare overlays the original sin of transgressive desire with the intractability of social antagonism, which impose competing frames onto this core encounter.

"Adam" comes from *adamah*, "earth." *Adamah* is God's plastic medium for fashioning the first man, and it is also the ground, literally, of natural life in its avid fecundity and vermicular decomposition. In naming "the bigger light and . . . the less," Caliban creates his own star map in language that directly echoes Genesis 1:16.[27] Benjamin links Adam's naming of creation to the originary purity of Ideas:

> Adam's action of naming things [*Namengeben*] is so far removed from play or caprice that it actually confirms the state of paradise as a state in which there is as yet no need to struggle with the communicative significance of words. Ideas are displayed, without intention, in the act of naming, and they have to be renewed in philosophical contemplation. In this renewal the primordial mode of apprehending words is restored.[28]

Adamic Caliban is not only a natural lawyer turned natural historian but also a natural philosopher who enumerates the gifts of the cosmos. Unlike Adam, however, Caliban must be taught this language by Miranda and Prospero rather than finding it on his own, though he was not without language when the Italians discovered him. Showing the visitors the resources of the island, this polymorphous polyglot is more a translator between discourses than an original nominator of things. "A man or a fish?—dead or alive?" (2.2.23): amphibious Caliban swims in a post-Babel world while posing a problem of translation for others. Caliban's imprinting by the *imago dei* is not a birthright immediately recognized by the other human creatures onstage but rather an attribute that must be defensively demonstrated and performed by dint of an *Entstellung* (Shakespeare's "savage and deformed slave") that reflects grace, but only from the swamp.[29] That swamp is also an estuary, its brackish waters fed by multiple streams; in *Trauerspiel*, Benjamin wrote in 1916, "we find a word . . . that is subject to change, as it moves from its source [*Ursprung*] toward a different point, its estuary [*seiner Mündung*]. Language in the process of change is the linguistic principle of the mourning play."[30] When we first meet him, Caliban subsists in the estuary of words in transition, where "the fresh springs" of one language mix indeterminately with the "brine pits" of another.

Born in the swamp of Adam's guilt and subsisting in the estuary of gabble, Caliban is not a noble savage but a creature like others, destined to miss the good that he aims for: "Fate," writes Benjamin, "is the entelechy of events within the field of guilt."[31] Yet Miranda and Prospero refuse to acknowledge that they wade in the same swamp. Siding with Prospero, Shakespeare rezones the creatureliness of his Creature from a common condition in which good and evil mingle to a state of permanent exclusion from human society and its virtues. Yet Caliban's ability to mount a compelling counternarrative, to organize a coup, and to articulate an aesthetic project worthy of the island establishes the creature as a kind of prince.

Sons of Noah: Prospero's Dogs

Caliban twice calls Prospero a tyrant, a word given new power in defenses of tyrannicide in the sixteenth and seventeenth centuries, as Benjamin notes.[32] The brute Caliban is also a Brutus, a plaintiff who desires freedom and justice, not simply power.[33] The word "tyrant" also appears in the mouth of Prospero, as part of an antimasque of violence that both squashes the coup and begins the process by which Prospero and Shakespeare begin to acknowledge Caliban's faults as their own. Prospero abruptly dissolves the marriage masque when he remembers the gang of conspirators. As part of the counterattack, he calls his hounds on the rebels: "Fury, Fury! There, Tyrant, there! Hark, hark!" (4.1.249). These dogs of war materialize Prospero's own disavowed *Drang*, beginning to draw into visibility his complicity in Caliban's degradation. The inventory of dog names stems from Ovid's tale of Actaeon, in which hounds trained for the hunt dutifully dismember the beast who had been their master. From Giordano Bruno to Aby Warburg, the ritual dismemberments of Actaeon, Orpheus, and Osiris allegorize ancient wisdom dispersed by the events of history and reconstructed by the heroic scholar-philosopher, who himself, however, risks being torn apart by the dark powers unleashed by the esoteric enterprise.[34] In Shakespeare's allegorical antimasque, the Ovidian tale of a beast-man torn apart by his own hounds graphs both the violence that threatens the martyr Caliban and the mutant inhumanity of the tyrant Prospero while linking that violence to the play's own allegorical search for ideas.

Prospero's dogs also recall the seventh of the Noahide commandments, which prohibits the tearing and eating of flesh from a living animal.[35] These laws are derived from a terse set of pronouncements that follow God's recovenanting with creation after the Flood (Gen. 9:1–7). In *The Tempest*, positive law has dissolved into archaic arrangements of hospitality and hostility after a great storm, followed by the rainbow of covenant in the marriage masque and its promise of a renewed civil society. The seventh law assures the minimal rights of creatures to a humane death and sets the table for the Jewish dietary laws. In setting the dogs of Fury and Tyranny against other human beings *after* the masque of Juno and Iris has taken place, Prospero is abrogating the Noahide laws associated with the heavenly rainbow. The greatest seventeenth-century English reader of the Noahide laws, the jurist and parliamentarian John Selden (1584–1654), pieced together a body of natural law from the Noahide laws, derived from his reading of the Talmud while locked in the Tower in 1629 for his parliamentary activities.[36] Through his Hebraic researches, Selden learned to "look for continuities among the cultures of pagans, Jews, Muslims, and Christians."[37] In a more intuitive and allegorical mode, the same might be claimed for Shakespeare, who unleashes the specter of dismemberment in the biopastoral of the hunt in order to newly articulate and emancipate multiple mythographic and exegetical dispensations within a posttragic *Denkraum* organized around the passion of the creature, who is also a prince.

Son of David, Song of Jonah: Caliban's Project

As a type of Adam, Caliban secures his relation to the *imago dei*, but in the postreflective mode of *Entstellung* and translation. As a Noahide, Caliban is identified with a primitive natural law suited to the pluralization of peoples in the epoch between Flood and Sinai. Prospero's tyranny raises Caliban's revolt into what Ariel suggestively calls "their project" (4.1.175). The word "project" appears more often in *The Tempest* than in any other play by Shakespeare: three times in relation to Prospero's plans (2.1.284, 5.1.1) and the overarching intentions of the theatrical work (Epilogue 12), and once to characterize the conspiracy. Shakespeare's "project" comes close to Benjamin's notion of an *Aufgabe*, or "task": the *Aufgabe*, writes Rokem, concerns not only the aim of a particular project but also "how to give an account of the processes of thinking and reflection . . . even accepting that this self-reflexive process does not in itself guarantee that it is possible to carry out this particular task."[38] Caliban's project fails, but his very possession of a motivating task asserts his dignity and affiliates his actions with the Baroque intriguer: "The organizer of its plot, the precursor of the choreographer, is the intriguer. He stands as the third type alongside the despot and the martyr."[39] Caliban takes all three roles: he is an intriguer who acts like a tyrant when, like Macbeth, he plots to kill the duke in his sleep, an action that also recalls Cham's viewing of the naked Noah. Suffering the stigmata of Prospero's spite on his inflamed and suffering body, he incarnates, like the Sigismundo of Calderón and Hofmannsthal, "the martyrdom of princely existence."[40]

It is neither as Adam nor as Noahide but as a son of David that Caliban begins to articulate the reflective aspect of his project in the sounds and sweet airs passage. Unsettled by Ariel's music as it mixes with the uncanny noises of the island, Trinculo and Stephano are assured by Caliban that their anxieties are groundless. (Of course it is precisely the groundlessness of anxiety that makes it so hard to overcome.) Caliban reassures them,

> Be not afeard, the isle is full of noises,
> Sounds, and sweet airs, that give delight and hurt not.
> Sometimes a thousand twangling instruments
> Will hum about mine ears, and sometime voices
> That if I then had waked after long sleep
> Will make me sleep again; and then in dreaming
> The clouds methought would open and show riches
> Ready to drop upon me, that when I waked
> I cried to dream again. (3.2.126–34)

Caliban accedes here to a new and higher order of translation, what Benjamin calls *die Aufgabe des Übersetzers*, "the task of the translator." Benjamin describes translation as an emancipation: "It is the task of the translator to release in his own language that pure language which is under the spell of another, to liberate the language imprisoned in a work in his re-creation of that work."[41] This and other passages associate the task of the translator with Adam's primal naming of creation; whereas before translation had put Caliban at a remove from the world whose things he named, in this passage Caliban uses language to release the sounds of the island, cribbed and cabined like Ariel in his pine, into a form of artful coherence that takes Aeolian autopoiesis as its emancipatory prompt. Translating the island's primal sonority as it burgeons toward meaningfulness, Caliban's habits of audition allow "work, image and tone [to] converge" in a neo-Adamic consonance.[42]

Indeed, Caliban's praise song is a free translation of Psalm 131:2 (AV): "Surely I have behaved and quieted myself, / As a child that is weaned of its mother: My soul is even as a weaned child." Sung by David to the sound of the lute, the psalm imagines an infant learning to comfort itself in the absence of its parent by rhythmic crooning and rocking, sucking and sighing.[43] It is one of fifteen Songs of Ascent, also called Gradual Psalms, Songs of Degrees, and Pilgrim Songs, perhaps sung by worshippers in their journey to Jerusalem on the three pilgrimage festivals (the *hagim* of Passover, Shavuot, and Sukkot).[44] Caliban's rendering is drenched with memories of the mother. Benjamin compares the Idea to a mother surrounded by her children who gather at a distance from her: already weaned, already comforted, they are on the road to becoming *auto nomos* through the work of rhythmic symbolization. This is a new and different order of self-rule from Caliban's presentation of himself as his own king. Neither sovereignty nor resistance is the dominant motif; instead, Caliban practices spiritual techniques that endow the ensouled creature with heightened cognitive and affective capacities.

Benjamin associated opera with the dissolution of *Trauerspiel*: "In the north the *Haupt- und Staatsaktionen* eventually merged into the opera"; "That which is initially present in the *Trauerspiel* as a dancing chorus . . . openly displays its operatic character in the pastoral play."[45] As Sigrid Weigel argues, what Benjamin presents as a narrative of decline also harbors the deeper affinity between *Trauerspiel* and opera that Benjamin himself could only partly acknowledge.[46] In his early essay "Trauerspiel und Tragödie," Benjamin writes that "der Rest des Trauerspiels heißt Musik."[47] Benjamin's dictum plays on Hamlet's last words: "The rest is silence." Silence and music, tragedy and opera, are the twin extremes, the origin and the end, that *Trauerspiel* holds in tension. Opera becomes the mother of all art forms, around whom the children of music, theater, dance, and design cluster and confabulate, in order, in Benjamin's words, "to secure for music" its rightful place as "the last remaining universal language since the tower of Babel."[48]

Caliban composes his "sounds and sweet airs" in response to the music of Ariel, both within the scene and across the soundscape of the play.[49] Ariel's "Full fathom five" is itself a free translation of Jonah's prayer of thanksgiving. A man in a fish, Jonah delivers his prayer from the belly of the whale yet writes it in the past tense; likely added later to the text as a votive offering, the poem enacts prophetic time as the leap into a future that will have been.[50] In this hymn, writes Benjamin's friend Gershom Scholem, "the movement [of the book of Jonah] rises to its original-unitary height."[51] At once man *and* fish, Caliban channels both the refugee's terror and the whale's answering presence, the twangle and hum of somatic processes coming to comfort rather than terrify the soul huddling in the cavern of creaturely being as he tunes his own rhythms to the life force of Leviathan. Caliban's song sounds the depths of the play, sending sonic and semantic waves through its many layers of loss and allusion in search of answering ideas. Caliban's poignant echolocation orchestrates the psychic and the somatic, the cosmic and the creaturely, within the anticipatory time of awakening, which Benjamin took as a paradigm of dialectical thinking.[52] In Caliban's sonic reverie, reason, imagination, memory, perception, and emotion resonate with one another like so many strings on the lute of the soul (see Psalm 108:1–2). In and between Caliban, Ariel, the island, and their Scriptural proof texts, the proprioceptive and the alio-ceptive touch each other, if only through and under water, while the pastoral elegy crests into operatic duet. If in desiring to people the island with Calibans, the princely creature had sought one type of eternity, in this call-and-response with the unsexed or trans-sexed Ariel, Caliban seeks the eternity of the Idea through aesthetic means that are also political, since in concert with Ariel he seeks a new, emancipatory harmony among persons, places, times, and modes of being.[53] In composing his own whale song, Caliban son of Noah becomes Caliban son of David, *mashiach ben David*, capable of messianic yearnings.

Wisdom and Grace

In "sounds and sweet airs," Caliban already begins to practice what he will lay out as his new project in his penultimate lines in the drama:

> I'll be wise hereafter,
> And seek for grace. What a thrice-double ass
> Was I to take this drunkard for a god
> And worship this dull fool! (5.1.292–95)

Caliban's opening promise lays out in the simplest words possible the creaturely relationship to the Idea established by Benjamin in the "Epistemo-Critical Prologue." To be wise *hereafter* and *to seek* for grace means to assume an aspirational stance toward the Idea that takes alienation and even anxiety as its precondition but uses the very distance and tension maintained by their constellation as a navigational map for action in the world. Wisdom names a fidelity toward the Idea that takes knowledge as enterprise, not possession: the *sophos*, the "sage" or "sophist," only believes he is wise (think Prospero), whereas the *philo-sophos* loves wisdom because he knows that he does not have it. Grace soothes the wound of regret into a vessel that receives what is given, whether conceived as flowing from heaven, from fellow humans, or from the mysteries of the created world. Alain Badiou defines grace as simply "agreeing to work through the (generally unprecedented) consequences of what happens"; like Benjamin, he links grace to the affirmation of "eternal truths and their fragmented creation in the present of worlds."[54] This is a world in which, in the words of Edgar/Albany at the end of *King Lear*, we must prepare ourselves to "Speak what we feel, not what we ought to say" (5.1.320–21), to try to restore significance in the face of its horrific dispersal rather than disappear into skeptical equivocation or the consolations of bare life.[55] Recall Benjamin: "The light of grace is still reflected from the state of creation. But it is mirrored in the swamp of Adam's guilt." At the end of *The Tempest*, Caliban remains in the same swamp, but the light has changed: it shines more warmly, and the days have grown longer.

Caliban's search for wisdom and grace ends with his renouncement of idolatry: "What a thrice-double ass / Was I to take this drunkard for a god, /And worship this dull fool!" Iconoclasm is the signature of the prophet's commitment to the renewal of language in the face of all priestly, statist, and utilitarian reductions. In *The Origin of the German Tragic Drama*, Benjamin warns against the fetishization of characters or the search for moral meanings: "'Thou shalt not make unto thee any graven image'—this is not only a warning against idolatry. With incomparable essence the prohibition of the representation of the human body obviates any suggestion that the sphere in which the moral essence of man is perceptible can be reproduced."[56] A prophet of literary criticism, Benjamin reminds us to treat literary works as themselves constellations that cannot be reduced to single meanings because they approach the Idea only through the total set of tensions that they manage. Although I have focused here on the passion of Caliban, I have tried to place his speech and personhood in a sonorous geology of epochs, allusions, translations, and duets that seek ideas in the place of idols.

At the end of *The Tempest*, Caliban has a new project, an *Aufgabe* that is also a *Gabe*, or "gift." His project is the task of the translator, *die Aufgabe des Übersetzers*, whose tonality has shifted from curse to benediction, from rage at the suppression of his mother tongue to a form of listening and speaking that "gives voice to the *intentio* of the original not as reproduction but as harmony."[57] This is a translation that proceeds by way of language but also veers into music, dance, pantomime, and opera, lifting Caliban above the gabble and babel of tongues toward the Idea that the choreography of dispersal recollects.[58] The task of the translator is not to celebrate pluralism as an end in itself but to approximate the "pure language" that lies in the virtual zone between the original and its rendering. Robert Brandom describes this articulation over time of the animating references that discourses share as "magnanimous forgiving recollection."[59] So, too, the task of natural law and natural theology is to acknowledge the variety of the human search for justice by seeking what reason and imagination strive to share everywhere they appear.

The rippling, resonant text of *The Tempest* reflects the constellation and translation of ideas over time, and the play has been made to host many sets of ideas, from angelology and alchemy to psychomachia and kabbalah. Subtending these glittering displays of virtuoso ideation is the passion of the Idea as such, whether in the form of Platonic truth, Adamic language, or natural law. In the scenes of *Trauerspiel*, sublunar beings seek, avoid, or respond to the idea traces impressed in their souls, secreted by their somatic processes, mapped by their dwelling places, and infusing their relationships with other creatures and communities. In *The Tempest*, natural law is encountered as natural history—that is, as a body of ideas painfully reconstructed from a past in pieces, in a landscape fractured by disavowed domination. In *The Tempest*, natural law inspires philosophical inquiry, legal reform, and political revolution within a scene of action shaped by the *Sturm und Drang* of original sin and social antagonism. Like Calderón's Sigismundo, Caliban has begun to assume his princely prerogative at the play's close; like Hofmannsthal's Sigismund, however, this accession passes by way of conspiracy, the threat of violence, and class warfare. Stigmatized, misrecognized, and enslaved, the Adamic creature nonetheless finds resources within his own damaged being to transform rage and regret into the occasion for a new project of renewal.[60]

Caliban's story indexes the Scriptural motifs of creation, fall, flood, and messianic hope, and Caliban himself becomes a gracious translator as well as a living allegory of the play's many ideas. Both Benjamin's messianic criticism and Shakespeare's romances draw on Hellenistic, Jewish, and Christian philosophies in order to acknowledge the *Drang* of envy, anger, hatred, and fear as the conditions but not the ends of human being. As *Der Sturm* ends, Caliban is not "his own king" so much as a new (fresh) prince, entering from a truncated childhood and an enforced minority into the beckoning fullness of his capacities. Seeking wisdom and grace, this *fürstliche* Caliban is poised to accede from the *Mündung* (estuary) of languages in transition to the *Mündigkeit* (majority, maturity) that Kant identifies with Enlightenment.[61] This *Mund* calf's Enlightenment, however, might be called, echoing Hugh Grady's "impure aesthetics," an *impure Enlightenment*, in which sunlight and eveningtide, reason and imagination, mix indeterminately in a gritty messianic dawn.[62] And Caliban's natural law, following Vincent Lloyd, might be rechristened *black natural law*, in which the deepest truths disclosed by reason are those recovered in the struggle for freedom.[63]

Notes

A version of this essay was first presented at a conference on Shakespeare and Benjamin (University of London and Warburg Institute, November 2018). My deep thanks to Julia Ng, Andrew Benjamin, Freddie Rokem, and Anat Messing Marcus, among other participants in the event, and special thanks to Jane O. Newman and Eric Santner for additional commentary, references, and intellectual friendship.

1. Walter Benjamin, *Gesammelte Schriften*, II.2, ed. Rolf Tiedemann and Hermann Schweppenhäuser, *Werkausgabe*, vol. 5 (Frankfurt: Suhrkamp, 1980), 610–11. Translation by Freddie Rokem, in "'But a storm is blowing from Paradise'/'*Aber ein Sturm weht vom Paradiese her*': Walter Benjamin and Shakespeare's *The Tempest*," paper presented at a conference on Benjamin and Shakespeare, Goldsmiths, London, November 2018. Translation modified at the suggestion of Eric Santner.

2. Rokem, "'A storm is blowing,'" 3.

3. Walter Benjamin, *The Origin of the German Tragic Drama*, trans. John Osborne (London: Verso, 1998), 44. German citations from this volume are taken from *Ursprung des deutschen Trauerspiels*, ed. Rolf Tiedemann (Frankfurt: Suhrkamp, 1978).

4. Christopher Pye, *The Storm at Sea: Political Aesthetics in the Age of Shakespeare* (New York: Fordham University Press, 2015), 78; emphasis added.

5. Pye, *The Storm at Sea*, 145.

6. Pye, *The Storm at Sea*, 143.

7. Pye, *The Storm at Sea*, 145.

8. Walter Benjamin, *Hugo von Hofmannsthal, Der Turm: Ein Trauerspiel in fünf Aufzügen* (Munich: Verlag der Bremer Presse, 1925), in Walter Benjamin, *Gesammelte Schriften*, III, ed. Hella Tiedemann-Bartels, *Werkausgabe*, vol. 8 (Frankfurt: Suhrkamp, 1980), 29–33.

9. On Hofmannsthal's play, Benjamin's review, and the prince as creature, see Eric Santner, *The Royal Remains: The People's Two Bodies and the Endgames of Sovereignty* (Chicago: University of Chicago Press, 2011), 177–87.

10. On Hamlet as prince and Caliban as minor, see Julia Reinhard Lupton, *Thinking with Shakespeare: Essays on Politics and Life* (Chicago: University of Chicago Press, 2011), 69–95, 187–218. On Caliban as creature, see Julia Reinhard Lupton, *Citizen-Saints: Shakespeare and Political Theology* (Chicago: University of Chicago Press, 2005), 159–80.

11. Benjamin, *Origin*, 38.

12. Benjamin, *Origin*, 38.

13. Benjamin, *Origin*, 37.

14. Benjamin, *Origin*, 34–35.

15. Jane O. Newman, *Benjamin's Library: Modernity, Nation, and the Baroque* (Ithaca, N.Y.: Cornell University Press, 2011), 78. See also Hugh Grady, who describes *Trauerspiel* as "a changing process which takes place over time" (*Shakespeare and Impure Aesthetics* [Cambridge: Cambridge University Press, 2009], 141.

16. Benjamin, *Origin*, 47.

17. Benjamin, *Origin*, 92.

18. Hannah Arendt, introduction to *Illuminations: Essays and Reflections*, by Walter Benjamin, ed. Hannah Arendt, trans. Harry Zohn (New York: Schocken Books, 2007), 50–51.

19. This is the argument of Sigrid Weigel: "The *messianic* aims at redemption through the fulfillment of history; *secularization* here means the withdrawal of sacred significance within history, the transformation of existence back into the creaturely state or of history back into nature" (*Walter Benjamin: Images, the Creaturely, and the Holy*, trans. Chadwick Truscott Smith [Stanford, Calif.:

Stanford University Press, 2013], 12; emphasis in original). On Benjamin's account of virtue, see p. 8.

20. On Benjamin and presentism, see Hugh Grady, *John Donne and Baroque Allegory: The Aesthetics of Fragmentation* (Cambridge: Cambridge University Press, 2017), 10–12.

21. William Shakespeare, *The Tempest* (1611), in Gary Taylor, John Jowett, Terri Bourus, and Gabriel Egan, eds., *The New Oxford Shakespeare: Modern Critical Edition* (Oxford: Oxford University Press, 2016). All citations taken from the online version of this edition, https://www.oxfordscholarlyeditions.com/nos.

22. Benjamin, *Origin*, 85.

23. On autonomy, see Grotius: "For God created man αυτονόμος, 'free and *sui iuris*,' so that the actions of each individual and the use of his possessions were made subject not to another's will but to his own." Cited in Janne E. Nijman, "Grotius' *Imago Dei* Anthropology: Grounding *Ius Naturae and Gentium*," in *International Law and Religion: Historical and Contemporary Perspectives*, ed. Martti Koskenniemi, Mónica García-Salmones Rovira, and Paolo Amorosa (Oxford: Oxford University Press, 2017), 104. For maxims of natural law, see Richard Hooker, *Of the Lawes of Ecclesiastical Politie, Eight Books*, ed. John Kemble (1883), 1.8.3, Kindle.

24. Georg Cavallar, *The Rights of Strangers: Theories of International Hospitality, the Global Community, and Political Justice Since Vitoria* (Aldershot, Hampshire, U.K.: Ashgate Publishing, 2002). *Ius naturale* and *ius gentium* blend into each other in both theory and practice. On the distinction, see the classic (1951) work by Alexander Passerin d'Entrèves, *Natural Law: An Introduction to Legal Philosophy* (London: Routledge, 2017).

25. Hooker, *Of the Lawes*, 1.9.5.

26. Hooker, *Of the Lawes*, 1.10.1.

27. Stephen Orgel, ed., notes the prooftext, *The Tempest* (Oxford: Oxford University Press, 1987), 119n.

28. Benjamin, *Origin*, 37.

29. See Weigel on *Entstellung* in Benjamin, which, she argues, operates as both a distortion and a messianic *Erlösung*; *Body- and Image-Space: Re-reading Walter Benjamin*, trans. Georgina Paul with Rachel McNicholl and Jeremy Gaines (London: Routledge, 2005), 25.

30. Walter Benjamin, "The Role of Language in *Trauerspiel* and Tragedy," in *Selected Writings, Volume 1: 1913–1926*, ed. Marcus Bullock and Michael W. Jennings (Cambridge, Mass.: Harvard University Press, 1996), 60. German cited in Tamara Tagliacozzo, "Walter Benjamin und die Musik," *Jewish Studies Quarterly* 13, no. 3 (2006): 281. On the *Mündung* in this passage, Anat Messing Marcus says the following: "Language's manifestation as a voice is, interestingly, captured here in the figure of the 'Mündung,' the mouth—or perhaps mouthing—of the river, the point at which the opening and gathering of the lips could be imagined, that is, their rendition of ex-pression but also, their drawing nearer to the expression of silence" ("Antinomies of *Kinah* and of Translation: Gershom Scholem on *Hiobs Klage* and Walter Benjamin's '*Die Aufgabe des Übersetzers*,'" in *Rethinking the Book of Job*, ed. Simon Godart et al. [Berlin: Neofelis, forthcoming]).

31. Benjamin, *Origin*, 129.

32. Sarah Mortimer, "Protestantism, Resistance, and Natural Law," in Koskenniemi, Rovira, and Amorosa, *International Law and Religion*, 31–33. On Baroque tyrannicide, see Benjamin, *Origin*, 215.

33. Ewan Fernie, *Shakespeare for Freedom: Why the Plays Matter* (Cambridge: Cambridge University Press, 2017), 10–12.

34. See Christopher Johnson on Warburg's identification with Actaeon via Giordano Bruno, *Memory, Metaphor, and Aby Warburg's Atlas of Images* (Ithaca, N.Y.: Cornell University Press, 2012), 213. On the English Talmudist John Selden as a modern Osiris, see Jason Rosenblatt, *Renaissance England's Chief Rabbi John Selden* (Oxford: Oxford University Press, 2006), 12.

35. David Novak, "Natural Law and Judaism," in Anver M. Emon, Matthew Levering, and David Novak, *Natural Law: A Jewish, Christian, and Islamic Trialogue* (Oxford: Oxford University Press, 2014), location 590. See also Ofir Haivry, "John Selden and the Jewish Religious Fountainhead of the International Law of the Sea," in Koskenniemi, Rovira, and Amorosa, *International Law and Religion*, 126.

36. Rosenblatt, *Renaissance England's Chief Rabbi*, 276.

37. Rosenblatt, *Renaissance England's Chief Rabbi*, 142.

38. Rokem, "'A storm is blowing,'" 15.

39. Benjamin, *Origin*, 95.

40. Benjamin, *Hugo von Hofmannsthal*, 30; translation mine.

41. Walter Benjamin, "The Task of the Translator," in *Illuminations: Essays and Reflections*, ed. Hannah Arendt, trans. Harry Zohn (Boston: Houghton Mifflin, 1968), 79.

42. Benjamin, "Task of the Translator," 81.

43. Winnicott's work on transitional objects illuminates the rhythms of Psalm 131, as several modern readers have noted; e.g., Sara Maitland, *How to Be Alone* (New York: MacMillan/Picador, 2014), 79–80.

44. On the psalms of ascent in ancient Jewish practice, see David C. Mitchell, *The Songs of Ascent: Psalms 120–134 in the Worship of Jerusalem's Temple* (Newton Mearns, Sct.: Campbell Publications, 2015). On the psalms of ascent in Christianity, see Gerald McLarney, *St. Augustine's Interpretation of the Psalms of Ascent* (Washington, D.C.: Catholic University of America Press, 2014).

45. Benjamin, *Origin*, 69, 211.

46. Sigrid Weigel and Joel Golb, "Brünhilde's Lament: The Mourning Play of the Gods," *Opera Quarterly* 31, nos. 1–2 (Winter–Spring 2015): 53–70.

47. German cited in Tagliacozzo, "Walter Benjamin," 280.

48. Benjamin, *Origin*, 214.

49. On the soundscape of *The Tempest*, see Colby Gordon's essay in the present volume.

50. Ariel's song takes off from a similar passage in *Pericles*, which is closely linked to Jonah's prayer. See Hannibal Hamlin, "The Acts of Pericles: Shakespeare's Biblical Romance," in *The Bible on the Shakespearean Stage: Cultures of Interpretation in Reformation England*, ed. Kristin Poole and Thomas Fulton, 140–55 (Cambridge: Cambridge University Press, 2018).

51. Gershom Scholem, "On Jonah and the Concept of Justice," trans. Eric J. Schwab, *Critical Inquiry* 25, no. 2 (Winter 1999): 354.

52. Weigel, *Body- and Image-Space*, 44.

53. Alain Badiou says the following: "A genuine creation, a historicity of exception, has no other criterion than to establish, between disparate worlds, the evidence of an eternity" (*Logics of Worlds*, trans. Alberto Toscano [New York: Continuum, 2008], 513).

54. Badiou, *Logics of Worlds*, 512.

55. Edgar in the Folio; Albany in Q1. Cited from William Shakespeare, *King Lear* (1605–1606): 24 (5.3) in Taylor et al., *The New Oxford Shakespeare*, online edition, https://www.oxfordscholarlyeditions.com/nos.

56. Benjamin, *Origin*, 105.

57. Benjamin, "Task of the Translator," 79.

58. In a 1916 piece, Benjamin insists on the close link between *Trauerspiel* and music: *Trauerspiel* "describes the path from natural sound via lament to music" ("Role of Language," 60). On ancient pantomime, see Ismene Lada-Richards, *Silent Eloquence: Lucian and Pantomime Dancing* (London : Bloomsbury, 2007).

59. Robert B. Brandom, *A Spirit of Trust: A Reading of Hegel's Phenomenology* (Cambridge, Mass.: Harvard University Press, 2019), 608.

60. On Shakespeare and stigma, see Jeffrey Wilson, "'Savage and Deformed': Stigma as Drama in *The Tempest*," *Medieval and Renaissance Drama in England* 31 (2018): 146–77.

61. In "What Is Enlightenment?" Kant identifies enlightenment with *Mündigkeit*, maturity; the ability to speak with reason; Immanuel Kant, *An Answer to the Question: 'What Is Enlightenment?,'* trans. H. B. Nisbet (London: Penguin, 2013).

62. Grady, *Shakespeare and Impure Aesthetics*. Grady draws extensively on Benjamin in this volume.

63. Vincent Lloyd, *Black Natural Law* (Oxford: Oxford University Press, 2016); Julia Reinhard Lupton, "*The Tempest* and Black Natural Law," *Religions* 9, no. 12 (2018), https://www.mdpi.com/2077-1444/10/2/91.

CONTRIBUTORS

Joel M. Dodson is an associate professor at Southern Connecticut State University, where he teaches early modern English literature. He has published articles on political theology and confession in the works of Sidney, Donne, and Foucault.

Colby Gordon is an assistant professor in the English Department of Bryn Mawr College. He is the author of multiple articles on Renaissance literature and transgender studies.

Hugh Grady is professor emeritus at Arcadia University in Glenside, Pennsylvania. He is the author of *The Modernist Shakespeare*; *Shakespeare, Machiavelli, and Montaigne*; *Shakespeare and Impure Aesthetics*; and *John Donne and Baroque Allegory*.

Lydia C. Heinrichs is a graduate student in early modern English literature at the University of Cambridge. She studies aesthetics and epistemology in early modern literature and natural philosophy.

Russ Leo is an associate professor at Princeton University. He is the author of *Tragedy as Philosophy in the Reformation World* and the translator of Jarig Jelles's *Preface* to Baruch Spinoza's *Opera Posthuma*.

Joan Pong Linton is an associate professor at Indiana University. She is the author of *The Romance of the New World*.

Julia Reinhard Lupton is a professor of English at the University of California, Irvine. Her current work is on Shakespeare and virtue.

Christopher Pye is a professor of English at Williams College and has written several books on Shakespeare and early modernity, including *The Storm at Sea: Political Aesthetics in the Time of Shakespeare*.

Jennifer R. Rust is the Georgia K. Johnston Professor of English at Saint Louis University. She is the author of *The Body in Mystery: The Political Theology of the* Corpus Mysticum *in the Literature of Reformation England* (Northwestern University Press).

Tracey Sedinger is a professor of English at the University of Northern Colorado. She has published essays in *ELH*, *LIT*, *Cultural Critique*, and *Shakespeare Quarterly*.

Andrew Sisson has taught at Williams College, Emory University, and the University of Richmond. His work on early modern aesthetics and political thought has appeared in *Shakespeare Quarterly* and *Spenser Studies*.